W9-CME-991

MYTHOLOGY

AND

THE RENAISSANCE TRADITION

IN ENGLISH POETRY

DOUGLAS BUSH

PAGEANT BOOK COMPANY

New York

1957

Published by Pageant Book Company
59 Fourth Avenue, New York 3, N. Y.

Printed in U.S.A. by
NOBLE OFFSET PRINTERS, Inc.
400 Lafayette Street
New York 3, N. Y.

TO
MY MOTHER
AND
THE MEMORY OF
MY FATHER

PREFACE

THIS study set out, with Elizabethan confidence, to describe the uses of mythology in English non-dramatic poetry from the Middle Ages to the present. The result of such an ambition can perhaps be suggested in the apt words of a university poet concerning Actaeon:

> His hands were changed to feet, and he in short
> Became a stag.

In plain prose, this volume ends at 1680; I hope in another volume to complete the tale.

The purpose of the book is to follow some threads through the rich web of the classical tradition in English poetry of the sixteenth and seventeenth centuries. Not of course that mythological poetry and the classical tradition are equivalent terms, or have indeed any essential connection. The truism may be emphasized at the beginning that *In Time of "the Breaking of Nations"* or *The Death of the Hired Man* is far more truly classical than a multitude of poems inspired by a vision of Olympus. That, however, was not the general attitude in the period covered by this book, and historically, though not absolutely, mythology is a part of the classical tradition in European poetry.

The material had to be limited, and, unless incidentally or for a special reason, nothing has been said of classical influences in general, of formal translations from the classics, of dramatic treatments of classical themes; such huge subjects would need volumes to themselves. Some space is necessarily given to minor figures who bulk larger in relation to the mythological genre than they do in the history of English poetry. But while a number of corpses have been disinterred, almost all of these are on view in the Appendix, and the curious may satisfy their "gowlish gusto" (in Mr. Polly's phrase) by wandering through the morgue. At any rate it can be honestly affirmed, if one may profane Browne's solemn music, that the author, who hath an art to make dust of all things, hath yet spared some minor monuments.

For abbreviations used in footnotes see the bibliography, page 327.

It is pleasant to acknowledge the kindness of officers and attendants of the British Museum, the Bodleian, the Harvard University Library, and the University of Minnesota Library; and to express my gratitude to the authorities of Harvard University for a fellowship which enabled me some years ago to work in England. I am under special obligations to the governing board and editorial staff of the University of Minnesota Press. For criticisms of some chapters I am indebted to Professor Charles G. Osgood of Princeton University and Professor Warner G. Rice of the University of Michigan.

I would emphasize the responsibility of Professor Lowes as the only begetter of this book if it were not for some fear that even so wise a father might not know such a child. What his encouragement means his pupils best know, even if their feet move more easily down to Avernus than along the road to Xanadu.

Finally, my wife did not compile the index; her manifold help in other ways I am not allowed to acknowledge.

DOUGLAS BUSH

University of Minnesota.

CONTENTS

MYTHOLOGY
AND THE RENAISSANCE TRADITION
IN ENGLISH POETRY

INTRODUCTION

THERE are always readers and writers who know, like Peacock, that there are no dryads in Hyde Park, nor naiads in the Regent's Canal; who rejoice with Mr. Weller when they find in a poem "no Wenuses, nor nothin' o' that kind"; who echo Whitman's familiar prayer,

> Come Muse migrate from Greece and Ionia,
> Cross out please those immensely overpaid accounts,
> That matter of Troy and Achilles' wrath, and Æneas', Odysseus'
>   wanderings,
> Placard "Removed" and "To Let" on the rocks of your snowy
>   Parnassus . . .
> For know a better, fresher, busier sphere, a wide, untried domain
>   awaits, demands you.

But Peacock was the author of *Rhododaphne,* a good deal of Whitman is a close parallel to the Homeric catalogue of the ships, and, in general, a particular subject matter should not be blamed for the faults of its compromising votaries. Myths and tales can hardly be banished to the museum when they have attracted almost all the major English poets, not to mention minor ones, from Chaucer to the present.

Poetry is largely a matter of symbol, and the complete rebel, like Blake, who flouts tradition and insists on making his own symbols, may achieve originality of a kind, but at a high price, as the most ardent devotee of the prophetic books must admit. The greatest artists, I think Mr. Clive Bell has remarked, always look forward. It is equally true that they always look backward. Of course feeble poets who try to write in a great tradition remain feeble poets, and the bright world of classic myth has allured a number of persons who, in the words of Coleridge, mistake an intense desire to possess the reputation of poetic genius for the actual powers. But what is called realism has its own compromising army of camp followers, who, in our day, forget that the din of riveters in poetry may become as smooth a cliché as Phoebus or Diana. An authentic poet may be moved to authentic utterance by the excitement of reading— witness such diverse examples as Chapman and Swinburne—and the more original he is the more he gains from drawing upon the accumulated artistic heritage, which is surely as essential a part of "life" as any aspect of human behavior.

Hundreds of poets have written about Helen of Troy; she is the rich source of a many-colored stream of associations. One thinks at once of Marlowe's rapturous lines, or of that astonishing lyric from the most boisterous of Elizabethan pens:

> Brightness falls from the air;
> Queens have died young and fair;
> Dust hath closed Helen's eye:
> I am sick, I must die.
> *Lord, have mercy on us!*

Here the one name evokes glamor and romance, the brevity of life and love and beauty, with such concentrated suggestion that the imagination is filled with undertones and overtones which no "original" image or cumbrous circumlocution could give. We have even a Celtic Helen, in the inspired talk of the "playboy": "If the mitred bishops seen you that time, they'd be the like of the holy prophets, I'm thinking, do be straining the bars of Paradise to lay eyes on the Lady Helen of Troy, and she abroad, pacing back and forward, with a nosegay in her golden shawl." Hundreds of poets have written of Leda, but the theme is far from threadbare when touched by Mr. Yeats. And perhaps Mr. Eliot is nowhere so poetic and so moving as in those lines about the nightingales singing near the Convent of the Sacred Heart, which

> sang within the bloody wood
> When Agamemnon cried aloud,
> And let their liquid siftings fall
> To stain the stiff dishonoured shroud.

Helen, Leda, Agamemnon are only a few symbols from the inexhaustible treasury of classic myth. Beautiful simply as tales, the myths have constituted for modern poets a kind of poetic shorthand of infinite imaginative and emotional value. Mythological allusions have not lost their spell merely because at times bad poets turn them into glass beads. We are in this book concerned partly with allusions, but mainly with more elaborate manifestations of the same impulse, narrative poems on classical themes. One has only to run over the list of English poets to see that myths have appealed to the most diverse minds, have been put to the most diverse uses. They have been the vehicle for sermons on morality, for revolts against morality, for mystical theology, for obscene burlesque, for decorative tapestry, for human comedy and tragedy, for poems of escape from life, for humanitarian amelioration of life.

We moderns have a pleasant way of using, and using interchangeably, such phrases as "the Greek spirit," "the classic spirit," "the pagan spirit," and doubtless often with a meaning. Our instinct for synthesis welcomes an expression that sums up in a couple of words the essential kinship of Pindar and Sappho, Aeschylus and Lucian, Plato and Aristotle, Herodotus and Thucydides, Sophocles and Euripides—not to mention the Romans. While we are possibly nearer than our ancestors ever were to a definition of the Greek mind—to take it for the moment, as more elusive and un-English than the Roman—we continue, as they did, to make the Greeks in our own image, to see in the ancient as well as in the modern classics the reflection of our changing philosophies and prejudices. The strictly neoclassic intelligence, admiring if not fully understanding Virgil, regarded Homer as a genius, though a somewhat rude and uncouth one; for the sentimental primitivists of the eighteenth century Homer's faults of incorrectness became the virtues which proclaimed him an inspired child of nature, a true primitive bard, finally a whole committee of bards. Demosthenes, said Dr. Johnson, spoke to brutes. The German Hellenists saw the Greek as a being of superhuman beauty of body and mind, of godlike serenity and calm. In our own time we have had an anthropological and corybantic Hellenism that makes Dionysus more potent than Zeus or Apollo. And so the search for truth proceeds.

Of the writers to be discussed here the earlier ones at least, less philosophic than we, were content with a rather vague apprehension of the classic genius, but, like us, they did find in ancient literature the reflection of themselves. When we think of "unclassical" variations of theme and treatment in English mythological poems, we may well qualify our judgments in the recollection that ancient mythology was not a rigidly fixed body of "authentic" material which only in the Middle Ages began to be wondrously transmogrified. The Greek dramatists, when they cut slices from the banquet of Homer (the whole body of cyclic poems, that is), trimmed and seasoned them, within limits, to suit their own purposes. To summarize a good many centuries, the names of Aeschylus, Sophocles, Euripides, Theocritus, Virgil, Ovid, Lucian, testify to the widest variety of conception and handling. However poetic mood and poetic genius may vary, such material has enduring vitality. In spite of the vast bulk of Arthurian stuff, old and new, we can imagine a world without Arthur; we can hardly conceive of a world without Apollo.

This volume attempts to outline both the changing moral and intellectual conceptions of myth and the changing fashions in artistic

6 MYTHOLOGY AND THE RENAISSANCE TRADITION

treatment, for the two are of course inseparable. The cycle of taste is roughly parallel to that represented by the ancient writers already named; it begins with religious seriousness and ends with irreverent burlesque. We shall follow the poetic handling of myth from the period of infant simplicity through that of adolescent exuberance to the mature and chastened splendor of the last poet of the English Renaissance, and, finally, sink by a logical anticlimax to the immature and unchaste travesties of the Restoration.

We shall not arrive at any startling conclusions; on the contrary everyone knows the direction to be taken and at least the chief landmarks along the way. But by surveying a single aspect of the Renaissance tradition that is not unrelated to the central principles of neoclassicism we may be able to see a little more clearly and consecutively the struggle between the virtues and vices for possession of the soul of poetry. One moral that will emerge, a moral which might be called a truism if it were not so often ignored, is that in the history of English poetry there is no absolute classicism, there are only conceptions—perhaps misconceptions—of classicism. Critics who write of the changeless laws of taste must have in mind a set of tables laid up in some Platonic heaven, for the literature of earth, which, in the absence of an aesthetic revelation, must be our criterion, does not warrant such comfortable doctrine.

But there is a stream of continuity, and for that reason, as well as from the academic instinct to commence *ab ovo,* the first chapter is devoted to a sketch of mythology in the Middle Ages. For another moral, to be perhaps relentlessly emphasized, is that the essential quality of Renaissance poetry, at the best as well as at the worst, is its medievalism. We shall find ourselves dealing continually with the heritage of medieval religion, with the spirit and technique of medieval art. The bulk of the poetry surveyed may be described, with due reservations, as a "Gothic" and edifying tapestry into which are woven more and more silver threads from Ovid and threads of gilt from Italy. Such poetry, heavily encrusted with Renaissance brocade, is obviously seldom "classical." But how many of the Latin poets are classical, when tried by the standards that we catalogue so glibly? However, the genial Ovid would probably have been less disturbed than scholars if he had known not merely that he would not wholly die, but that through the centuries he would be, like Caesar's wife, all things to all men. For a history of mythology and the Renaissance tradition must be largely an account of the metamorphoses of Ovid.

CHAPTER ONE

CLASSICAL THEMES IN THE MIDDLE AGES

I. THE STORY OF TROY

WITHOUT going into evidence which suggests that a few men were acquainted with Homer, one may safely assert that the *Iliad* and *Odyssey* were virtually unknown in western Europe during the Middle Ages. Of course men praised him, as we still do, without having read him. Dante, master of the learning of his time, saluted Homer as lord of the loftiest song who soars above the others like an eagle, but knew him only vaguely as a great name. The mass of readers were as ignorant of Greek as they are today.

Trojan saga, therefore, reached the medieval man by devious paths. Passing over the brief epitome of the *Iliad* by "Pindarus Thebanus" (Silius Italicus), which was read in the sixteenth century as well as in the sixth, we come to the great twin brethren, Dictys Cretensis and Dares Phrygius, who were the sources of nearly all medieval and many Renaissance versions of the Trojan story. Our Latin text of Dictys (fourth century A. D.), which is orderly and adequate in style, describes events from the rape of Helen to the death of Ulysses. Dares (sixth century), though much briefer, takes in everything from the Argonautic expedition to the destruction of Troy; his prose style has been sufficiently damned.

These books had an enduring popularity far beyond that of our modern outlines of the universe; they were exactly what the public wanted. The reasons are worth noting, for their potency did not end with the Middle Ages. One has been mentioned, the general ignorance of Greek. There were also abundant positive reasons. Both writers had taken part in the Trojan war and derived information from experience or from eyewitnesses; they said so themselves. Benoit de Sainte-Maure expressed the common opinion when he commended the absolute veracity of Dares and observed that Homer, though a marvelous clerk, did not live until a hundred years after the war.

These truthful historians had the gifts requisite for popularizing material. The supernatural events of the story were freely rationalized. Dictys omitted debates in heaven, divine assistance given to the heroes, fights among the gods. Even the wooden horse ceased to be hollow. Homer in his simplicity had described characters with a few broad strokes. Dares and Dictys sprinkled their work with convincing touches of realism, the kind of corroborative detail of which Pooh-Bah was such a master. Thus in Dares Aeneas has sparkling black eyes, and Polyxena is cursed with large hands. Dictys, with no less journalistic skill, gives the satisfying information that at the time of the elopement Paris was thirty-three and Helen twenty-six. The motivation is sometimes made more plausible and human; Menelaus is less disturbed because his wife left him than because two of his female relations helped her to leave.

Homeric heroes undergo a curious transformation, the last becoming first and the first last. Troilus, hardly mentioned by Homer, is described in Dares as equal to Hector. Achilles is far from heroic when he stabs Hector in the back, strangles Troilus, and is ready to betray the Greeks for the sake of Polyxena. Naturally Dictys, one of the Greek force, and Dares, a Trojan, viewed the facts from different standpoints, as historians of wars generally do. Dictys sneered at the Trojans as barbarians, and Dares placed responsibility for the war on the shoulders of the Greeks, since Paris had only taken revenge for the abduction of his aunt, Hesione. Such divergence of opinion did not weaken the authority of the historians. Dictys became the oracle of truth in the East, while Dares was preferred in the West—since many western nations were descended from Trojan heroes. Before leaving the pair in the mire of disrepute where they used to be thrown, we may remember that, however slight their literary merits, they do derive material from heroic tradition and have some "authority."

Another un-Homeric element in Dares and Dictys, which became much more important in works based on them, was romantic love. The story of that evolution has been told many times, and only a few landmarks need be noticed here. In the vast *Roman de Troie* Benoit de Sainte-Maure developed the romance of Achilles and Polyxena and invented or elaborated the story of Troilus, Briseida, and Diomede. Like other western authors Benoit used Dares chiefly, but had recourse to Dictys for events beyond the point where Dares stopped. The manners and setting were of the twelfth century, and Hector appeared as the ideal knight of medieval chivalry.

Another version of Dares that Chaucer knew was a paraphrase in Latin verse by Joseph of Exeter, written toward the end of the twelfth century. The style and technique of the *Bellum Troianum* remind one frequently of both post-classical and Renaissance poetry; in other words it is typically medieval. The versification, modeled especially on that of Lucan and Claudian, has been pronounced "little, if any, inferior to the average of the Silver Age." [1] Colors of rhetoric, as prescribed in medieval textbooks, are laid on in profusion. We have a catalogue of trees, and, in connection with Helen, the orthodox medieval catalogue of female beauties, along with "a physio-psychological description of her interior." Mr. Sedgwick remarks that Joseph's style displays "the luxuriance of the young Shakespeare of *Lucrece* and *Venus and Adonis,* or of the young Pindar who 'sowed not with the hand but with the whole sack.'" The *Bellum Troianum* continued to be read for centuries; it was praised, for instance, by Samuel Daniel, William Browne, and Milton. [2]

We need not rehearse the familiar story of the paraphrase of Benoit by Guido delle Colonne and the development by Boccaccio and Chaucer of the tragic romance of Troilus and Cressida, though it is of interest to recall that Boccaccio's account of the enamorment drew not only upon the author's always useful experience but upon Benoit's episode of Achilles and Polyxena. Of those formidable saurians, the Middle English redactions of the whole story of Troy, the best is that of the much-enduring if not over-cunning hero, John Lydgate. His *Troy Book* (1412–20) is a solid performance of more than thirty thousand lines. While most of us, like Mr. Wegg in the matter of Gibbon, have not been "right slap through him very lately," one can by searching find bits of something like poetry.

II. VIRGIL IN THE MIDDLE AGES

The reasons for Virgil's unique authority in the Middle Ages were manifold and sometimes strange. Very early he became a textbook, and the stateliest measure ever moulded by the lips of man was chanted by rows of grubby children in hot schoolrooms. The beauty and subtlety of Virgil's language delivered him into the remorseless hands of grammarians. Rhetoric, too, claimed Virgil for her own. The speeches of his characters were studied and spouted in the schools of declamation; the question could be debated, "Was Virgil a poet or an orator?" There is testimony to his literary pre-eminence in the practice of making centos

---

[1] W. B. Sedgwick, "The *Bellum Troianum* of Joseph of Exeter," *Speculum,* V, 49–76. Cf. R. K. Root, "Chaucer's Dares," *M. P.,* XV, 1; N. Griffin, *J. E. G. P.,* XX, 45, note. My sketch of Dares and Dictys is indebted to the studies of Mr. Griffin cited in the bibliography. See also the reference to the thesis by Mr. J. C. McGalliard.

[2] Gregory Smith, *Elizabethan Critical Essays,* II, 370; *Prose Works of John Milton* (Bohn ed.), V, 172; and see below, page 176.

of Virgilian lines and phrases, such as the partly roguish composition of Ausonius.

But Virgil's universal sway did not rest merely on literary and artistic greatness. The purity of his writing, his ethical and philosophic tone, commended him to Christians who recoiled from Catullus or Lucretius. The lines that sounded forever of imperial Rome could not cease to inspire members of a church whose rulers were the successors of Augustus as well as of St. Peter. Then, like Homer among the Greeks, and Shakespeare among nineteenth-century critics, Virgil came to be regarded as an encyclopedia of knowledge, a complete guide to life. The *sortes Vergilianae,* which we may associate with Panurge's anxious project of matrimony, could be invoked by a Roman emperor. Hints of allegory in the early commentators were developed into a complete allegorization of the *Aeneid;* of this something will be said later. Finally, as everyone knows, on the strength of the fourth eclogue Virgil was revered as a prophet of the Messiah and hence came to occupy a place apart from other pagan poets; the traditional belief appears among scholars of the Renaissance. We need not concern ourselves with the popular metamorphosis of the poet into a wizard and hero of ignoble amorous adventures.

It was inevitable that the chief work of the universal poet should be adapted to medieval taste, and the latter half of the twelfth century produced the *Roman d'Eneas.* The very elaborate episode of Lavinia and Aeneas, which is the redactor's invention, is familiar, yet it is such a significant example of the medievalizing process that it must be summarized. For the technique of situation, dialogue, soliloquy, analysis of love and its effects, all this and more shows that for the medieval writer the successful reworking of Virgil consists to a large degree in borrowing from and imitating Ovid.

The queen visits Lavinia in order to speak to her about Turnus and tell her what love is. Aeneas happens to come out of his tent and Lavinia, seeing him, suddenly understands more than her mother could impart. She pours forth long amorous lamentations. When Aeneas pays no attention to her, she faints; recovering, she goes on again. She passes a restless night. The queen, calling the next day, sees that her daughter is in love, and is furious on learning that the object is Aeneas instead of Turnus. She rails at Aeneas, accusing him of unnatural vice. Lavinia faints, and revives to consider what she shall do. She has a letter sent to her unsuspecting idol. He reads it, turns toward Lavinia, who is on the watch, and salutes her. Going back to his tent, he feels so stricken that he has to take to the medieval lover's usual refuge, his bed. The next day

Lavinia waits in the tower to see Aeneas come under the walls. Not knowing of his prostration she fears coldness, and begins to believe her mother's charges. But when Aeneas, weak and pale, rides out and shows himself to Lavinia, she repents of her lack of faith. The two gaze lovingly at each other. Aeneas' fellow warriors observe his passion and mock him. The lovers turn away, trembling. Here the author takes up Virgil, in order to describe the battle in which Turnus is killed. But for an adequate conclusion, the removal of the last doubts and obstacles and the happy marriage, he has to abandon Virgil again. Thus is a slow-moving classic speeded up to please sophisticated taste.

The whole setting of the romance is of course medievalized. Supernatural machinery, in Virgil decorative or symbolic or both, is reduced to a minimum, though romancers were fond enough of some kinds of wonders. For instance, whereas in Virgil Venus substitutes Cupid for Ascanius, in the romance Venus gives to Ascanius the power of exciting Dido's love. In general, of the *Aeneid* that we know the poet sees, or chooses to see, nothing. A religious epic, celebrating the divine mission of the Roman Empire, the venerable traditions and the ancient loveliness of Italy, touched everywhere with Virgil's sense of the burthen of the mystery and with the intricate beauty of Virgilian style — all this goes over the head of the redactor. For him and his readers the *Aeneid* is a thin tale of knightly deeds and romantic love. And yet, before shuddering at such medieval obtuseness, we may remember again that, if the romance is far from Virgil's conception and handling of the Trojan story, it is by no means so far from Ovid's.[3]

III. OVID

"Next to Virgil in the Middle Ages came Ovid," says Mr. Haskins, "indeed, one suspects that with the more carnally minded Ovid often

[3] Edmond Faral, *Recherches sur les sources latines des contes et romans courtois du moyen age* (1913), pp. 125 ff. Writing on "Ovid's *Aeneid* and Vergil's," Mr. F. J. Miller finds the essential difference in motivation, and contrasts with the *Aeneid* "Ovid's presentation of a humdrum story, or what had, traditionally, become so; in a humdrum manner; with an un-heroic hero; his slurring over or entire omission of pertinent, important incidents, and his over expansion of entirely unrelated tales" (*Classical Journal*, XXIII, 33 ff.).

To mention one more item, in the *Roman de Jules César,* developed out of Lucan, Caesar's *Civil War,* and minor sources, the most notable episode is the love of Caesar and Cleopatra. An ample picture of Cleopatra's beauty, which resembles that of Iseult, prepares us for Caesar's immediate subjugation and consequent insomnia. A friend, acting as ambassador for the prostrated lover, is well received. When Caesar declares his passion Cleopatra, though already won, desires to consult her chamberlain. The conqueror of hearts and empires hastens to bribe this functionary, and victory is achieved. It seems hardly fair to regard this as more naïve than Shakespeare or Shaw, whatever its literary quality.

came first. First he seems to have been in the twelfth century, that 'age of Ovid' which followed the Carolingian 'age of Virgil.' Any one who still believes that the Latin classics were a sealed book to the men of the Middle Ages, who cared only for the next world and had no appreciation of the beauties of literary art and the joys of the realm of sense, should ponder the popularity of Ovid and grow wiser."[4]

Some, though by no means all, of the elements of that popularity were alien to the real Ovid, but we can ill afford to patronize medieval students who, whatever their occasional vagaries, had a vital contact with Latin literature. Their classical past was a usable one—as ours hardly is— and the diversity of uses that the Latin authors served is the best proof of a fruitful tradition. The influence of Ovid ranged from the wandering scholars' very practical eulogies of Venus to the idealisms of the *Roman de la Rose,* from mythological romances to allegories of Christ's love for the human soul, from fairy tales to treatises on amatory etiquette.

To glance for a moment at these last works, how was a medieval translator, living in the midst of feudal society, to understand and make intelligible to readers such a poem as the *Ars Amatoria,* a detailed picture of the gilded life of Augustan Rome? With the self-confidence and independence that is sometimes called medieval naïveté he made over Ovid for his own purposes, and to suit his own world. It is significant that the *Ars Amatoria* was translated by Chrétien de Troyes, that twelfth-century master of the female heart; his version is not extant. A version entitled *Clef d'Amors* opens with a dream; instead of Roman entertainments we have dances, carols, tournaments; where Ovid suggests that a moistened hand may give the effect of tears our practical author recommends an onion. Still another redaction, by Jacques d'Amiens, gives models of amorous conversation. With Chesterfieldian detail he tells how to approach an old woman, a woman of rank, a young girl.

Ovidian irony was not always carried over into these pieces, for the didactic form was congenial and might be taken rather seriously. Ovid, like other ancients, was considered a repository of wisdom, as in truth he was. "I am love's professor," he had said, and his works, which bear such testimony to a lifetime of research, might well serve as a guide to a society becoming conscious of love as the finest of fine arts. For Ovid and the courtly poets assumed that love is an art, subject to laws—artistic laws —and that the novice may take lessons in it. The redactors of the *Ars Amatoria* might miss Ovid's wit and mock-seriousness, but their medievalizing of the poem was both inevitable and rational.

The Renaissance of the Twelfth Century (1928), p. 107.

The *Metamorphoses* offered a different problem. A highly romantic version, in Old French, of the story of Pyramus and Thisbe is discussed in a later chapter, for the good but perhaps unexpected reason that an English poem derived from it appeared in an Elizabethan miscellany.[5] We have some indication of the character of *Piramus et Tisbé* in the fact that it was of service to the author of *Aucassin et Nicolette*.[6] The *Narcisse*, also of the twelfth century, is another illustration of the humanizing of a myth.

More elaborate than either of these poems is the *Philomena*.[7] Every reader of Chrétien de Troyes knows how dear to his heart, and to the courtly circle for whom he wrote, were amorous dialogue and psychological analysis. Whether or not Chrétien was the author, such elements are conspicuous in *Philomena*. The changes made in the Ovidian story are much the same as those favored in the sixteenth century. The most obvious one is that the Old French poem is six times as long as Ovid's. While Ovid has only a few words about Philomela's beauty, the medieval poet gives an exhaustive catalogue of her charms, from her nose to her knowledge of grammar. There is a long debate whether Philomela shall accompany Tereus or not, and the author discusses the metaphysics of love and madness. Tereus' growing passion is recorded through all its stages. Rhetoric is everywhere. Tereus first tries to win Philomela with a flood of eloquence. When he gives to his wife a circumstantial report of the supposed death of her sister, Progne delivers a harangue against death. She greets the discovery of her husband's villainy with a compendious tirade against men. Although there is an elaborate account of her funeral sacrifices, the general setting is medieval. Tereus in Ovid is *opibusque virisque potentem,* Pandion becomes *poissanz et larges et cortois*. While it is Ovid's great vice that he will always be clever, in this grim tale even he seems to be a trifle moved; there is no emotion at all in the ambling little couplets of the French poem. Thus the Ovidian story, rhetorical enough in itself, but still neat, compact, objective, is richly embellished with romantic, courtly, and even more rhetorical decorations.

Another mode of treating myth is illustrated at its best in the well-known tale *Sir Orfeo*. Instead of Hades we have the Celtic otherworld; instead of Pluto a fairy king with a band of knights and ladies clad in white and riding white horses; and "Heurodis" does not die, she is won by the king of the otherworld because she falls asleep under a

---

[5] Page 50.   [6] Faral, *Recherches*, p. 27.
[7] Since we are concerned only with the technique of the poem, the question of authorship may be left to the experts, who disagree. See, for example, Voretzsch, *Einführung in das Studium der altfranzösischen Literatur* (1925), p. 256; and De Boer's edition of *Philomena* (Paris, 1909).

fairy tree.[8] Chaucer, who is so rationally minded in his treatment of classic story, speaks of Pluto as "the king of fayërye." Henryson's poem on Orpheus and Eurydice mixes "goddes Infernall" and the "quene of fary."[9] In the not altogether dry light of the later sixteenth century this hybrid blossom, so far from withering, took on new life and color.

To follow the fortunes of individual Ovidian tales would lead us everywhere, but one example may be noticed. The myth of Io traveled as far as, in the drama, the gnat-stung damsel herself did. The *Gesta Romanorum* has a version that shuns connection with the pagan gods. A nobleman gives a favorite heifer to a hundred-eyed servant, Argus. A covetous man, Mercury, who wants this animal with golden horns, tries to charm and bribe the shepherd. The latter, whose integrity is shaken by opportunity, holds an imaginary dialogue with his master, represented by his staff set up in front of him. The rest of the tale is closer to the myth.[10] There are other versions in Latin, Italian, Spanish, German, Turkish, sometimes so remote from the original that it is only through knowledge of the intervening links that the relationship can be recognized. But the debatable land of folklore we may contemplate from afar.

Though medieval readers and writers liked Ovid the story-teller, they worshiped Ovid the poet of love. Chaucer's tribute illustrates the common opinion:

> And next him on a piler was,
> Of coper, Venus clerk, Ovyde,
> That hath y-sowen wonder wyde
> The grete god of Loves name.[11]

Not merely the troubadours and their successors, but clerics, historians, moralists, bear testimony, joyously or reluctantly, to the great teacher of the art of love, the painter of women who were faithful to at least one god. In fact the most potent of deities might be regarded as the son of Venus and Ovid.

[8] The story of Orpheus and Eurydice was known in the Middle Ages through Virgil (*Georg.* iv. 454), Ovid, and Boethius (bk. iii, met. 12). See L. Hibbard, *Mediæval Romance in England* (1924), p. 197; J. Wirl, *Orpheus in der englischen Literatur,* Wiener Beiträge, XL, 18.

[9] *Poems of Robert Henryson,* ed. Gregory Smith, III (Edinburgh and London, 1908), 35; Wirl, p. 26.

[10] *Gesta Romanorum,* ed. Oesterley, c. 111, p. 451. See E. Bourne, "Mediæval Wanderings of a Greek Myth," *J. E. G. P.,* XXIV, 184; and "Classical Elements in the *Gesta Romanorum,*" *Vassar Mediæval Studies* (1923), p. 345.

The allegorical interpretation is this: the nobleman is Christ, the heifer the soul, Argus a prelate, and Mercury, of course, the devil. The music with which Mercury captivates Argus is the wanton charms of women.

[11] *Hous of Fame,* ll. 1486 ff.

If medieval authors generally missed the witty, ironic, cynical tone of the sophisticated poet of love, they also read the *Metamorphoses* in their own way. They were less likely than a modern reader to see Ovid plain, since they often met him in expanded paraphrases or abridgments, often, too, encrusted with astrological, allegorical, euhemeristic deposits. They were less likely to perceive Ovid's firm control of his material, his rhetorical tricks, his sustained verve, his creation of a clear daylight world of magic. Scholars such as John of Salisbury may praise Ovid's *levitatem versificandi,*[12] poets such as Chaucer may learn artistic lessons, but in comparison with later ages—for these statements are only relative— it is the substance of the *Metamorphoses* rather than its spirit or the niceties of its technique that the medieval writer lays hold of.

IV. ALLEGORY

Allegory might almost be said to constitute the bone, muscle, and nerves of serious medieval literature. The medieval mind, inhabiting a more intelligible world than ours, saw everywhere correspondences between sets of facts and ideas that to us seem unrelated. Knowledge was of three kinds, material, moral, spiritual, and up and down the ladder joining these three planes the allegorists moved like the angels in Jacob's dream. Yet the habit of allegorizing—for us the word means the reading of allegory into literature—was by no means purely medieval. It was common before Plato, and Plato himself counts as one of the germinal forces. And we shall escape from it only toward the end of this book, when the rationalism of the later seventeenth century bores through things mysterious with a cool hard stare. The octopus of allegory, then, lies floating many a rood, and at intervals we shall pause and survey the creature, though we must be content with a few prominent features of the great anatomy.

Since Homer was the Greek Bible in almost everything except the claim of divine authority, the time arrived when the devout or the skeptical reader had difficulty in reconciling the ideals of religion or the dictates of reason with the behavior of Zeus and Ares and Aphrodite. An avenue of escape opened up in the doctrine that things were not what they seemed, that underneath the fiction was concealed precious truth. However particular modes of interpretation might differ, the allegorical reading of myths became almost universal.

Such a magical sword and shield were naturally seized by Neo-Platonists and Christian apologists. Philo Judaeus and his school tried

[12] Migne, *Patrologiæ Latinæ,* CXCIX, 484.

to show that the Pentateuch contained Greek philosophy, and Christian writers proved that the Hebrew prophets and poets contained Christianity. The Old Testament includes episodes of doubtful religious quality, and allegory came to the rescue. The most familiar example is the conversion of a sensuous love song (perhaps a survival from a liturgy of the fertility cult) into an allegory of Christ and the church. The invaluable method was carried over into the New Testament as well; the five barley loaves and two fishes, for instance, might become the law and the prophets. Despite protests from some of the fathers such an instrument of exegesis was too effective to be laid down. Augustine tells how the allegorical expositions of Ambrose removed his difficulties, and illuminated passages "which when I understood literally, I was slain." [13]

Although, after the first battles between classical literature and Christianity, the practical necessities of education established Latin authors in the medieval curriculum, they were never so secure that they did not need defenders. Allegorical interpretation could be used by both friends and foes of classical writings and classical mythology. Euhemerism, for example, might be turned against pagan religion; gods who had originally been mere men were no fit objects of worship. With or without polemical motives euhemeristic interpretation continued to be popular throughout the Middle Ages and long afterward. Still other modes of thought turned the ancient gods into demons, or into astrological influences. Such topics are alluring, but have less concern for us than the religious and ethical methods of interpreting the classics. Apologists invoked the doctrine which had proved its strength, and classical literature was found to contain Christian truth hidden under the attractive coating of fable. The *Virgiliana continentia* of Fulgentius, written apparently in the early sixth century, launched an interpretation of the *Aeneid*—the pilgrimage of the soul through life—that was to be accepted for many centuries. In various forms this notion appeared in John of Salisbury, in Petrarch (who had moments of doubt), and other "modern men." And indeed, apart from the arid literalness of the allegorizers, is it in essence altogether un-Virgilian? [14]

[13] *Confessions* (Loeb Classical Library), bk. v, c. 14 (I, 259); bk. vi, c. 4 (I, 279).

[14] "Vergil set before himself a Ulysses, perhaps even an Achilles. Nature set before him a St. Louis—a crusading knight and a 'holy' war.' In the issue he hovers between the two conceptions—and fails. Yet there emerges from the failure something greater, at any rate in hope and suggestion, than any epical success: an ideal and mystical figure standing outside time and place, that seems to be now Aeneas, now Rome, now the soul of Man setting forth doubtfully on the pilgrimage of a dimly descried eternal glory." H. W. Garrod, "Vergil," *English Literature and the Classics*, ed. Gordon (1912), p. 152.

Fulgentius also wrote a handbook of classical mythology, and his interpretations we shall meet again, for they lived more than a thousand years. In his hands the judgment of Paris, for instance, became a sermon on three modes of life, the contemplative, active, and sensual. This association with Minerva of the contemplative life (*quæ ad sapientiam & ad veritatis inquisitionem pertinet*) seems the most probable source of the medieval and modern version of the myth. In classical literature the offer of Minerva or Pallas is victory in war, in the medieval and modern tradition it is wisdom.[15]

The sprightly Ovid might seem to offer intractable material to the most devout and ingenious interpreter, yet all things were possible when the *Ars Amatoria* could be reproduced as a sober didactic manual. The *Heroides* also contributed moral lessons; in his picture of Penelope Ovid was upholding chaste love, while guilty passion was condemned in the person of Phaedra.[16] Much more important was the immense reworking of the *Metamorphoses* called the *Ovide moralisé*, produced somewhere around the end of the thirteenth century. No tale was too sensuous and pagan to yield its quota of theological and moral lessons, not to mention other kinds.[17] Since the *Philomena*, which has been outlined already, was incorporated in the *Ovide moralisé*, we may ask what the interpreter makes of it. Pandion is God, who marries the soul, Progne, to the body, Tereus, in order that their offspring may replace the wicked angels who were cast out of heaven (these being the barbarians who were besieging Athens). The soul and body lived well together, and had a son Itys, "le bon fruit de sainte vie." But Progne longed to see her sister (the world and its pleasures), and sent Tereus over land and sea to obtain those earthly delights which God

[15] W. C. Curry, *M. L. N.*, XXXI, 114–16. The first literary appearance of the offer of wisdom Mr. Curry finds in *Floir et Blancefloir* (*ca.* 1160), and it occurs in the Middle English *Destruction of Troy* (*ca.* 1375). The source of the various Middle English versions is probably, sometimes certainly, Guido delle Colonne. Cf. Edmond Faral, "Le récit du jugement de Paris dans l'Énéas et ses sources," *Romania*, XLI (1912), 100–02.

Fulgentius is quoted from *Mythographi Latini*, ed. T. Muncker (Amsterdam, 1681). For Paris, see ii. 1. As an instance of survival I might quote the allegory of L. Scoto prefixed to the second canto of Marino's *L'Adone* (Amsterdam, 1679, p. 45), where there are remarks on the three ways of life, "l'attiva, la contemplativa, & la voluntaria."

[16] S. B. Meech, "Chaucer and an Italian Translation of the *Heroides*," *P. M. L. A.*, XLV, 110 ff.

[17] The method of allegorizing, as formulated by Origen, Pope Gregory, and others, involved the elucidation of three or four meanings. A convenient exposition of fourfold interpretation, literal, allegorical, moral, anagogical, is given in Dante's *Il Convivio* (Trattato Secondo, c. 1). For some remarks on the fourth or anagogical value as containing the whole meaning of metaphysical poetry, see Herbert Read, *Reason and Romanticism* (1926), p. 45. For authorities on ancient and medieval mythographers and allegory see my bibliography (under "General" and "Chapter One"), in particular H. J. Rose, Sir J. E. Sandys, E. E. Sikes, O. Gruppe, L. Rick, E. C. Knowlton, and C. G. Osgood.

had granted to be used in moderation. The body, however, fixed all its thoughts upon these (Tereus' violation of Philomela), and hoarded them with avaricious care (the immuring of Philomela in the charge of an old woman). The soul forsakes the good for the evil life (Progne sacrifices to Pluto and doffs her golden robes to put on black ones), and gives itself up to sin (the releasing of Philomela). The fruit of good life is destroyed (the murder of Itys). The soul flies to hell, the vile body becomes a hoopoe, and Philomela is changed into a nightingale.[18]

Another allegorized version of the *Metamorphoses,* composed in the fourteenth century, was the Latin prose work that went under the name of Thomas Waleys but was written by Petrus Berchorius. The story of Pyramus and Thisbe, for example, seems almost made to the interpreter's hand. Pyramus, the son of God, loves Thisbe, the human soul, but the wall (sin) stands between them. Through the blessed incarnation they are to come together under the cross (the mulberry tree), at the baptismal font (the fountain). But the soul cannot approach the font because of the devil (the lion), and awaits the coming of Christ in silence. The son of God endures death for the human soul (Pyramus commits suicide). The soul should imitate his death, as Thisbe kills herself, and suffer the same anguish mentally. Or, to take an alternative exposition, Thisbe is the maiden to whom the son came in the flesh; he died on the cross, and she in compassion transfixed herself with a sword.[19]

There was an unbroken chain of such works which extends into the seventeenth century. In addition to miscellaneous compilations of allegorized myths, such as those of Boccaccio and Christine de Pisan, there were successive moralized versions of the *Metamorphoses* in Latin and the vernaculars. About 1370 Giovanni dei Buonsignori put together a volume based on an earlier translation of Ovid and the allegories of Giovanni del Virgilio. In 1484 the house of Colard Mansion issued a French rendering of Ovid, with bits from Waleys, Guido, and others woven into the text. And so we reach Caxton. But this is to anticipate, and we shall return to some of these books later.

The religious and moral and other lessons embodied in the *Ovide moralisé* and kindred works would of course have made Ovid stare and gasp. Mr. Haskins remarks that such Ovidian exegesis "must ordinarily

---

[18] *Ovide moralisé,* ed. De Boer, vi. 3719 ff.

[19] *Metamorphosis Ovidiana moraliter explanata* (Paris, 1509), fol. xxxvi. It was possibly another edition of "Waleys" that Richard Inglesant, ancestor of John, found in the Prior's room of the monastery he was investigating as the envoy of Thomas Cromwell.

I might mention the romance of *Amoryus and Cleopes,* by John Metham, apparently written in 1448–49 (*Works of John Metham,* ed. H. Craig, E. E. T. S., 1916). The author

have been the rationalizing effort to find justification for what men were reading for other reasons." [20] While an amateur may well hesitate to question any observation of Mr. Haskins concerning the Middle Ages, I cannot help thinking that, in his rehabilitation of an abused period, he inclines to make it too modern, to underestimate the sincerity of the moralizers and their public. No doubt many deceived themselves, but surely many more read the allegories in good faith. What proportion of the Victorian middle class honestly believed it was reading poetry when it was only looking for Great Thoughts? In the first place, there is the sheer appalling bulk of allegorical commentary, far too large to spring from a perfunctory official piety. Then, if one habitually thinks in terms of allegory, if the physical world and everything else are an allegory of the spiritual, mythology becomes a natural part of one's subject matter. Finally, a mode of thought which maintained a vigorous life well into the seventeenth century—indeed far beyond—must have had deep and authentic roots. Of course this is not to say that Ovid the poet was not enjoyed. Nor can one generalize about medieval simplicity in the age of the Freudians.

V. CHAUCER

If Chaucer had lived in the sixteenth century or in the twentieth his classical erudition would probably not have been infallible, for, though learned, he was not a mousing scholar, and he read with the swift and selective eye of a poet. But there were more than temperamental reasons for inaccuracy in the fourteenth century. Though much scholarly exploration has been done, it is still often difficult to ascertain how far Chaucer and other medieval men got information directly from the classical texts, and how far indirectly, through medieval redactions, books of extracts, quotations in grammars, and such things. Chaucer's sixty books constituted a large library, and his knowledge of Latin, French, and Italian was more than respectable. If he does sometimes make errors in classical matters he has also sometimes been wrongfully accused.[21] In any case such details have little to do with his art.

makes use of the story of Pyramus and Thisbe, though with some remarkable changes. The lovers are revived through the prayer of a hermit, are baptized, married, and enjoy a long life.

[20] *Renaissance of the Twelfth Century*, p. 108.

[21] For instance, there is classical authority, probably known to Chaucer, for the uncertain identity of Ascanius, so that he cannot be safely charged with a schoolboy blunder in making Ascanius and Iulus two persons. See E. K. Rand, "Chaucer in Error," *Speculum*, I (1926), 222. As for the telescoping of Brutus and Cassius, there was at least an established medieval tradition, which is a mitigating circumstance. See H. T. Silverstein, *M. L. N.*, XLVII (1932), 148. I think Thomas Phaer, the Elizabethan translator of Virgil, regarded Pyrrhus and Neoptolemus as two men.

We can here only recall a few well-worn illustrations of Chaucer's attitude toward classical themes and classical authors. To begin with the outline of the *Aeneid* in the *Hous of Fame,* the first three books receive about a hundred and eighteen lines in Chaucer; the fourth book, the story of Dido, receives ninety-two lines, of which sixty are taken up with Dido's complaint; the remaining eight books are dispatched in thirty-five lines. Arithmetic alone indicates that epic has become romance. The *Legend of Dido,* though closer to the corresponding portion of Virgil, reveals a similar shift of emphasis, which of course is justified by the title. Dido's violation of her oath of loyalty to her husband is not mentioned, and much is made of Aeneas' broken vows. In neither poem does Chaucer present Aeneas as the prospective founder of Rome, traveling under divine guidance, temporarily seduced from his high destiny by a grandly passionate woman. Dido is a faithful saint of Cupid deceived and abandoned by a treacherous man, and the conception is in obvious accord with medieval romance—and Ovid.[22]

Another medieval element, likewise already encountered in romance, is the rationalization of the pagan supernatural. Chaucer relates, but with strong misgivings, that in "the book" Venus makes Aeneas invisible; he omits the divine agencies which secured a welcome for the Trojans; and he questions Cupid's personal activity in the kindling of Dido's love. In connection with Chaucer's rationalistic attitude it may be noted that his armor of common sense leaves him almost untouched by the allegorical mania.[23] Of course the setting of the poems is medievalized.

Thus Virgil is a source of material for Chaucer, but of spiritual affinity between the two there is not much. Chaucer's favorite ancient, one of his three or four favorite authors, was Ovid, whose influence ranges from decorative allusions to narrative method and conception of character. The familiar list of concrete borrowings need not be repeated here, but one question may be dwelt upon for a moment. Since we shall be much concerned with the technique and style of mythological poems in the sixteenth century, I should like to quote here an analysis of one of Chaucer's Ovidian pieces which, in almost every detail except the precise arithmetical figures, will be found true of *Venus and Adonis* and *Lucrece.* Mr. Manly thus dissects the Manciple's Tale:

[22] See E. K. Rand, *Ovid and His Influence* (1925), pp. 24–26; Elizabeth Nitchie, *Vergil and the English Poets* (1919).

[23] J. D. Cooke, "Euhemerism," *Speculum,* II, 396 ff. Chaucer does of course make use of the "astrologised" gods. See W. C. Curry, "Astrologising the Gods," *Anglia,* XLVII, 213, and *Chaucer and the Mediaeval Sciences* (New York, 1926).

It consists of 258 lines, of which 41 are devoted to describing Phebus, his wife, and the crow, and 50 to telling the incidents of the story. The remaining 167 lines—61 per cent. of the tale—are patches of rhetoric. Even this high percentage is perhaps too low, for the 25 lines of description devoted to Phebus are so conventional, so much in accordance with rhetorical formulas, that they might fairly be added to our estimate of the percentage of rhetoric. No effort was made by the author to conceive any of his characters as living beings or to visualize the action of the tale . . . Instead of attempting to realize his characters psychologically and conceive their actions and words as elements of a dramatic situation, he padded the tale with rhetoric. Thus he thrust into it and around it 32 lines of *sententiae*, 36 of *exempla*, 18 of *exclamatio*, 14 of *sermocinatio*, 3 of technical transition, 17 of *demonstratio*, and 63 of *applicatio*—all external and mechanical additions, clever enough as mere writing, but entirely devoid of life.[24]

To this general pattern Shakespeare, writing in the convention of his day, added pagan and pictorial sensuousness, but not much more. Further, Shakespeare carried to excess the balance and antithesis of the Ovidian line, but the trick is common in Chaucer; he learned it both from Ovid and from poets nourished on Ovid.[25]

Chaucer gathered his classical materials with an impartial hand. Statements regarding his sources are constantly subject to revision, but we need not go into detail. The legends of good women are compounded from a variety of authors, Ovid, Virgil, Guido delle Colonne, Boccaccio, the *Ovide moralisé,* Filippo "Ceffi," and others. The story of Ceyx and Alcyone in *The Book of the Duchesse* combines, with original variations, Ovid and a dash of Machaut. The Physician's Tale of Virginia, along with its attribution to Livy, comes from the *Roman de la Rose.* Trojan material is taken from Joseph of Exeter's version of Dares, from Guido and Benoit. Sometimes, as Mr. Lowes pointed out, mythological allusions are colored by Dante. The classical purist might accuse Chaucer of sowing cockles in his clean corn, but the charge would of course only exhibit a quite uncritical conception of medieval ways. Chaucer was not writing works like Becker's *Gallus,* he was a story-teller looking for stories; he assumed, as Shakespeare did, that human nature is the same in all times and places.

But, with all his classical borrowings, Chaucer was on the whole least Chaucerian and most medieval in his treatment of ancient stories. The tales of good women are perfunctory and contain frequent admissions of haste and boredom; he never finished the book. Nor are the classical

[24] "Chaucer and the Rhetoricians," *Proceedings of the British Academy,* XII (1926), 108.
[25] M. A. Hill, "Rhetorical Balance in Chaucer's Poetry," *P.M.L.A.,* XLII (1927), 845. Cf. C. S. Baldwin, "Cicero on Parnassus," *ibid.,* p. 106.

stories told by the pilgrims among his successes. Yet would one expect anything else? The ironic observer of the human comedy moved more easily and happily among creatures of flesh and blood than in the less substantial world of mythological figures. Here and there, to be sure, are pleasant touches of simplicity and pathos, and the inimitable irony is not wholly wanting:

> She fledde her-self into a litel cave,
> And with her wente this Eneas al-so;
> I noot, with hem if ther wente any mo;
> The autour maketh of hit no mencioun.

But the comment is in the vein of Ovid rather than Virgil.

We cannot linger over the more elaborate "mythological" poems, the Knight's Tale and *Troilus,* since they are of medieval origin. In the latter Chaucer had the room and the material he needed; his characters live as they never could in brief Ovidian tales. Here and in the best of the *Canterbury Tales* Chaucer revealed himself as, in the main, a classic artist, and Dryden with his usual insight said so, finding the medieval poet more simple and natural, in a word, more classical, than Ovid. Yet to say that Chaucer is nearest to classical art when he is furthest from classical material, that his Dido is less classical than his Wife of Bath, is only to say that the deepest influence of the ancients upon him cannot be measured. For would the Wife be what she is if Chaucer had not learned much from Ovid and the poets whom the classics taught, such as Jean de Meung and the rest?

If Chaucer represents the incalculable accident of genius, his friend the moral Gower represents something better than the average mind of the fourteenth century. His knowledge of the Latin classics was considerable, though not invulnerable; he could make two persons of "Tullius" and "Cithero," and was content to write of Virgil the wizard and his magic mirror. Gower is assuredly not a tricksy spirit, but as a story-teller he has virtues, in spite of the portentously didactic framework of the *Confessio Amantis*. While, except in a few moments of pathos, classic myths left Chaucer cold, they found in Gower an often spirited and sympathetic narrator; he was really moved by the fate of Medea, Canace, Lucrece. Besides, he had command of pure and simple English. Altogether his tales are much better than many later mythological poems. The remarkable evenness of Gower's thousands of lines has been unkindly described as the fluency of running lead, and doubtless he is not for continuous reading; but neither is William Morris.

VI. THE MEDIEVAL ATTITUDE

Although the fallacious implications of such a heading as "the medieval attitude" arouse the just ire of scholars, the phrase may serve to introduce a few words on certain important aspects of classical culture in the Middle Ages. Some familiar generalizations have a bearing on the medieval heritage of the sixteenth century. In the first place knowledge of classical, that is, Latin literature, was limited to a small minority. Then, although the range of Latin authors known was wide, it was often only partial. Horace's *Epistles* and *Satires,* for instance, had a considerable circulation, while the *Odes* were almost unread. Ovid's *Amores* was little known, though his other major works had such an immense popularity. The list might be extended indefinitely. Further, if the Latin authors were seldom read as wholes, and if spurious works had got into the canon, they could not be appreciated as distinct personalities. Nor could the classical writers be seen in a historical setting. Horace and Lucan, Virgil and Statius, were simply lumped together; they were all ancients.

But in the absence of our historical and critical view of antiquity the story-teller did not greatly suffer. Classical epics and romances based on them were read side by side, and were equally useful as sources. A story was a story, wherever found, though an ancient name, such as Lollius, might add weight and prestige. Whatever went into the capacious melting pot, the *Aeneid* or a tale from the *Metamorphoses,* came out a romance, or a sermon, or both.

Since medieval art in general is characterized by the mixture of alien elements, we have abundant illustrations in the treatment of classic and pseudo-classic themes. The mingling of the classical and medieval includes of course the mingling of the pagan and the Christian. "I am not Aeneas, I am not Paul," says Dante to his master and guide. In his untroubled use of classic myth the most religious of poets is typical of the reconciling spirit of the best medieval minds; perhaps one should say typical of a spirit unconscious of the need for reconciliation. Chaucer may exclaim

> Lo here, the fyn and guerdon for travaille
> Of Iove, Appollo, of Mars, of swich rascaille!

But these lines occur in that remarkable epilogue to *Troilus,* where, recoiling from his own vivid presentation of physical passion, Chaucer exhorts young people to turn from earthly loves to the abiding love of God. That is not the normal mood of Chaucer or other secular writers.

Chaucer is normal when he casually dubs Amphiaraus a bishop,[26] or thinks of Ovidian love stories as "the Seintes Legende of Cupyde."

The untroubled assimilation of all manner of things, so evident in the mixture of sources and of Christian and pagan ideas, has an obvious bearing upon critical appreciation of classical art. The timeless virtues of clear vision, disinterested reasonableness, precision of line, architectonic form, are not the most conspicuous qualities of medieval writing, though they are not wholly absent. Even Chaucer, in many ways truly classical, is sometimes naïve in matters of form. Despite the plentiful evidence of rich enjoyment of the classics, and despite the intensive study of rhetoric, it was not in the main aesthetic lessons that the medieval writer absorbed from his reading. John of Salisbury, the best scholar and one of the best minds of the twelfth century, read the *Aeneid* as an allegory of the life of man, found precepts of morality in the *Georgics,* and drew wisdom even from the talk of shepherds in the *Eclogues.* He esteemed Lucan highly as a moral teacher; Ovid also, with reservations. Horace is *ethicus;* likewise Juvenal and Persius. Terence contains excellent lessons in morals and manners. Altogether, for this Christian humanist, the ancients transmit *informationem virtutis quae facit bonum virum.*[27] Such an approach to the classics does not preclude aesthetic appreciation, but it certainly does not emphasize those qualities which would have helped to restrain and mold and rationalize medieval literature. On the other hand it proves that the classics, however altered and Christianized, were a living source of culture to a degree which we with all our knowledge hardly attain.

While the nineteenth century in general saw the Middle Ages and the Renaissance in terms of black and white, modern scholars have in the first place shown the importance of medieval achievement, and, in the second, have made it clear that the Renaissance was no sudden break with the medieval past. In all fields of activity men of the Renaissance were much less emancipated than they thought they were; most of them, even such heralds of modernity as Bacon and Descartes, were rooted in medieval tradition. The medieval mind accepted the irrational if it came in the guise of religion, we accept the irrational if it comes in the guise of science; the difference is called progress. Though, in relation to the general march of mind, the study of myths is a bypath, a main effort in this book will be to show the persistence, for good and ill, of the medieval spirit.

[26] Golding, by the way, renders *sacerdos* as "bisshop" (*Metam.* xv. 778; Golding, ed. Rouse, p. 311, l. 855).

[27] A. C. Krey, "John of Salisbury's Knowledge of the Classics," *Wisconsin Academy of Sciences,* XVI, Part 2 (1910), 948 ff.; Migne, *Patrologiæ Latinæ,* CXCIX, *passim.*

CHAPTER TWO

THE BACKGROUND OF CLASSICAL MYTHOLOGY IN THE SIXTEENTH CENTURY

I. THE CHARACTER OF ENGLISH HUMANISM

THOUGH the religious and ethical quality of early Tudor humanism is a commonplace, it is one that must be emphasized here. Without it Spenser and Milton, even Marlowe and Shakespeare, are inconceivable. For what vitalized the Renaissance in Europe generally was the spiritual energy inherited from medieval religion. That energy, however disguised or transmuted, made possible, for a time, a Christian humanism more liberal and cultivated—and perhaps less devout—than the Middle Ages had developed. But for it the revived classical culture would have been less solid, less fruitful, less enduring; the fact will find illustration even in these pages.

From the very beginning the movement revealed some dangerous symptoms. The spiritual chaos of the present day may leave it open to question whether the separation that finally took place between humanism and religion was both an inevitable and a triumphant stride forward, or, on the part of humanism, a self-destructive cutting off of its own life-giving roots. There can at any rate be no question about the fatal results of the divorce between literary humanism and life. At first the classics mirrored an ideal of civilized sweetness and light, a world in which man enjoyed dignity and freedom; in the hands of dilettanti and pedagogues they became too often an ideal of *eloquentia*. Humanism ceased to be humanistic when it made style a supreme object, when Bembo could give his well-known advice to Sadoleto. For one bold mind like Valla, who had absorbed the critical spirit (if not the urbanity) of the ancients, there were a thousand sedulous apes of Cicero; and Latin was slain in the house of its friends. The humanists, at first the party of progress, became the party of academic orthodoxy and reaction, while scientists and other more legitimate heirs of antiquity took the lead.

The paganism of the Italian Renaissance has usually been exaggerated by glowing or gushing pens, for popular writers still embellish some fundamental misconceptions of Burckhardt and Symonds. But certain large differences between Italian and English religion and culture cannot be overlooked. Religious instincts in many leaders of the Italian Renaissance flowed into mystic or "heretical" channels; we recall such names as Ficino, Pico della Mirandola, Pomponio Leto, Pomponazzi, Agostino Nifo, Giordano Bruno, not to mention the ascetic fervor of Savonarola. Among classical scholars, humanists in the special sense of the word, a soul is not always to be discerned, though one Vittorino had more influence than a score of Poggios and Filelfos.

But early Tudor Englishmen felt no great urge toward mystic ecstasy, high philosophic speculation, or bold and critical rationalism. Instead we find orthodox Catholicism followed by more or less orthodox Calvinism, and an unceasing preoccupation with practical morals. Paganism, real or affected, did not flourish among English scholars of the fifteenth and sixteenth centuries. The first generations of English students, with such rare exceptions as the luckless Tiptoft, brought back from Italy serious books and ideas, not the empty purse, queasy stomach, and naughty conscience of the later Italianate Englishman. The names of most early Tudor humanists are virtually a roll call of religious leaders, or at any rate sober and pious teachers. As a pendant to Bembo and Sadoleto we may think of Erasmus and Colet walking in Colet's garden and talking of Christ.

Not only was the early English Renaissance extremely religious, it was also extremely practical. The shallow elegances of some continental culture were alien to the English temper. Besides, in barbarous Britain, "situated outside the world," as Battista Guarino said, it was natural that the fruits of the movement should for some time be devoted mainly to education. Humanism in England did not of course altogether escape the dangers of inbreeding. No one could seek more eagerly than Ascham to relate literature to life, yet even he could utter the astonishing complaint: "Ye know not, what hurt ye do to learning, that care not for wordes, but for matter." A little more than a generation later the Moses of the new science pronounced sentence against the Egyptians who had kept the children of Israel in the house of bondage: "Here therefore is the first distemper of learning, when men study words and not matter." But if humanism sometimes lapsed into sterile pedantry, for the most part it labored in the best spirit of learning and patriotism to spread enlightenment.

Propagation and popularization of classical literature was a first necessity. Over and over again the translators lament that England lags

behind other countries in making classical wisdom available for the
mass of unlearned readers; their own desires, they say, exceed their
competence, but they go manfully to work. And these translators were
not merely or mainly university teachers, official custodians of the
classics, but ardent unofficial scholars, young authors and Inns of Court
men.[1] A chronological summary of works translated from the classics
might try the reader's patience, but a very brief survey may be allowed.

To pass over the beginnings in the first quarter of the century, we
find about thirty-five translations in the second quarter. There are half
a dozen medical books, some history (including Thucydides, done from
a French version of a Latin version), but the largest group is that of
moral and philosophical works, Aristotle, Cicero, Seneca, Plutarch,
"Cato," and others. In the third quarter about eighty translations appear,
and we have, in addition to such perennials as Galen, more history, some
science, textbooks on rhetoric; moral works are still prominent, from
Cicero, with seven or eight pieces, to Philo Judaeus. So far the century
is running true to form.

But now there is also a considerable bulk of translation from ancient
fiction, drama, and poetry. Many of these works, to be sure, were not
officially labeled as entertainment, since the early Elizabethans hardly
admitted such a category. At any rate we have Adlington's *Apuleius,*
Underdowne's *Heliodorus,* the classical tales in Painter's *Palace of
Pleasure,* and other such books, though Italian and French fiction is
taking the lead. There are numerous renderings of Ovid and Virgil,
some of which will be noticed later, and most of the Senecan plays
appear in English. Some treatments of Horace are significant. The
versions of two odes in Tottel's *Miscellany* represent, not the urbane
observer of life or the heart-whole lover, but the sober moralist who
flees extremes and meditates on the brevity of life and the approach of
death.[2] And in his version of the *Satires* and *Epistles* (1566–67) Thomas
Drant, who complacently "wyped awaye" all of Horace's "vanitie and
superfluitie of matter," turned the sophisticated ironist into a Tudor
preacher.

The fourth quarter of the century shows some decline in the number
of classical translations; there are only about sixty. Most of the works

---

[1] In addition to Whibley's chapter in the *Cambridge History of English Literature* and
H. R. Palmer's invaluable *List of English Editions and Translations of Greek and Latin
Classics* (1911), see such later special studies as F. R. Amos, *Early Theories of Translation*
(1920); C. H. Conley, *The First English Translators of the Classics* (1927); F. O. Matthiessen, *Translation: An Elizabethan Art* (1931).

[2] The odes are ii. 10 and iv. 7. See *Miscellany,* ed. Rollins, II, 152, 273, and index.

which attracted Elizabethan readers were already in English, and there was increasing competition in a multitude of translations from modern languages. Besides, the first phase of the English Renaissance, that of education and assimilation, had passed into the second, that of re-expression, and the immense creative energy of the time was pouring along a dozen channels. Yet the same kinds of books were being read, and in about the same proportions. One work alone would have made the fortune of the period, North's *Plutarch* (1579), and in 1600 came Livy, announcing the arrival of the translator-general, Philemon Holland. More translations of the Greek romances bear witness to an interest reflected in Elizabethan fiction, yet Greek tragedy and comedy and Plato had not yet found their way into English. Among many versions of classical poets we may remember that Homer first appeared in Arthur Hall's ten books of the *Iliad,* done from the French, and before the end of the century came the first installments of Chapman's *Homer,* one of the uncertain glories of that April day.

Most of the works mentioned indicate not only popularization of classic story but increasing knowledge and understanding of antiquity. When we come to Philemon Holland we have reached the beginnings of modern scholarship. Yet men had not laid aside the ethical spectacles of John of Salisbury. Even if Tudor writers and readers, like their medieval predecessors, fell short of the modern in aesthetic appreciation of the classics—an assumption that we may make too easily—they had a far more immediate and vivid sense of ancient literature as a part of their life, of ancient civilization as a not unattainable ideal. It is a commonplace that to North Brutus and Antony are as real as Cecil and Leicester. In 1570 Thomas Wilson issued a translation of Demosthenes' orations against Philip, "most nedefull to be redde in these daungerous dayes, of all them that loue their Countries libertie, and desire to take warning for their better auayle, by example of others." The Macedonian was not the only King Philip Englishmen thought of when they read Demosthenes.

If the ancients, who in general held a rather didactic view of literature, had returned to earth in the sixteenth century, they would not have complained, as I think Ruskin did, "I show men their plain duty, and they reply that I have a beautiful style." Ciceronians were relatively few in England, experiments with classical meters were largely a coterie affair (nor were they so irrational around 1580 as they might seem a decade later), and the general influence of the classics was solid and healthy. That their direct influence on poetic theory and practice was somewhat weak is partly, but not altogether, a matter for regret. The native and medieval tradition was too strong to be subdued; thanks to that Elizabethan drama, for instance, displayed a vitality lacking in the classicized drama of France. Poetry in general owed more directly to the older English poets and modern continental writers than to the classics, and the classics were read by a half-medieval light. But even if a characteristic of Elizabethan writing is a rich lawlessness, such an earnest and sometimes moving poem as *Musophilus,* a sixteenth-century *Culture and Anarchy* in verse, shows both the fertilizing and the disciplinary power of classical literature over sober minds. Nor was Daniel ever a more authentic classicist than when in his prose essay he spoke out against slavish imitation of the ancients and declared that English literature must develop in accordance with its own genius.

A word more must be said on the matter of imitation or plagiarism, especially since we are following in mythological poems a very imitative tradition. Mr. Saintsbury once ranked source-hunting with the sport of worrying cats, and it is a popular attitude among the foes of pedantry. But in studying poetry of the Renaissance it is somewhat uncritical to ignore one of the main tenets of the poetical creed. Imitation, which for Aristotle meant ideal imitation of life, by the first century B. C. had come to mean, for Dionysius of Halicarnassus, imitation of authors. This early perversion of the Aristotelian doctrine was encouraged by the strong tendency of Greek and Roman critics to link poetry with rhetoric. The precept of literary imitation appeared in Cicero's *De Oratore,* and in the pseudo-Ciceronian *Ad Herennium,* which was extremely popular in the Middle Ages. It was approved by Quintilian and even by "Longinus." [3] Having flourished throughout the medieval period, the doctrine of plagiarism was powerfully reinforced by such Italian critics as Bembo, Vida, Daniello, Minturno. The modern author, it was said again and again, learns his craft from the masters; if he improves what he borrows he justifies his theft.

The critical tradition was of course carried on by English writers— Ascham was a notable early exponent—and although, as in Italy, there was a growing reaction against servility, a growing confidence in native genius, the doctrine of imitation was abundantly preached and practiced. Consistency was not always observed. Lodge could write in an essay

[3] *Instit.* x. i–ii; *On the Sublime,* xiii. 2–4; xiv. 1. See G. Fiske, *Lucilius and Horace* (University of Wisconsin Studies, 1920), c. 1, "The Classical Theory of Imitation"; W. L. Bullock, "The Precept of Plagiarism in the Cinquecento," *M. P.,* XXV, 293; H. O. White, *Plagiarism and Imitation in English Literature, 1558–1625,* in *Harvard University Summaries of Theses, 1930,* pp. 218–21.

of the *furor poeticus;* when he wrote verse the divine and presumably original inspiration was not incompatible with wholesale thefts. On some levels, naturally, plagiarism was vicious, as a mass of sonnets makes clear, but it was imitation of great poets that made possible great Elizabethan poetry. E. K. pointed out that Spenser in his first book was devoutly following literary tradition, and in the strength of maturity Spenser invaded authors like a monarch. He went to school to some ancients and the best moderns, and, having done so, he created a style, a style essentially original. If English poetry was to be great it had to be not merely English but European, and Spenser more than anyone else made it so. Whatever sins, therefore, are to be traced to the Renaissance theory of imitation, and we find a good many, it may be remembered that the two greatest non-dramatic poets of the English Renaissance are also, to use our disparaging term, the most derivative.

II. THE SOURCES OF CLASSICAL MYTHOLOGY

Sources were of course vastly more abundant in the sixteenth century than in the Middle Ages. More ancient authors were known, and they were better known. Of these Ovid was the most important, and it would need many volumes to catalogue the adventures of that most capricious poet among the Goths. But the use of Ovid and some other ancient sources will be noticed in connection with individual poets. In this section I shall try to indicate the nature of what may be called popular authorities, for, as every student of the Renaissance knows, medieval sources and medieval ideas were not abandoned in a general return to the pure fountains of classical literature.

Since a large share of mythological and historical allusion was given a didactic turn in both prose and verse, we find a large debt to such books as Plutarch's *Lives* and *Morals,* the collections of Valerius Maximus, Aelian, Aulus Gellius. The sixteenth-century reader had a keen relish for the sober shrewdness and point of ancient anecdote. Then there were countless modern compilations, such as the *Adagia* of Erasmus, a book which helped as much as any to reveal to Europe the intellectual and moral character of antiquity. To the ordinary reader such books may not always have brought emancipation, but they were inexhaustible treasuries of classical story.[4]

Medieval redactions of classic stories reached the English reader mainly

[4] For instance, the story of Ulysses' stopping his own ears with wax appears in Ascham, Lyly, Pettie's translation of Guazzo, and Chapman. The un-Homeric detail seems to come from Erasmus (*Similia*), who was imperfectly recollecting an allusion in Plutarch. See M. P. Tilley, *Classical Philology*, XXI, 162. Even Ben Jonson accepts the variant (*Bartholo-*

through the paraphrases of Caxton and Lydgate, but in the sixteenth century the originals continued to be printed and read—Dares and Dictys, "Pindarus Thebanus," Guido, and Joseph of Exeter. Such writers, especially Dares and Dictys, were still authorities on the Trojan war, and they survived, though with diminishing prestige, far beyond the age of Scaliger and Casaubon. Sidney contrasts "the fayned Aeneas" of Virgil with "the right Aeneas" of Dares.[5]

In spite of more modern rivals Boccaccio's respectable labors, the *De Genealogia Deorum*, *De Claris Mulieribus*, and *De Casibus*, were constantly reprinted, translated, and borrowed from. Mythological handbooks later in date, and more learned, but not much more modern in spirit, were the *De Deis Gentium* of Lilius Giraldus (1548), the *Mythologiae* of Natalis Comes (1551), and *Le Imagini, con la Spositione de i Dei degli Antichi* of Vincenzo Cartari (1556).[6] These books, especially the last two, had an enormous influence throughout literary Europe, and the number of editions perplexes the bibliographer. Natalis Comes (Natale Conti) is perhaps the most attractive of the compilers, and he has his merits. He summarized mythological tales in easy Latin, assembled abundant references, quoted and translated Greek authors, and altogether provided the means which enabled many men, such as Chapman, to appear more learned than they were. Of the value of such books to writers Marston gives a satirical hint:

> Reach me some poets' index that will show.
> *Imagines Deorum,* Book of Epithets,
> Natalis Comes, thou I know recites,
> And makest anatomy of poesy . . .[7]

But well-arranged stories and references, however inviting, would not in themselves have given such works the authority they had. The great mass of sixteenth-century readers were far from pagan in their tastes, and mythology was especially appetizing when the cup was coated with the honey of morality. Comes and the rest carried on the tradition of Fulgentius, Neckam, Boccaccio, and the whole tribe of authors who had made mythology safe for the world. The myths were enriched with

mew Fair, III. i). One finds everywhere a similar process of transmission going on; we do the same thing ourselves.

[6] *Elizabethan Critical Essays,* I, 168. Geffrey Whitney compares the treatment of Hector by Dares, the eyewitness, and that of Achilles by the later Homer (*Choice of Emblemes,* 1586, dedicatory epistle). See the Appendix, under Thomas Fenne (1590) and Thomas Milles (1613).

[6] In addition to Gruppe (pp. 22, 32) and other authorities, see H. Pinard de la Boullaye, *L'étude comparée des religions* (3d ed., Paris, 1929), pp. 146 ff.

[7] *Works,* ed. Bullen, III, 270. *Imagines Deorum* is the title of the Latin editions of Cartari.

edifying interpretations, sufficiently medieval in character, though now moral expositions replaced theological. It was this allegorical element in Comes which commended itself to Chapman, and Chapman was not unique, unless perhaps in the magnitude of his debt.

There were some small English books of similar character. Stephen Batman's *Golden Booke of the Leaden Goddes* (1577) was a didactic compendium of mythology which described the appearance and insignia of the gods (not without glances at "sectarian gods" and misguided Anabaptists) and appended their "signification." Abraham Fraunce's *Third part of the Countesse of Pembrokes Ivychurch* (1592) contained sixteen Ovidian tales in verse and the fullest allegorical commentary which appeared in English before that of Sandys; Fraunce's "philosophi-call explications" were drawn from Cartari, Comes, and others. Richard Linche's *Fountaine of Ancient Fiction* (1599) was an abridged version of Cartari.

There was plenty of mythological lore in older English books. Chaucer, Gower, and Lydgate were widely read in the sixteenth century, but, so far as classical tales are concerned, it does not appear that Chaucer (apart from *Troilus*) and Gower had much influence. For earlier Tudor readers at least Lydgate often stood first in the trinity—he was a master of aureate diction—and his staggering paraphrases had a popularity out of proportion to anything but their length. His *Troy Book,* however, was overshadowed by Caxton's *Recuyell;* we shall return to Caxton in a moment.

The mythological compilations of Christine de Pisan, that doughty feminine invader of Grub Street, had some slight importance in the fifteenth and early sixteenth centuries, if several translations are adequate evidence. The first one was made about 1444–50 by Stephen Scrope, a stepson of Sir John Fastolf, from Christine's *L'Epistre d'Othea a Hector de Troie,* and, as one would expect, the book was included in the Pastons' library.[8] Drawing upon Ovid, the *Ovide moralisé,* Boccaccio, Dante, Machaut, and others, Christine recounted numerous myths and appended a moralization to each. Andromeda stands for the soul, Penthesilea is the virtue of charity, Bacchus the sin of gluttony; one may wonder if the lessons took effect on the rather mundane Pastons.

Equally medieval was the pedigree of Caxton's vastly more important versions of classic stories. His *Recuyell of the Historyes of Troye* was done from the French of Raoul le Fevre, who had embellished Guido.

---

[8] Ed. Sir George Warner, Roxburghe Club, 1904. See P. G. C. Campbell, Jeanroy, Laigle, and Pinet, in the bibliography to this chapter. For other translations from Christine, see the Appendix, under 1521 and 1536–45.

The choice of such a book to inaugurate Caxton's publishing career is significant enough regarding popular interest in the matter of Troy. It was frequently reprinted during the next two and a half centuries; the last of the twenty or so editions appeared thirteen years after the town had welcomed the *Iliad* of Pope.[9] Far more than any other book the *Recuyell* established the Elizabethan conception of the Trojan story. We shall often encounter it in pages to come.

In 1480 Caxton finished translating *Ovyde Hys Booke of Methamorphose* but apparently he did not print it.[10] The French original sometimes incorporated the moralizations of Berchorius, which Caxton mostly omitted, and Trojan matter was considerably expanded by passages interpolated from Guido delle Colonne and others. But the stories and the pictorial quality of Ovid remain; if they have lost a good deal of their polished art and sophistication, they have gained something rich and strange. Hector and Achilles are medieval knights, of course, and romance is more romantic, magic more magical, than in Ovid. But Ovid, whose text Caxton probably never looked at, might not have been displeased by a rendering so spirited and so opulent in style.

Other medievalized tales which Caxton translated from the French were *Jason* (*ca.* 1477) and *Eneydos* (1490). The French redactor had treated Virgil with the usual freedom, omitting, abridging, changing, adding matter from Boccaccio and similar indispensable sources. Some of the most familiar Virgilian episodes—Sinon and the wooden horse, the loss of Creusa—do not appear at all, while there is a long account, taken from Boccaccio, of the life and death of Dido. Epic elements are slighted, but the work was not conceived of as an epic; such a scholar as Gavin Douglas might well exclaim in his wrath that it was no more like Virgil than the devil like St. Austin. Though the *Eneydos* was not so popular as the *Recuyell,* we shall meet it again.

The multitude of later and more direct translations from the classics cannot be considered here. The influence of particular works, such as the all-important *Metamorphoses* of Golding, will be noticed in subsequent chapters. Such formal and relatively accurate versions had an immense and obvious share in the popularization of classical culture. They did not always catch the spirit of an author, and had a tendency

[9] A. Esdaile, *English Tales and Prose Romances Printed before 1740,* p. xii.

[10] There is only one MS extant, containing books x–xv, which may have been Caxton's own copy. It had an eventful history before it reached the hands of that lover of books, women, and song, Samuel Pepys. See the handsome reprint (1924) edited by Mr. S. Gaselee and Mr. H. F. B. Brett-Smith. Caxton translated from the French version—which was published by Colard Mansion in 1484—perhaps from Mansion's own MS, since the two men had been associated at Bruges.

to reduce the ancients to a common denominator, but they had the not negligible advantage of enthusiasm and a rich, fresh, vigorous idiom. They also enabled a number of persons, in Nashe's words, to vaunt "Ouids and Plutarchs plumes as theyr owne" and "feed on nought but the crums that fall from the Translators trencher" [11]—which is a rather good instance of Satan rebuking sin.

A few words may be added concerning miscellaneous books which, increasing in number as the century advanced, helped to make mythological allusions more familiar to the reading and theater-going public than they have ever been since. No one in the period could set pen to paper without invoking classical authority—"this pitch, as ancient writers do report, doth defile"—and a multitude of anecdotes and allusions passed from hand to hand in English books. Such ornaments, either in a journalist like Nashe or a scholarly poet like Chapman, cannot, any more than in the Middle Ages, be taken as evidence of profound learning. The mass of this material in Elizabethan books is quite overwhelming, and it will be enough to mention a few titles by way of emphasizing the fact that mythology reached both readers and writers by circuitous paths.

When one is told of the seething current of ideas that swept through Elizabethan England it is well to remember some of the best-selling books, such as *A Mirror for Magistrates,* which had many offspring, or the works of the most episcopal Guevara. The chief translations from the latter, Lord Berners' *Golden Boke* (1534) and North's *Diall of Princes* (1557), with their appalling prolixity, unwearied sententiousness, and hundreds of classical anecdotes, perfectly suited Tudor taste.[12] Manuals of rhetoric, such as those of Leonard Cox (1524) and Thomas Wilson (1553), illustrated their more or less classic principles with classic examples. Mindful of the rhetorical value of illustrations, Wilson explains the allegorical meaning of Danae and Isis, Tantalus and Icarus, Midas and Hercules. From Wilson came the story of Zaleuch and his son which is versified in *The Paradise of Dainty Devices;*[13] and from Elyot's *Governour* was taken the subject of a companion poem, also by

[11] Preface to *Menaphon (Works,* ed. McKerrow, III, 312). One might mention such a book as Underdowne's translation of Ovid's *Ibis* (1569), the notes to which constitute a small dictionary of myth.

[12] It may be put down to Guevara's credit that he pleased Montaigne's excellent father *(Essays,* ii. 2). And he contributed something to Burton, Jeremy Taylor, and Sterne (E. Bensly, *T.L.S.,* February 13, 1920, p. 106). Of course he influenced such earlier writers as Pettie and Lyly and others, though the theory of his euphuism has long been exploded.

[13] *Paradise,* ed. Rollins, pp. 58, 221; *Wilson's Arte of Rhetorique,* ed. G. H. Mair, p. 28.

Richard Edwards, *A yong man of Ægipt and Valerian.*[14] An Italian work based on Plutarch, Baptista Gelli's *Circe,* made the story of Ulysses and Circe the vehicle for a series of debates on the comparative merits of human and bestial life.[15] Such are a random few of the innumerable works which have unexpected dealings with mythology. Elizabethan prose and verse were sometimes dropsical with classical allusions, and, while a portion of such lore was honestly begotten by the ancients, a goodly portion also was of more recent parentage. The Elizabethan reader and writer could no more escape it, whatever they read, than the modern can escape the jargon of psychology.

III. CLASSICAL TALES IN ENGLISH PROSE

Painter's *Palace of Pleasure* (1566–67), which introduced Italian and French *novelle* to English readers and especially to English drama-tists, concerns us here on account of its forty-one classical stories. The sources make a significant list: Herodotus (two stories); Aelian (three); Plutarch's *Morals* (one); Aulus Gellius (twelve); Livy (eight); Quintus Curtius (three); Xenophon (one); Pedro Mexia (two); Guevara's *Letters* (three); Bandello (six).[16] The collection was indeed put together to be "delectable . . . for al sortes of men."

With one exception [17] the twenty-eight classical tales of Part One are taken from ancient sources; in Part Two only four are from ancient

[14] *Paradise,* pp. 57, 220; *The Governour,* ed. Croft, II, 315.

[15] The book was translated into English in 1557. See M. A. Scott, *Elizabethan Transla-tions from the Italian* (1916), pp. 10–11, and Collier, *Bibl. Acct.* (New York, 1866), II, 155–57.

[16] This correct list of sources is taken from my article on Painter, *J. E. G. P.,* XXIII, 331 ff. The list in Jacobs' edition (1890), which is repeated in the *D. N. B.,* is full of errors, including such an absurdity as making Tacitus the source of the account of Queen Zenobia. These errors are repeated again in Mr. Peter Haworth's volume of selections from Painter, *An Elizabethan Story-Book* (London and New York, 1928); and, when he touches on sources, in Mr. E. A. Baker's *History of the English Novel,* II (London, 1929). I have not seen the edition of Painter issued in 1929 by the Cresset Press.

From Livy Painter took the stories of the Horatii and Curiatii, Lucrece, Mucius Scaevola, Coriolanus, Appius and Virginia, Camillus, Tanaquil, and Theoxena; from Herodotus (Valla's translation, apparently) the stories of Candaules and Gyges, Solon and Croesus; from Xenophon the story of Panthea; from Plutarch that of Timoclea; from Bandello, Antiochus, Ariobarzanes, Aristotimus, Sophonisba, Pompey and the lady of Hidrusa, Faustina; from Guevara the correspondence of Trajan and Plutarch, the lives of the courtesans Lamia, Lais, and Flora (as examples to be avoided), and the energetic Queen Zenobia; from a French version of Mexia, the accounts of Timon and the Amazons; and so forth.

Greek authors were translated from Latin versions. In rendering Xenophon, Painter even made wholesale use of William Barkar's English translation of six books of the *Cyropaedia.* He likewise took some liberal extracts from Brende's version of Quintus Curtius.

[17] Novel 27. There are two exceptions if one counts the story of Timon, but it differs from Plutarch in arrangement rather than substance.

authors, the other nine from Bandello, Guevara, and Mexia. In Part One Painter was feeling his way, and nearly half of the classical stories belonged to the jest book category; in fact several had appeared in the *Mery Tales, Wittie Questions, and Quicke Answeres (ca.* 1535). But the reception of his book apparently showed the compiler what the public wanted, and in Part Two classical sobriety gave way to more modern tales of love and hot blood; even classical stories were mostly taken from modern versions adapted to modern taste. Thus Painter's solid tomes in a manner epitomize the changing literary fashions of the age, and this new appetite for amorous intrigue, courtly romance, lurid action, other translators quickly endeavored to satisfy, to the scandalizing of middle-aged puritans and patriots, such as Ascham.

Painter attempted to forestall the moralists, and his didactic motives, or professions, were expounded with fervor and fluency in the preface; stories of intrigue and rape and murder show young and old what not to do. (The useful word "frank" had not yet come into vogue.) Painter's additions to stories taken from classical sources were nearly all in the way of "morals"; a number of the longest ones, which introduce tales drawn from Belleforest, were carried over from the original. Otherwise, apart from occasional words of explanation, and occasional abridgment of historical matter, Painter was an almost colorless medium.

A Petite Pallace of Pettie his Pleasure (1576) has a small niche in literary history because it is the most notable document before *Euphues* in the development of euphuism.[18] It is of interest here as a collection of prose tales, all but one classical in subject and all highly unclassical in manner. Ovid was apparently Pettie's main quarry for plots, and from him came a good many incidental bits as well; Pettie, an Elizabethan professor of love, could not overlook the first and greatest incumbent of the chair.[19] Pettie's treatment of his plots is so very free, and most of them are familiar in so many versions, that sometimes one can only guess at his sources.[20]

As his title implies, Pettie was one of the numerous followers of

[18] Ed. Gollancz, London, 1908.

[19] Speaking of Lyly Miss Jeffery remarks that "within this system of reasoning the turning to classical mythology, especially to Ovid, for arguments and illustrations, is probably derived originally from Boccaccio" (*John Lyly and the Italian Renaissance,* p. 129). But it is difficult to name any one original model.

[20] With the proviso indicated, one can summarize the certain or probable sources thus:
Sinorix and Camma: *The Courtier* (Tudor Translations, p. 236).
Tereus and Progne: *Metam.* vi. 424 ff.
Germanicus and Agrippina: Tacitus, *Ann.* i. 33, 69; ii. 43, 72 ff.; iii. 1–6; etc. (though Tacitus would never have recognized his characters).
Amphiaraus and Eriphile: Hyginus, *Fab.* 69–73.
Icilius and Virginia: Livy, iii. 44–58. Pettie (I, 161–62) paraphrases and expands the

Painter, but his method was quite different. So far from being a mere translator, Pettie often changed his stories out of all likeness to the originals. A few examples may be outlined, though outlines involve the loss of most of what Pettie adds. The tale of Tereus and Progne, opening with three pages on the misery of the human lot, proceeds through five pages of courtship; of all this Ovid knows nothing. The marriage is dispatched "out of hand" in one sentence. Tereus' report to Progne preserves the spirit of Ovid, but the dialogue is expanded to emphasize his hypocrisy. Philomela sends her message through a chivalrous gentleman, not through a mere woman. Progne, planning revenge, soliloquizes for two pages, with copious classical allusions.[21] Another invention, a little scene between Progne and Itys—who talks of his "Christcross"—has some tender pathos which reminds one of Greene. Pettie spares his readers some of the more repulsive elements; he omits the evil omens which attended the wedding and the details regarding the Bacchic costume; he allegorizes the metamorphoses. One third of the story is occupied with dialogue and soliloquy. In general though not in particular features such a psychologized and romanticized version recalls the medieval *Philomena*.

Amphiaraus and Eriphile are both rich, and both afflicted with the desire of having. After declining a proposal from the fortune-hunting Amphiaraus, Eriphile, in two pages of soliloquy, decides to unite their estates. A young suitor, Infortunio, appears, and the experienced widow makes use of him to stir up Amphiaraus to renew his plea. This time he is accepted, and Infortunio relieves his mind in a tirade of three pages. Now, for the first time, Pettie turns to the classic myth, to tell of Adrastus and the bribe, though even this is simplified. On learning of his betrayal Amphiaraus "fell to raging against his wife, and other like women for her sake," and in two angry pages he denounces female deceivers from Eve and Circe to the maid who tempted Peter.

speech of Virginius which is only summarized in Painter (I, 38).

Admetus and Alcest: Hyginus, *Fab.* 50–51.
Scilla and Minos: *Metam.* viii. 1 ff.
Curiatius and Horatia: Livy, i. 24 ff., or Painter's first novel.
Cephalus and Procris: *Metam.* vii. 690 ff., and perhaps *Ars Amat.* iii. 707–08, 731–32, 737–44.
Minos and Pasiphae: *Ars Amat.* i. 289 ff., 313 ff.
Pygmalion's Friend: *Metam.* x. 243 ff.
Pettie's sources and technique are discussed in *J. E. G. P.*, XXVII, 162 ff. A number of these stories are told in the notes of Servius, and Pettie (II, 105) quotes Servius on *Ecl.* vi. 46.

[21] "Without doubt, Boccaccio was the original source of inspiration for another motive used freely by Lyly,—the motive of depicting the lover shutting himself up in his chamber, and locking his door, to fling himself on his bed and indulge in a sad soliloquy" (V. M. Jeffery, pp. 63–64). But the motive is also that of Old French romance, which was revived by Belleforest and others. Pettie is full of such soliloquies.

Amphiaraus disposed of, Eriphile decides to take Infortunio, but that youth is now too wise, and the lady "in very choleric conceits consumed away, and died."

The title *Icilius and Virginia* shows the bent of Pettie's mind; a tragedy in which Icilius is a mere lay-figure becomes a romantic love story. Icilius meets Virginia at a house party, falls in love, and seeks fame and fortune in order to win her as a bride. Although at the moment of death Pettie gives Virginia a long speech, he ends the tale with dispatch, in order to address his Gentlewomen Readers on the texts that virtue is to be preferred above wealth, and that girls should not marry old men. The story of Scilla and Minos crams almost all the action of the Ovidian tale into twelve lines. It becomes a romance in which a girl, having repulsed one lover (of the author's invention), falls in love with a stranger, and goes through acute distress in wondering if she can tell him so and win him. The myth of Cephalus and Procris is localized in "the Duke's court of Venice"; the supernatural elements are omitted or rationalized.

Thus, whatever the original plot, Pettie creates a romantic love story concerned with the difficulties of young lovers, the obduracy of parents, the problems of matrimony. Action counts for little, and Pettie hastens over it in order to develop psychology. He always has his Gentlewomen Readers in mind, and he bows and smirks and rallies them like an old master of ceremonies. He presents, in the form of entertaining fiction, a manual of the ethics and etiquette of courtship and marriage. His story-telling technique Pettie might have learned partly from the versions of Bandello done by Boaistuau and Belleforest; a number of these had been included in Painter's book, not to mention Fenton's, and Pettie often refers to them. The elements which Pettie makes so much of are the elements which Belleforest in particular added to the usually plain *novelle,* moralizing, romantic love-making, dialogue, soliloquies, letters, tirades—these last Pettie delivers with a wink. This technique takes us back to Chrétien and the classical romances and tales of the Middle Ages.

There is another strain in Pettie's little stories which becomes more obvious in Lyly. It was not a mere accident that Pettie's first tale should have been borrowed from *The Courtier,* or that his other literary work should have been a translation of Guazzo's *Civile Conversation.* Pettie's endless discussions of the problems of love owe a great deal to the social customs of Renaissance Italy, customs reflected in the many books which testify to Italian interest and success in making an art of life.[22]

[22] See T. F. Crane, *Italian Social Customs of the Sixteenth Century* (Yale University Press, 1920), and Miss Jeffery.

The *Petite Pallace* is one of the books which, stemming from *The Courtier* and lesser works, made possible the birth of Benedick and Beatrice. And this has led us a long way from classical mythology.

Equally remote from antiquity is such a tale as Greene's *Euphues his Censure to Philautus* (1587).[23] Greek and Trojan knights and ladies entertain each other at the Greek camp and in Troy, where they discuss the ideal soldier and other topics in the Italianate manner. Ovid and Caxton's *Recuyell* contribute to the setting, but not a great deal to the subject matter. In *Penelopes Web* (1587) Greene does not attempt a re-creation of Homeric Ithaca, but takes Penelope's name as a peg on which to hang tales and conversations about feminine virtues.

Thus the Elizabethan reader found mythology and pseudo-mythology even in prose fiction. Writers like Pettie and Greene were better classical scholars than their medieval progenitors, but in dressing up more or less classical material in the Franco-Italian manner they were following a medieval tradition; we have had similar novels in our own day, with flippancy and satire in place of courtly romance and moral ballast. Pettie and Greene help to prepare us for quite unclassical poems on classical subjects.

IV. NEW TROY

A sketch of the Elizabethan attitude toward classic myth would leave a gap if it passed over a myth that is not strictly classic, the story of the Trojan origin of Britain.[24] The legend flourished for at least five hundred years, and we are limited to about five paragraphs. Whether Geoffrey of Monmouth was or was not "a master of grave, imperturbable lying,"[25] he started on its way the tale which was to inspire for centuries almost equal quantities of poetry and controversy.

Brutus, the descendant of Aeneas, having involuntarily killed his father, was driven out of Italy. Collecting in Greece a band of Trojans, which was augmented during the westward voyage, he landed in Albion. The first task was to rid the country of giants, and the sportive Corineus,

[23] *Works*, ed. Grosart, VI, 147–284. See J. S. P. Tatlock, "The Siege of Troy in Elizabethan Literature," *P. M. L. A.*, XXX, 682.

[24] This section owes several references to the charming essay by Mr. George Gordon, "The Trojans in Britain," *Essays and Studies by Members of the English Association*, IX (1924), 9 ff.

See also Greenlaw's "The Battle of the Books" (*Studies in Spenser's Historical Allegory*), and Miss Roberta F. Brinkley's *Arthurian Legend in the Seventeenth Century;* both volumes were issued by the Johns Hopkins Press after my work had gone to the printer.

[25] On the questions regarding Archdeacon Walter and the British book see Mr. Acton Griscom's edition of the *Historia Regum Britanniae* (London and New York, 1929), and Mr. J. J. Parry's review, *J. E. G. P.*, XXX (1931), 95. Cf. Mr. Parry's "The Welsh Texts of Geoffrey of Monmouth's *Historia*," *Speculum*, V (1930), 424.

having his choice of districts to rule, chose Cornwall, since nothing gave him greater pleasure than to wrestle with the giants, who were especially numerous there. Brutus built a city on the Thames which was called Troia Nova, later Trinovantum or Troynovant, and finally Lud's Town; the country itself was called Britain, after the Trojan leader. Brutus was followed by the long and famous line of kings, Locrine, Lear, Gorboduc, and the rest.

Geoffrey's book was a patriotic monument, and Spenser, when he came to glorify the Tudor house, was moved by a similar spirit. Everyone read Geoffrey's history, and it was paraphrased and elaborated in endless ways. Skeptics there were from the beginning; witness William of Newburgh, and the familiar tale of Giraldus Cambrensis about the man troubled by demons. But what the skeptics disliked was the Arthurian matter; throughout the Middle Ages the Trojan dynasty stood unshaken. Since Englishmen, like other western nations, found it agreeable to trace their origin to Troy, it is not surprising that the first important iconoclast was a foreigner, the historian Polydore Vergil, who worked in England under Henry VII and Henry VIII. (There was an earlier English skeptic, but he, happily for himself, failed to draw fire.) Polydore discussed the silence of the Roman historians, of Gildas and Bede, and cited William of Newburgh's animadversions upon Geoffrey's "most impudent lyeing." But he felt the strength of popular sentiment, and, for "the avoydinge of evel will," decided that he could not escape rehearsing the story, "albeit not altogether without indignation." [26] Alas for his hopes of avoiding evil will! He had said enough, and the curses of loyal antiquaries rained upon him. If he had not quite sapped a solemn creed with solemn sneer, he had questioned the entire holiness of the Pilgrim Fathers and laid a sacrilegious hand upon the cherry tree.

Grafton's *Chronicle* considered opinions pro and con, and mentioned among the skeptics the learned Thomas Cooper. But Grafton's heart is with the Trojans. After citing Cooper he proceeds: "And nowe I will returne to the Historie of Brute where I left. . . ." [27] Holinshed accepted the Trojan pedigree with confidence. The great Camden did not, but showed a diplomatic discretion which attests the weight of traditional belief. John Stow achieves a compromise. Attacking Polydore, not without thoughts of Camden, he exclaims that "this man with one dash

[26] *Polydore Vergil's English History, from an Early Translation,* ed. Sir H. Ellis (Camden Society, 1846), p. 33.
[27] Ed. Sir H. Ellis (1809), I, 27.

of a pen, cashireth threescore Princes together," but, while he will not insist on the descent of Brutus from Aeneas, he does maintain that there was a King Brute or Brito.[28]

John Speed has an encyclopedic discussion of the subject. Like Stow he cites perhaps the earliest English skeptic, "Iohn Weathamstead Abbat of Saint Albanes, a most judicious man that wrote in *Anno* 1440," who had pronounced the story of Brute "rather poeticall, then historicall" and "built more upon opinion then truth." [29] Speed, a thorough patriot, declares that it is no honor to be descended from the Trojans, who lasted for only six reigns and were three times vanquished. He is also a thorough moralist, and these words are of interest not only in this connection, but as one of the increasingly numerous expressions of hostility toward pagan myth:

And therefore as France hath cast off their Francio King Priamus his sonne, Scotland their Scotia King Pharaoes daughter, Denmarke their Danus, Ireland their Hiberus, and other Countries their Demi-gods; so let Britaines likewise with them disclaime their Brute, that bringeth no honour to so renowned a Nation, but rather cloudeth their glory in the murders of his parents, and imbaseth their descents, as sprung from Venus that lascivious Adulteresse: of whom saith du Plessis, I am ashamed that the heathen were not ashamed of this shamefulnesse; but much more that Christians blush not to name her in their verses.

Meanwhile the British kings and their numerous relations had appeared again and again in dramatic and non-dramatic writings, from *Gorboduc* and *A Mirror for Magistrates* to less weighty productions. We meet the story in Spenser, William Warner, Drayton, Thomas Heywood. But it could not retain its hold upon intelligent opinion in the face of the critical antiquarianism of the seventeenth century. The name of Drayton reminds us that the omniscient Selden could argue for Brute "but as an advocate for the Muse." And it was mainly advocacy for the muse that inspired kind treatment of the legend in the *History of Britain,* at the hand of one who had already sung of the

> Virgin, daughter of Locrine,
> Sprung of old Anchises' line . . .

Here we may end, though this is not the end of the tradition.

[28] *Annales* (ed. 1631), pp. 6–7. One might give ear to loud if not authoritative skepticism, the remarks of Nashe on one of the Harveys whose sins included a Trojan bias: "Dick the true Brute or noble Troian, or Dick that hath vowd to liue and die in defence of Brute, and this our Iles first offspring from the Troians" (*Works*, ed. McKerrow, III, 85). In 1593 Richard Harvey produced *Philadelphus, or a defence of Brutes and the Brutan history.*

[29] *The History of Great Britaine* (ed. 1627), pp. 164 ff. Cf. Stow, p. 7.

V. THE GREEK SPIRIT

As a challenging text for a brief consideration of the Greek element in the Renaissance one might take the dictum of a nineteenth-century scholar: "Greece rose from the dead with a New Testament in her hand." This is still a popular notion, whether or not it may be called a classic myth.

The renaissance of the twelfth and thirteenth centuries did not accomplish a great deal for the study of Greek. Aristotle became a bulwark of Catholic theology, but the mass of Greek literature remained buried; I am speaking of course of literature only, not of science and philosophy proper. A slender Greek tradition persisted in southern Italy and Sicily, and it was through a Calabrian monk that Petrarch was introduced to Greek. Petrarch scarcely knew the alphabet, but Boccaccio gained some knowledge of Homer at least, and took honest pride in being the first Italian Grecian. Everyone has read the words of Leonardo Bruni on hearing that Chrysoloras was coming to Florence, and his enthusiasm was shared by other young men. The revival of Platonism, which Plato might not have fully understood, encouraged the new fashion. By assembling utterances like that of Bruni one might suggest that fifteenth-century Italy was a new Athens, but as a matter of fact or inference there was probably at any one time only a handful of men who could read Greek with ease. All the charges that are now made against the study of Greek were made then, and there were reasons besides. Lack of adequate grammars and dictionaries, the decline of an enthusiasm which had been something of a high-brow fad, the multiplication of translations, the lessening prestige of Greek teachers, all these factors combined to make a knowledge of Greek the possession of a few. Nor did the study of Greek in Italy have the patriotic stimulus that helped to revive Latin. Most men who knew anything of the language read a little with a teacher—if especially ambitious they produced a translation as a *specimen eruditionis*—and thereafter relied upon Latin or vernacular renderings. The evidence of printing is clear enough. By 1500 about five thousand books had been printed in Italy, and, before 1495, only a dozen were Greek.[30] Here and there a man like Poliziano might seem to have breathed Athenian air, but there were not many Polizianos.

In France—if one can survey French Hellenism in a paragraph— Greek was better known than elsewhere, in the sixteenth century as

[30] Sandys, *History of Classical Scholarship*, II, 97.

well as later. There were illustrious scholars from Budé onward. But among the great writers of the century perhaps only Montaigne would have been at ease in Athens, and Montaigne's Greek culture was decidedly indirect. In general, what Hellenic current there was in France soon flowed into the narrower and shallower channel of neoclassicism.

Greek studies in England, if we can believe Anthony à Wood, were of more than respectable antiquity, for when Brute came to the land about 1108 B.C. he had some Greek scholars in his train. This efflorescence of Hellenism must be passed over; likewise the more authentic if not very extensive revivals connected with various individuals from Archbishop Theodore to Grosseteste. After about 1300 the English universities declined from the high position they had occupied in the thirteenth century; the scholastic program was entering upon its long period of decay. The catalogue of Oriel College Library in 1375 contains, among about a hundred titles, not a single reference to classic Latin literature, much less Greek.[31] Concerning Duke Humphrey's gifts to Oxford it has been said: "Of 130 books which he presented to the University in 1439, not one is Greek; of 135 given in 1443, only one—a vocabulary— is certainly Greek, four more are possibly, but not probably so." [32] And even this library did not remain intact. The situation at Cambridge was still worse. Some catalogues of college libraries in the fifteenth century reveal no Greek books at all, and almost no classical Latin.[33]

But Duke Humphrey's interest in humanism had not been fruitless at Oxford, especially at Balliol. Such Oxonians as Grey, Free, Gunthorp, Flemming, Selling, studied in Italy. Of these only Free and Flemming seem to have been productive. Flemming is credited with a Latin-Greek dictionary, and Free made a Latin version of Synesius' treatise on baldness; one could have wished for a more inspiring introduction to the glory that was Greece. There are several candidates for the honor of having first taught Greek in England. Perhaps the first teacher was Emmanuel of Constantinople, a Greek who was working in England as a copyist, before 1470.[34] At least as early as 1475 the Italian Vitelli taught *bonae literae* at Oxford, and the phrase, which is Polydore

[31] M. W. Wallace, *The Birthe of Hercules* (Chicago, 1903), p. 8. See *Collectanea* (ed. C. R. L. Fletcher, Oxford Historical Society, 1885), I, 61. There are some translations from Aristotle and Euclid in the catalogue.

[32] P. S. Allen, *The Age of Erasmus* (1914), p. 121. See also W. F. Schirmer, *Der englische Frühhumanismus* (1931), pp. 55 ff.

[33] J. Bass Mullinger, *The University of Cambridge*, I (1873), 323 ff., 327; Wallace, p. 10.

[34] H. L. Gray, "Greek Visitors to England in 1455–56," *Haskins Anniversary Essays* (1929), pp. 81 ff. Schirmer's recent book, already cited, is invaluable on the whole subject of early English humanism.

Vergil's, may or may not include Greek. William Grocyn knew some Greek before he went to Italy, as a middle-aged man, in 1488, and he might have learned it from Emmanuel or Vitelli. The names of Grocyn, Linacre, William Latimer, bring us to a less misty period in the history of Greek studies. Yet the group of competent Grecians was small, and the instruction in Greek given by Erasmus at Cambridge in 1511 was rudimentary. As Mr. Allen says, "eminent scholars do not teach the elements at a university if boys are already learning them at school."

But from this time onward the fortunes of Greek rose. Corpus Christi College was founded in 1516, the first permanent establishment for the teaching of Greek in England, and, in spite of "Trojan" opposition, Greek made its way in the universities. Under Colet and Lily Greek was taught in St. Paul's School, but it was not until Elizabeth's time that the precedent was followed in public schools. Such men as Elyot pleaded for the study of Greek. Ascham even set Greek literature above Latin. The Greek lectures of Cheke and Smith gave Cambridge an international repute. And of course everyone knows of Lady Jane Grey and other learned women, though their names, as evidence of the state of scholarship, have been somewhat overworked.

Unhappily this flowering in the first half of the century was followed by a decline. Religious strife between Catholics and Protestants was the main cause. The dissolution of the monasteries had helped to cut off the supply of students for the universities. The minds of scholars were more or less preoccupied with religious controversy. The city of the violet crown might well seem a remote fairy tale when Latimer and Ridley were burned outside college walls. Then from about the middle of the century we have the successive phases of controversy between prelacy and puritanism. The central tenet of puritanism, that the Bible was the only and sufficient guide in ecclesiastical government, ritual, and doctrine, and in personal conduct, was not favorable to the study of ancient literature. In the sixteenth and early seventeenth centuries the steady enlargement of the reading public, which included puritans, involved, as it always does, the rise of middle-class illiberality and morality, and the aristocratic humanism of the Renaissance was hardly intelligible to the new masses. Erasmus, with his ideal of Christian culture, had foreseen the dangers of purely religious fervor, of uneducated passion and prejudice.

In Elizabethan England we do not, at any rate, find Grecians like Budé, or scholar-printers like the Estiennes. The materials for Greek study were nearly all of foreign origin. The first Greek text of the *Iliad*

printed in England seems to have appeared as late as 1591; the first
scholarly English *Homer* was the celebrated edition of Joshua Barnes
(1711), which is said to have been financed by Mrs. Barnes on the
understanding that the *Iliad* was the work of Solomon. Nor, in the
later sixteenth century, was the general level of Greek studies high
enough to lead to much scholarly research; the domain of Hellenism
was on the whole bounded by educational requirements. Even among
scholars learning was less disinterested than it was on the continent,
for few were untouched by religious controversy. Besides, Greek was
often studied merely as a key to the New Testament. Similar reasons
supported the claims of Hebrew, which became an increasingly formidable rival; on this point orthodox divine and puritan could agree. Thus
a movement which had promised well had not gathered sufficient
momentum to make head against a variety of obstacles.[35]

A real knowledge of Greek was obviously rare among Elizabethan
writers. We have observed the usual procedure of translators, such as
Painter, Nicolls,[36] North, and Hall. Even Chapman, who worshiped
Homer, used Latin aids, and worked humanistic commentary into his
text. The almost total ignorance of Greek drama, which was not
translated at all—except for one play of Euripides taken from Italian—
is a commonplace.[37]

In such circumstances there could be little understanding of the special
virtues of Greek art, virtues moreover which have always been alien to
the English genius. Not merely the qualities which Greek authors
possessed in common, but their wide individual differences, had small
chance of surviving when the text filtered through one or more diffuse
mediums. If translators failed to perceive and reproduce Greek clarity
of line, the mass of readers, who depended upon translations, were
still further removed from the manner and spirit of the originals. It is
perhaps ungrateful to quarrel with a theory of translation which gave
us North's *Plutarch* and Chapman's *Homer,* yet the bad results are
obvious. The freest sort of paraphrase or redaction might pass as a
translation, and there was no established standard of scholarly judgment

---

[35] "The Elizabethan age is almost a blank in the history of Greek learning in England.
It produced a few translations—mostly of books bearing on matters of theological controversy—but there is hardly a trace in it of that large interest in Greek antiquity which
characterized the humanists of the early part of the century.

"Whatever the explanation may be, the situation changes when we come to James I's
reign, and from that moment there is no dearth of distinguished names in the annals of
English learning." I. Bywater (*Oxford Lectures on Classical Subjects,* 1919, p. 13).

[36] The translator of Thucydides. See above, page 27.

[37] In addition to Gascoigne's *Jocasta* one might mention Peele's translation of one of the
Iphigenia plays of Euripides. See T. Larsen, *Library,* Fourth Series, XI (1931), 310.

such as nowadays, for instance, distinguishes between Plato and Jowett's Plato, between Euripides and Mr. Murray's Euripides. Of course even in the eighteenth century, the age of generally diffused scholarship, translators had a way of missing some essential qualities of their originals, not only Greek but Latin, and most people had no very clear conception of the real virtues of classic art.

While an author of any age may possess Greek virtues without knowing Greek, the point here is that those virtues were in general neither understood nor admired by men of the Renaissance. The note of Renaissance art was not restraint but excess. The period nourished every kind of stylistic extravagance—Ciceronianism, euphuism, Gongorism, Marinism. Writers seldom saw an object quietly or described it temperately. Form is perhaps the last quality that one looks for in the mass of Renaissance literature, even in the greatest. Taste was not Attic but Asiatic, or rather Alexandrian. While the literature of the golden age of Athens was comparatively neglected, that of the silver and brass ages—the Greek romance, for example—was highly popular. We constantly find Renaissance authors attracted by the florid and rhetorical in late Greek writing. If these facts were true of the continent, they were even more true of Elizabethan England. The virtues which the Elizabethans admired and possessed were at the opposite pole from the Greek, and they lacked the first-hand knowledge of the best Greek literature which might have supplied a corrective and an ideal. The dramatists, from the greatest down, were addicted to over-expression; in both central conceptions and details one misses a severe, rational, critical instinct. Nothing could be less Greek than *The Faerie Queene,* or almost any typical work of the period. The prodigal excellences of Elizabethan literature, which are a large if not a full compensation, do not need to be discussed.

In short, the resurrection of Greece was a slow process, not accomplished in the sixteenth century. And the mere revival of Greek was not enough to establish it on an independent footing. Greek learning was valued not only for theological reasons, but as an aid to Latin; Battista Guarino esteemed the dialogues of Plato as collateral reading for the student of Cicero. The classical revival was mainly a Latin revival, and it was not over-discriminating, as the welcome accorded the Senecan dramas indicates. In England solid critical scholarship came with the seventeenth century, and antiquity began to be understood, by the few, as we understand it today. But English culture, so far as it was derived from the ancients, continued throughout the neoclassic period to be

Latin rather than Greek. In the matter of style poets in general preferred Latin rhetoric to Greek simplicity. The codifying habit of the neoclassic mind, moreover, had early begun to reduce Aristotelian principles to neat Horatian rules, with so many half-medieval and modern additions that not merely the Greeks but the Romans would have had difficulty in recognizing the aesthetic laws fathered upon them. The Renaissance, far from being Hellenic, was only imperfectly Latin, but this Latin culture so greatly predominated over Greek that only in the romantic period did the pendulum swing in the other direction. In modern times the tendency has been, especially among persons with a tincture of Greek and anthropology, to depreciate and neglect the real legacy of Rome.

CHAPTER THREE

MYTHS IN EARLIER ELIZABETHAN VERSE

WHEN a period of sterility occurs in the progress of poesy it is customary for literary historians to call it a seedtime and discover abundant promise of harvests to come. We shall, however, skip the long interval between Chaucer and the early sixteenth century without examining such modest seeds as the works of Lydgate. The practice of versifying tales from Ovid had virtually expired, and the genre was born anew in the Elizabethan age. But the medieval manner had not expired, and this chapter may achieve some coherence through the fact that the pieces described are almost untouched by Italian influence. Very few of those pieces are of more than historical interest, but they demand some attention because the origins of the modern mythological poem lie in the period from 1557 to 1589. It is hard to classify representative types, for the early Elizabethans were quite indifferent to the scholarly pigeonholes of posterity, and did not distinguish between translation and the freest kind of redaction. With this proviso the poems to be discussed may be divided into five groups, mythological tales proper, miscellaneous pieces, amatory pieces, ballads, and long poems. A survey of these, if it does nothing more, should give one a new appreciation of Spenser and Marlowe.

I. MYTHOLOGICAL TALES

An interest out of proportion to literary merit attaches to *The fable of Ouid treting of Narcissus, translated out of Latin into Englysh Mytre, with a moral ther unto* (1560).[1] The narrative, which follows Ovid closely, and apparently at first hand, occupies one hundred and ninety-two lines, while the moral receives eight hundred and ninety-six, in seven-line stanzas. The matter of edification consists of sermonizing on

---

[1] Reprinted in full by W. E. Buckley in his edition of Thomas Edwards (Roxburghe Club, 1882), pp. 133 ff.; the narrative portion by O. Jiriczek, *Specimens of Tudor Translations from the Classics* (1923), pp. 77 ff. The piece is discussed by Corser, *Collectanea,* IX, 101 ff.; Brydges, *Restituta,* III, 265–67, and *Censura Literaria,* VIII, 337–41; E. Witz, *Die englischen Ovidübersetzungen des 16. Jahrhunderts* (1915), pp. 27–29; L. Rick, *Ovids Metamorphosen in der englischen Renaissance* (1915), pp. 29–32.

The author is unknown. The piece ends with "Finis. Quod. T. H.," and it was therefore assigned by Ritson and others to Thomas Howell. This ascription is repeated in

the topics traditionally connected with the story of Narcissus—"richis and bewty be vayne"; "the transitory thinges of this world are not to be trustyd"; "all dysdayne ful folkes are compared unto Narcyssus."

The preacher is good enough to name some of his sources. Thirty-five lines elaborate Boccaccio's interpretation of Echo, the voice of earthly delights and vanities which lures men to their ruin.[2] We have a Platonic discourse on the power of the soul over the body, taken from "Ficius," that is, Ficino.[3] There is a reference to one who

>   asence deuine, doth make
> No foole he semethe, that walles hath to name
> And englyshe man, whych thus doth undertake
> For sowles behoufe, to deskant on this same . . .

"Walles" is no other than the moralized *Metamorphoses* which, as we have already noticed, passed under the name of Thomas Waleys, so that we receive a sufficiently instructive "deskant."[4] Our author also deals with an interpretation of the story put forth by one "whome Italye dyd brede," namely, Buonsignori or Niccolò degli Agostini; it does not matter which, since Agostini's work was a version of Buonsignori's.[5]

It is clear that the author has got up the literature of his subject with commendable zeal. The whole sermon is of course plastered with examples, from Helen, Cleopatra, and Phaethon to Lucifer, Dives, and David. As poetry it is naught, but it remains a not insignificant congeries of ancient, medieval, and Renaissance elements. And in the narrative the versifier does make some attempt to carry the Ovidian manner over into English. At any rate Golding, who to be sure was only loosely Ovidian in style, did not disdain, when he reached the story of Narcissus, to borrow a good many phrases from this version.

the *Cambridge History of English Literature*, IV, 438; in the *Short-Title Catalogue* edited by Messrs. Pollard and Redgrave (1926); in C. H. Conley, *First English Translators of the Classics* (1927); and elsewhere. But the poem is not like Howell's known work, and one may agree with the note added to Warton's *History of English Poetry* (London, 1871), IV, 298: "It is supposed that T. H. may be the initials of the printer Hacket: the work appears to have been written some years before it was published, from the unpolished and archaic style." Even the few quotations given in the text should confirm this judgment.

[2] Buckley, p. 150; Boccaccio, *De Genealogia Deorum* (Venice, 1511), bk. vii, c. 59, p. 60.

[3] Buckley, pp. 165 ff. The reference is apparently to the passage on Narcissus in Ficino, *Comm. in Convivium* (*Omnia Divini Platonis Opera*, Lyons, 1548), vi. 17, p. 277.

[4] Buckley, p. 168. Buckley reprints the passage from Waleys, page 176; see fol. xxxv in the edition of Waleys already cited (Paris, 1509). Echo represents flatterers who frequent prelates (mountains), and others in high place; or, Echo signifies quarrelsome women and servants who must have the last word, etc. The story of Narcissus shows that pride leads to aloofness. People see in the fountain of worldly prosperity the shadow of their condition, which passes away like a shadow and destroys the life of the soul.

[5] See above, page 18. For the passage in the English poem, see Buckley, page 169. Cf. Agostini, *Tutti gli Libri de Ouidio Metamorphoseos tradotti dal litteral in uerso uulgar con le sue Allegorie in prosa*, Venice, 1522 (no pagination).

A Gorgeous Gallery of Gallant Inventions (1578), a miscellany which does not live up to the fine Elizabethan swagger of its title, contains a poem of about four hundred and fifty lines called *The History of Pyramus and Thisbie truely translated*.[6] I have not found any version from which it could be said, at least in our sense of the words, to be truly translated, but it derives ultimately from the Old French redaction of Ovid, *Piramus et Tisbé*.[7]

Both the Old French and the English poem have much to say about the childhood of the pair, who were touched by love at the age of seven, and were consumed by desperate passion at fourteen. In the French piece Pyramus utters a long complaint and then goes to the temple of Venus to pray, though the substance of his prayer is not given; in the English, Pyramus does not make a complaint, but he does go to the temple, and his prayer is set down. In both Thisbe finds a hole in the wall and hangs the pendant of her girdle through it; Pyramus, returning from the temple, catches sight of the pendant and begins to talk. Thus the Ovidian tale is spun out with amorous dialogue and soliloquy and romantic incidents. It may be a little surprising to find in a miscellany of 1578 a

[6] *Gorgeous Gallery*, ed. Rollins (1926), p. 103.

[7] Ed. De Boer (Paris, 1921). Of later foreign versions of the story there are many, and a number I have not seen. Georg Hart throws no light on our poem (*Die Pyramus-&-Thisbe-Sage*, 1891). The essential un-Ovidian details mentioned in my outline occur in the version in *Les XV. liures de la Metamorphose D'ouide . . . contenans L'olympe des Histoires poëtiques traduictz de Latin en Francoys* (Paris, 1539), pp. 54 ff.; and in *Les Histoires des Poetes: comprises au Grand Olympe* (1595). These works derive from the *Bible des Poetes*—a significant title, by the way, as regards the reputation of Ovid.

Some of the details, though not the visit to the temple, had already appeared in English, in the two translations of Christine de Pisan's *Epistre d'Othea* (chapter 38), and in Anslay's *Boke of the Cyte of Ladyes*, translated from another work of Christine's (see above, page 32). Anslay's chapter is reprinted in *Anglia*, XII (1889), 14.

Among other versions of the tale before 1578 were Chaucer's, in the *Legend;* that of Gower, *Confessio Amantis*, iii. 1331–1494; Lydgate, *Reson and Sensuallyte*, ll. 3960–4001; a poem taken from Gower (printed in *Anglia*, XII, 16 ff., 631); *La conusaunce damours*, printed before 1531 (see the Appendix); a mysterious book "intituled Perymus and Thesbye" of 1562–63 (see *Gorgeous Gallery*, pp. 198, 203); *A New Sonet of Pyramus and Thisbie* in *A Handful of Pleasant Delights* (see below, page 58); and of course Golding's translation.

Not even the exalted consciousness of knowing more about Pyramus and Thisbe than anyone else gives warrant for setting down here a detailed comparison of countless versions of the tale, from notes compiled in my lusty youth, but a word may be said about Gower. G. C. Macaulay (*Works of Gower*, I, 497–98) remarks, for example, that in his story the lovers make the hole in the wall; that Ninus' tomb is not named; that (to be Irish) the lioness is a lion; that Thisbe hides in a bush, not a cave; that Pyramus dies before Thisbe returns, etc. In such items Gower is closer to Christine's versions than to others. Thus in Anslay Thisbe sees a small hole and makes it larger; Ninus' tomb is not mentioned; there is a lion; Thisbe hides in a bush; Pyramus dies at once. Some, though not all, of these un-Ovidian details are, as we see, in *Piramus et Tisbé* (and in the tale in the *Gorgeous Gallery*); cf. Boccaccio, *De Claris Mulieribus* (Berne, 1539), c. xii. Since this note was written Mr. S. B. Meech has discussed some details (*P. M. L. A.*, XLVI, 201, note 105).

poem which, whatever its immediate original, is directly descended from
a French work of the twelfth century, and, what is more, retains its
medieval character.

In 1589 George Peele published together a *Farewell* to Norris and
Drake and a *Tale of Troy*. The latter piece was included ostensibly to
rouse his countrymen to emulate "their glorious and renowned predecessors, the Trojans," but really, it would appear, in order to swell the
volume to a respectable size.[8]

In nearly five hundred lines Peele narrates events from Hecuba's
dream to the departure of Aeneas from Troy. The story lacks continuity
and coherence, and the verse, apart from a few lines, is far from Peele's
best. In its treatment of classical material, however, the poem has
interest. We might not expect an Oxford man, publishing in 1589, to
handle the Trojan saga in this manner:

> How many Greeks, how many Troyan knights,
> As chivalry by kind in love delights,
> Upon their helmets can their plumes advance,
> And twist their ladies' colours on their lance . . .[9]

We are in the world of the *Roman de Troie*. The presence of incongruous
materials is explained when we examine Peele's sources. Ovid contributes
some events and details, Virgil most of the description of the fall of
Troy, but the groundwork of the whole, and many incidents, appear
to be derived from Caxton's *Recuyell*.[10] The narrative method, the
medieval and chivalric tone, of Caxton are clearly reflected in Peele.

Along with romance we have the pastoral note, especially in the
passage describing that "jolly swain," Paris:

> How he can nymphs and shepherds' trulls beguile,
> And pipen songs, and whet his wits on books,
> And rape poor maids with sweet-alluring looks:
> So couth he sing his lays among them all,
> And tune his pipe unto the water's fall,
> And wear his coat of grey and lusty green,
> That had the fair Œnone never seen
> His ticing curlèd hair, his front of ivory,
> The careless nymph had ne'er been so unhappy . . .

---

[8] *Works of Peele,* ed. Dyce (London, 1829), I, xvi; ed. Bullen (1888), I, xxix. The text
is quoted from Bullen, II, 241 ff.

Peele refers to the piece as "an old poem," and it has been conjecturally assigned to
his undergraduate days, 1572–81 (Dyce, I, ii; Bullen, I, xvii; J. S. P. Tatlock, "The Siege
of Troy in Elizabethan Literature," *P. M. L. A.*, XXX, 679). Possibly, in view of the
parallels between them, the poem and *The Arraignment of Paris* (published 1584) were
written about the same time, whether revised later or not.

[9] Ll. 276 ff. Cf. ll. 289–90, 295–96.   [10] For details see Tatlock, pp. 680–82.

Nearly all these lines, and more that follow, are pieced together (to ignore the question of dates of composition) from the pastoral drama, *The Arraignment of Paris*.[11] The close relations between the Italian pastoral and the Italian mythological poem will be noticed later.[12] Here we may observe that the pastoral element, though slight, is a trifle incongruous in an un-Italianate and medieval story of Troy.[13] A casual bit of Platonism adds further variety; the idea is elaborated by the thrifty author in the *Arraignment*.[14]

From the play Peele also carried over some archaisms in diction, which form a noticeable element in the poem. In addition to the general influence of Caxton Peele seems to have had both Chaucer and Spenser in mind.[15] In fact a number of the archaisms are words that E. K. saw fit to explain—but the details may be left to a footnote.[16]

The poem as a whole is poor enough, and lacks the charm and lyrical sweetness of much of the *Arraignment*. But the pastoral bits are pleasant, and there are occasional other good lines. A happy addition in the

[11] With the passage quoted (ll. 66 ff.) compare, in the play, III. i. 55–56, 116 ff., I. i. 49 ff.

[12] See below, pages 72, 84.

[13] Paris appears in a pastoral background in Ovid's epistle of Oenone, and in Colluthus' *Rape of Helen* (trans. A. W. Mair, Loeb Classical Library, ll. 102 ff.). This latter piece was popular enough in the period to attract two translators (see the Appendix, under 1586, 1587).

Miss V. M. Jeffery (*M. L. R.*, XIX, 175 ff.) has argued that Peele based his *Arraignment* on *Il Giuditio di Paride* (1566), by Anello Paulilli. Mr. A. H. Gilbert offered reasons against this view (*M. L. N.*, XLI, 36 ff.). Miss Jeffery is least convincing in regard to the judgment scene proper, since the material is traditional, and her parallels could be multiplied from other versions than Paulilli's. Mr. Gilbert also fails to take account of the number and variety of sources. For instance, he remarks that Euripides and Paulilli make Hermes the guide of the three goddesses, while Ovid (epistle of Oenone) and Peele do not. But Hermes appears in Ovid's epistle of Paris, in Colluthus, in Lucian's dialogue, in Apuleius (x. 30), in Lydgate's *Reson and Sensuallyte* (ll. 1601 ff.), in a pseudo-Chaucerian piece (see the Appendix, under 1561), and in pageants. Pageantry is especially important in connection with Peele's compliment to Elizabeth, though the critics do not deal with it, apart from Miss Jeffery's mention of Gascoigne's *The Grief of Joy* (page 176). See below, page 79 and T. S. Graves, "*The Arraignment of Paris* and Sixteenth Century Flattery," *M. L. N.*, XXVIII (1913), 48–49. Cf. also a poem in the *Gorgeous Gallery*, page 63. Miss Jeffery's case is plausible on some points, and one may accept her argument for the general influence of Italian pastoral on English even if it is difficult to prove a connection between Peele and Paulilli.

[14] *Tale*, ll. 117 ff.; *Arraignment*, II. i. 68 ff. The whole passage on the judgment of Paris in the *Tale*, though relatively short, has numerous correspondences with the play.

[15] The 1589 version has a reference to the story of Troilus and Cressida, while the 1604 edition has a direct allusion to Chaucer and another to the "House of Fame." (The version published in 1604 was apparently written in 1595–96; see Bullen, I, xxix; II, 241, 255.)

One line in the passage quoted above was taken from Spenser's *April* (l. 36): "And tuned it unto the Waters fall." Though variations on the phrase later became conventional, they were not in 1589 and earlier. (Spenser also liked it well enough to use it in other places.)

[16] Peele uses "y-clyppèd" (l. 11), "y-blinded" (l. 120), etc. E. K. explains "y" as "a poeticall addition" (*April, May*). Other words occurring in Peele which E. K. glosses are

revised text describes Paris' flight with Helen—"As blithe as bird of morning's light in May." The Greeks set sail from Aulis "As shoots a streaming star in winter's night." [17] But the significance of the piece is not in its few gleams of poetry. It appears rather, as I have said, in the medieval substance and spirit. In narrative method the poem is the exact opposite of Lodge's mythological poem issued in the same year, for while Lodge, inaugurating the Italianate style, slighted action in favor of sensuous picture-making, Peele crammed the matter of half a dozen epics into a chronicle of five hundred lines. Whether or not *The Arraignment of Paris* had a particular Italian source, almost everything in *The Tale of Troy* is in accord with the native tradition.

II. MISCELLANEOUS PIECES

The poems so far mentioned represent the more strictly narrative species. "Strictly" is a relative term, since the *Narcissus* of 1560, and some other tales noticed in the Appendix, were adorned with an impressive caudal member in the form of a sermon. The early Elizabethans were equally fond of what may be called sermons with a mere prefatory hint of narrative. Indeed a single example, from the *Gorgeous Gallery*, testifies that the Helen of Troy who haunted pedestrian imaginations was not the vision beheld by Marlowe; in *The reward of Whoredome by the fall of Helen* the repentant sinner avows all her errors in lurid language. The *Mirror for Magistrates*, like Falstaff, was not only witty in itself but the cause that wit was in other men.

George Turberville was one of the most typical and popular writers of the pre-Spenserian generation. His talents show to better advantage in his translation of the *Heroides* than in original work. He anticipated Keats in handling the war of gods and Titans, and his treatment of this high argument bears the very Elizabethan title *A Myrrour of the*

"of yore," "couth," "dight," "swain," "won" (i.e., "dwell"), "uncouth," "hight," "surquedry," "hent," "mickle." Peele's revised text seems slightly more archaic than the first one.

[17] The simile, like the phenomenon, was not new. For example, cf. *Pearl*, ll. 115-16; *Canterbury Tales*, A 267-68; see also *Venus and Adonis*, l. 815 (quoted below, page 141).

A possible instance of Marlowe's influence on Peele is the expansion of ll. 25-26, which in the 1589 text read thus:

> His court presenting to our earthlie eyes
> A skye of starres or shyning paradise.

The revised version was:

> His court presenting to our human eyes
> An earthly heaven or shining paradise,
> Where ladies troop'd in rich disguised attire,
> Glistering like stars of pure immortal fire.

Cf. *Hero and Leander*, i. 97 ff.; and also *Romeo and Juliet*, I. ii. 25.

fall of Pride.[18] The war is dispatched in one and a half pages, but the
real theme requires five and a half more.

> Let giants fall and shipmens case
> a myrrour be, therefore,
> To such as seeke to hie a place,
> for like shall be their lore.

This specimen may relieve us from the need of describing the story of
Aristotimus in Turberville's *Tragical Tales.*[19]

Another representative of the mob of gentlemen who wrote with ease
is Thomas Howell. He treated the story of Cressida twice, the second
poem being a recasting of the first. Their character is indicated in the
titles, *The britlenesse of thinges mortall, and the trustinesse of Vertue*
and *Ruine the rewarde of Vice.*[20] There is the usual debt to Chaucer and
Henryson, but in place of Chaucer's subtle irony and Henryson's grim
tragedy we have only flat moralizing.[21] Yet Howell had a spark somewhere in him. His editor, Sir Walter Raleigh, justly praised these lines:

> At strife to whom I might
> Commit my secret tears,
> My heart the mountains' sight
> And hollow Echo fears.

> I doubt the Dryades
> Amidst the forest chace,
> And thinking on the Seas,
> I dread the Mermaids' grace.[22]

The brief suggestion, the gleam of magic, in that second stanza are
beyond the conscientious poet's normal reach.

Such a heading as "miscellaneous" may justify our turning for a
moment to that Theocritean translation called *Sixe Idillia*, which was

---

[18] *Epitaphes, Epigrams, Songs and Sonets* (1567), ed. Collier, pp. 152 ff. There was
an earlier edition apparently, published in or after 1565 (H. E. Rollins, *M. P.*, XV, 518).

[19] Ed. Edinburgh (1837), pp. 203 ff. Extant copies of the book were printed in 1587,
but the first edition must have appeared in 1574–75 (Rollins, pp. 520 ff.). Bandello's novel
of Aristotimus (iii. 5) had been translated by Painter (ii. 5), and a version of the story
was included in Thomas Fortescue's *The Foreste*, 1571. Turberville follows Bandello quite
closely. An envoy of twelve stanzas makes clear the evils of despotism.

[20] *Poems of Thomas Howell*, ed. Grosart, pp. 121–22; *Howell's Devises*, ed. W. Raleigh,
pp. 18–19. See below, page 56, note 29.

[21] Another piece of didactic earnestness, evidently inspired by the *Mirror for Magistrates*,
is *The infortunate ende of Cresus Kynge of Lydia, a worthy note for Couetousnesse sake*
(ed. Grosart, "Newe Sonets," p. 124). Howell has two versions of *The lamentable ende
of Iulia Pompeis Wyfe* (*ibid.*, p. 138; *Devises*, p. 26). He probably took the story from
Valerius Maximus (iv. 6. 4) rather than from Plutarch (*Pompey*, 53; North, *Tudor
Translations*, IV, 263). It is also in Boccaccio, *De Claris Mulieribus*, c. 79. Cf. Lucan,
Pharsalia, i. 111 ff.

[22] *Devises*, pp. xvii, 64.

published anonymously at Oxford in 1588.[23] The translator chose an author who was relatively little read, and his work is attractive. Although Bullen with unwonted sourness pronounced it worthy of Turberville or Googe, the transparent ease of the *Sixe Idillia* is far removed from the heavy flatness of the older generation. The style has some charm and grace, and occasional rustic words add vividness and flavor. Thus Polyphemus consoles himself:

> For many Maidens in the evening tide with me will play,
> And all do sweetly laugh, when I stand heark'ning
>   what they say . . .

The singers of the bridal hymn to Helen

> will, every Spring, unto the leaves in meadow go
> To gather garlands sweet; and there, not with a little woe,
> Will often think of thee, O Helen! as the suckling lambs
> Desire the strouting bags and presence of their tender dams.[24]

III. AMATORY PIECES

Even amatory verse shows the influence of the study of rhetoric and the long rhetorical tradition in poetry. The courtly lover's first object was to convince his mistress, real or imaginary, of the sincerity of his passion and the hardness of her heart. Ovid had been a master of the *suasoria,* and in his various poems about love he had shown himself not only a brilliant wit and psychologist but a superlatively clever rhetorician. The Elizabethan amorists were portentously serious—the Petrarchan mood was not altogether favorable to levity—and they borrowed Ovidian myths to incorporate in their own special kind of *suasoria.* Gascoigne gives this advice to the poet-lover:

> Likewise, if I should disclose my pretence in loue, I would eyther make a strange discourse of some intollerable passion, or finde occasion to pleade by the example of some historie, or discouer my disquiet in shadowes *per Allegoriam* . . .[25]

For versifiers seeking "the example of some historie" no matter lay readier to hand than the familiar tales of mythological lovers.

---

[23] The six pieces are reprinted in Bullen's *Longer Elizabethan Poems* (1903), pp. 125 ff. The one on Adonis is given by O. L. Jiriczek in *Jahrbuch der Deutschen Shakespeare-Gesellschaft* (1919), p. 30; parts of others are in Ward's *English Poets,* I, 379. See R. T. Kerlin, *Theocritus in English Literature* (1910), p. 27.

[24] The translator, by the way, in a note prefaced to his last idyll, that on Venus and Adonis, gives an allegorical interpretation of the story:

"The Poet's drift is to shew the power of Love, not only in men, but also in brute beasts: although in the last two verses, by the burning of the Boar's amorous teeth, he intimateth that extravagant and unorderly passions are to be restrained by reason."

[25] Smith, *Elizabethan Critical Essays,* I, 48.

Tottel's *Miscellany* contained a number of short poems exploiting what was to remain a popular formula, that is, the narration of a mythological tale and the application of it to the lover's own hard lot. The pattern soon became sufficiently stereotyped to find a place in a practical manual on the art of writing letters.[26] Rosalind advised lovers who were gravelled for lack of matter to kiss; the courtly lover who lacked not only matter but a mistress at hand was compelled to use mythology. Thus we meet in Tottel's *Miscellany* such self-explanatory titles as *The tale of Pigmalion with conclusion upon the beautye of his loue; The louer praieth his seruice to be accepted and his defaultes pardoned* (concerning Cephalus and Procris); *The louer complaineth his harty loue not requited* (Phoebus and Daphne).[27] In harmony with such themes is a translation of the first twelve lines of Ovid's epistle from Penelope to Ulysses, apparently the first published version of any part of the *Heroides*.[28]

One of the most popular stories to be adapted to the amatory formula was that of Troilus and Cressida. The tale was, as the poets testify, in every man's mouth, and allusions to it are spread like a rash over Elizabethan verse.[29] Turberville and the rest wrote amorous plaints on various mythological themes, but we must put wax in our ears and pass by. In addition to poems outlining a single myth brief allusions were fashionable too. In one passionate "sonnet" Thomas Watson mentions Leander, Hero, Pyramus, Thisbe, Haemon, Antigone, Orpheus, Eurydice, Cerberus, "the Wheele, the Stone, the Fire and Furies." [30] Any further illustration would be an anticlimax. Sidney might well complain that the "swelling phrases" of literary lovers would never persuade a mistress.[31]

One more author, George Gascoigne, must be noticed, not because he sometimes wrote poetry but because he wrote *The complaynt of Phylomene* (1576).[32] This poem, begun when the author was riding, was broken off when he was "overtaken with a sodaine dash of Raine."

---

[26] See the Appendix, under William Fulwood (1568).

[27] Ed. Rollins, I, 125, 202, 253.

[28] *Ibid.*, p. 219. But see the Appendix, under 1526.

[29] For example, Tottel's *Miscellany*, I, 183. On the debasement of Cressida's character between Chaucer and Shakespeare, a process started mainly by Henryson's beautiful *Testament,* see H. E. Rollins, "The Troilus-Cressida Story," *P. M. L. A.,* XXXII, 383 ff.; F. Haynes and J. S. P. Tatlock, in my bibliography, under "General"; W. W. Lawrence, *Shakespeare's Problem Comedies* (New York, 1931), c. 4, especially pp. 144 ff.

[30] *Poems,* ed. Arber, p. 66.

[31] Smith, *Elizabethan Critical Essays,* I, 201. Even King James wrote a lyric invoking the examples of Leander and Pyramus (*New Poems by James I of England,* ed. A. F. Westcott, 1911, p. 24).

[32] *Works,* ed. Cunliffe, II, 177 ff. One might mention also *Davids salutacions to Berzabe* (I, 463), which quaintly links Apuleius and the Bible, Fotis and David.

The narrator listens to the nightingale, which declares that she sings for true lovers, of whom one is not far away. While she sings the poet falls asleep and dreams that a nymph appears to "paraphrase" the song We. may observe that the author uses the medieval dream-convention, and also associates himself with the piece in the character of a lover.

In the narrative, which occupies twenty-three pages, Gascoigne's management of an unhappily popular meter suggests that his ride to London was in the right butter-women's rank to market. He follows Ovid closely, except in a few details, but adds an abundance of sententious morality. In his long analysis of the nightingale's notes he may have been the first to isolate *Tereu,* a doleful and dubious mark of originality.[33] The poem ends with the departure of the nymph, the awakening of the poet, and the application of a sermon to him; though Gascoigne was rather a gay blade in private life he could be heavily didactic in public.[34] To appreciate the incredibly swift maturing of Elizabethan poetic art —in other words, the accident of genius—one may set this piece beside Sidney's *The Nightingale.*

IV. BALLADS

In that eloquent testimonial to the breadth of Elizabethan literary interests, the Stationers' Register, among "ballets" on monstrous pigs and still more monstrous children, on maids undone and maids who would like to be, we find dozens of pieces on classical themes. A list of ballad titles, if we had room for it, would show that classic myths which, in more pretentious versions, appealed to the polite, were known in racier form to the eager customers of Autolycus. When all shops were stuffed with rhyming pamphlets, anecdotes, sermons, critics who had the good of literature at heart groaned aloud over the mangling of poetry by rude smatterers. "Scarce a cat can look out of a gutter," snorted one enemy of popular journalism, "but out starts a halfpenny chronicler, and presently A propper new ballet of a strange sight is endited." [35]

When mythological ballads kept such company one would not look in them for the qualities of Spenser and Marlowe. But it would be a

---

[33] H. W. Garrod, *The Profession of Poetry* (Oxford, 1929), p. 150.

[34] In the introduction to his *Steele Glas* (*Works,* II, 144) Gascoigne allegorizes the story of Philomela in a cumbrously medieval way:

> My Systers name, was pleasant Poesys,
> And I my selfe had Satyra to name.

They are the daughters of "Playne dealyng" and "Simplycitie." Tereus turned from Progne to Philomela; that is, "Satyrical Poetry is somtimes ravished by vayne Delight." In his comments on Ovid's tale George Sandys takes the sisters as representing poetry and oratory (*Ovid's Metamorphosis,* 1632, pp. 228–29).

[35] *Epistle to Martin Mar-sixtus,* 1592 (quoted by F. O. Mann, *Works of Thomas Deloney,* Oxford, 1912, p. x).

mistake to regard the early Elizabethan ballads as a distinct stratum of verse quite different from and inferior to the "sonets" written by the courtly poets. It must be remembered that in the first half of Elizabeth's reign ballads were being composed by such men of letters as Turberville, Googe, Gascoigne, and Howell. Many pieces in the miscellanies, from Tottel's onward, were ballads; many were entered separately, as such, in the Stationers' Register. There was not, then, in this period an impassable gulf between the courtly ballads and their poor relations of the street. In later times, as the mention of Autolycus suggests, ballads as a class did come down in the world.

Since the character of the Elizabethan broadside is familiar, and since pieces on classical subjects possess the generic qualities, it will be enough to recall a very few specimens. Some, either real or virtual ballads of the courtly type, have been noticed already in this chapter. Mythological ballads were fairly numerous through most of the period covered in this book, but they were especially abundant between 1560 and 1575. They must have helped greatly to popularize the commoner myths among people who did not keep Ovid under their pillow.

The most representative collection of what may be called upper-class ballads was *A Handful of Pleasant Delights,* which first appeared in 1566 and was enlarged in 1584.[36] One piece of particularly tragical mirth is *A New Sonet of Pyramus and Thisbie. To the, Downe right Squier.*[37] This affecting version of one of the most popular myths may have been in Shakespeare's mind when, in providing a tragic vehicle for Bottom, he burlesqued the theatrical heroics of an earlier age. Here at any rate is Ercles' vein, a part to tear a cat in:

> Oh Gods aboue, my faithfull loue
> shal neuer faile this need:
> For this my breath by fatall death,
> shal weaue Atropos threed.
> Then from his sheathe he drew his blade,
> and to his hart
> He thrust the point, and life did vade,
> with painfull smart.

Ballad narratives may pause for moralizing, or for bursts of rhetoric, but they seldom waste time in mere decoration; the story must march. In a piece on Diana and Actaeon (sung "To the Quarter Braules"),

[36] Ed. Rollins, 1924. See Mr. Baskervill's review, *M. P.,* XXIII, 119 ff., and his own *Elizabethan Jig* (Chicago, 1929), pp. 30–31.

[37] *Handful,* ed. Rollins, pp. 35, 99. See G. Hart, *Die Pyramus-&-Thisbe-Sage* (1891), pp. 22–23, and *Cambridge History of English Literature,* III, 191. Mr. Rollins remarks that this ballad "could have been, and probably was, in the 1566 *Pleasant Sonnets.*"

which was reprinted or imitated many times, the crisis of the tale is thus dispatched:

> As she began to shoot, Acteon ran about,
> To hide he thought no boote,
>   his sights were dim:
> And as he thought to scape,
> Changed was Acteons shape,
> Such was unluckie fate,
>   yeelded to him.[38]

Longer but hardly more moving is Thomas Howell's *The lamentable historie of Sephalus with the Unfortunat end of Procris. To the tune of Appelles (ca.* 1568).[39] It discards all of the Ovidian story except the catastrophe, and, for the earlier part, transfers to Cephalus and Procris the experiences of Pyramus and Thisbe. And at the end the Ovidian motive of Procris' jealousy is abandoned in favor of pure romantic tragedy, in the style of the other pair of lovers:

> When Sephalus his Procris founde,
> Imbrude with blood on euery side,
> The arowe stickinge in the wounde,
> That bleedinge sore did gape full wyde,
>   He curst the gods that skies possesst
>   The systers three and all the rest.

Indeed Shakespeare had only too many models for his Pyramus and Thisbe.

One more specimen must be enough. *The Wandering Prince of Troy* was an extremely popular ballad, or rather ballads, for there were many issues or versions from 1564–65 onward. The text of 1624 has two parts. The first follows the Virgilian story, from the arrival of Aeneas to the death of Dido. The second part opens with Dido's funeral. Her sister wrote to Aeneas, who was sojourning on an island of Greece, and the hero's "lofty courage then did fall." Dido's ghost appeared and foretold his death.

> And like one being in a Trance,
> A multitude of ugly fiends
> About this wofull Prince did dance,
> No help he had of any friends:
>   His body then they tooke away,
>   And no man knew his dying day.

We may smile with Bishop Percy over the engrafting of "a Gothic

---

[38] *Handful,* pp. 25, 91.

[39] *Poems of Thomas Howell,* ed. Grosart ("Newe Sonets," pp. 146 ff.). For the story of Cephalus and Procris see *Metam.* vii. 694 ff., and *Ars Amat.* iii. 685 ff. A brief love poem in Tottel makes use of the death of Procris, omitting the rest of the tale (ed. Rollins, I, 202–03; II, 309).

conclusion" upon the story, and agree that the author of the ballad "dealt out his poetical justice with a more impartial hand" than Virgil.[40]

Sound morality was generally a strong point with ballad-makers, whether courtly or popular, as it was with almost any writer of the Tudor age. Middle-class virtue was the special concern of the puritans, who had no love for courtly and worldly ballads, and, since they could not banish them, they could at least try to moralize them. If a multitude of readers clung to the old songs and, like Sir Andrew Aguecheek, cared not for good life, the old songs might be made to yield a lesson. Thus we find a number of moralized ballads registered in the fifteen-sixties. These years seem to have witnessed special efforts to snatch merry tunes from the devil. Some of the titles are rather pathetic examples of popular paganism conquered by the stern daughter of the voice of God— *I myghte have leved meryly morralysed* (1564–65); *O Sweete Olyver altered to ye scriptures* (1586).[41]

The moral fervor of this period, so clearly marked in the ballads, had other manifestations, some of which we have already encountered, such as the *Fable of Narcissus* (published in 1560) and the works of Peend (1565), Underdowne (1566), Golding (1565–67), Painter (1566–67).[42] While the classical translators inherited a moralistic tradition, the warm professions of such men as Golding and Painter were doubtless heightened by the consciousness that popularizers of pagan and immoral stories needed to be on the defensive.

There is no need of citing ballads of later periods. Religious and political and topical broadsides might undergo some changes of style, or at least of sentiment, but those on classical themes have a strong family likeness in all ages. Moralistic or romantic or sentimental, they lived on—as the chapbook stories of Leander or Hercules did—into the eighteenth century. Their increasingly subterranean existence was hardly touched by changing fashions in poetry in the world above.

V. LONG POEMS

Sackville's *Induction,* though only incidentally mythological, is an early and highly significant example of the working of classical influences, and is moreover the most important poem between Skelton—

---

[40] *Roxburghe Ballads,* VI, 547; Percy's *Reliques* (Everyman's Library), II, 307; Rollins, *Analytical Index,* 2710, 2839 ff.

[41] Rollins, *Analytical Index,* 1193, 1994. See also 819, 820, 1051, 1175, 1627, 1693, 2033, 2035, 2331, 2332, 2333, 2334, 2612, 2840, 2921. Only one of these is on a classical theme, *The wanderynge prynce moralyzed* (2840).

[42] For Peend and Underdowne see the Appendix. The ungodly *Couurte of Venus* (1557) provoked two attempts to counteract its pernicious influence. One was John Hall's *The*

some would say Chaucer—and Spenser. It was published in 1563.[43] In this really noble work of the young lawyer we have, treated with dignity and somber emotion, that theme which above all others haunted the Renaissance mind, mutability, the theme which links together Spenser's *Cantos,* Hamlet's speeches in the graveyard, Ralegh's apostrophe to death, so much of the prose of Drummond, Donne, Burton, Browne, Taylor, and those lines from the last of the great race,

> The glories of our blood and state
> Are shadows, not substantial things . . .

Walking forth into the fields on a bleak winter evening, and thinking of "the sundry changes that in earth we find," the poet sees a woman, clad in black, who is overcome with grief. She is Sorrow, and she will guide him to the underworld where he may see those who have fallen from pomp and power, and may learn that there is no duration in earthly happiness. They enter Hades by "an hideous hole, all vast, withouten shape," and meet a series of figures, Remorse of Conscience, Dread, Revenge, Misery, Care, Sleep, Old Age, Malady, Famine, Death, War, all of whom are described with vivid physical detail. The shield of War is pictured at still greater length, for it contains scenes from ancient history, especially the fall of Troy. The poet and his guide pass on, cross over Acheron in Charon's boat, appease Cerberus, and enter Pluto's realm, where the air is filled with groans and wailing of babes and maids unwed, and princes of renown

> That whilom sat on top of fortune's wheel,
> Now laid full low . . .

Then the Duke of Buckingham appears, to commence his story.

Even this brief summary reveals the combination of medieval and classical motives. At the outset we have for example the dream-allegory convention, echoes of Chaucerian language, four stanzas about the signs of the zodiac to emphasize the fact that it is evening. The theme of the

---

Couurte of vertu contaynynge many holy or spretuall songes Sonettes psalmes ballettes shorte sentences as well of holy scriptures as others &c. (1565; *Stat. Reg.,* I, 268). The other was *The Couurte of Venus moralized,* by Thomas Bryce (1567; *Stat. Reg.,* I, 343).

[43] In a letter to the *T. L. S.* (April 18, 1929, p. 315) Miss Marguerite Hearsey reported the discovery, in the library of St. John's College, Cambridge, of a MS, apparently Sackville's own, containing the *Induction* and *The Complaint of Henrie, Duke of Buckingham* as one continuous poem under the latter title. This, Miss Hearsey believes, "invalidates definitely the contention made in the past that Sackville was 'the primary inventor' of the *Mirror* plan, and that he wrote 'The Induction' for an introduction to the whole series." See *Cambridge History of English Literature,* III, 192–93. In her letter Miss Hearsey printed some stanzas, in praise of Chaucer, Wyatt, and Surrey, out of a number in the new MS hitherto unknown. Since this note was written, Miss Hearsey has printed the MS; see *R. E. S.,* VIII (1932), 282.

whole, the fickleness of fortune and the tragedy of fall from high estate, recalls Chaucer's droning monk and other medieval preachers.[44]

But when he approaches the underworld the author inevitably recalls Aeneas. The description of Avernus is obviously based on Virgil, yet Sackville's phrasing and slight additional details almost suggest the hell-mouth so popular in the Corpus Christi plays. Virgil's personified abstractions are given epithets only. Sackville's list roughly corresponds, so that the passage has a classical rather than a Christian tinge, but his treatment is quite different from Virgil's. This is only one of a number of stanzas describing Old Age, the *tristis Senectus* of Virgil:

> Crookbacked he was, tooth-shaken, and blear-eyed,
> Went on three feet, and sometimes crept on four,
> With old lame bones that rattled by his side,
> His scalp all pilled and he with eld forlore;
> His withered fist still knocking at Death's door,
> Fumbling and drivelling as he draws his breath;
> For brief, the shape and messenger of Death.

One is reminded at once of the much-discussed old man in the Pardoner's Tale; in fact both pictures have been traced to a common source, an elegy of Maximian.[45] Such technique is a medieval development of the post-classical, and is most familiar to us in Spenser. Sackville's lines have a concrete, half-Dantesque actuality, yet the very fullness of physical detail loses something of the timeless universality and vague horror of Virgil's personifications.

Some other imitations and borrowings are palpable—the shield of War, suggested by the shield of Aeneas; the account of the fall of Troy, with the capture of Cassandra and the death of Priam; the embarkation with Charon; the subduing of Cerberus; the lamentations of the shades. Sackville shares the Virgilian mood more keenly than Spenser,[46] but he lacks the power of suggestion, the sustained greatness of style, which raise the commonplaces of death to the Virgilian level. "Here puled the babes" hardly approaches

[44] Sackville is quoted from the text in Hebel and Hudson, *Poetry of the English Renaissance* (1929), pp. 56 ff.

[45] Koeppel pointed out (*Archiv*, CI, 145–46) that some lines in Sackville's description of Sorrow (87, 90–91, 123) echo phrases in Chaucer's *Romaunt of the Rose* (312, 336 ff.) which describe a painting of "Sorowe." Reminiscences of Sackville in *The Faerie Queene* have been noticed by commentators, but not, I think, in *The Shepheardes Calender*. Cf. the pictures of winter in Sackville (ll. 1, 5, 13, 16–17), and Spenser's *January* (ll. 19, 24, 31, 35). Courthope, *History of English Poetry* (II, 122–23), notices Sackville's debt, in this description of winter, to the lines of Gavin Douglas prefixed to his version of *Aen.* vii.

[45] Chaucer's debt was pointed out by Mr. Kittredge (*American Journal of Philology*, IX, 1888, 84–85; see Skeat, V, 287). Mr. A. M. Clark added Sackville (*T. L. S.*, January 23, 1920, p. 52).

[46] See below, pages 103–06.

> Continuo auditae voces vagitus et ingens
> infantumque animae flentes, in limine primo
> quos dulcis vitae exsortis et ab ubere raptos
> abstulit atra dies et funere mersit acerbo.

Nor does

> the maids unwed
> With folded hands their sorry chance bewailed,

attain the concentration of the one word *innuptae* with which Virgil
suggests the untimely blighting of rose-lipt maidens; Sackville's maids
might almost be disappointed wallflowers. But then, in the expression
of pity, who does not fall short of Virgil? And as a whole Sackville's
poem is moving.

It would be odd if the young man who collaborated in *Gorboduc*
did not reveal Senecan influence in this poem also. The stanzas concerning the zodiac have many parallels in medieval writers, but the passage,
more mythological than mathematical, is nearer Seneca than Chaucer.[47]
The main theme of the *Induction* is no less Senecan than medieval, and
the sketch of the fall of Troy, though Virgilian in substance, yields the
Senecan moral of mutability.[48] While Seneca's personified abstractions
are generally labeled in an epithet or a phrase,[49] his apostrophe to sleep
suggested Sackville's finest stanza, the second of these two:

> By him lay heavy Sleep, the cousin of Death,
> Flat on the ground and still as any stone,
> A very corpse, save yielding forth a breath;
> Small keep took he whom fortune frownëd on
> Or whom she lifted up into the throne
>   Of high renown; but as a living death,
>   So, dead alive, of life he drew the breath.
>
> The body's rest, the quiet of the heart,
> The travail's ease, the still night's fere was he,
> And of our life in earth the better part;
> Reaver of sight, and yet in whom we see
> Things oft that tide, and oft that never be;
>   Without respect, esteeming equally
>   King Crœsus' pomp, and Irus' poverty.[50]

[47] Cf. the opening of *Hercules Furens*, or *Thyestes*, ll. 844 ff.
[48] For example, see the opening of the *Troades*, or the first chorus in *Agamemnon*. The
description of Avernus may be compared not only with Virgil, but with *Hercules Furens*,
ll. 664 ff.
[49] E.g., *Herc. Fur.*, ll. 96 ff., 690 ff. (Tudor Translations, I, 12, 31).
[50] Cf. *Herc. Fur.* (Tudor Translations, I, 43):
>   . . . and thou O tamer best
> O sleepe of toyles, the quietnesse of mynde,
> Of all the lyfe of man the better parte . . .

Although there is nothing in the first stanza which might not have arisen naturally
out of Sackville's theme, it may have been partly inspired by the picture of the sleeping
Hercules which motivates the Senecan chorus.

Chaucer, Virgil, Seneca—it is a characteristic Tudor combination. And Sackville is not a mere stumbling translator or imitator, like most of the men treated earlier in this chapter. His borrowings are wrought into an original poem, at once medieval and classical, which is the most ample poetic expression before Spenser of the moral seriousness of Tudor humanism.

To subsist in bones, says Browne, and be but pyramidally extant, is a fallacy in duration, yet that mortuary monument, the *Mirror for Magistrates,* demands a sigh from the passing reader, if only because of its size and influence. The 1587 edition contained a number of pieces on Roman emperors, from the pen of the worthy John Higgins. They vary in length from six to over fifty stanzas; variations in style are less readily discernible. The narratives in this group, like the rest, embody the medieval conception of tragedy as a dolorous fall from high estate, and Julius Caesar begins his tale of sin with a reference to the medieval models of the book, "Bocas" and Lydgate.

Among this nice derangement of epitaphs the life of Tiberius will serve for illustration. After some inevitable stanzas on the dangers of fortune we learn of the divorce of Agrippina, of wars in Illyria, of professed hesitation to accept the throne. Less familiar to classical students is a letter written by Pilate to Tiberius, reporting the birth, miracles, death, and resurrection of Christ. It is translated literally from the *Flores Historiarum,* with a comment from Higgins by way of higher criticism.[51] Then the fate of Sejanus, Drusus, and Germanicus is mentioned, and some lines are given to the depravities of the court. With a literary tact unusual in the *Mirror* Tiberius decides to tell no more of his life now, since his evil deeds do not bear repetition.

Such an imperial precedent may absolve us from the necessity of gazing any longer into a mirror which, says its compiler to the reader, shows "the slipery deceiptes of the wavering lady, and the due rewarde of all kinde of vices." The motive of the book is medieval, the manner is medieval, and even in these Lives of Roman emperors much of the substance is medieval too. The bulk of it is taken from Suetonius and Herodian, but some details and episodes are drawn from the *Flores Historiarum,* Grafton's *Chronicle,* and Lanquet's *Chronicle.*[52] Such a combination of ancient, medieval, and Renaissance sources, done in a medieval spirit, is still another illustration of the more sluggish of the innumerable cross-currents in sixteenth-century literature. And here we

[51] *Mirror,* ed. Haslewood, I, 279; *Flores Historiarum,* ed. Luard, I, 108.
[52] The sources of the classical Lives are discussed in detail in my article in *S. P.,* XXII, 256 ff.

may leave the *Mirror,* floundering, as Mr. Birrell somewhere says of Hannah More, like a huge conger eel in an ocean of dingy morality.

One would not at first thought expect to find classical myths in a versified history, but in his *Albion's England* William Warner, like medieval chroniclers (not to mention Ralegh and others), thought it well to get a flying start by beginning at the beginning.[53] So Warner, with little of Ralegh's knowledge, imagination, or eloquence, but with a sincere desire to glorify the nation's ancestry, began with the father of Saturn. The birth of Jupiter, the overthrow of Saturn, and kindred matters lying at the root of British history, lead on to the career of Hercules, whose labors are amply described. One of several inset tales narrated by the daughters of King Picus has romantic touches:

> Wheare braue aspects of louely dames
>   Tantara to the fight,
> Whose forms perhaps are weg'd in harts,
>   When fauours wag in sight . . .
>
> Wheare ladies doffe their champions' helmes,
>   And kisse their beauers hid,
> And parlie under canapies
>   How well or ill they did.[54]

The chivalric note is frequently sounded in the poem. Warner was, according to Anthony à Wood, "a friend to poetry, history, and romance." [55] Taste as well as the habit of the times would lead him to Caxton, and in the first two books he did little more than versify the *Recuyell.*[56] In addition to the relics of chivalry there are other non-classical details. One of the inset tales is that of Callisto, and we might expect an Ovidian interlude, but even this story is based on Caxton.[57] Caxton's version, however, is serious, pathetic, courtly; Warner develops the motive of Jupiter's feminine disguise and the progress of the seduction with sportive and rakish detail, his Jupiter is a Don Juan in the harem.[58]

Jogging along at an even trot Warner deals with the Trojan war and the death of Aeneas, and reaches at length the all-important Brute.

[53] *Albion's England* appeared in successively enlarged editions, the first four books and the prose history of Aeneas in 1586, the first six books in 1589, the first nine in 1592, and so on.
[54] Chalmers, *English Poets,* IV, 527. Most of the first stanza, by the way, is woven into Baron's *An Apologie for Paris* (1649, p. 55); see the Appendix.
[55] *Athen. Oxon.,* ed. Bliss (London, 1813–20), I, 766.
[56] See Hans Huf, in the bibliography.
[57] Chalmers, pp. 531–33; *Recuyell,* pp. 48 ff.
[58] Both in *Troia Britanica* and in *The Golden Age* Heywood, in his episode of Jupiter and Callisto, follows Warner, and elaborates the details of dalliance in the same spirit. There are even verbal correspondences.

And thus the Brutons bring
Their petigree from Iupiter,
Of pagane gods the king.

And thus two books are filled. The rest of the work, apart from some inset tales, is devoted to Brute's successors on the British throne.

In the sixth book Owen Tudor relates to Queen Katherine several classical or pseudo-classical stories, and the spirit of them is rather more Jacobean than Elizabethan. The thirtieth chapter tells of Venus and Vulcan, with a good deal of dialogue and realistic or burlesque detail. The gods proceed to consider the case, and Pan, Mercury, and Mars contribute tales and opinions which reveal the disconcerting ways of women. In the forty-sixth chapter the story of Narcissus and Echo follows Ovid, with variations,[59] but Ovidian myth fades away when the ghost of Narcissus and the voice of Echo are sent, with the Furies, to do what damage they can on earth. Mythological machinery becomes a vehicle for satire.

The chief claim of *Albion's England* to the title of epic is that it has twelve books. Francis Meres, with characteristic exuberance, declared that "the best wits of both our Universities" regarded Warner as "our English Homer." For us Warner's interest lies mainly in the medieval and English quality of his work which appears not only in his treatment of myth but in the poem as a whole; in an age of borrowing Warner reveals only a few traces of Italian influence.[60]

A further illustration of Warner's medievalism is the prose "breuiate of the true historie of Aeneas" which was appended to the second book.[61] In the poem, in accordance with a venerable tradition, Aeneas appears as a traitor. In the first sentence of his "true historie" Warner repudiates this view. After that we might look for an abstract of the *Aeneid;* instead we get a summary of Caxton's *Eneydos,* with a few borrowings from Virgil.

The narrative, following Caxton, proceeds by the chronicle, not the epic method. Epic portions are condensed, for Warner frankly avows his desire to reach the love story; speeches and dialogue are altered and expanded. In addition to chivalric touches we have rationalizing of the supernatural; even though Caxton, like Virgil, has Mercury sent with a warning message, here "a noble Troian" is substituted. Then there are realistic details which add verisimilitude; Ascanius is twelve years old.

[59] For example, Echo cries "Let's meete," and Narcissus, thinking that his shadow in the pool has spoken, jumps in and drowns. See below, page 137, note.
[60] See Huf, and F. Brie, *Archiv,* CXXVII, 328 ff.
[61] For a fuller account see *M. L. N.,* XLIV, 40–41.

Thus in following Caxton Warner treats the classical epic exactly as Chaucer did in the *Legend of Dido*.

Looking back over the mass of material touched upon in this chapter, one remains certain at least of the great and increasing popularity of classical themes. They furnish wings (or pattens) to the translator and the literary aspirant, the story-teller and the puritan preacher, the courtly amorist and the ballad-monger, the patriotic chronicler and the philo-sophic moralist. Every quill-driver of the age has slept, more or less soundly, on Parnassus hill. In two types of writing especially we find the beginnings of the mythological poem proper, in paraphrases of single tales from the *Metamorphoses,* and in mythological narratives used to decorate the plea of a despairing lover. The former were natural products of an age of translation. The latter were partly responsible for the style and tone of mythological poems, which inherited the rhetorical tricks and conceits of the courtly lover.

The most pronounced and consistent quality of this body of writing is its medievalism, usually in the bad sense of the word. It is often heavily didactic, and a poem may embody a sermon or an allegory or both. Ancient, medieval, and modern sources are mingled with medieval indifference—Ovid, the *Ovide moralisé,* "Waleys," Boccaccio, Ficino, Chaucer, Virgil, Caxton's *Recuyell* and *Eneydos,* Seneca, Herodian, Suetonius, Geoffrey of Monmouth. Even in those narratives which are free from a moral the manner of treating myths is medieval. The authors want a story, find it in Ovid or elsewhere, and retell it as best they can, with little originality and no attempt at rich decoration. Before turning to Lodge and later exponents of the Italianate Ovidian poem we must take fuller account of old and new conceptions of Ovid.

CHAPTER FOUR

OVID OLD AND NEW

I. ALLEGORY

THE persistence of the habit of allegorizing myths has been and will be noticed in connection with individual poems, but here we may pause to invoke a few out of the cloud of witnesses by way of reminding ourselves that most Elizabethans, in their whole theory of poetry, relied upon the medieval method of defense. There is no need of more than a reminder, since the subject has often been discussed.

Although, as Mr. Spingarn has said, the first problem of Renaissance criticism was the justification of imaginative literature, the victory of aesthetic disinterestedness (a victory which has proved something of a great illusion) was long delayed. The tradition of many centuries could not be quickly overthrown. Aristotelian doctrine, considerably modified by Horatian and medieval ideas, gradually changed the status of literature from what had been a dubious province of heaven into a bravely independent kingdom of man. The process was not completed in the sixteenth century—in England it was only beginning—for the allegorical defense could not become obsolete so long as the conditions which created it still subsisted. When historical criticism of the Bible, for instance, was only faintly stirring, allegory might be needed, even by such a clear-eyed ironic humanist as Erasmus, to explain biblical stories. As for classical myths, Erasmus seems to have wavered, sometimes accepting allegory, sometimes laughing at it.[1]

The allegorizing of Virgil and Ovid flourished on the continent in the sixteenth century.[2] The medieval version of the *Metamorphoses* by Buonsignori was revamped by Agostini. The free translations of Dolce (1539–53) and Anguillara (1554–61) had their moral baggage. Hand-

---

[1] "And here they bring in some foolish insipid Fable out of *Speculum Historiale* or *Gesta Romanorum*, and Expound it Allegorically, Tropologically, and Anagogically . . ." (*Praise of Folly*, trans. J. Wilson, ed. Mrs. P. S. Allen, Oxford, 1913, p. 135). But the allegorical commentary in Sandys' *Ovid* (1632) draws upon Erasmus two or three times.

Our concern is with prevailing orthodoxy rather than with sporadic hints of skepticism, but we may recall something more than a hint in the prologue to *Gargantua*, and the amusing mockery in *Epistolæ Obscurorum Virorum*, Letter 28 (ed. F. G. Stokes, London, 1925, pp. 72 ff.).

[2] For the continent, see, in addition to Rick, Gruppe, pp. 26 ff. And see the chapter on allegorical interpretation of the *Aeneid* in M. Y. Hughes, *Virgil and Spenser* (1929).

books of moralized mythology, such as those of Comes and Cartari, have been mentioned already; they were widely read not only in the sixteenth but throughout the seventeenth century. In France, to mention one item, Barthélemy Aneau translated part of the *Metamorphoses* (1556), and, though reacting to some degree against religious interpretations, he was rationalistic mainly in a Pickwickian sense. Jupiter's amorous exploits signified for him the effort of the world-soul to unite all things in itself. The general tendency of interpretation in the sixteenth century was ethical rather than theological; the fact marks both the strength and the limitations of the secularizing spirit of the Renaissance. On the other hand there was the mystical vein which, branching out from Pico and other Platonists (to go no further back), was inextricably mixed with Cabbalism; the mixture was likely to be more fantastic than fruitful.

Perhaps the best proof of the dominance of allegory is found in the notorious cases of the two chief poets of sixteenth-century Italy. Ariosto had incorporated some actual and obvious allegories in the *Orlando,* but the intuitions of pious commentators soon uncovered many more which the gay and gallant author would not have recognized.[3] And Tasso, harassed by criticism and by his own morbid conscience, declared, to save his poem, that it was allegorical throughout.[4]

In England the medieval notion of allegory held firm sway. The opinions of Thomas Wilson we have met already. The poets, says Ascham, "oftentymes under the couering of a fable, do hyde & wrappe in goodlie preceptes of philosophie."[5] The Elizabethan critics who defended poetry against puritans and ballad-mongers had commonly no better argument than the allegory underlying poetical fiction. Lodge, Webbe, "Puttenham" (perhaps Lord Lumley), are quite orthodox. The mystical Tom Nashe accounts poetry a hidden and divine kind of philosophy, and duly interprets the tales of Ovid.[6]

Sidney, with more important ideas to expound, only glanced at allegory, and perhaps did not have much faith in it. He found parables and allegories edifying, but his parables were Christian, and his allegories the fables of Aesop. Yet his strong moralizing instinct is apparent. He sees in the *Aeneid* a picture of the excellent man, and in the *Cyropaedia*

---

[3] S. J. McMurphy, *Spenser's Use of Ariosto for Allegory* (1924).

[4] Angelo Solerti, *Vita di Torquato Tasso* (Turin and Rome, 1895), I, 233; Courthope, *History of English Poetry*, III, 113–15.

[5] *English Works of Ascham,* ed. W. A. Wright, p. 17.

[6] *Works,* ed. McKerrow, I, 25, 28, 286. On the identity of "Puttenham" see B. M. Ward, "The Authorship of the *Arte of English Poesie:* A Suggestion," *R.E.S.,* I (1925), 284.

"an absolute heroicall Poem" designed to give us *effigiem iusti imperii;* he embodied similar ideas in the revised *Arcadia.* Further, at the very end of the *Apology* Sidney seems to endorse the current view when he cites Clauser and Cornutus and agrees that the fables of Hesiod and Homer "giue us all knowledge." [7]

A moralist no less versatile than Nashe was Sir John Harington, author of the *Metamorphosis of Ajax* and of a version of Ariosto which did not bowdlerize erotic passages. In his preface to the latter work (1591) he borrows both from Fornari, the allegorical interpreter of Ariosto, and from Leo Hebraeus.[8] Following Leo he moralizes the myth of Perseus and Andromeda. "The weaker capacities" will be content with the story, "stronger stomackes" will taste the moral sense, while "a third sort, more high conceited then they, will digest the Allegorie."

For Elizabethan orthodoxy concerning Ovid one may turn back to Golding's "Epistle" and "Preface," where the translator expounds his author's "dark Philosophie." He marches resolutely through the fifteen books, demonstrating the moral lessons of the tales, reducing them to "ryght of Christian law." Ovid is reconciled with the Bible quite satis-factorily. In the "Preface" Golding explains the meaning of the gods in such a way as not to offend Christian scruples, and further celebrates the rule of reason over the flesh. Gavin Douglas had pronounced Ovid "expert of all thing as it semit," [9] and Golding is of the same mind. He proclaims that Ovid is a repository of all knowledge, that he has profitable lessons for all classes of people, young and old, rich and poor, learned and unlearned. Such words are not a mere blurb (done in Elizabethan fashion by the author instead of the publisher), they spring from real conviction; though some allowance may be made for humanistic exuberance of expression, and also for a consciousness of censors in the offing.[10]

These representative opinions are enough to show that the Elizabethan conception of poetry, and of myth in particular, was on the whole the medieval substitute for an aesthetic theory. Yet, as on the continent,

[7] *Elizabethan Critical Essays,* I, 206. An appeal, in the same passage, to supposed Aristotelian authority, is apparently taken from Boccaccio's *De Genealogia Deorum.*

[8] McMurphy, pp. 19–20 (on Fornari). As for Leo, see his *Dialoghi d'Amore,* ed. Caramella (1929), pp. 98–99; and *Elizabethan Critical Essays,* II, 201 ff. See the Appendix, under Abraham Fraunce, 1592.

[9] *The Palice of Honour (Works,* ed. Small, I, 47).

[10] Symptoms of puritan sobriety have been noticed already in connection with ballads, and puritan dislike of mythology becomes increasingly significant. Warton quotes *The Ungodlinesse of the Hethnicke Goddes or The Downfall of Diana of the Ephesians, by J. D. an exile for the word, late a minister in London, MDLIV,* and says: "The writer, whose arguments are as weak as his poetry, attempts to prove that the customary mode of training youths in the Roman poets encouraged idolatry and pagan superstition"; see *History of English Poetry* (1871), IV, 231. Warton also mentions one "H. G.," "a painfull minister

interpretations of myth are mainly ethical and humanistic. The Elizabethan love of morality is manifest everywhere, in the briefest allusion and in the plan of *The Faerie Queene*. In the matter of allusions it is often hard to say—as it is in the case of preachers' use of the Bible— whether an author is consciously allegorical, whether he is employing a poetic symbol or metaphor, or whether a petrified allegory has become a mere conceit. A single familiar example will do:

> O! when mine eyes did see Olivia first,
> Methought she purg'd the air of pestilence.
> That instant was I turn'd into a hart,
> And my desires, like fell and cruel hounds,
> E'er since pursue me.

So well-worn an idea could not retain much allegorical edification.[11]

There is a serious purpose in Spenser's summary of the ethical allegory of the great heroic poets:

> In which I haue followed all the antique Poets historicall, first Homere, who in the Persons of Agamemnon and Ulysses hath ensampled a good gouernour and a vertuous man, the one in his Ilias, the other in his Odysseis: then Virgil, whose like intention was to doe in the person of Aeneas: after him Ariosto comprised them both in his Orlando: and lately Tasso disseuered them againe, and formed both parts in two persons, namely that part which they in Philosophy call Ethice, or vertues of a priuate man, coloured in his Rinaldo: The other named Politice in his Godfredo . . .

The didactic attitude must be accepted if we wish to understand a large share of Elizabethan literature. It may amuse or offend our aesthetic sophistication, but it would have been understood, and partly endorsed, by Plato and even Aristotle as well as Horace. If the classics received sometimes wrong-headed appreciation from Elizabethan readers, they were not a mere innocuous genteel tradition. Besides, moral theory did not hamper Elizabethan freedom of feeling and expression. When

of God's word in Kent," who condemned Linche's *Fountaine of Ancient Fiction* or some similar book as "spawne of Italian Gallimawfry" (*ibid.*, p. 351). Thomas Bryce exclaims

> We are not Ethnickes, we forsoth at least professe not so;
> Why range we then to Ethnickes' trade? Come back, where will ye go?
> Tel me, is Christe or Cupide lord? Doth God or Venus reign?

(Quoted by Raleigh, *Milton*, London, 1909, pp. 173–74.) See the Appendix under Thomas Salter, 1579; and the quotation from Speed, page 41 above.

[11] The interpretation of Actaeon's hounds as his own emotions appears, for example, in the Epistle Dedicatory of Adlington's *Golden Asse* (1566); Whitney's *Choice of Emblemes* (1586), p. 15; the fifth sonnet of Daniel's *Delia* (1592); Fraunce, *Third part of the Countesse of Pembrokes Ivychurch* (1592), p. 43; B. Barnes, *El.* iii (Lee, *Elizabethan Sonnets*, I, 240); B. Griffin, *ibid.*, II, 269; Drayton, *Heroical Epistles*, "Rosamond to Henry" (Chalmers, IV, 58). Cf. *Adonais*, st. xxxi.

In this period, as earlier, euhemerism is common, but it has not much interest for us and may be neglected. One might cite examples ranging from Greene's *Planetomachia* to the travel books of Moryson and George Sandys.

Spenser exhausts the resources of a luscious imagination in painting the Bower of Bliss, is he, as he thought, an ethical teacher exposing the meretricious allurements of vice, or, in the phrase of our more liberal age, a frank pagan celebrating sensuous beauty? At any rate didactic zeal did not hinder him from doing the job thoroughly.[12]

II. THE NEW OVID

With full recognition of the fact that in the sixteenth century a large proportion of readers and writers regarded, or professed to regard, Ovid as a moral teacher, we may here outline the growth of a more aesthetic and "pagan" conception of mythology in general and the *Metamorphoses* in particular. It is of the first importance for the mythological poem throughout its history that from the beginning the new mythology was closely associated with the developing pastoral conventions. Further, the new and warmer treatment of myth was often not incompatible, outwardly at least, with didactic allegory.

We may recall the character of Boccaccio's elaborate pastoral, the *Ameto* (*ca.* 1341). Ameto, a rough hunter, comes upon a group of nymphs sitting by a stream, and, overhearing the song of one of them, Lia, he falls in love. Later, at the feast of Venus, Ameto listens while each nymph, at Lia's suggestion, tells the story of her love, and his pulse is considerably stirred by their tales. Then, after what has appeared to be a celebration of very earthly love, a pillar of fire is seen—it is likened to that which led the Israelites—and the voice of Venus explains,

> Io son luce del cielo unica e trina,
> Principio e fine di ciascuna cosa,
> Del qual nè fu nè fia nulla vicina.[13]

The faces of the nymphs shine with unearthly beauty, and the dazzled Ameto becomes aware that it is the goddess of sacred, not profane, love who has spoken. Baptized with elaborate rites by the nymphs, he, the representative of untaught humanity, can now comprehend the heavenly mysteries and feel the divine fire. The work is an early illustration of

[12] To take a minor example, Peele's *The praise of Chastitie* includes a passage which was apparently imitated in *Venus and Adonis* (397 ff.). Thus Peele (*Phœnix Nest*, ed. Rollins, p. 22; ed. Macdonald, p. 14):

> Who hath beheld faire Venus in hir pride,
> Of nakednes all Alablaster white,
> In Iuorie bed, strait laid by Mars his side,
> And hath not bin enchanted with the sight . . .

This, however sincere, is not the vein of *Comus* or *A Dialogue between the Resolved Soul and Created Pleasure*.

[13] *Opere Volgari* (Florence, 1833), XV, 186.

what was to be a widespread and enduring quality of Renaissance writing, the mixture of sensuous paganism (not to mention erotic realism) with a more or less Christian allegory. Such a combination, one might say, is more congenial to the Latin than to the English temperament, yet no Renaissance author is a more notable exemplar than the creator of *The Faerie Queene.*

Closer to the mythological poem was Boccaccio's *Ninfale fiesolano,* which "uses a pagan allegory to convey a favourite *novella* theme. The shepherd Affrico loves a nymph of Diana, and the tale ends by the goddess changing her faithless votary into a fountain."[14] A similar Ovidian motive appeared in the *Ambra* of Lorenzo de' Medici, for the poem is virtually a redaction of the story of Apollo and Daphne.[15] Likewise Ovidian was Sannazaro's graceful *Salices,* which described the flight of nymphs from pursuing satyrs and their metamorphosis, through Diana's power, into willows. Pastoral and mythological poems shade into each other, for pastoral writing in both prose and verse was drenched with mythology, and the mythological poem obviously owed much to the pastoral. In both is an artificial Arcadian scene, exhaustively described, inhabited by artificial nymphs and swains and mythological figures, also—especially the nymphs—exhaustively described, and of course there is interminable sensuous or sensual love-making.

Among mythological poems must be mentioned the *Giostra* of Poliziano.[16] In it the thread of narrative hardly does more than unite mythological pictures of the richest ornamentation. In Italy, as later in England, the ornate manner rapidly became a convention, and the mythological poem was one of the most popular genres in the fifteenth and sixteenth centuries.[17] The style was encouraged by Ariosto, whose *Orlando* contained elaborately sensuous variations on Ovidian and Virgilian themes. And then, in addition to many versions of tales from the *Metamorphoses,* there were such large works as the paraphrases, often freely expanded, of Dolce, Anguillara, Maretti.[18]

The weaknesses of the Italian mythological poem, amply evident in English pieces, were almost inevitable. Emphasis on luscious descriptions

[14] W. W. Greg, *Pastoral Poetry and Pastoral Drama* (1906), p. 37. For Boccaccio's poëm, see *Opere Volgari,* XVII, 1 ff., and the separate edition, ed. A. F. Massèra (1926). See also the works on Boccaccio by Edward Hutton (1910) and T. C. Chubb (1930); and of course Symonds, *Italian Literature* (1909), I, 103–04, 108, and *passim.*

[15] *Opere,* ed. A. Simioni (Bari, 1913), I, 291 ff.

[16] *Le Stanze per la Giostra: L'Orfeo,* ed. E. Rho (Milan, 1927). See Greg, p. 37, and De Sanctis, *Storia della Letteratura Italiana,* ed. B. Croce (Bari, 1912), I, 339 ff.

[17] See A. Belloni, *Il Poema Epico e Mitologico* (1912), especially chapter xii.

[18] For a convenient list of Italian versions of Ovid, see R. Schevill, *Ovid and the Renascence in Spain* (1913), pp. 234 ff.

of the beauties of art, nature, the human and especially the female body, resulted often in long invertebrate poems compounded of voluptuous imagery and word-spinning.[19] In their pictorial richness, artificial rhetoric, erotic themes, and general slightness of content, they were typical young man's poetry, beautiful words about beautiful things, things and bodies which can be seen and touched. Style cultivated smooth softness of diction and rhythm, diffuseness instead of concentration, bookishness instead of emotion. Love of color and detail was not favorable to purity of line and pattern. But poetry needed a rediscovery of sensuous beauty, and not all poets ran to excess.

Though the inexhaustible Ovid was far and away the chief source of themes, there were other tales, such as the late Greek *Hero and Leander*. Boscán's *Leandro y Hero* (1543), which was inspired by Bernardo Tasso's much superior Italian version, established the elaborate mythological poem in Spain.[20] In both countries Ovidian narratives multiplied with a rapidity quite appalling to the investigator. In France the Italianate fashion took less hold, though mythology was rampant there as elsewhere, and the works of Ronsard and others are full of mythological pieces.

Conservative humanistic tradition might prefer to follow the narrative method of the Latin epic, without frills, except those sanctioned by the *Aeneid,* and Petrarch's *Africa* was the first of many neoclassic epics which, as Porson said of Southey's, will be read when Homer and Virgil are forgotten, and not till then. Conservatism also, supported by the principle of *utile et dulce,* found expression in half-mythological or pastoral didactic pieces, such as the *Scacchiae Ludus* of Vida or the extraordinary work of Fracastoro. But in general the sensuous Italian fancy applied itself to decorative embellishment of Ovid.

Although, as neoclassic principles hardened into a rigid convention, Virgil became the ideal heroic poet, and although, on the strength of critical dicta, he might be given that place even in the sixteenth century, the more concrete testimony of imitation proclaims Ovid the favorite of the Renaissance. The fact explains a good deal in the history of poetry. Renaissance dramatists, even if they sometimes knew Greek, were much better able to imitate or surpass the rhetoric, the sententiousness, and the violence of Seneca than to fathom the spiritual depths of Greek

[19] For instance, see Symonds' account of Molza's *Ninfa Tiberina*, in his *Italian Literature* (1909), II, 199 ff.

[20] Menéndez y Pelayo, *Antología de Poetas Líricos Castellanos (Tomo XIII), Juan Boscán* (Madrid, 1908), 334 ff.; F. Flamini, *Studi di Storia Letteraria* (1895), pp. 385 ff.; F. Pintor, *Delle liriche di B. Tasso* (1900), pp. 137 ff.; M. H. Jellinek, *Die Sage von Hero und Leander in der Dichtung* (1890). For the general influence of Ovid in Spain, see Schevill.

tragedy. The most Virgilian qualities of Virgil, when appreciated, were
not within easy reach, but an unhappily large number of men throughout
the neoclassic period thought that a combination of "correctness,"
funeral games, historical prophecy, and "machines" made an epic poem.
Thus the very defects of Ovid, as well as his real virtues, contributed
to his popularity in the sixteenth century.

While the strength of medievalism continued to manifest itself, Ovid
did by degrees slough off his didactic and allegorical skin sufficiently
to emerge as something more like the poet we know.[21] Increasing
scholarship placed him, for some men, in a recognizable milieu, and gave
to readers a tolerably authentic text of his work. Despite layers of
allegorical interpretation Ovid could be better appreciated as a personality. Although his narrative and stylistic technique were by no means
wasted on medieval scholars and writers, knowledge, understanding,
the capacity for imitation, were now more generally diffused. Ovid's
morality was less of a stumbling-block. In short, his combination of
brilliant rhetoric and soulless subject matter was exactly suited to
Renaissance taste.

The foundation of Ovid's medieval fame shifted somewhat in the
later period. Advancing knowledge and aesthetic appreciation put the
Metamorphoses definitely in the forefront of the poet's work, not merely
as a great body of narrative matter, but as the revelation of a carefree
world of the imagination inhabited by beings who live only for love
and beauty. As Gilbert Murray has said, in an admirable characterization
of Ovid,

He was a poet utterly in love with poetry: not perhaps with the soul of
poetry — to be in love with souls is a feeble and somewhat morbid condition —
but with the real face and voice and body and clothes and accessories of
poetry. He loved the actual technique of the verse . . . He loved most the
whole world of mimesis which he made . . .

What a world it is that he has created in the *Metamorphoses!* It draws its
denizens from all the boundless resources of Greek mythology, a world of live
forests and mountains and rivers, in which every plant and flower has a story,
and nearly always a love story; where the moon is indeed not a moon but an
orbèd maiden, and the Sunrise weeps because she is still young and her
belovèd is old; and the stars are human souls; and the Sun sees human virgins
in the depths of forests and almost swoons at their beauty and pursues them;
and other virgins, who feel in the same way about him, commit great sins
from jealousy and then fling themselves on the ground in grief and fix their
eyes on him, weeping and weeping till they waste away and turn into flowers;

[21] For the survival in our day of popular legends of Ovid as "magician, trader, prophet,
preacher, saint, paladin," see R. H. Coon, "The Vogue of Ovid since the Renaissance,"
Classical Journal, XXV, 277–90.

and all the youths and maidens are indescribably beautiful and adventurous and passionate, though not well brought up, and, I fear, somewhat lacking in the first elements of self-control; and they all fall in love with each other, or, failing that, with fountains or stars or trees; and are always met by enormous obstacles, and are liable to commit crimes and cause tragedies, but always forgive each other, or else die. A world of wonderful children where nobody is really cross or wicked except the grown-ups; Juno, for instance, and people's parents, and of course a certain number of Furies and Witches. I think among all the poets who take rank merely as story-tellers and creators of mimic worlds, Ovid still stands supreme. His criticism of life is very slight; it is the criticism passed by a child, playing alone and peopling the summer evening with delightful shapes, upon the stupid nurse who drags it off to bed. And that too is a criticism that deserves attention.[22]

The pure story-telling faculty, when not actually despised, is nowadays generally regarded as a half-spurious thing, within the reach of those who are not true poets. Yet the gift for narration, at its best, is rare enough to be valued more highly. How many great poetic story-tellers can one count up? At any rate Ovid possessed that gift in a supreme degree. He may not appeal to the immortal in man, but he has stirred to enthusiasm such various poets as Dante, Chaucer, Shakespeare, Milton, Wordsworth. And the writers of the Renaissance accepted Ovid without damaging reservations. His limitless invention and untiring verve, his delight in the sensuous, his taste for scenery at once pleasing and conventional, his easy mastery of every rhetorical artifice, such qualities were more fully enjoyed in the sixteenth than in any other century. Further, we now hear less of Ovid the respectable professor of the theory of love, and more of Ovid the guide to not quite respectable practice. The tolerant but scarcely Bohemian Roman gentleman is on his way to becoming the patron saint of neo-pagans.

Such a brief outline of a general tendency through a long period, or rather different periods in different countries, must of course be qualified at every point. As we have seen, and shall see, the moralized Ovid enjoyed a prolonged euthanasia. While the complete works in the original text were read by more people than in the Middle Ages, numerous translations had a still wider circulation, and Elizabethan translations were even less likely than modern ones to preserve the special character of an ancient classic. A diligent and moderately faithful translator, like Golding, often missed or blunted Ovidian points, while many versifiers freely expanded and altered the original.

In Elizabethan England opposed attitudes toward Ovid existed side

[22] "Poesis and Mimesis," *Tradition and Progress* (1922), pp. 116–17. See also E. K. Rand, *Ovid and His Influence*, 54 ff., 172.

by side, even within the same mind. He was a treasury of moral wisdom, and he was the archetype of the loose and immoral poet. In the course of a quite un-Ovidian anatomical catalogue, Sidney, reaching thighs, pronounces them for Ovid's song more fit.[23] Lodge found moral lessons in Ovid, but in his own *Glaucus and Scilla* he slighted that aspect of his master in favor of sensuous picture-making. Spenser, whose soul moved above Ovid's mundane level, constantly wrote in the Ovidian tradition. No literary compliment was more esteemed than the bestowal of Ovid's crown, and the names of poets who received it—Shakespeare, Daniel, Drayton, Chapman—suggest rather mixed notions of the real Ovid.[24] For Ovid was inextricably entangled with the work of his Renaissance imitators, who often exaggerated or distorted Ovidian qualities.

Ovidian influence on the mythological poem was not that of the *Metamorphoses* alone. The *Amores* contributed erotic suggestions. The *Heroides* taught the arts of amatory rhetoric and complaint. From Ovid too came the trick of scattering moral aphorisms through immoral poems, for, as the Middle Ages well knew, Ovid was a keen observer of human behavior, and, intermittently, a sound moralist.

Then there was the poet's immense indirect influence, which reached the mythological poem through such various intermediaries as pastoral verse and prose, Greek romances, Italian discussions of love, courtly fiction, Petrarchan sonnets, painting, tapestry. Pastorals and Franco-Italian fiction we have glanced at already. Greek romances stimulated both the erotic and the pictorial impulses in mythological verse.[25] The sonneteering tradition contributed its familiar virtues and vices to the technique of mythological poems, for these, dealing with amatory themes, naturally absorbed the whole jargon, Ovidian, chivalric, Petrarchan, which composed the rhetorical pleading of very articulate lovers. The numerous parallels, for instance, between Ovid and Shakespeare's sonnets, between the sonnets and *Venus and Adonis,* are a commonplace. In general the style of mythological poems inclined to the artificial and

[23] *Arcadia*, ed. Feuillerat (1912), p. 220.
[24] Of course it might be a particular rather than a general appellation. Drayton was Ovidian by virtue of his *Heroical Epistles*, Chapman on the strength of *Ovid's Banquet of Sense*.
[25] Here may be mentioned the half-medieval *Hypnerotomachia* (1499) of Colonna, which was translated into English in 1592. As Andrew Lang said, it "is a specimen of the Renaissance in its fever of paganism. He is a Christian monk, vowed to poverty and chastity, and nothing is dear to him but heathenism and luxury in all its forms. Beautiful naked bodies, beautiful faces, beautiful buildings, fountains, temples, triumphs of dead gods, a Venus of onyx and sardonyx, nursing a Cupid above the sepulchre of Adonis, these things and such as these are his sole delight" (Introduction to the reprint, 1890, of the English translation). See Symonds, *Italian Literature* (1909), I, 190.

bookish, and it is significant that two eminent practitioners in this genre were Marino and Góngora.[26]

As for painting, the brush and the pen stimulated each other. Poets of all kinds subscribed to the dogma *ut pictura poesis*. One cannot race too quickly through the Louvre or the Italian galleries to observe that Ovid rivaled, or excelled, the Bible as a storehouse of subjects. While even lean Madonnas acquired a figure, they might, in their ample robes, be less attractive than buxom Venuses clad in sunshine. And mythological poets vied with painters in rich ornamentation and warm flesh tints. The body had come into its own, although in mythological verse it often seems to be under glass.

The Renaissance conception of mythological characters was by no means wholly bookish. There were popular and alien influences which help considerably to explain unclassical qualities. In England especially, where paintings were less familiar than on the continent, tapestries were common, and the myths pictured in them are not always recognizable at first sight. Whatever the popularity of Ovid and the mythographers, they could not altogether counteract the effect of a tapestry on the wall which more often than not showed mythological figures in modern dress. Or, even if such figures were classical to the extent of having no dress at all, the pictorial details and conventions of tapestry were transferred to verse; one has only to recall the character of the pictures promised to the bewildered Christopher Sly.[27]

Thus tapestries might simply vivify a traditional myth with abundant pictorial detail, or might embellish or alter it in various unorthodox or romantic ways. Another powerful influence of a similar kind came from the living pictures of pageants and masques, which made the Elizabethan eye familiar with mythological figures placed in strange settings and combinations. Pageantry had a long native tradition behind it, and when, under the impulse of Renaissance classicism, mythological characters were introduced, they naturally took color from the older and stronger popular conventions.

French influence may account for the fact that the first mythological

---

[26] Góngora, though he could use mythology abundantly and seriously, could also burlesque Boscán's poem on Hero and Leander. See Jellinek, *Die Sage von Hero und Leander*, p. 16.

[27] There is no need of citing other familiar examples, especially as we shall meet them from time to time, but Sandys' remark concerning Ovid's palace of the sun may be quoted: "In this description our Poet imitates Homer in the sheild of Achilles; and is imitated by the moderne in their Screenes and Arasses" (*Ovid*, 1632, p. 65).

See F. Hard, "Spenser's 'Clothes of Arras and of Toure,' " *S. P.*, XXVII, 162 ff.; Joan Evans, "Chaucer and Decorative Art," *R. E. S.*, VI (1930), 408 ff.

pageant was performed, not in England, but in Scotland.[28] At Edinburgh
in 1503 the daughter of Henry VII was welcomed with a representation
of the judgment of Paris. The pageant included, in addition to Paris,
Mercury, and the goddesses, the salutation of Gabriel to Mary, and the
four virtues, Justice, Fortitude, Temperance, Prudence, treading upon
Nero, Holofernes, Epicurus, and Sardanapalus respectively—surely a
comprehensive scheme.[29] Thirty years later, at the coronation of Anne
Boleyn we have, among other things, Apollo and the Muses sitting on
Parnassus, St. Anne, the three Marys, the three Graces, and Udall's
elaborate pageant, "almost a play," on the judgment of Paris. The three
goddesses of course were unworthy to receive the apple in the presence
of their superior, Anne [30]—a courtly compliment which Peele repeated,
to Anne's daughter.

Under Elizabeth, who loved shows if they did not "put her to charges,"
pageants and masques became more and more lavish. In the entertainments at Kenilworth old English and Arthurian characters rubbed
shoulders with Arion and Proteus. The shows at Elvetham (1591)
opened with an oration, "during which six virgins, representing the
Graces and the Hours, removed blocks from her majesty's path, which
Envy had placed there to impede Virtue's progress." [31] On the second
day there were water sports. "From a bower, built at the further end of
the pond, rose Nereus, Neptune, and Oceanus, Phorcus and Glaucus
with a pinnace, in which three virgins played Scottish jigs with their
cornets." Later Sylvanus appeared, to be "spilt into the lake by Nereus,
then ducked by the hooting sea-gods."

Obviously mythological characters underwent a sea-change. They
were similarly "romanticized," if the term be adequate, when they
appeared in drama both courtly and popular. At Dublin in 1528 there
was at Christmas a dramatic festival "wherein the taylors acted the part
of Adam and Eve; the shoemakers represented the story of Crispin and
Crispinianus; the vintners acted Bacchus and his story; the Carpenters
that of Joseph and Mary; Vulcan, and what related to him, was acted
by the Smiths; and the comedy of Ceres, the goddess of corn, by the
Bakers." [32] We cannot, however, either here or elsewhere take time to

---

[28] Robert Withington, *English Pageantry*, I (1918), 81.   [29] *Ibid.*, I, 169.

[30] *Ibid.*, I, 180 ff. A contemporary account is printed in Arber, *English Garner*, II, 41 ff.
For a list of dramatic treatments of the judgment of Paris, see C. R. Baskervill, *M. P.*,
XIV, 483. Cf. above, page 52.

[31] Withington, I, 216; on Kenilworth, I, 207. For further accounts of Kenilworth, etc.,
see E. Greenlaw, *S. P.*, XV, 105 ff., and C. R. Baskervill, *M. P.*, XVIII, 49 ff.

[32] Sir E. K. Chambers, *The Mediaeval Stage*, II, 365. Concerning this list Mr. Baskervill
remarks: "The treatment in these plays in spite of their classical themes, was probably as

do more than record a phenomenon which must be studied in scores of plays, and may fall back on a summary of some results of the mixture of classical and native traditions:

> . . . An argument for old traditions can be made in the case of practically every mythological play before 1600. Moreover, the particular combination of material in these plays suggests dramatic tradition. Like love allegory of the Middle Ages, they show divergences from classical story toward the conventions of mediaeval pageantry and festival play; but the presence of clowns, pages, fairies, and shepherds is suggestive of the melting pot of earlier romantic drama rather than of the somewhat more harmonious court of love poems. Some such mingling of elements must have appeared in the pastoral presented before Elizabeth by Italian actors in 1574, features of which were a scythe for Saturn, shepherds, a wild man, arrows for nymphs, and garlands, the last possibly for festival dances and games.[33]

Lyly of course combined mythological, pastoral, and romantic elements. In Marlowe's *Edward II* Gaveston, considering how to bend the pliant king as he wishes, plans Italian masques, and pages, clothed or unclothed, to represent nymphs, satyrs, Diana and Actaeon.[34] "At Pentecost," says Julia to Silvia, in *The Two Gentlemen of Verona,*

> When all our pageants of delight were play'd,
> Our youth got me to play the woman's part . . .

> Madam, 'twas Ariadne passioning
> For Theseus' perjury and unjust flight;
> Which I so lively acted with my tears . . .

And that marvelous evocation of a purely romantic mood, the allusion to Dido with a willow in her hand, is so un-Virgilian that Shakespeare is thought to have had Ovid's or Chaucer's Ariadne in mind. Probably he did, but may he not also have recalled some Dido of "Pentecost"? One has only to think of *A Midsummer Night's Dream* to see how apparently heterogeneous elements could be wrought into a harmonious whole, to understand the potency of the tradition which romanticized classical figures and stories in a way that no reading of the classics could "correct." [35]

free and romantic as that of Venus and Diana in court of love romance, of Venus in *The tryumpe of Love and Bewte,* 1514, or of classical figures in plays about the middle of the sixteenth century, particularly in Lyly" ("Some Evidence for Early Romantic Plays in England," *M. P.,* XIV, 479). Mr. Baskervill's article, especially pp. 245 ff., 478 ff., 483 ff., has much material on the mixture of classical and native tradition in drama.

[33] Baskervill, pp. 483–84.

[34] *Works of Marlowe,* ed. T. Brooke, p. 315. One line in this passage, "Crownets of pearle about his naked armes," is recalled in *Hero and Leander,* i. 375–76.

[35] In connection with the play of Pyramus and Thisbe may be mentioned a border-piece used by Tottel, a "double-timed" picture of the lovers in modern costume. See R. B. McKerrow, "Border-pieces used by English Printers before 1641," *Library,* Fourth Series, V (1924–25), 17–18.

These few references must serve to indicate the highly romantic influence of tapestries, pageants, and plays upon Elizabethan conceptions of mythological figures. Writing at such a time the authors of mythological poems could hardly sit down to their desks without being consciously or unconsciously affected by the mixture of classical, romantic, pastoral, and folk motives which, for generations of spectators in both palace and market place, had been the accepted and very acceptable rendering of classic story. In view of such facts Spenser's frequently "Gothic" treatment of myth appears more natural and intelligible, and, in general, the reading of Elizabethan mythological poems may leave one less surprised at finding alien elements than at not finding more of them.

III. THOMAS LODGE

In the evolution of the mythological poem Lodge's *Scillaes Metamorphosis* or *Glaucus and Scilla* (1589) has an importance independent of intrinsic merits.[36] Apart from his real titles to fame Lodge has long enjoyed a certain eminence as one of the chief of the light-fingered Elizabethan gentry who pillaged foreign authors to adorn their country, their mistresses, and themselves. As earlier pages have made very clear, what the mythological poem needed if it was to rise above feeble paraphrases and moralizations of Ovid was the influence of continental art and style, and above all, of course, something nearer poetic genius than an earnest desire to write or to edify. These desiderata Lodge supplied, after a fashion.

In Ovid, Lodge's main source, Scilla, while bathing in her favorite pool, is seen, loved, and pursued by Glaucus, who tells how he was changed into a sea-god, and urges his suit. But Scilla flees again, and Glaucus in anger betakes himself to Circe, begging that the nymph may, in Golding's words, be made partner of his smart. Circe's obliging offer of herself as a substitute being rejected, she mixes a "grisly jewce" which, when dropped into Scilla's pool, transforms the damsel into the traditional monster. Glaucus "wept therat," and Scilla remained to wreak her spite on passing mariners.[37]

Ovid's hundred and forty-three lines are metamorphosed by Lodge's magic into nearly eight hundred. The poet is wandering near the Isis, lamenting misfortunes which, we later infer, are those of one crossed in love. Glaucus comes out of the water, lays his head upon the knee of the poet (who had sat down under a willow), and they mingle their

---

[36] *Works of Lodge,* ed. Gosse, Hunterian Society, Vol. I.

[37] *Metam.* xiii. 900 ff., xiv. 1 ff.; Golding, ed. Rouse, pp. 272 ff.

tears. Glaucus offers comfort in several stanzas on mutability in nature and life.[38] A band of nymphs appear from the water and dance about the disconsolate pair. Glaucus again becomes vocal, on the subject of nature's sympathy, and we have the not wholly Ovidian situation of a Greek sea-god, lying beside an Oxford stream, with his head on the knee of Thomas Lodge, complaining of love with citations from Ariosto. Fifteen stanzas of lamentation have their effect upon Glaucus, and he faints. Urged by the sympathetic nymphs, he recovers and launches on his story.

We have now reached the point where Ovid begins. In his tale the heroine, when seen by Glaucus, merely *sine vestibus errat*. Lodge gives one of those luscious catalogues of feminine beauties which were to be extensively cultivated in the next decades; the convention was medieval, but Renaissance poets made it much warmer and more anatomical.[39] Glaucus proceeds with the story of his love and Scilla's proud disdain until he is again overcome. The nymphs raise a pretty litany to Venus, and a few lines will show, in their delicate allusiveness and sensuous rhythm, how far the Italianate style has gone beyond the jigging verses of earlier Ovidian poems:

> Borne of the Sea, thou Paphian Queene of loue,
> Mistris of sweete conspiring harmonie:
> Lady of Cipris, for whose sweete behoue
> The Seepeheards praise the youth of Thessallie:
> Daughter of Ioue and Sister to the Sonne,
> Assist poore Glaucus late by loue undone.

In answer to the prayer Venus appears with Cupid and gives another opportunity for luxuriant description. Cupid transfixes Glaucus with an arrow, and he starts up, completely cured of his infatuation. In the midst of general rejoicing Scilla approaches, and is punished with a shaft from Cupid, whereupon she "gan claspe the Sea-god in her amorous armes." Nine stanzas describe her unavailing attempts to win the love of disdainful Glaucus. With a shriek she flies out to sea, and the company prepare to follow, including the narrator, who rides with Glaucus on a dolphin. While Scilla proclaims her sorrows there appear Fury, Rage, Despair, Woe, and Wan-hope, who bind her to the rocks, and she undergoes a metamorphosis. Glaucus and the rest repair to Neptune's

---

[38] The theme was a commonplace, but Lodge may have had in mind the passage in *Metam.* xv which was one of Spenser's sources in *Mutability*.

[39] The Renaissance catalogue is based on patterns ranging from the *Song of Songs* (chapter 4) to some Anacreontics. On Boccaccio's use of it, see Symonds, *Italian Literature* (1909), I, 98 ff. Thomas Watson, one of the many English practitioners, says that he imitated Aeneas Sylvius (later Pope Pius II) and Ariosto (*Poems of Thomas Watson*, ed. Arber, p. 43).

bower to celebrate the happy event, and the poet accompanies them, but sits apart to

> write this storie
> With many a sigh and heart full sad and sorie.

Finally Glaucus conveys him on the useful dolphin back to where he was at first,

> Willing me let the world and ladies knowe
> Of Scillas pride,

and the moral is enforced

> That Nimphs must yeeld, when faithfull louers straie not.

Lodge has been justly credited with introducing into English a new genre, the minor epic in which a classical subject is treated in a romantic manner. But if we look at the poem from the dubious vantage point of the last chapter we may also say that Lodge was only developing a form and subject already common in Elizabethan verse, that *Glaucus and Scilla* was not so much the first poem in a new genre as one of the last in an old one. It is less a minor epic than a love-complaint, and its pedigree takes us as far back as the Theocritean idyll of Polyphemus and Galatea.[40] Lodge of course owed more to French and Italian writers than to the classics.[41]

The relationship between *Glaucus and Scilla* and Elizabethan lyrics is concealed by the poem's abundant draperies, but the beginning and end hint at a broken heart. We have observed the Elizabethans' fondness for recounting briefly the story of an Ovidian lover and then applying it to their own case. Lodge keeps his professed, one might say professional, pangs in the background, and the mythological example is greatly elaborated, but the poem has an evident connection with the orthodox formula. Indeed it might almost be regarded as a sonnet sequence strung on a mythological thread.[42] The style also is in harmony with the amatory tradition; it is a mosaic of Petrarchan conceits.

On one side then Lodge's theme is related to the sonneteering tradition; for centuries the coy dame had been, despite her proud virginity, the

[40] See Lodge's lyric on this theme in *Rosalynde* (*England's Helicon*, ed. H. Macdonald, p. 61).

[41] Since *Glaucus and Scilla* is immediately followed by a short piece, *Glaucus Complaint*, and since his other work shows thefts from Ronsard, Lodge must have known Ronsard's *Complainte de Glauce a Scylle Nimphe* (*Œuvres*, ed. Laumonier, II, 57; ed. Marty-Laveaux, II, 285). Although the French poem is brief its general tone is like that of *Glaucus and Scilla*; in fact Lodge seems to echo it in several places. Lodge may also have read Ronsard's *Le Ravissement de Cephale* (Laumonier, II, 133 ff.; Marty-Laveaux, II, 329 ff.), which treats the pursuit of a reluctant man by an amorous goddess.

[42] The full title of the first edition was:
"Scillaes Metamorphosis: Enterlaced with the unfortunate loue of Glaucus. Whereunto

mother of a vast amount of poetic invention. But courtship of a disdainful mistress who in turn pleads in vain opens up other literary vistas. It was not a mere accident that such a subject should have been chosen for the first Italianate mythological poem. Amorous and argumentative women were familiar in all kinds of fiction, from Achilles Tatius to Sidney's *Arcadia,* in Ovid's *Heroides* and *Metamorphoses.* The reversal of the rôle of wooer had been common in English, from *Robin and Makyne* to courtly ballads in *A Handful of Pleasant Delights.*[43] Though *Robin and Makyne* is remote in treatment from Lodge, it indicates the genus if not the species to which *Glaucus and Scilla* belongs. Both in subject matter and mode of handling Lodge's poem is related to the Italian pastoral. "In fact the idea of a Nemesis overtaking the disdainful nymph or shepherd is the fundamental theme of the Italian pastoral, though the tragedy is generally averted by his or her ultimate yielding."[44] Lodge's wide reading in continental literature precludes any doubt of his acquaintance with foreign pastorals, but for an illustration of his theme and manner it is enough to cite Peele's *Arraignment of Paris.* Parts of that work are closer to *Glaucus and Scilla* than are any of the mythological narratives so far considered.[45] Lodge's pattern in the main resulted from a combination of the stock theme and style of Italian pastoral with the stock conventions of love poetry. The marriage could not be regarded as altogether eugenic, and most of the English mythological poems which followed bore obvious marks of heredity.

The outline of *Glaucus and Scilla* will have made clear its formal defects. Indeed, of it and a number of its descendants one might use that celebrated dictum of an agonized aesthete, "The two countesses had no outlines at all, and the dowager's was a demd outline." The poem has its skeleton framework, but otherwise, to quote the author,

is annexed the delectable discourse of the discontented Satyre: with sundrie other most absolute Poems and Sonnets.

Contayning the detestable tyrannie of Disdaine, and Comicall Triumph of Constancie: Verie fit for young Courtiers to peruse, and coy Dames to remember."

Many of the short pieces in the volume are in the same key as the moans of Glaucus.

[43] In one pair of poems we have "The scoffe of a Ladie" and "An answer as pretie to the scof of his Lady"; the wooer, repulsed, scoffs in his turn, "being glad he went without her" (*Handful,* ed. Rollins, pp. 12–15). Another and fragmentary piece, one of the many imitations of Elderton's "Pangs of Love and Lovers' Fits," uses the story of Narcissus' disdain of love and his fate to show that the cold mistress may become the vain suitor (*ibid.,* pp. 29 ff., 96–97).

[44] V. M. Jeffery, *M. L. R.,* XIX (1924), 180. Miss Jeffery gives examples from Guarini, Tasso, etc. Cf. F. W. Moorman, *William Browne* (1897), p. 31; W. W. Greg, *Pastoral Poetry and Pastoral Drama, passim;* Hector Genouy, *L'élément pastoral dans la poésie narrative et le drame en Angleterre, de 1579 à 1640* (1928).

[45] *Works of Peele,* ed. Bullen, I, 46.

Discourse was steeresman while my barke did saile,
My ship conceit, and fancie was my bay . . .

Incongruities of costume and allusion have been partly indicated; not the least remarkable is the combination of an Ovidian metamorphosis with figures from medieval allegory.

But the poem as a whole is not medieval, except in the large sense that most of its Italianate elements have a medieval origin. If set beside Peele's *Tale of Troy,* published in the same year, *Glaucus and Scilla* shows the break with the English and medieval manner. Instead of a sketchy chronicle of many events we have eight hundred lines made out of one bare circumstance. Instead of the more or less bald narrative and plain diction of Peele and the other writers discussed in the last chapter, we find that Lodge loads every rift with ore, or at least pyrites, in the form of amatory rhetoric and description, of Italianate language both luscious and precious. If in this poem a man capable of lovely lyrics seldom rose above facile prettiness, and often sank below it, he did show the way to the stronger poets who were to follow. Except in parts of *The Shepheardes Calender* English poetry had as yet nothing so smooth and warmly pictorial as this:

He that hath seene the sweete Arcadian boy
Wiping the purple from his forced wound,
His pretie teares betokening his annoy,
His sighes, his cries, his falling on the ground,
    The Ecchoes ringing from the rockes his fall.
    The trees with teares reporting of his thrall:

And Venus starting at her loue-mates crie,
Forcing hir birds to hast her chariot on;
And full of griefe at last with piteous eie
Seene where all pale with death he lay alone,
    Whose beautie quaild, as wont the Lillies droop
    When wastfull winter windes doo make them stoop:

Her daintie hand addrest to dawe her deere,
Her roseall lip alied to his pale cheeke,
Her sighes, and then her lookes and heauie cheere,
Her bitter threates, and then her passions meeke;
    How on his senseles corpes she lay a crying,
    As if the boy were then but new a dying.

We may as we go on in this book be surfeited with honey, whereof a little more than a little is by much too much, but, unless the reader has skipped most of chapter three, he should be convinced that the earlier Elizabethan verse was in need of some refining.

CHAPTER FIVE

SPENSER

ALTHOUGH Spenser has no single poem that belongs to our genre —unless in a sense the *Cantos of Mutability* may be so regarded— his works are such an endless gallery of mythological paintings that a chapter, however inadequate, must be given to him. Many books and essays have been written, many are still to be written, concerning the influence of particular authors upon a poet whose receptivity is equaled only by his originality, and he in turn has been a more potent and continuous influence than any other English poet with the possible exception of his chief disciple. Even the subject of this chapter, Spenser's treatment of mythology, needs a stout volume or two, and one must be content to set up a few headings. No attempt can be made at a general estimate of classical influences, though some of these are naturally touched upon. The main theme of this book, the way in which ancient, medieval, and modern elements are mingled in one current of poetic expression, is nowhere better illustrated than in Spenser. Even at the cost of being repetitious, therefore, it may not be amiss to emphasize those qualities in him which sum up the past as well as those which look toward the future.

I

Nowadays, especially in the United States, if a poet is "literary" and writes in the consciousness of a great tradition, his work, if not absolutely blasted as "derivative," is likely to be eyed askance. As Fielding would say, all the young critics of the age, the clerks, apprentices, etc., call it traditional and fall a-groaning. The important question is whether the poet is the master or the servant of tradition. Renaissance poets, good or bad, seldom desired or received a higher tribute than the epithet "learned." The association of learning and poetry was no novelty; we meet it in ancient Alexandria and Rome and in the Middle Ages. But in the Renaissance the union became especially close and self-conscious, and it was productive of both good and ill. Elizabethan critics, distressed by the "fardles" of broadsides on sale in St. Paul's churchyard, lamented the degradation of poetry, and urged, wisely enough, that poets should elevate their art through study, discipline, imitation of the ancients and the best moderns. Learning was a wall that the profane rabble of poetasters could not scale. Here, it may be repeated, we have a main reason for the wholesale "plagiarism" that confronts us everywhere in Renaissance writing. Spenser, justly hailed by his own and later ages as the much-desired regenerator of English poetry, was learned both in his rich assimilation of imaginative literature of the past and in his very deliberate following of critical precept. He was a royal borrower, and why not? He was linking English poetry with the European tradition; he was re-creating in English the themes and devices consecrated by centuries of poetic handling. If in one sense his work is a mosaic of traditional materials, in another it is greatly original; for to almost everything he appropriated he gave his own interpretation and coloring.

A no less essential part of the task which Spenser set himself is revealed in the fact that at every turn we find him working in the light of the best critical opinion of his age. From the theory and practice of pastoral to the theory and practice of the heroic poem he is aware of what Italians and Frenchmen have been doing. Yet he was not at any time merely an imitator. Though the Pléiade turned away from medieval literature, except as a source of words, Spenser in *The Shepheardes Calender* proudly announces discipleship to Chaucer. His own critical utterances are mostly lost, but we have such things as the letter to Ralegh, and anyhow his creative work affords sufficient proof of a substantial if eclectic artistic theory. The "dewe obseruing of Decorum euerye where," which E. K. praised as one of the chief virtues of the new poet, has been well emphasized by Mr. Renwick as a dominant principle in all Spenser's work.[1] In his various modes of writing, not merely in the shorter pieces but within *The Faerie Queene*, Spenser's choice and variation of style, partly suggested by the model of the moment, are governed by the principle of congruity. Spenser rather than Ben Jonson is the first modern English poet in whom critical theory supports and controls imaginative expression.

On the other hand the mention of Ben Jonson along with Spenser indicates the distance between them, between the dim figure of the poet of the half-medieval English Renaissance and the substantial personality of the first modern neoclassicist (for the amateur Sidney was hardly modern). Spenser is not of our world, Jonson is, though Spenser's junior by only twenty years. The mold of Jonson's thought and expression was formed mainly by the ancients, whom he knew so familiarly, and by

[1] W. L. Renwick, *Edmund Spenser* (1925), p. 74.

the Dutch Latinists of his own day, and of course he owed something to the classicist strain in Sidney; the medieval tradition, however, and the modern literature of Italy and France counted for little. And the fruits of Jonson's relatively pure classicism—the word "relatively" is emphatic—are obvious in almost all his work, from his theory and practice of comedy to the clear-cut symmetry and diction of his lyrics. With Spenser, on the contrary, the medieval tradition and the critical and creative literature of modern Italy and France counted for much more than the classical, and his classicism was rather an acquisition than a mental habit. His formative ideas were those of a period which was only beginning to discriminate and define, which had not yet taken stock of its intellectual possessions. Like many of his modern preceptors, Spenser himself was too much a part of the medieval tradition to understand his own situation. Living at a time when the omnivorous and uncritical assimilation of the earlier Renaissance was giving way to something like modern scholarship and criticism, he was neither medieval nor modern. He had a body of critical theory, but, drawing ideas and material from all kinds of sources, he lacked generally the critical sophistication needed to reconcile and unify. Indeed he was not of a nature to be conscious, as Tasso was, of disturbing conflicts. He remains, among other things, the wistful panegyrist of an imagined chivalry, the bold satirist of ugly actuality, cosmic philosopher and pastoral dreamer, didactic moralist and voluptuous pagan, puritan preacher and Catholic worshiper, eager lover and mystical Neo-Platonist. To ask "Which is Edmund Spenser?" would be to misunderstand the spirit of an age when, in life no less than in literature, a man could be all these at once.

II

But some of these generalizations must be translated into more specific terms. It is a textbook commonplace that Spenser's poetry gathers many-colored threads from ancient, medieval, and modern worlds into one shimmering web. Nowadays, however, scholars speak less certainly than they once did of his familiarity with ancient literature. While his acquaintance with medieval and Renaissance writing has been extended, his supposed classical learning has been reduced here and there. We do not speak of Spenser's Platonism as if it came from the fountainhead, for there is hardly any evidence that he knew Plato at first hand. Doubtless, like most men of his time, he read Ficino and similar authors, and slighted the Greek. At any rate the so-called

Platonism which runs through so much of his work, and constantly kindles his idealistic nature, is thoroughly of the Renaissance.[2]

It has been proved that the ethical scheme of *The Faerie Queene* is based directly upon Aristotle; it has also been proved, more lately, that it is not based upon Aristotle. Again, for Spenser as for most men of his age, Aristotle meant not so much the body of writings that we know as the numerous strata of medieval and Renaissance commentary; and his name might be attached to pagan doctrines of morality implicit in the Christian tradition.

Or there is *The Shepheardes Calender*. A critical legend, started by E. K. and repeated with embellishments by later generations, has found Greek influence in Spenser's pastorals. But it has been conclusively shown that "direct Greek influence on the *Calender,* if it existed at all, was negligible"; that Spenser's chief models were Marot and the poets of the Pléiade, along with Chaucer and Mantuan; and that even Virgil's influence "seems to have been slight, indirect, and distorted." [3]

These are some instances of the way in which Spenser's direct debt to classical, especially Greek, literature has been shrinking. Few modern readers have brought to Spenser the classical equipment of Mr. Mackail, and Mr. Mackail has said that "even for traces of any influence on him from Homer, from the Greek lyrists, or from Attic tragedians we may search through him in vain." [4] The exceptions which can be lodged against that statement seem to be relatively few and unimportant.

On the other hand, as I have remarked, Spenser's debt to medieval and Renaissance literature has been steadily illuminated and extended. Such facts are no reflection upon the genuineness of the poet's wide culture, but they do involve a shift of emphasis. The process of investigation, still far from complete, has not been mere barren source-hunting; it has helped to clarify our understanding of Spenser's art and thought, to root him more solidly in his own age. Closer scrutiny of dozens of Renaissance figures, along with fuller knowledge of the Middle Ages

[2] Mr. A. E. Taylor (*M. L. R.*, XIX, 208–10) called attention to the curious medley of blunders in Spenser's allusions to Socrates (*F. Q.*, II. vii. 52, and IV, introduction, st. 3). Spenser had apparently a confused recollection of two passages in Cicero. One cannot of course infer too much from this, since Spenser had no great head for facts.

[3] M. Y. Hughes, "Spenser and the Greek Pastoral Triad," *S. P.*, XX, 187; *Virgil and Spenser* (1929), p. 307.

[4] *Springs of Helicon* (1909), p. 98. Mr. H. M. Belden, objecting to such an assertion, offers a rather tenuous argument for the influence of Euripides' *Helen* upon Spenser's account of Proteus and Florimell (*M. L. N.*, XLIV, 526 ff.). Mrs. J. W. Bennett has lately shown that Spenser's list of the Nereids (*F. Q.*, IV. xi. 48–51) probably followed the Latin verse translation of Hesiod's *Theogony* by Boninus Mombritius; see *American Journal of Philology*, LII (1931), 176 ff. Cf. Natalis Comes, *Mythologiae*, viii. 6 (Padua, 1616, pp. 439–40).

and the medieval tradition, has exploded the older conception of the Renaissance as a sudden awakening, a complete break with the medieval past. The Elizabethan author, as we have frequent occasion to observe, was, in his treatment of mythology and his general mental habit, nearer 1400 than 1700. Spenser would have been more at ease with Chaucer than with Dryden.

Though internal evidence is our only guide to the sources of Spenser's mythology in general, the glosses of the *Calender* provide a suggestive basis of concrete fact. A gloss on *March* begins: "Flora, the Goddesse of flowres, but indede (as saith Tacitus) a famous harlot . . ." But Tacitus does not say so; the information comes from the *De Genealogia Deorum* of Boccaccio, who got it from Lactantius.[5] On *July*, E. K. refers to Diodorus Siculus for the story of "the hyl Ida," but Spenser is following Mantuan, who reflects a medieval tradition based on Ezekiel.[6] An example of allegory is the note on *March* which relates the story of Achilles' heel (and assigns it to Homer!). The exposition, derived ultimately from Fulgentius, is that, since the heel is connected by veins and sinews with the genitals, "by wounding in the hele, is meant lustfull loue."

It is significant, though not in the least surprising, that we find two young men, fresh from the university, accepting very mixed mythology with no more hesitation than was shown by medieval writers. They have of course a wider acquaintance with ancient literature, but they are often inaccurate, and their allusions are mainly to Latin authors. In addition to examples cited already—in addition also to many correct references—there are items attributed to Hesiod, Plato, Theocritus, Virgil, Ovid, Mantuan, that cannot be found in modern texts. All these straws indicate how the wind blows, and the impression given by Spenser's first book is not essentially altered by study of his later work.

When we move on to *The Faerie Queene* and other poems we accumulate a list of "errors" in mythology not remarkable in a voluminous Elizabethan poet, yet rather damaging to any exaggerated estimate of the solidity of Spenser's classical learning. Some of these may be ascribed, like our own, to slips of memory or "Ignorance, Madam, pure ignorance"; besides, as Gascoigne said, poetic license is a shrewd fellow, and many "errors" must have been deliberate. It is a question in which category one should put such an example of contamination as that in

[5] C. C. Coulter, "Two of E. K.'s Classical Allusions," *M. L. N.*, XXXV, 55–56. Other examples are taken from Mr. W. P. Mustard, "E. K.'s Classical Allusions," *M. L. N.*, XXXIV, 193 ff. In the *April* gloss a note on the nymph Chloris, as Miss Coulter showed, comes from the same passage in Boccaccio. See also Mustard, p. 197, and *M. L. N.*, XLV, 168–69.

[6] Mustard, p. 199.

Daphnaïda; Spenser was familiar with the myths of Orpheus and Eurydice, Cybele, and Ceres and Proserpine, yet he has the mother of the gods seeking Eurydice through the world.[7]

Further, Spenser was no more troubled than Chaucer by the modern pedantry that distinguishes between ancient myth and later accretion or variation. He could borrow freely without feeling the scholar's obligation to verify his references. We may be surprised to read that Hercules took the distaff in hand "for Iolas sake," instead of Omphale's. But in *Gerusalemme Liberata,* in one of the cantos upon which Spenser drew for the Bower of Bliss, we find Iole and the distaff; she had appeared more than once in Boccaccio's Italian works.[8] The Elizabethans, despite their generally superior knowledge of Latin and sometimes Greek authors, were very often content, like their medieval predecessors, to gather their mythological nosegays from the nearest conservatory. The mythographers, as we have seen, were not merely convenient for reference, like a classical dictionary; their allegorical interpretations were highly attractive. Spenser's desk evidently contained well-thumbed copies of *De Genealogia Deorum* and some similar books.[9]

III

In approaching the more important question of Spenser's artistic handling of myth we may ask how far the medievalism apparent in matters of fact extends to spirit and mode of treatment. No English poet has employed myth in more various ways than Spenser, and the mere bulk of his mythological lore is so great that even an irreducible minimum of illustrations spreads out like the Spenserian lists of Gloriana's progenitors.

Ornamentation ranges from allusions, similes, periphrases, to narratives or pictures occupying a number of stanzas. Like bookish poets before and after him Spenser used the names of classical divinities instead of the natural phenomena they represented, and such allusions even in him were often conventional and colorless. Yet, artificial as these flowers of rhetoric are, in the better poetry of the sixteenth century they

---

[7] Ll. 463 ff. See E. K.'s gloss on Orpheus (*October*), and Mustard, *M. L. N.,* XXXIV, 201.
[8] *F. Q.,* V. v. 24; *G. L.,* XVI. 3. The point was noticed by Mr. Mustard (*M. L. N.,* XX, 127).
[9] Spenser certainly knew Natalis Comes, as commentators have long recognized. The extent of his use of the *Mythologiae* is doubtful in respect to ordinary mythology, since his tracks would be covered. When, however, he takes over from a handbook some post-classical accretion or allegorical exposition, he may afford clues. Mr. C. W. Lemmi, in a study of Spenser's debt to Comes (P. Q., VIII, 270), recorded as borrowings some twenty-nine allegorical interpretations. A good many of these seem to me dubious, but some can be taken as proved. Even a single example throws some light on Spenser's treatment of classical matter.

are almost if not quite saved by a touch of freshness, of unspoiled gusto, which we miss in later times when the flowers had gone to seed. So we may prefer Spenser's

> As gentle Shepheard in sweete euen-tide,
> When ruddy Phœbus gins to welke in west,

to Gray's similar but shopworn phrasing,

> In vain to me the smiling mornings shine,
> And redd'ning Phoebus lifts his golden fire.

The first English heroic poet could not fail to employ the detailed simile sanctioned by poetic precedent and critical doctrine. The long and unclassical catalogue of Belphoebe's charms of person and dress ends with a pair of similes of which the first may be compared with Virgil:

> Such as Diana by the sandie shore
> Of swift Eurotas, or on Cynthus greene,
> Where all the Nymphes haue her unwares forlore,
> Wandreth alone with bow and arrowes keene,
> To seeke her game. . . .[10]

The mildly and vaguely sensuous adjectives, "sandie," "swift," "greene," "keene," are characteristic Spenserian additions.

Ancient epic similes, however, were not usually mythological. Rather they were bits of observed nature or familiar experience, and such "spaces of cool air and quiet daylight," as Mr. Mackail says of the Homeric similes, have a magical effect—the horse breaking from the stall, the flight of birds, Odysseus covering himself with leaves as a peasant thrusts a brand into the ashes. The majority of Spenser's similes are of this sort, though more "poetical" and detachable. Here is a random specimen which, prefixed with a "So have I seen . . . ," might almost be Jeremy Taylor's:

> Like as a tender Rose in open plaine,
> That with untimely drought nigh withered was,
> And hung the head, soone as few drops of raine
> Thereon distill, and deaw her daintie face,
> Gins to looke up, and with fresh wonted grace
> Dispreds the glorie of her leaues gay;
> Such was Irenas countenance, such her case,
> When Artegall she saw in that array . . .[11]

This is quite lovely, but overloaded, and it does not approach "the portion of weeds and outworn faces," nor can it be set beside Virgil on the

---

[10] *F. Q.*, II. iii. 31. Cf. *Aen.* i. 498 ff.
[11] *F. Q.*, V. xii. 13. A less luxuriant and more successful example from Spenser would be *F. Q.*, VI. ii. 35. Cf. *F. Q.*, II. xii. 74–75, and Tasso, *G. L.*, XVI. 14–15.

death of Euryalus. Thus Spenser's similes, whether or not they involve
mythology, have a diffuse richness and lack of salience. They are—and
this is true of most of his incidental allusions to myth—patches stuck
on rather than a growth from within. To say that is of course only to
say that Spenser was a poet of the Renaissance.

The decorative circumlocution we commonly think of as an eighteenth-
century disease, but the seeds from which sprang those wax flowers had
been planted long before. Du Bellay described the art of periphrasis in
1549 with a fullness of detail which suggests that he believed himself to
be inaugurating a fashion new in France. It is more graceful, he says,
to write "the thundering father" for Jupiter, "the virgin huntress" for
Diana; instead of the prosaic "from east to west" let us have "From
those who first see Aurora blush to where Thetis receives in her waves
the son of Hyperion." [12] Nor is the trick merely a result of the classical
measles of the Renaissance, it had really never been absent from the
European tradition since Roman times. For a convenient account of the
medieval esteem for this "color of rhetoric" I may quote Mr. Manly's
remarks on several rhetorical treatises written by Matthieu de Vendôme
and Gaufred de Vinsauf:

> The first two are prose treatises, carefully defining and discussing all
> processes and terms and illustrating them by examples, in part drawn from
> earlier writers, such as Virgil, Horace, Ovid, Statius, and Sidonius, and in
> part composed by the rhetorician himself, either to show his skill or to pay
> off a grudge . . . Gaufred, illustrating the beauties of *circumlocutio*, says it
> is of special value when we wish to praise or diffame a person: thus if any one
> were speaking of William de Guines, the disreputable butler of the king, he
> might, instead of his name, more elegantly use this circumlocution, *Regis ille
> pincerna, pudor et opprobrium, pincernarum faex, et inquinamentum domus
> regiae* . . .
> *Circumlocutio* was highly regarded as one of the best means, both of ampli-
> fying discourse and of raising commonplace or low ideas to a high stylistic
> level . . .[13]

Everyone remembers how Chaucer, having launched an unwonted
bubble of high-flown style, catches himself in the act, and, with a quiet
wink, punctures it before proceeding:

> Til that the brighte sonne loste his hewe;
> For thorisonte hath reft the sonne his lyght;
> This is as muche to seye as it was night.

[12] *La défense et illustration de la langue française,* ed. L. Séché (1905), pp. 152–53.
Cf. Boileau, *L'art poétique,* iii. 165 ff.
[13] "Chaucer and the Rhetoricians," *Proceedings of the British Academy,* XII (1926),
99, 105.

Chaucer does of course make astronomical calculations in public, as it were, but that is not a wholly decorative trick. Anyhow Renaissance critics and poets, molding classic example into sacred law, allowed no Chaucerian instinct for simple directness to stand in the way of ornate amplitude, and in this as in other matters they went beyond the limits of their Roman models; both ancient and modern excesses were to receive attention from Scarron and Butler. This brief sketch of the pedigree of circumlocution has rather more relation to some of Spenser's successors than to Spenser himself, though he has a good many examples. One of the most elaborate introduces the second canto: "By this the Northerne wagoner had set . . ."—and this way of saying that it was morning suited Spenser's leisurely style. Most of his several dozen periphrases are statements of time—the majority occurring in the first two books, where the action is more closely knit—and their mythology is warmer and more romantic than Chaucer's.

Purely descriptive periphrases, which are such a splendid ornament in Milton, are not characteristic of Spenser, whose style, however loose, is generally straightforward and avoids rhetorical indirectness. Once at least he anticipates Milton's manner of introducing mythological allusions:

> Not that great Champion of the antique world,
> Whom famous Poetes verse so much doth vaunt,
> And hath for twelue huge labours high extold,
> So many furies and sharpe fits did haunt,
> When him the poysoned garment did enchaunt
> With Centaures bloud, and bloudie verses charm'd,
> As did this knight twelue thousand dolours daunt.[14]

But Spenser, as usual, is more detailed. Spenser's few periphrases of this kind have a less deliberate and conventional air than many later efforts, and of the small change of the neoclassical treasury—"Venus' train" and the like—he has hardly any. He can say that in Belphoebe's eyes "The Christall humour stood congealed rownd," but this is not his characteristic style.

IV

Very characteristic of Spenser and the Renaissance tradition is the combination or juxtaposition of classical and biblical characters, allusions, and turns of phrase. So Spenser's loveliest description of the dawn mixes classic myth with the language and imagery of the nineteenth psalm:

[14] *F. Q.*, I. xi. 27.

At last the golden Orientall gate
Of greatest heauen gan to open faire,
And Phœbus fresh, as bridegrome to his mate,
Came dauncing forth, shaking his deawie haire:
And hurld his glistring beames through gloomy aire.[15]

Here there is no incongruity; Hebraic and classic images are fused in
the alembic of a Renaissance imagination.

Everywhere Spenser freely mingles allusions fictitious and historical,
Hebraic and classical. Seeking parallels for the warlike Britomart, he
cites Penthesilea, Deborah, and Camilla. The well of life which renewed
the strength of the knight of holiness—that is, the sacrament of baptism
—excels, as it well may, "Silo" and Jordan, Bath, "the german Spau,"
Cephisus and Hebrus. The hill from which the same Christian soldier
surveys "the new Hierusalem" is

> like that sacred hill, whose head full hie,
> Adornd with fruitfull Oliues all arownd,
> Is, as it were for endlesse memory
> Of that deare Lord, who oft thereon was fownd,
> For euer with a flowring girlond crownd:
> Or like that pleasaunt Mount, that is for ay
> Through famous Poets verse each where renownd,
> On which the thrise three learned Ladies play
> Their heauenly notes, and make full many a louely lay.[16]

These musical lines carry their own justification, but when, within the
compass of the *Calender,* we find that Pan is at various times Henry VIII,
the pope, and Christ, we may be disconcerted. If the procedure is medieval and casts back to Petrarch's allegorical eclogues, it is also of the
full-blown Renaissance and looks forward to Hippotades, Camus, and
the pilot of the Galilean lake. In this connection a critic of Spenser has
quoted an apt passage from Vernon Lee:

[15] *F. Q.,* I. v. 2. Cf. Psalm xix. 5: "In them hath he set a tabernacle for the sun: which
cometh forth as a bridegroom out of his chamber, and rejoiceth as a giant to run his
course."

The same combination appears again, in a place where decoration is enlisted in the
service of the poet's deepest personal emotions:
> Loe where she comes along with portly pace
> Lyke Phœbe from her chamber of the East,
> Arysing forth to run her mighty race . . .

[16] Incidentally, while the minutest speculation about Shakespeare's sonnets is hazardous
(with or without a review of a few hundred books and articles), one may wonder if the
"olives of endless age" in Sonnet 107 (the dating of which has been so much discussed)
is not an echo of Spenser's second and third lines. At any rate in Sonnet 106 is the
apparent allusion to *The Faerie Queene,* which suggests that the two sonnets were written
not far apart. Cf. Chambers, *William Shakespeare,* I, 563; G. B. Harrison, *T. L. S.,* November 29, 1928, p. 938.

There is, inside Ara Cœli—itself commemorating the legend of Augustus and the Sibyl—the tomb of Dominus Pandulphus Sabelli, its borrowed vine-garlands and satyrs and Cupids surmounted by mosaic crosses and Gothic inscriptions; and outside the same church, on a ground of green and gold, a Mother of God looking down from among gurgoyles and escutcheons on to the marble river-god of the yard of the Capitol below.[17]

This instinctive fusing of apparently alien elements is not a mere matter of random allusions, it lies at the very center of Spenser's work. Everywhere the question is "Christ or Apollo?"—or should it be "Aphrodite?" While the real Spenser cannot be understood without his didacticism and allegories, the average modern reader believes with Hazlitt that the allegory if left alone will not bite him; he reads Spenser, he would say, "for the poetry." Such an attitude Spenser himself, for all his delight in love and beauty, would have repudiated. Like other poets of his time he probably was not fully conscious of the opposed impulses within him; at any rate he gratified both, and we have the results not merely side by side but inextricably mixed.

While one has a general impression that Spenser's work is a tissue of decorative episodes, closer scrutiny makes it clear that not many are wholly decorative. Again and again passages which to the casual reader seem to be ornamental excrescences, existing for their own sake, are found to be related, however tenuously, to the allegory. The appearance of otiose though delightful ornament is often due to the fact that the allegorical or didactic purpose is overlaid and obscured by elaborate and sensuous descriptive detail. In his account of the three temptations which Guyon undergoes at the hands of Mammon Spenser has in mind, along with many other things, both the familiar three tests of Celtic folklore and Satan's three temptations of Christ. It is to this episode that Milton refers when he calls Spenser "sage and serious," "a better teacher than Scotus or Aquinas." Here if anywhere Spenser is in a soberly didactic mood, and this is the scene of the final temptation:

> The Gardin of Proserpina this hight;
> And in the midst thereof a siluer seat,
> With a thicke Arber goodly ouer dight,
> In which she often usd from open heat
> Her selfe to shroud, and pleasures to entreat.
> Next thereunto did grow a goodly tree,

[17] *Renaissance Fancies and Studies* (London, 1896), p. 165; quoted in W. M. Dixon, *English Epic and Heroic Poetry* (London and New York, 1912), p. 151. Concerning the *Calender*, it will be recalled that in Marot's pastoral poems Pan is both God and Francis I. Of course such things are a commonplace of Renaissance art of all kinds.

See the opinions of Pigna, Cinthio, and Ronsard cited by Mr. Renwick, *Edmund Spenser*, pp. 143–44.

With braunches broad dispred and body great,
Clothed with leaues, that none the wood mote see
And loaden all with fruit as thicke as it might bee.

Their fruit were golden apples glistring bright,
  That goodly was their glory to behold,
  On earth like neuer grew, ne liuing wight
  Like euer saw, but they from hence were sold;
  For those, which Hercules with conquest bold
  Got from great Atlas daughters, hence began,
  And planted there, did bring forth fruit of gold:
  And those with which th' Eubœan young man wan
Swift Atalanta, when through craft he her out ran.

Here also sprong that goodly golden fruit,
  With which Acontius got his louer trew,
  Whom he had long time sought with fruitlesse suit:
  Here eke that famous golden Apple grew,
  The which emongst the gods false Ate threw;
  For which th' Idæan Ladies disagreed,
  Till partiall Paris dempt it Venus dew,
  And had of her, faire Helen for his meed,
That many noble Greekes and Troians made to bleed.[18]

After these melodious lines, laden with glamorous suggestion of earthly beauty, do we remember that the knight of temperance is winning a hard victory over avarice and ambition, have we an ear for the groans of Tantalus and Pilate?

The *locus classicus* is of course the voyage to the Bower of Bliss. The groundwork of the allegory in the whole book is the traditional psychology of Plato and Aristotle and Christian moralists. The groundwork of this episode is the story of Circe, but there is far less of Homer than of the allegorical tradition which interpreted the myth as the war of flesh and spirit. Spenser uses the theme, as Milton does in *Comus,* in the orthodox way, to show the conquest of sensual appetite by the virtuous will. But Milton tries not to let us forget that vice is ugly, and his Lady is icy and unassailable; we are uncertain how Guyon might behave if the Palmer were not with him. When Spenser's sirens sing

  O turne thy rudder hither-ward a while:
  Here may thy storme-bet vessell safely ride;
  This is the Port of rest from troublous toyle,
The worlds sweet In, from paine and wearisome turmoyle,

is it any wonder that Guyon's senses are "softly tickeled," that the commands of impeccable "reason" seem a little over-righteous? (It is,

[18] II. vii. 53–55.

by the way, worth noting that Spenser's most uniformly beautiful lines, apart from pageantry, are those which either summon to high endeavor or invite to sensuous ease!) And would Milton, for all his love of beauty, permit himself the naked wanton damsels whom Spenser here and elsewhere depicts with an exuberance which, however serious his intention, leaves the moral a trifle pallid?

In the first canto of the third book Spenser wishes to suggest the sensual atmosphere of the Castle Joyous, and accordingly devotes five luscious stanzas to pictures of Venus and Adonis. In the sixth canto it is perhaps necessary that Venus should call upon Diana—but less necessary that she should find Diana bathing. The eleventh canto of the same book has a long series of mythological paintings which "shew Dan Cupids powre and great effort." These pictures, "all of loue, and all of lusty-hed," hang in the mansion of the evil enchanter Busyrane, that foe of chastity. But does "profane" love seem so unlovely when it appears in Spenser's tapestries depicting Europa on the bull's back, Danae in her tower, and many more?

> Then was he turnd into a snowy Swan,
> To win faire Leda to his louely trade:
> O wondrous skill, and sweet wit of the man,
> That her in daffadillies sleeping made,
> From scorching heat her daintie limbes to shade:
> Whiles the proud Bird ruffing his fethers wyde,
> And brushing his faire brest, did her inuade;
> She slept, yet twixt her eyelids closely spyde,
> How towards her he rusht, and smiled at his pryde.

Never on Olympus did Jove's exploits receive such mild censure.

But too many passages demand quotation, and we must end with Calidore, who beheld such a sight

> That euen he him selfe his eyes enuyde,
> An hundred naked maidens lilly white,
> All raunged in a ring, and dauncing in delight.

The beauty of this vision of the Graces is Spenser's own, though the materials are drawn from manifold sources, classical, modern, Celtic. While our eyes are still bewitched, a shepherd proceeds, with the aid of Natalis Comes, Servius, Boccaccio, to expound the relation of the Graces to Courtesy—if we can give him our attention.[19]

Spenser was of course a very conscious and responsible inheritor of

[19] See *F. Q.* VI. x. 10 ff.; Renwick, p. 135; W. P. Mustard, *M. L. N.,* XLV, 168–69; E. Greenlaw, *S. P.,* XV, 108–09; H. H. Blanchard, *P. M. L. A.,* XL, 848.

the traditional conception, powerfully reinforced by Renaissance criticism, of the poet, especially the heroic poet, as a moral teacher, whose combination of the *utile* and the *dulce* both instructs and delights. But Spenser was in the paradoxical situation of many artists of the Renaissance; his right hand remains untroubled by what his left hand does. Our Protestant and puritan tradition has made most of us incapable of entering naturally into the state of mind which, from the *Ameto* downward, unites religious or didactic allegory and luxuriant fleshliness. And many old-fashioned evangelical families read Spenser, though they would have recoiled from Ariosto; yet it is a question if Ariosto's morality is less healthy than Spenser's. What Mr. L. P. Smith has admirably said of Jeremy Taylor, who preached in the sunset glow of the Renaissance tradition, is even more true of the poet of noontide:

> It is a dangerous thing for him to denounce evil in lovely chimes of words . . . A sin which is damned with too much eloquence may arouse more interest than holy execration; and when we read in Jeremy Taylor of "the falling stars and little glow-worms of the world," we, too, are tempted to turn from the altar and gaze on them with worldly eyes; "the harlots' hands that build the fairy castle" are hardly regarded by us with all the reprobation they deserve, and a sinner who, with a heart full of wine and rage and folly goes "singing to the grave" may seem to have made what is after all a not inglorious end . . . The preacher may be preaching with the most solemn emphasis of the four great last things, of Death and Judgement and Hell and Heaven, but if the poet within his cassock is singing at the same time of the dew on the leaves of the rose, it is to the song rather than the sermon that we listen.[20]

V

This chapter is a sketch of some aspects of Spenser's treatment of mythology, not a monograph on his *Belesenheit,* but a few sections may be devoted to his use of certain ancient poets. There is not here any more than elsewhere room for anything except the briefest illustrations.

The customary claims for Spenser's fairly extensive knowledge of Greek literature have already been questioned, and we might now take a brief glance at his debt to Homer. Finsler, without offering much in the way of proof, remarks: "Umfassend ist seine Kenntnis Homers." [21] "Homer," says Miss Winstanley, "was one of Spenser's favourite authors," and she too cites some more or less familiar Homeric themes.[22]

[20] "Jeremy Taylor," *Life and Letters,* II (1929), 261; and *The Golden Grove* (Oxford, 1930), pp. xlviii–xlix, lxii.
[21] *Homer in der Neuzeit* (1912), p. 278.
[22] *The Faerie Queene,* Bk. II (1914), p. xxxiv. See pp. xiv–xv, xxviii ff.

But we remember Achilles' heel, and when the poet burns

> To heare the warlike feates, which Homere spake
> Of bold Penthesilee,

we may conclude that his Homer, even if not, like the Rev. Mr. Portpipe's, clothed in the dust of thirty years, has at any rate not been opened very lately.

That Spenser sometimes uses material which is in Homer is obvious, but that he got it from Homer, as Miss Winstanley assumes, is another question. That he knew some Greek is also obvious; that he was in the habit of reading Greek literature is very unlikely. When one collects and examines the evidence for Spenser's use of Homer it proves to be slight. The voyage to the Bower of Bliss, for instance, has often been related to the *Odyssey,* and of course it is, ultimately, but here as in other cases there are far too many intermediaries. That canto is in the matter of sources a veritable gulf of greediness, yet it seems safe to argue that there are not ten lines in it which derive directly from Homer; it is a question if there be any. When ancient Latin or modern sources account for Spenser's material and his moral coloring, it seems best to leave Homer in the background.[23]

Whether he takes material directly from Homer or not, he is constantly un-Homeric in the handling of it. His ethical attitude, his conception of Agamemnon and Ulysses as, in Homer's intention, "a good gouernour and a vertuous man," is of course Renaissance orthodoxy, but it explains the way—a not ignoble way—in which Homeric as well as other classical matter is reinterpreted. Explicit moral and allegorical teaching, which turns characters and incidents into symbols, at once separates Spenser from the forthright objectivity, simple realism (and unobtrusive but healthy morality) of Homer. So the girdle of Aphrodite, becoming the girdle of Florimell, becomes also, by way of folklore and Renaissance

---

[23] See page 114 below, note. To mention one item, Miss Winstanley cites the Homeric description of Scylla and Charybdis in connection with the gulf of greediness and the rock of vile reproach. Spenser's rock (xii. 4) is magnetic—Homer's is not—and belongs in part at least to travelers' tales. Miss Lois Whitney quotes Mandeville (*M. P.,* XIX, 156). Besides, we know that Spenser in writing this canto had Natalis Comes at hand, and Comes quotes Virgil's description of Scylla, and both quotes and translates Homer's (viii. 12; Padua, 1616, pp. 455–56). For the allegory Mr. Lemmi (*P. Q.,* VIII, 278) cites Comes. Spenser's moral is partly suggested in some lines from B. Anulus (Aneau) quoted and translated by Sandys in his comment on *Metam.* xiv (ed. 1632, p. 475):

> Detracting envy Scylla's curres imply;
> Charybdis, the deepe Gulph of pouerty,
> Who shun Charybdis, upon Scylla fall:
> Still snarling Envy barks, Want swallowes all:
> If prudent, of two evills choose the least:
> Rather be enui'd, then by need opprest.

For a medieval analogue, see F. M. Padelford, *S. P.,* XXVIII (1931), 213.

Platonism, a test for distinguishing true from spurious beauty. The golden chain of the *Iliad* is associated with Philotime in the cave of Mammon as a symbol of avarice and ambition; thus Comes interprets it.[24] The meaning of the golden apples in the same canto is explained by Comes, who makes the apples of the Hesperides symbols of wealth, "which is given to men almost as a touchstone by which to test their souls." [25] The episode of Circe, though probably felt by Homer [26] as partly didactic, becomes much more so when incorporated in a book devoted to temperance. Thus, however much or little Spenser knew of the Homeric poems, he regularly alters the spirit of what he borrows, and so far as these items are concerned he needed no more of Homer than he could find, translated and moralized, in Comes and other higher critics.

VI

The influence of Virgil on Spenser can hardly be discussed in a few pages, but a sixteenth-century poet's reaction to Virgil is such an important index to some major aspects of his mind and art that an attempt must be made. Fortunately there is a recent and scholarly work to lean upon.[27] It goes without saying that one great poet's influence on another is often not of the demonstrable kind; rather it is like one of the forces of nature the effect of which even the poet himself could not analyze. But any Renaissance poet, especially so self-conscious and eclectic an artist as Spenser, reveals literary influences in tangible ways. The more elusive and generally more essential kind may be there too, and doubtless is in this case, yet Spenser does obviously borrow material from Virgil, and we may ask how he handles it.

The influence of the *Eclogues* we have already seen to be "slight, indirect, and distorted." The *Georgics,* than which even the *Aeneid* is hardly a surer touchstone for the appreciation of Virgil, left no, or almost no, trace in Spenser.[28] He was attracted by the *Culex* and the *Ciris,* a fact which suggests the Alexandrian taste of the Renaissance rather than an instinct for the true Virgil. *Virgils Gnat* is negligible, except as a biographical puzzle. The material borrowed from the *Ciris,* for the episode of Britomart and Glauce, is however Spenser's chief debt, as

[24] *F. Q.,* II. vii. 46–48; Comes, ii. 4 (Padua, 1616, p. 72). See C. W. Lemmi, *P. Q.,* VIII, 277. Chapman, that great borrower from Comes, has the same interpretation in his *Hymnus in Noctem* (F. Schoell, *Études sur l'humanisme continental en Angleterre,* p. 35).
[25] St. 54. The lines are quoted above, p. 97. See Lemmi; I have quoted part of his translation of Comes (vii. 7, p. 385).
[26] E. E. Sikes, *The Greek View of Poetry* (1931), p. 14.
[27] M. Y. Hughes, *Virgil and Spenser* (1929).
[28] Mr. Renwick (page 56) suggests a possible imitation in the *Epithalamion Thamesis* which was worked up into the eleventh canto of the fourth book. See Hughes, pp. 300–01.

regards bulk, to Virgil.[29] Though the *Ciris* as a whole is unattractive, Virgil does depict the anxious care of the old nurse with touches of homely pathos and dramatic truth of detail, and Spenser follows him with tender feeling.[30]

There remains the *Aeneid*. E. K., in pointing out that the new poet was following Virgil and others in beginning with pastoral, had established him as "the English Maro." The identification, accepted by admirers, was confirmed when, in the opening lines of *The Faerie Queene,* Spenser echoed the *Ille ego qui quondam gracili modulatus avena*—though it was the voice of Ariosto that promised to sing "of Knights and Ladies gentle deeds."

The chief Virgilian item in Spenser's first book is the Red Cross Knight's encounter with the bleeding tree, whose story of Duessa fails to warn the untried Christian soldier. While there are some Virgilian touches, the incident is closer to Ariosto's version than to the tale of Polydorus. It is, moreover, closer to Ariosto in spirit, for Ariosto, though enjoying the tale simply as another marvel, makes use of it in his most elaborate allegory, the series of episodes which show the temptations confronting the temperate man.[31]

In the second book Spenser's description of the dying Amavia is partly modeled on the suicide of Dido, but Amavia is not a grand heroine, she is an intemperate and fatal excess of "spirit"; her story may be based on Ariosto, though it is given a sterner meaning.[32] In the second canto of the same book Medina entertains Guyon—"the mean" has no heart to be captured by a guest!—and her desire to hear the story of his adventures corresponds to that of Dido. In the *Aeneid* of course we have the structural device of recapitulation that follows the plunge

[29] *F. Q.*, III. ii. The story of Britomart and Artegall of course owes much to Ariosto.
[30] Compare stanza 47 and *Ciris* (*P. Vergili Maronis Opera*, Teubner ed.), ll. 340 ff.:

> His ubi sollicitos animi relevaverat aestus
> vocibus et blanda pectus spe luserat aegrum,
> paulatim tremebunda genis obducere vestem
> virginis et placidam tenebris captare quietem
> inverso bibulum restinguens lumen olivo
> incipit ad crebrosque insani pectoris ictus
> ferre manum, adsiduis mulcens praecordia palmis.
> noctem illam sic maesta super morientis alumnae
> frigidulos cubito subnixa pependit ocellos.

See also ll. 250–51.
[31] *F. Q.*, I. ii. 30–32; *Aen.* iii. 27; *O. F.*, vi. 27; S. J. McMurphy, *Spenser's Use of Ariosto for Allegory*, pp. 24–25; Hughes, pp. 368–69; E. Greenlaw, *The Province of Literary History* (Baltimore, 1931), pp. 113–17. For Spenser's general relation to Ariosto, which lies outside our range, it is needless to cite Mr. Dodge's standard articles and Mr. Gilbert's supplement.
[32] *F. Q.*, II. i. 38–40; McMurphy, pp. 25–26.

in medias res; but Guyon has no epic narrative to recount, and Spenser seems merely to have taken over a bit of technique for which he has no real use.[33]

In the third canto Braggadocchio, who is compounded out of Ariosto's braggarts, and his man Trompart encounter the dazzling Belphoebe. The meeting recalls that of Aeneas, Achates, and Venus, and Trompart even echoes the words of Aeneas, but Spenser's scene is partly burlesque. Here as elsewhere Belphoebe has some kinship with the Virgilian Venus, but the description of her is based mainly on Ariosto's Alcina, with significant Platonic additions taken perhaps from the Clarice of Tasso's *Rinaldo*.[34] Venus does not praise the arduous life of seekers after honor; the theme was a poetic and especially a pastoral commonplace, and one very congenial to Spenser.[35]

Spenser's attitude toward the *Aeneid* is doubtfully illuminated by his summary in the ninth canto of the third book. Chaucer missed or avoided the epic story in order to make Dido a romantic and pathetic heroine; Spenser omits her entirely, unless she is comprehended in the phrase "fatall errour." One stanza takes Aeneas from Troy to Latium. The omission, as Mr. Hughes remarks, "may have been due to the allegorical interpretation of the *Aeneid* which represented Dido as a mere Circe, set to tempt Aeneas from his heaven-appointed way; but it was probably due to his desire to relate the legend of Rome's Trojan origin to the tradition that the Trojan Brutus established the British kingdom." [36] Such a patriotic motive was common enough, but Spenser's general lack of interest in the Trojan war is rather odd, since in his age it was the most popular of classic themes. At any rate in this summary we find him approaching Virgil in a manner more independent than sympathetic.

Finally we may notice the parallels between the underworld of Virgil's sixth book and Spenser's partial imitations, which are no less than three. The first passage is the description of "Plutoes house." [37] Spenser's

[33] Hughes, p. 331.

[34] H. H. Blanchard, "Imitations from Tasso in the 'Faerie Queene,' " *S. P.*, XXII (1925), 205–07.

[35] Greenlaw (*M. L. N.*, XLI, 325) traced Spenser's forty-first stanza to the *Works and Days*, i. 287 ff.; the parallel had been noticed by Charles A. Elton in his translation of Hesiod (2d ed., London, 1815, p. 37). Since Spenser was apparently acquainted with a Latin version of Hesiod (see above, p. 89, note 4), Hesiod may be the source. Mr. Blanchard had recorded parallels in Boiardo and Tasso (*P. M. L. A.*, XL, 832–34). Cf. Seneca, *Hipp.*, ll. 483 ff.; the first scene of Tasso's *Aminta;* and *Pastor Fido* (1590), iv. 6 (ed. Brognoligo, p. 147; trans. Fanshawe, ed. 1676, p. 135).

[36] Page 336.

[37] I. v. 32–35. The Virgilian lines quoted are *Aen.* vi. 306–07. See the remarks on Sackville, above, page 62.

shades may stir our hair (if we are of delicate sensibility), but not our
hearts:

> The trembling ghosts with sad amazed mood,
> Chattring their yron teeth, and staring wide
> With stonie eyes; and all the hellish brood
> Of feends infernall flockt on euery side . . .

These medieval specters are far from

> matres atque viri defunctaque corpora vita
> magnanimum heroum, pueri innuptaeque puellae.

Spenser's thirty-fifth stanza contains a list of mythological sinners:

> There was Ixion turned on a wheele,
>   For daring tempt the Queene of heauen to sin;
> And Sisyphus an huge round stone did reele
>   Against an hill, ne might from labour lin;
> There thirstie Tantalus hong by the chin;
>   And Tityus fed a vulture on his maw;
> Typhœus ioynts were stretched on a gin,
>   Theseus condemned to endlesse slouth by law,
> And fifty sisters water in leake vessels draw.

Virgil describes several of these victims, and the line about Theseus
points to him, but how soft and flat it is compared with the mingled
pathos and sternness of

> sedet aeternumque sedebit
> infelix Theseus.

The perfunctory catalogue as a whole is one of the elements in Spenser's
pagan hell which are fatal to any real emotion, and the clue appears to
be the fact that it is derived from either Ovid or Seneca.[38] One cannot
with impunity add patches from those authors to Virgil—at least the
mature Virgil, for Spenser's hell suggests not only Ovid and Seneca
but the *Culex,* in which hell is "a mere catalogue without visual imagination or geography . . . pure boyish pedantry." [39] It gives one pause when
a poet of Spenser's sensitive nature, who, one would say, must have felt
the quality of Virgil's most beautiful and moving book, can pass so
easily, unconscious of any jar, from the spirituality and humanity of
the Virgilian underworld to the mythological catalogues of Ovid and
Seneca. The mythological allusions in Virgil's picture of hell are not,

---

[38] *Metam.* iv. 457 ff. (and cf. *Metam.* x. 41 ff.; *Ibis,* ll. 173 ff.); Seneca, *Herc. Fur.,*
ll. 750 ff. (in the Elizabethan version, Tudor Translations, I, 33). Such lists, derived
ultimately from *Od.* xi. 576 ff., lost their human quality when they became mythological
trappings. Cf. Thomas Watson, Sonnet lxii. The list in Lucretius (iii. 978 ff.) is "moralized" with all its author's passionate sympathy for humanity.

[39] N. W. DeWitt, *Virgil's Biographia Litteraria* (Toronto and New York, 1923). p. 17.

to be sure, its most affecting parts, but they are carried along on the wave of emotion which Virgil raises and sustains. There is no such wave of human feeling to animate Spenser's lines.

Then there are Virgil's personified abstractions:

> vestibulum ante ipsum primis in faucibus Orci
> Luctus et ultrices posuere cubilia Curae;
> pallentesque habitant Morbi tristisque Senectus,
> et Metus et malesuada Fames ac turpis Egestas,
> terribiles visu formae, Letumque Labosque . . .[40]

In Spenser, in the dungeon of the House of Pride, the dwarf beholds the victims of "couetise," wrath, envy.[41] Such allusions to the deadly sins are quite consistent with Spenser's plan, since the structure of his first book resembles that of a morality play, but the Virgilian philosophy is rather less cramped and schematic. Virgil's pity is so profound that even his abstractions, which represent not man's sins but his wretched lot, give utterance, in Newman's words, as the voice of Nature herself, to that pain and weariness, yet hope of better things, which is the experience of her children in every time.

There is a more elaborate list of personifications in Spenser's second account of the underworld, which is occasioned by Guyon's experience in the cave of Mammon. Spenser's figures are mostly theatrical properties:

> By that wayes side, there sate infernall Payne,
> And fast beside him sat tumultuous Strife:
> The one in hand an yron whip did straine,
> The other brandished a bloudy knife,
> And both did gnash their teeth, and both did threaten life.

> On thother side in one consort there sate,
> Cruell Reuenge, and rancorous Despight,
> Disloyall Treason, and hart-burning Hate,
> But gnawing Gealousie out of their sight
> Sitting alone, his bitter lips did bight,
> And trembling Feare still to and fro did fly,
> And found no place, where safe he shroud him might,
> Lamenting Sorrow did in darknesse lye,
> And Shame his ugly face did hide from liuing eye.[42]

Again there are a few faint suggestions of Virgil, but the manner is post-classical and medieval. The whole passage, in tone and in details, reminds one of Theseus' account of the underworld in *Hercules Furens*. Spenser's personifications, in short, are cold and dead in comparison with Virgil's; the latter carry a weight of genuine feeling and suggestion, the

[40] *Aen.* vi. 273 ff.   [41] I. v. 46 ff.   [42] II. vii. 21-22.

former are mostly conventional tags that inspire no emotion in the borrower.[43]

We need not linger over the third picture of the underworld and its essential differences from Virgil's.[44] Spenser was undeniably attracted by Virgil's sixth book, but how unhappily he changed what he took over! "Every one of his imitations was inspired directly by the *Aeneid*, yet in every one he failed to understand Virgil's mood of reverent pity for the dead and of curious, speculative faith hardly distinguishable from doubt about the immortality of the soul. Spenser's first imitation of Virgil's hell, if the allegory be taken seriously, should be even more impressive than its original. In his two later imitations he dissolved Virgil's most moving elements into stark allegory." [45]

Even the barest summary of some main parallels between Virgil and Spenser shows that the borrower hardly ever approaches or perhaps quite understands the spirit of his original. There are certain large general resemblances; both poets embody their deepest thoughts about life in material based on a romantic body of legend, both use patriotic myth to glorify their country and the ruling house; and so on. But such things do not go very far, indeed they were constituent elements in the Renaissance conception of the heroic poem; Spenser's treatment of national history, moreover, is quite different from Virgil's. His debt to Virgil is, then, mainly external; he takes over incidents, details, phrases, and greatly alters them, in important matters seldom happily. The two poets differ in workmanship. With some reservations it may be said that while Virgil has the grandeur of generality Spenser is minute and circumstantial, and where Virgil is concentrated and suggestive Spenser is diffuse and transparent. As Dryden finely remarked, Virgil has the art of "expressing much in little, and often in silence"; Spenser, like most poets of his age, rarely leaves anything unsaid. Of course Spenser has his own peculiar virtues which are not in Virgil.

One important general question can be asked, though hardly answered. We cannot tell how much Spenser's high seriousness owes directly to Virgil. His survey of epic heroes in the letter to Ralegh is, however, enough to show his acceptance of the didactic and allegorical conception of the *Aeneid* which had flourished in the Middle Ages and was reinforced rather than weakened by Renaissance commentators.[46] This

---

[43] "Strife" comes perhaps from Chaucer's "Contek, with blody knyf and sharpe manace" (Knight's Tale, A 2003). "Payne" is akin to the *frendens Dolor* of Seneca; "Shame" also resembles Seneca's *Pudorque serus conscios vultus tegit* (*Herc. Fur.*, ll. 692–93). In the Elizabethan version this phrase is rendered "And shame to late doth hide his face that knowes what crimes it hath" (Tudor Translations, I, 31). "Fear," in this and a later passage (III. xii. 12), recalls the medievalized "Dread" of Sackville's *Induction*.

[44] *F. Q.*, IV. i. 20 ff. See Hughes, pp. 379–80.

[45] Hughes, p. 371.   [46] See Mr. Hughes' final chapter.

kind of seriousness was by no means wholly bad; without the moral
energy and high purpose of the medieval and Christian tradition
Renaissance classicism would have been far less fruitful than it was.
Yet it must be admitted that in his outlook upon life Virgil is more
maturely philosophic than Spenser, more modern in his sad uncertainties.
Spenser is assuredly sage and serious, and his idealism is always fresh
and attractive, but his moral earnestness is rather that of the confident
teacher than the questioner. He expounds, however sincerely, an official
morality which is not quite the universal humanity of the purest of
pagans. Virgil has a more truly religious and sympathetic imagination.
And Spenser is nearest to Virgil not when he is borrowing something,
but when, contemplating the ruthless course of time and change, he
feels the *lacrimae rerum* and utters the moving cry:

> When I bethinke me on that speech whyleare,
>   Of Mutability, and well it way:
>   Me seemes, that though she all unworthy were
>   Of the Heav'ns Rule; yet very sooth to say,
>   In all things else she beares the greatest sway.
>   Which makes me loath this state of life so tickle,
>   And loue of things so vaine to cast away;
>   Whose flowring pride, so fading and so fickle,
> Short Time shall soon cut down with his consuming sickle.
>
> Then gin I thinke on that which Nature sayd,
>   Of that same time when no more Change shall be,
>   But stedfast rest of all things firmely stayd
>   Upon the pillours of Eternity,
>   That is contrayr to Mutabilitie:
>   For, all that moueth, doth in Change delight:
>   But thence-forth all shall rest eternally
>   With Him that is the God of Sabbaoth hight:
> O that great Sabbaoth God, graunt me that Sabaoths sight.

Yet even this is not Virgilian, for Spenser has no language but a cry.
His mood touches that of disillusioned romantics who turn from life to
rest in the bosom of the church. When the world fails him Spenser yearns
to fall asleep, and then the care is over.

VII

Spenser would not be an Elizabethan if he had not felt the charm of
Ovid's sensuous grace and brightness, the stimulus of his inexhaustible
invention. He responded to the *Metamorphoses* in various ways.[47] He
adapted Ovidian matter for didactic purposes, as, for instance, when

---

[47] There are traces of Ovid's other works. Paridell's seduction of Hellenore seems to be
modeled partly on the seduction of Helen as described in the two epistles of the *Heroides;*
Spenser's choice of names may be taken as confirmation. See *F. Q.,* III. ix–x. For some items

he converts a forest in Ovid into a Wood of Error—and carries the not wholly instructive tree-list along with it.[48] There is perhaps no better proof of Spenser's liking for the *Metamorphoses* than his habit of introducing invented myths on the Ovidian pattern, and no better proof of his Elizabethan character than the fact that he often gives them an allegorical application.[49] Even Ovidian rhetoric left its mark in the "turn"—"Meat fit for such a monsters monsterous dyeat." [50]

For our purpose it will be enough to notice the pictorial quality of Spenser's Ovidian adaptations. Here are some lines from *Muiopotmos* that describe Europa:

> Arachne figur'd how Ioue did abuse
> Europa like a Bull, and on his backe
> Her through the sea did beare; so liuely seene,
> That it true Sea, and true Bull ye would weene.
>
> She seem'd still backe unto the land to looke,
> And her play-fellowes aide to call, and feare
> The dashing of the waues, that up she tooke
> Her daintie feete, and garments gathered neare:
> But (Lord) how she in euerie member shooke,
> When as the land she saw no more appeare,
> But a wilde wildernes of waters deepe:
> Then gan she greatly to lament and weepe.
>
> Before the Bull she pictur'd winged Loue,
> With his yong brother Sport, light fluttering
> Upon the waues, as each had been a Doue;
> The one his bowe and shafts, the other Spring
> A burning Teade about his head did moue,
> As in their Syres new loue both triumphing:
> And manie Nymphes about them flocking round,
> And manie Tritons, which their hornes did sound.

The first twelve lines are a paraphrase of two passages about Europa in Ovid:

> Maeonis elusam designat imagine tauri
> Europam: verum taurum, freta vera putares;

in the episode see Mr. Dodge's "Spenser's Imitations from Ariosto," *P.M.L.A.*, XII, 201–02; and Miss McMurphy, p. 33. Cf. also Hughes, *Virgil and Spenser*, pp. 333, 339.

[48] *F. Q.*, I. i. 7–9; *Metam.* x. 86 ff. See Skeat's notes on the *Parlement of Foules*, ll. 176–82; *Classical Weekly*, XXII (1928), 91–92, 166, 184; and Miss Winstanley's notes on the Spenserian lines. For the convention of the list of trees, see below, page 161.

[49] E.g., *F. Q.*, I. vii. 4; II. ii. 7.

[50] *F. Q.*, V. xii. 31. Some early readers thought Spenser's turns Virgilian (see the preface by "R. C." to Bosworth's *Arcadius and Sepha, Minor Caroline Poets*, II, 526, and below, page 194) but, as Mr. Hughes says, Spenser's plays on words are more Ovidian in character (*Virgil and Spenser*, pp. 382 ff.). The turn is not altogether suited to the smooth flow of the Spenserian stanza.

Ipsa videbatur terras spectare relictas
Et comites clamare suas tactumque vereri
Adsilientis aquae timidasque reducere plantas.[51]

pavet haec litusque ablata relictum
Respicit et dextra cornum tenet, altera dorso
Inposita est; tremulae sinuantur flamine vestes.[52]

For other items Spenser may have had in mind some tapestry or a description more detailed than Ovid's. The attendant Love might come from the elaborate painting of Europa in the opening pages of Achilles Tatius:

About the bull dolphins gambolled, Cupids sported: they actually seemed to move in the picture. Love himself led the bull — Love, in the guise of a tiny boy, his wings stretched out, wearing his quiver, his lighted torch in his hands: he was turning towards Zeus with a smile . . .[53]

If so, Spenser transfers the torch to Love's companion, whose presence may have been suggested by Horace's second ode:

Erycina ridens,
quam Iocus circum volat et Cupido.[54]

The nymphs and Tritons, and the wilderness of waters, are almost inevitable in such a picture; we have these items in Moschus' second idyll, on Europa. At any rate Spenser's own tapestry is more finely woven, more Alexandrian and more Italianate, than Ovid's.[55]

A less elaborate example of the process is in Spenser's treatment of the House of Sleep. Chaucer, following Ovid at a distance, is plain and "primitive":

Beste, ne man, ne nothing elles,
Save ther were a fewe welles
Came renning fro the cliffes adoun,
That made a deedly sleping soun . . .[56]

[51] *Metam.* vi. 103 ff.   [52] *Metam.* ii. 873–75.
[53] Trans. S. Gaselee (Loeb Classical Library), p. 9. For a long quotation from this passage, see page 127 below. And cf. Lucian, *Dialogues of the Sea-Gods*, xv (trans. Fowler, I, 105–06); *Aen.* v. 822–26.
[54] These lines, by the way, are quoted by both Comes and Cartari in their accounts of Venus.
[55] In *F. Q.*, III. xi. 30, the picture of Europa is for once slighter than that in Ovid:
Now like a Bull, Europa to withdraw:
Ah, how the fearefull Ladies tender hart
Did liuely seeme to tremble, when she saw
The huge seas under her t'obay her seruaunts law.
The idea of the last line is in Moschus, but Spenser gives it an Ovidian "turn."
[56] *Book of the Duchesse*, ll. 159 ff. Cf. *Hous of Fame*, i. 66–80. The Ovidian passage is *Metam.* xi. 600 ff. For traditional treatments of the theme see A. S. Cook, *M. L. N.*, V, 9 ff.

Between Chaucer and Spenser Poliziano and Ariosto—and such Ovidian "translators" as Anguillara—have handled the theme, and Spenser is neither plain nor primitive:

> And more, to lulle him in his slumber soft,
> A trickling streame from high rocke tumbling downe
> And euer-drizling raine upon the loft,
> Mixt with a murmuring winde, much like the sowne
> Of swarming Bees, did cast him in a swowne:
> No other noyse, nor peoples troublous cryes,
> As still are wont t'annoy the walled towne,
> Might there be heard: but carelesse Quiet lyes,
> Wrapt in eternall silence farre from enemyes.[57]

How much of Spenser's mythological painting was inspired by the recollection of actual tapestries or pictures we cannot say, but there is no doubt that his set descriptions are regularly executed in the spirit of the tapestry worker.[58] Reference has already been made to the pictures showing the power of Cupid which hang in the palace of the enchanter Busyrane. Spenser starts, like many other poets, from the list of Jove's amours given in Ovid, but he multiplies and greatly expands Ovid's brief allusions. For the stanza on Leda quoted above [59] Ovid supplies only this hint: *Fecit olorinis Ledam recubare sub alis.* Similarly Ovid has *Aureus ut Danaën . . . luserit,* while Spenser builds up a stanza. Spenser's picture-making is less heady and energetic, less economical, too, than Marlowe's in *Hero and Leander,* but in its softer way it is no less warmly voluptuous, and evidently done *con amore.* Only an Elizabethan could pass from the mood of Calvin to that of Giulio Romano.

Of course the formal description of a series of mural paintings or tapestries has a long literary tradition behind it, to which Ovid as usual contributed. The several examples in Chaucer are familiar, and there are innumerable others in medieval literature, especially court-of-love poems and romances.[60] The Italian poets of the Renaissance, in taking over the convention, gave it a new warmth and lusciousness.

Another example of Spenser's exuberant expansion is the pageant—how his spirits rise when he has a processional in hand!—in the second of the *Cantos of Mutability.* In Ovid Phaethon's arrival at the palace of the sun gives occasion for a brief but suggestive picture of the scene:

---

[57] *F. Q.,* I. i. 41. See Poliziano, *La Giostra,* ii. 22 ff. (the lines are translated in Cook); *Orlando Furioso,* xiv. 92 ff.; Anguillara, *Metamorfosi* (1575), p. 201ᵛ.
[58] F. Hard, "Spenser's 'Clothes of Arras and of Toure,'" *S. P.,* XXVII, 162 ff.
[59] Page 98. See *F. Q.,* III. xi. 32, and *Metam.* vi. 109.
[60] See Hard, p. 163, and E. B. Fowler, *Spenser and the Courts of Love* (Menasha, Wisconsin, 1921).

purpurea velatus veste sedebat
In solio Phoebus claris lucente smaragdis.
A dextra laevaque Dies et Mensis et Annus
Saeculaque et positae spatiis aequalibus Horae
Verque novum stabat cinctum florente corona,
Stabat nuda Aestas et spicea serta gerebat,
Stabat et Autumnus calcatis sordidus uvis
Et glacialis Hiems canos hirsuta capillos.[61]

Shakespeare adapts the last line in an Ovidian way:

And on old Hiems' thin and icy crown
An odorous chaplet of sweet summer buds . . .[62]

That is not Spenser's way. With this and a similar list from Ovid's fifteenth book in his mind he creates the sumptuous pageant of the seasons, months, and the rest; its purpose, one may or may not remember, is to prove that all things are subject to Mutability. But even numerous classical allusions do not make a classical atmosphere, and Ovid is left far behind.

And after her, came iolly Iune, arrayd
All in greene leaues, as he a Player were;
Yet in his time, he wrought as well as playd,
That by his plough-yrons mote right well appeare:
Upon a Crab he rode, that him did beare
With crooked crawling steps an uncouth pase,
And backward yode, as Bargemen wont to fare
Bending their force contrary to their face,
Like that ungracious crew which faines demurest grace.

Folk players, bargemen, puritans! "The symbolic figures of the months are, as Ruskin showed, the traditional figures illuminated in mediaeval Books of Hours, and the reader is reminded often, in such passages as the Masque of Cupid, not only of court masques which Spenser may have seen, but of the woodcuts of the *Hypnerotomachia Poliphili* and those in the old editions of Petrarch's *Trionfi.*"[63]

[61] *Metam.* ii. 23 ff. The other passage referred to just below is *Metam.* xv. 199 ff. There are also details from the *Fasti* (W. P. Cumming, *S. P.*, XXVIII, 249, note).
[62] *Midsummer Night's Dream*, II. i. 109–10. See Root, *Classical Mythology in Shakespeare*, p. 75.
[63] Renwick, *Spenser*, p. 119. See *Stones of Venice* (*Works*, ed. Cook and Wedderburn), II. vii. 52–53.
Anguillara, in his translation of the *Metamorphoses*, expands Ovid's description of the palace of the sun, giving a stanza to each of the seasons and more to Time.
For the resemblance between Spenser's descriptions and figures in pageants, see above, pp. 78 ff., and also H. R. Patch, "Notes on Spenser and Chaucer," *M. L. N.*, XXXIII (1918), 177; C. R. Baskervill, "Dramatic Aspects of Medieval Folk Festivals in England," *S. P.*, XVII, 19 ff.; R. Heffner, "Spenser's Allegory in Book I of the *Faerie Queene*," *S. P.*,

If we leave out of account the didactic intention which sometimes lies behind Spenser's use of both Ovid and Virgil, it is clear that in general Ovid undergoes less alteration than Virgil. He may be Italianized or medievalized, but he remains for the most part a recognizable Ovid. If it is less difficult to reach the level of Ovid than of Virgil, it is still easier to imitate Seneca. We have glanced already at some Senecan elements in Spenser, and the matter deserves a word more. Cerberus does not in himself invite prolonged contemplation, but he will serve to illustrate a feature of Spenserian technique. Virgil's picture of the beast in the *Culex* has some lurid concrete detail, and Spenser's translation heightens the effect. Since in *The Faerie Queene* he is, in his description of the underworld, more or less following the *Aeneid,* one might expect him to use Virgil's later account, which slights realistic physical horrors and relies mainly on suggestion.[64] Instead Spenser reverts to a multiplicity of horrid detail such as he had used in *Virgils Gnat.*[65] The method of the *Culex* is virtually the method of Seneca, and even Dante.[66] In a word, the more general and suggestive art of the mature Virgil is less attractive to Spenser than the post-classical and medieval accumulation of detail which achieves a coarser and more obviously striking effect. Most of Spenser's pictures owe their beauty to their wealth of detail; on the other hand we may have an unhappy excess. For good or ill Renaissance poets insisted on numbering the streaks of the tulip—and Seneca had done it at the top of his voice.[67]

Or, if there were room, one might quote Spenser's stanza on Tantalus for comparison with the accounts given by Homer and Seneca.[68] Homer feels the situation and his details deepen our impression of suffering,

XXVII (1930), 142 ff. Mr. Baskervill (page 39) quotes an account of a Shrovetide procession, from a Norwich record of 1443, which tells how one John Gladman rode as "King of Kristmesse in token that all merthe shuld end with ye twelve monthes of ye yer, afore hym eche moneth disgysed after ye seson yerof . . ."

[64] *Aen.* vi. 417 ff. Cf. *Culex,* ll. 220–22.

[65] *F. Q.,* I. v. 34. Ovid treats Cerberus briefly (*Metam.* iv. 450, vii. 413). See Hughes, p. 310.

[66] *Herc. Fur.,* ll. 782 ff. (Tudor Translations, I, 34); Dante, *Inferno,* vi. 13 ff.

[67] In the stanzas following Spenser relates the story of Hippolytus. Almost all of the facts seem to be drawn from Seneca's play. Miss Sawtelle (*The Sources of Spenser's Classical Mythology,* p. 66) mistakenly says there is nothing in Seneca about Theseus' gathering of his son's bones; see ll. 1247 ff. Seneca's text mentions only one monster, but the argument to the Elizabethan translation speaks of "certaine great Sea-monsters, or Whirlepooles" (Tudor Translations, I, 136). Further, the argument states that "shee turned hir former love into extreame hatred"; cf. Spenser (I. v. 37): "Her loue she turnd to hate." Spenser's diction seems occasionally to echo that of the translation, though it may be only coincidence. Seneca makes Hippolytus a hunter, but Spenser presents him as an Adonis or Narcissus. While Spenser is fond enough of violent grief, his Theseus is content with long speeches; Spenser's Theseus, more Senecan than Seneca, tears his hair and tongue.

[68] *F. Q.,* II. vii. 58; *Od.* xi. 582; *Thyestes,* ll. 152 ff., and *Herc. Fur.,* ll. 752 ff.

of the life and beauty of earth from which a human being is cut off. Seneca has read of the story in a book and duly places the item in his mythological museum. Instead of the Homeric sympathy, color, poetry, Spenser's antithetical lines have an unbeautiful and matter-of-fact opaqueness, a series of details which are more flat and arid than poetic and suggestive. It may be said that it is not fair to stress his accounts of a pagan hell, but they bulk rather large in his classical borrowings, and represent his own choice.

VIII

The most pervasive unclassical strain in Spenser's mythology is due to the character of the texture into which it is woven. Even if mythological tales and allusions were themselves treated with the limited measure of classical simplicity that appears in Ovid, they would take color from the romantic fabric of the whole poem. However important the classical sources, *The Faerie Queene* owes most of its material and more than a little of its narrative technique to medieval romance, and of course to Ariosto's version of romance as well. Throughout the poem there is the shifting panorama of gallant knights and lovely ladies, of magicians and monsters, of green forests and strange castles. Looking in that enchanted world for classical stories told with classical restraint, we can only, though with different feelings, echo Harvey's donnish complaint, "Hobgoblin runne away with the Garland from Apollo."

We cannot follow the moving row of magic shadow-shapes that come and go, but one large element in Spenser's romanticism may be emphasized, that is, the Celtic. For him the boundaries between the world of classic myth and the Celtic otherworld dissolve, and *The Faerie Queene* is the most notable example in our literature of the blending of the two mythologies. Spenser's pre-eminence over his contemporaries in this respect, however, is one of degree, not of kind, for the Elizabethans regularly mixed Celtic and classic lore. Philomela, says Ovid, was more beautiful than *naidas et dryadas,* and Golding renders "fairies." [69] Nashe as a matter of course links the sprites of English folklore with the woodland divinities of "idolatrous former daies and the fantasticall world of Greece." [70] Reginald Scot catalogues all kinds of "bugs" ranging from centaurs to Tom Thumb, and quotes a decree of a General Council about women who profess to "ride abroad with Diana, the goddess of

---

[69] *Metam.* vi. 452–53; Golding, ed. Rouse, p. 130, l. 579. In translating the *Culex* Spenser gives "many Fairies" for *naidum coetu.* See M. W. Latham, *The Elizabethan Fairies* (Columbia University Press, 1930).

[70] *Works,* ed. McKerrow, I, 347.

the Pagans, or else with Herodias."[71] But it is needless to mention examples when a single familiar one reveals the coalescence of two worlds —the significant name of the fairy queen who fell in love with that typical Athenian, Bully Bottom. As we have been reminded before, the mixture itself was a native tradition.

Naturally, then, in *The Faerie Queene* we constantly find Celtic motives woven into the narrative texture and into the allegory. Sometimes they proclaim their origin, sometimes they have become almost unrecognizable through combination with other material; yet always they contribute their unique quality of strangeness added to beauty. Spenser's second book draws more from the classics than any other, and expounds the classical virtue of temperance in terms of the classical divisions of the soul, but even here the three chief adventures involve Celtic motives. The wanton Phaedria is a lady of the lake, and not merely an adaptation of Tasso's Armida (who belongs anyhow to the same romantic sisterhood). The *Odyssey* is romantic enough, but it is not such a repository of wonders, such an *omnium gatherum*, as Spenser's twelfth canto. Here we have matter from modern books of travel, from Celtic *imrama*, from Mandeville and possibly Lucian's *True History*; we have Ovidian and Homeric myths and an apparent recollection of Christ calming the waters; strange beasts from Gesner and from Plutarch the hoggish Grill (to whose stubborn individuality the irrational part of one's soul accords a degree of admiration); the guide Reason from Ariosto, music and enticing damsels from Tasso; and the framework of the latter part of the book is apparently based on an allegorical episode in Trissino's epic, *L'Italia Liberata dai Gotti*.[72]

Finally, we may take Greenlaw's summary of the folklore involved in Guyon's trials in the cave of Mammon:

The old man who guards a fairy hill is a stock character; sometimes he is a *leprechaun*, who guards a treasure that he tries to hide when he is caught by a mortal; sometimes he is a fairy king. Again, the idea that to touch any object in the Underworld will necessitate remaining in the power of the fairy owner

---

[71] *The Discovery of Witchcraft* (London, 1665), bk. vii, c. 15, p. 85; bk. iii, c. 16, p. 36. (On Herodias, cf. Chambers, *The Mediaeval Stage*, I, 109). In the *Discourse concerning Devils* (i. 19, p. 17) Scot expatiates on the text that "the gods of the Gentiles are Devils."
[72] For Trissino, see C. W. Lemmi, *P. Q.*, VII, 220 ff. In another article (*P. Q.*, VIII, 270 ff.) Mr. Lemmi argues plausibly for the influence of Natalis Comes' interpretation of Circe. At any rate, as he points out (following Warton and others—see Greenlaw, *S. P.*, XX, 236), Spenser's Genius (*F. Q.*, II. xii. 47–49) was derived from Comes (iv. 3). Cf. E. C. Knowlton, "The Genii of Spenser," *S. P.*, XXV (1928), 439 ff.
For some of the other items mentioned, see Lois Whitney, "Spenser's Use of the Literature of Travel in the *Faerie Queene*," *M. P.*, XIX (1921), 143 ff.; E. Greenlaw, "Spenser's Fairy Mythology," *S. P.*, XV, 113; S. J. McMurphy, *Spenser's Use of Ariosto*, p. 28; Ariosto, *O. F.*, x. 43 ff.

is not only a part of the Proserpina myth, but of Celtic folk tradition generally. The very nature of Guyon's temptation: the offer of riches, love, fame, is in the story of Murrough. Guyon's sight of souls suffering the tortures of hell, which seems to owe something to Dante, is analogous to the legends about magic islands converted into places of eternal punishment. But the most significant detail is that of the apples. Since Warton's time the relation between Spenser's account of the Garden of Proserpina and Claudian's *De Raptu Proserpinae* has been recognized. In this we have the famous golden bough. But while Warton sees in the silver stool "a new circumstance of temptation," he does not explain it. In Celtic tradition resting beneath an apple tree subjected one to danger from fays. Lancelot, for example, is sleeping under an apple tree when he is seized by fays and carried into captivity. Ogier comes to an orchard, eats an apple, and is soon in the power of Morgain. Avalon is "apple land." [73]

Spenser's Celtic lore may not have embraced all these items but he must have known some. Such mixtures of Celtic and classical stories, with allegorical meanings implicit in the tales or added to them, can hardly remain strictly classical.

IX

In the "Gardens of Adonis," and on a larger scale in the *Cantos of Mutability,* Spenser employs classic myth in a way that is more symbolic than allegorical, though it springs from the allegorical or "parabolic" habit of mind. The earlier passage, the sixth canto of the third book, begins with the miraculous conception of Belphoebe and Amoret. Then we have Venus searching for Cupid, a theme that Renaissance poets loved to play with.[74] Venus encounters Diana, who, as we have already observed, is in that extreme dishabille so common among Spenserian ladies. During the hunt for Cupid the two infants, Belphoebe and Amoret, are found, and one is taken by each goddess, to be reared according to their respective standards.

Then comes the "scientific" part of the canto, the description of the Gardens of Adonis where Venus dwells. "A thousand thousand naked babes" are in this garden; some are clothed in flesh and sent to live in the world; after a time they return to be "planted" in the garden, and, in forgetfulness of their mortal life, they grow again during "some thousand yeares." These souls grow in the same way as animals and plants, under

[73] *S. P.,* XV, 111. The stanzas describing the Garden of Proserpina are quoted on pages 96–97 above.
[74] Spenser's handling of the theme again illustrates his taste. He had probably read Moschus at some time (see E. K.'s gloss on *March*), but he follows rather the embroidering of Moschus in the prologue of Tasso's *Aminta* (J. D. Bruce, *M. L. N.,* XXVII, 183–85). For imitations of the idyll of Moschus in ancient and modern poetry see James Hutton, *American Journal of Philology,* XLIX (1928), 105–36, and J. G. Fucilla, *ibid.,* L (1929), 190–93, and *Classical Philology,* XXVI (1931), 135–52.

the care of nature and the porter, "Old Genius." In the wide womb of
the world there lies

> An huge eternall Chaos, which supplyes
> The substances of natures fruitfull progenyes.

> All things from thence doe their first being fetch,
> And borrow matter, whereof they are made,
> Which when as forme and feature it does ketch,
> Becomes a bodie, and doth then inuade
> The state of life, out of the griesly shade.
> That substance is eterne, and bideth so,
> Ne when the life decayes, and forme does fade,
> Doth it consume, and into nothing go,
> But chaunged is, and often altred to and fro.

> The substance is not chaunged, nor altered,
> But th' only forme and outward fashion . . .

Even here Spenser has Ovid in mind, though it is Ovid versifying
Platonic ideas.[75]

Of this continual renewing of life the great enemy is Time, who mows
down "the flowring herbes and goodly things"; but for Time the garden
would be a cloudless paradise. Yet even Time cannot destroy a covert
on a hill where Venus lives eternally with Adonis,

> for he may not
> For euer die, and euer buried bee
> In balefull night, where all things are forgot;
> All be he subiect to mortalitie,
> Yet is eterne in mutabilitie,
> And by succession made perpetuall,
> Transformed oft, and chaunged diuerslie:
> For him the Father of all formes they call;
> Therefore needs mote he liue, that liuing giues to all.

> There now he liueth in eternall blis,
> Ioying his goddesse, and of her enioyd:
> Ne feareth he henceforth that foe of his,
> Which with his cruell tuske him deadly cloyd:
> For that wilde Bore, the which him once annoyd,
> She firmely hath emprisoned for ay,
> That her sweet loue his malice mote auoyd . . .

[75] *Metam.* xv. 252–60. See J. W. Bennett, "Spenser's Garden of Adonis," *P. M. L. A.*,
XLVII, 66–67. The canto is a repository of such a complex mass of traditional ideas
concerning otherworld paradises, chaos, creation, mutability, etc., that a glance at Mrs.
Bennett's learned discussion will explain why my few paragraphs can merely indicate
the general nature of Spenser's mythological-metaphysical symbolism. Greenlaw's argument
for strong Lucretian influence has been pretty well discredited, by Mrs. Bennett and others.
Since Du Bartas was a favorite of Spenser's, we might notice a passage in Sylvester

Thus Spenser bodies forth the idea of permanence underlying the eternal flux, and he does it through myth. In the first canto of the third book he had told the pictured story of Venus and Adonis in the best Italianate fashion, though with an eye to the state of morals in the Castle Joyous; here, however, the myth becomes a vehicle for a philosophic treatment, largely Neo-Platonic, of the problem of mutability, of the relation between form and matter. One may be left in some doubt concerning the precise nature of the mythological symbols.[76] In fact Spenser, who was not really a philosophic poet, though he felt the attraction of philosophic ideas, was in this canto allowing his imagination and fancy to play with mingled lightness and seriousness over the theme of mutability. It is an excellent specimen of his luxuriant mixture of diverse elements.

For a more elaborate and serious answer to the question of change and permanence we must turn to the *Cantos of Mutability,* which were first published in 1609, and were evidently among Spenser's last compositions,

which illustrates the prevalence of some ideas regarding form and matter (ed. Grosart, I, 28, ll. 164 ff.):

> Yet think not that this Too-too-Much remises
> Ought into nought: it but the Form disguises
> In hundred fashions, and the Substances
> Inly, or outly, neither win nor leese.

Cf., *ibid.,* ll. 219 ff.:

> Here's nothing constant: nothing still doth stay;
> For, Birth and Death have still successive sway.
> Here one thing springs not till another die:
> Onely the Matter lives immortally . . .
> Change-lesse in Essence; changeable in face . . .

I might add an irrelevant and rash query, whether Spenser's much-discussed Aetion might not be Sylvester? Drayton and Shakespeare seem to be the favored candidates, but the case for Shakespeare at least is very weak (Chambers, *William Shakespeare,* II, 187). Sylvester inserts in his text various eulogies of his patrons of Lambourne, under whose roof he worked at his translation (I, 43, ll. 380 ff.). At least twice he speaks of the eaglets on the Essex coat of arms, and says "For th' Eyrie's sake that ownes my Muse and me" (I, 69, l. 969), and "Let me deserve of my deer Eagle-Brood" (I, 50, l. 1162). There are two difficulties, the uncertain dates of Sylvester's sojourn with his patrons, and the uncertain dates of his writing and publication (see below, page 158, note 7). At any rate Spenser's allusion fits Sylvester (whose first name sounds heroical enough), and accords with Spenser's direct and reported praise of Du Bartas (*Ruines of Rome; Gabriel Harvey's Marginalia,* ed. G. C. M. Smith, p. 161).

[76] Following Upton, Greenlaw said that "the complete statement of the law is the symbol of Adonis as the personification of matter, mortal yet immortal, loved by the goddess of form, triumphant so long as the boar, symbol of the forces that would bring destruction, is held in check by law"; see *S. P.,* XVII (1920), 454. Spenser himself is less explicit. According to Mrs. Bennett (page 72) Adonis "represents the dynamic character of form, as Venus represents the preservative, or ruling character." Pico, by the way, says: "Venus is said to be born of the Sea; Matter the Inform Nature, whereof every Creature is compounded, is represented by Water, continually flowing, easily receptible of any form" (*A Platonick Discourse upon Love,* trans. T. Stanley, ed. E. G. Gardner, Boston, 1914, bk. ii, sec. xiii). Cf. Leo Hebraeus, *Dialoghi d'Amore,* ed. Caramella, pp. 131–32.

perhaps the very last.[77] A writer in the Elizabethan age had more than ordinary reason for being drawn to such a theme. During the century religion and politics had frequently changed their complexion over night, with a loss of benefices and heads. The block on Tower Hill was the very altar of Mutability. And if mutability in life and fortune was at once theatrical and commonplace—the Elizabethans never wearied of moralizing on both aspects—the inner life also, for thoughtful men, was becoming less stable and secure. From wicked Italy a dozen varieties of skepticism or atheism had been spreading over Europe. The reading of Lucretius, Cicero, Lucian, helped to revive and fortify medieval heresies. For the dominant philosophy of the Middle Ages God's world had been intelligible; the later sixteenth century was beginning to see the outlines of a problem which, in the seventeenth, was to be crystallized by the new science, namely, the problem of knowledge. While mathematical concepts of the universe lay beyond Spenser's horizon, it was plain to him and others of his time that orthodoxy in religion and ethics was being challenged, not by isolated rebels, but by strong groups of Renaissance thinkers, with compromising support from Renaissance pagans. The current of atheism—a rather crude and compendious term —was more or less subterranean in England, but its presence may be inferred from the frequent denunciations of it, and from the feeling aroused against such scapegoats as Marlowe and Ralegh.

One treatment of atheism and its usual companion, naturalistic ethics, is of special interest in relation to *Mutability*. Sidney's revised *Arcadia* was, like *The Faerie Queene,* by Elizabethan standards a "heroic poem," and into it the ideal knight, courtier, poet, statesman, Christian, put his most serious thoughts on such subjects as government, ethics, and religion. Thus the wicked queen Cecropia urges the maiden Pamela to enjoy the flower of her youth, since youth is made for love. When Pamela cites the injunctions of religion, Cecropia replies that religious restraints are foolish bogies in a world governed by chance. Pamela, whose motives are more exalted than those of her namesake, is stirred to a passionate affirmation of belief in the divine ordering of the world, and a passionate denial of the doctrine of chance.[78]

Spenser's *Mutability* is concerned with the divine government of the world, and one might predict that, nourished in the same tradition as

---

[77] For references to the numerous recent discussions see Mrs. Bennett's article cited above.

[78] *Arcadia*, ed. A. Feuillerat (1912), pp. 402–10; E. Greenlaw, "Sidney's *Arcadia* as an Example of Elizabethan Allegory," *Kittredge Anniversary Papers*, 1913; "The Captivity Episode in Sidney's *Arcadia*," *Manly Anniversary Studies*, 1923; L. Whitney, "Concerning Nature in *The Countesse of Pembrokes Arcadia*," *S. P.*, XXIV, 207 ff.; R. B. Levinson, "The 'Godlesse Minde' in Sidney's *Arcadia*," *M. P.*, XXIX (1931), 21–26.

Sidney, Spenser would make substantially the same reply. That his answer lacks the ringing clarity of Pamela-Sidney's is partly owing to the fact that the cantos are a fragment; and a mythological vehicle naturally does not keep to the highroad like Sidney's more direct discussion. Is it not also likely that Spenser, with his large responsiveness to all the currents of Renaissance thought and feeling, was less fully conscious than Sidney, with his decisive and militant Protestantism, of the irreconcilable conflict involved? But we had better look at the poem.

Spenser's presentation of the idea of eternal flux seems to be based mainly on the fifteenth book of the *Metamorphoses*.[79] His fable, a largely original offshoot of the story of war between gods and Titans, apparently combines suggestions from Ovid and Natalis Comes.[80] We are told that the Titaness Mutability, having brought all earth under her sway, conceives the ambition to rule heaven as well. She mounts up to the circle of the moon, and her attempt to thrust Cynthia from her throne leads to Jove's calling a celestial council. While the gods confer Mutability appears among them and challenges Jove's right to rule. She appeals to Nature, and Jove reluctantly grants that the case shall be heard before Nature, on the top of Arlo hill.

Now, with an apology for abating the sternness of his style, Spenser digresses in order to weave myth about the names of Arlo hill and "my old father Mole." Since we have not taken time to consider Spenser's original myths—apart from *Mutability* itself—we may notice this one. In old times in Ireland Cynthia and her nymphs used to delight in Arlo and its streams, where they bathed. The rustic god Faunus, desiring to "see her naked mongst her Nymphes," persuaded one of the nymphs, Molanna, to enable him to gratify his wish, and promised in return that he would make Molanna beloved of Fanchin. Faunus gazes to his satisfaction,

> But breaking forth in laughter, loud profest
> His foolish thought.

The goddess and her attendants find him, and, dressing him in a deerskin, pursue him with their hounds. Molanna they stone, but, through Faunus' aid, her stream is united with that of Fanchin. Diana "thence-forth abandond her delicious brooke." The story of course starts from the myth of Actaeon, to which Spenser alludes, and at the end recalls the union of Alpheus and Arethusa; it reminds one also in part of Marlowe's episode of Mercury and the country maid. Spenser's invented or adapted

---

[79] W. P. Cumming, *S. P.*, XXVIII, 241 ff.

[80] See A. E. Sawtelle, under "Titan"; Cumming, pp. 243–44; Comes, ii. 1, vi. 20 (ed. 1616, pp. 38, 53, 341).

myths usually have an allegorical purpose, but it is hard to find one here, and the tone of the digression is certainly out of key with the prevailing seriousness of *Mutability*. But Spenser's code of poetic decorum, though strict, is not ours, and such apparent incongruities are everywhere in *The Faerie Queene;* witness the difference between the search of Venus for Cupid and the account of creation and destructive Time in the "Gardens of Adonis."

Returning to his "greater Muse" in the seventh canto, Spenser tells of the assembly at Arlo hill; the setting is in the tradition of the medieval courts of love. Mutability pleads that all things are under her control. Vegetation flourishes and dies. Men slay animals, and themselves experience change in age and fortune and mind. The elements are perpetually changing. Then the Titaness calls forth as witnesses the seasons, months, and the rest of the figures which make up one of Spenser's finest pageants.[81] When these have gone by the plaintiff urges that all are subject to her, and that Time preys upon all. Jove replies that he controls Time. Mutability declares that the gods—Cynthia, who is a byword for changeableness, Mercury, Jove himself—are subject to change and motion. Nature, after reflection, gives her verdict:

> I well consider all that ye haue sayd,
>   And find that all things stedfastnes doe hate
>   And changed be: yet being rightly wayd
>   They are not changed from their first estate;
>   But by their change their being doe dilate:
>   And turning to themselues at length againe,
>   Doe worke their owne perfection so by fate:
>   Then ouer them Change doth not rule and raigne;
> But they raigne ouer change, and doe their states maintaine.
>
> Cease therefore daughter further to aspire,
>   And thee content thus to be rul'd by me:
>   For thy decay thou seekst by thy desire;
>   But time shall come that all shall changed bee,
>   And from thenceforth, none no more change shall see.
>   So was the Titaness put downe and whist,
>   And Ioue confirm'd in his imperiall see.
>   Then was that whole assembly quite dismist,
> And Natur's selfe did vanish, whither no man wist.

For his answer to the question of the one and the many, the question whether unity lies behind the eternal flux, Spenser, in the true vein of Renaissance reconcilers, seeks a compromise. That compromise is half "scientific," half Christian. All things work out the law of their being,

---

[81] See page 111 above.

not in the naturalistic sense, but under divine control; but there will come the eternal stability when all shall be changed for the last time. Yet the solution, however conventional, does not seem to have been wholly satisfying to Spenser. After Nature's reply come the two stanzas that were quoted above;[82] they are the voice of an infant crying in the night. Keats, writing in an era of Revolutionary optimism, made the defeat of the Titans by the gods a symbol of progress, but in the late sixteenth century the theory of progress was just coming to birth. From a world of medieval fixities Spenser contemplates the spectacle of endless change, and his answer comes more from his heart than his head. He was facing the Renaissance version of the doctrine that Whirl is king, and our own answers do not allow us to be patronizing.

It would be hard to find anywhere in *The Faerie Queene* two cantos that give stronger testimony of mature powers, or afford in such small compass a wider display of Spenser's particular gifts. Few readers are likely to dissent from Courthope's judgment, that *Mutability* is "both in conception and execution, the most sublime part" of the poem. It is to be sure the Elizabethan, not the Miltonic sublime; one does not expect from Spenser and his fellows a completely ordered and sustained nobility. When sources range from Ovid to Alanus de Insulis, and moods from the celestial to the earthy, when the poet pauses in his search for unity to paint gorgeous pictures of diversity, the total impression may well be somewhat clouded.

We can, perhaps, understand *Mutability* better if we glance at the *Four Hymns*. In the first two hymns Spenser, following Castiglione especially, had climbed through three or four of the orthodox six stages in the Platonic ascent, beginning with the love excited by a beautiful face and form.[83] Although the Renaissance religion of beauty achieved its culmination in mystical union with the divine essence, most adherents lingered on the lower rungs of the Platonic ladder, satisfying their sense of poetry with mystical rhapsodies and their other senses with mundane mistresses. Scholars disagree whether Spenser's two later hymns are a continuation or a repudiation of the earlier ones. It is a question if Spenser himself quite realized what he was doing; he was not really a mystic, though, like most poets of his time, he could deal in mystical language. At any rate we should be a little surprised if we met in Bembo's discourse

---

[82] Page 107. In connection with Spenser's reference to the changelessness of eternity one might quote the noble lines in Milton's *Ad Patrem* (30–31):

> Nos etiam, patrium tunc cum repetemus Olympum,
> Aeternaeque morae stabunt immobilis aevi . . .

[83] See R. W. Lee, *P. Q.*, VII, 65 ff.

what we have in Spenser, an account of the scheme of redemption made possible by the death of Christ, even though Bembo speaks of the sacrifice of our souls. Bembo's mystical experience can and does begin with the sensuous love of woman; Spenser's, in the later hymns, could not, for he is moving on a different plane.[84] In the earlier hymns he had been satisfied with the religion of beauty, so far as he outlined it, but now he is more definitely Christian. So too in the eighth canto of the second book of *The Faerie Queene*, there is a point beyond which the moral reason cannot go, and Guyon is saved, when the palmer is helpless, by Arthur, the grace of God.[85] And in *Mutability*, as we have seen, the philosophic assertion of permanence behind the flux is not enough for a poet who is Christian and medieval. He turns from such cold consolation to the refuge of faith.

It is at such moments, surely, that Spenser's inmost self is stirred, however richly he absorbed and re-expressed the worldliness of medieval romance and Renaissance culture. The mood may be more intelligible if we remember Chaucer's recoil not merely from the passions he had so subtly delineated in *Troilus*, but from all earthly love; if we remember his appeal to "yonge fresshe folkes" to turn their eyes to heaven alone. Or there is Sidney's "Leave me, O love which reachest but to dust . . ." It does not mean that Chaucer and Sidney and Spenser can permanently renounce the joys of earth, can deny for good the rights of half their nature, but that, in a moment of intense revulsion and spiritual insight, all things seem dross except God. Such moments, of course, are rare. The very names of Chaucer and Spenser suggest delight in all that the world can give. But we are in no doubt concerning the solid core in Chaucer. The contradictions in Spenser compel one to fasten upon him that definition of God which attracted Sir Thomas Browne, the circle whose center is everywhere and whose circumference nowhere. Only in a Renaissance poet, and only in Spenser among all English poets, could we have a poem about the government of the universe, based on a classic myth of gods and Titans, in the setting of a medieval court of love, including the mishaps of a mythological Peeping Tom, and ending with a heartfelt prayer to "that great Sabbaoth God."

One can hardly summarize a chapter which is itself a summary, and

[84] The view that Spenser's four hymns constitute a logical Neo-Platonic sequence has been reaffirmed by Mrs. Bennett, who gives special attention to Pico and Benivieni (*S. P.*, XXVIII, 1931, pp. 18 ff.). Mrs. Bennett's plea for continuity is opposed by Mr. Padelford, *S. P.*, XXIX (1932), 207 ff.

[85] See F. M. Padelford, *S. P.*, XVIII (1921), 342. This interpretation seems to be confirmed by the first eight stanzas of the canto, which describe a guardian angel (who, by the way, is said to resemble Cupid).

the attempt will not be made. Of Spenser's general cultural debt to the classics it is really impossible to say much, for such things do not always yield the "evidence" beloved of scholars. At the same time it is clear that a study of classical influences much fuller than this sketch includes would not make a rounded and just estimate of Spenser and his place in poetry. Spenser without the classics would be different, but his main outlines would be little changed; Spenser without medieval and modern literature would be inconceivable. To borrow a paragraph from Courthope:

Spenser's genius is inspired almost exclusively by the Middle Ages. The chivalrous matter of his poems is mediæval: so is his allegorical spirit: so is his quasi-archaic diction. Enthusiastic admirer of the classics as he is, all that he really draws from them is a frequent allusion to the tales of Greek mythology, and a certain concinnity in the metrical combination of words and phrases, which he imitates from the style of the Latin poets. The structure of his composition is in every sense of the word "romantic." [86]

There are very few passages in Spenser's work of which one can say, "Here he is writing like a classical ancient." Classical influence on him is much more indirect than direct. In the main it reaches him as already transmogrified, romanticized, by medieval, Italian, and French writers. Such classical "impurity" is of course the note of his age.

Spenser's treatment of myth, then, is largely colored by the medievalism apparent in his fable, in his narrative and descriptive technique, in his own thought and feeling, and by the theory and practice of continental literature of the sixteenth century. Myths are retold with Italian sensuousness, and allegorized with medieval seriousness. Spenser's romantic-didactic conception of poetry led him, as it led others, to borrow material from some ancients, to alter its form and spirit for his own purposes. "He shows no suspicion of Malherbe's rule, that if you borrow from the classics you must adhere rigidly to the traditional story or characteristics; that a dead mythology admits of no development; that to add new stories or new features only emphasizes the decorative, fantastic character of your material." [87] Nor did his borrowings from the classics teach him, any more than they taught most of his fellows, the lessons of form, selection, precision, restraint. It is needless to add that if he had learned those lessons he could not have written *The Faerie Queene.*

[86] *History of English Poetry*, III, 134. The romantic quality of Spenser has been admirably treated in an essay by Mr. E. E. Stoll in his *Poets and Playwrights* (1930). For a brief but suggestive note on medievalism in Spenser's treatment of myth, see Mr. Osgood's *Boccaccio on Poetry*, p. xxxix.

[87] H. J. C. Grierson, *The Background of English Literature* (London, 1925), p. 17. See Ferdinand Brunot, *La doctrine de Malherbe* (Paris, 1891), pp. 168–70.

CHAPTER SIX

MARLOWE : *HERO AND LEANDER*

ALL the best qualities of the Italianate Ovidian tradition are embodied, and transcended, in *Hero and Leander*. It is equally true that the poem exhibits in high relief all the vices of the tradition. Yet it remains for us the most beautiful short narrative poem of its age, and for Marlowe's contemporaries and followers the causes of our partial dissatisfaction did not exist. It was immensely admired before and after its formal publication, and was enthusiastically quoted and plagiarized for two generations.[1] In the heyday of the mythological poem men recognized that Marlowe had done superbly what many were trying to do, and that by imitating him—whose faults were more easily matched than his virtues—they might excel themselves.

Hero and Leander was entered in 1593, but apparently not published until 1598. The date of composition is not absolutely certain. It has been generally assumed that the poem was Marlowe's last work, and that its completion was prevented by his sudden death. Blount's dedication seems to say as much, but inferences from that strange document are doubtful.[2] While recent research has complicated problems to such a degree that even guesses are hazardous, the notion of a date earlier than 1593 does not seem untenable.[3] Marlowe's treatments of classical matter, the *Ovid, Dido* (most of it, at any rate), the lost version of Colluthus ascribed to him, are assigned to his bookish days at Cambridge (not wholly bookish, as we know now), or a shortly subsequent period.[4] Might not his enthusiasm for Musaeus belong to the same time?

[1] Allusions of the period 1593–98 are mentioned below. Later allusions which occur in the material treated in this book are listed in the index. See Tucker Brooke, "The Reputation of Christopher Marlowe," *Transactions of the Connecticut Academy of Arts and Sciences*, XXV (1922), 347–408; my note on the influence of *Hero and Leander*, M.L.N., XLII, 211; and the notes in Mr. L. C. Martin's valuable edition of Marlowe's poems (1931). Mr. Martin's edition became available just before this volume went to press, but it has not seemed necessary to make any alterations in this chapter.

[2] See Boas, *Marlowe and His Circle* (1929), pp. 130–32.

[3] See L. Chabalier, *Héro et Léandre* (1911). Mr. Martin (pp. 3–4) states the problem without attempting to decide; decision is of course impossible.

[4] In his edition of Marlowe (1910) Mr. Brooke regarded the *Lucan* as an early effort, but in his recent edition of *Dido* (page 51) he links it and *Hero and Leander* as productions of the poet's last months. His reasons, as he kindly informed me, are, in brief, the apparent maturity of style and the fact that the *Lucan*, a fragment also, was entered in September, 1593, along with *Hero and Leander*.

Internal evidence is conflicting and dubious. Parts of the poem show Marlowe's mastery of image and phrase at their impetuous best; other parts show an indifference to form and a fondness for puerile conceits which, in any age but the Elizabethan, would suggest the yeasty and uncontrolled imagination of youth. The translation of Ovid's *Amores*, which has its warm and felicitous lines, is accepted as an early work, yet its erotic tone is reflected in *Hero and Leander*, even to the extent of numerous verbal correspondences. On the other hand Marlowe has a way of echoing himself.[5]

Moreover, a classical poem was, and continued to be, an early rather than a late episode in an Elizabethan dramatic career. And, in comparison with Marlowe's best plays, *Hero and Leander*, for all its wealth of sensuous beauty, is spiritually poor, "a pretty piece of paganism," if the rather priggish phrase be allowed. Could it be the last and crowning work of a man who had entered into the agonized soul of Faustus? It is almost as if Shakespeare, after writing *King Lear*, had turned to *Venus and Adonis*—however inferior that poem is to Marlowe's. Yet literary history does record such disconcerting things, and in the Elizabethan age glorification of the senses was no mere phase of adolescence. Again, *Hero and Leander* seems a kind of inevitable fragment. If Marlowe had written it before 1593 it might well have remained incomplete, for we can hardly imagine how it could have been finished. What we have is no prelude to catastrophe, Hero and Leander are not star-crossed lovers; the poem in its total effect is an unclouded celebration of youthful passion and fullness of physical life. These various facts and speculations prove nothing one way or the other, but in the absence of positive testimony it seems possible to query the traditional date.

The numerous allusions to the poem, or imitations of it, between 1593 and 1598 show the influence it exerted even while circulating in manuscript; no allusion earlier than 1593 has been found.[6] We must assume that Shakespeare had early knowledge of it, since both *Venus and Adonis* (1593) and *The Rape of Lucrece* (1594) contain many obvious parallels. Traces of the poem appeared in Drayton's *Peirs Gaveston* (1593) and *Heroical Epistles* (1597), while his *Endimion and Phœbe* (1595) revealed its large debt in both style and details. In his

[5] For instance, Mr. Brooke remarks of *Dido* that parallels "are found most copiously in *Tamburlaine* and the translation of Ovid's Elegies, but some of the most striking link this play with such late works as *Edward II* and *Hero and Leander*" (*Dido*, p. 117).

[6] A microscope reveals a few slight resemblances in phrasing between the poem and Daniel's *Complaint of Rosamond* (1592), but they may be quite accidental. Anyhow such things would prove nothing as to priority.

Cephalus and Procris and *Narcissus* (1595)[7] Thomas Edwards not only made a direct acknowledgment to Marlowe but borrowed from his poem in dozens of passages. Dunstan Gale's *Pyramus and Thisbe*, the dedication of which is dated 1596, imitated Marlowe's description of Hero.[8] "About 1596 Richard Carew in a letter on the 'Excellencie of the English tongue' linked Shakespeare's poem [*Venus and Adonis*] with Marlowe's 'fragment,' and credited them jointly with the literary merit of Catullus." [9] The fifty-fourth sonnet of Bartholomew Griffin's *Fidessa* (1596) has two clear references.[10] Thus the fragment was uncommonly well known among the literary before it was published.

Marlowe chose a theme that had long been popular. Musaeus enjoyed a special fame among writers of the sixteenth century because he was regarded as the earliest of Greek poets, a contemporary of Orpheus. In addition to the immediate appeal of a tragic story of romantic love, the somewhat unclassical quality of the Greek poem commended itself to Renaissance taste. There were many modern versions of Musaeus, ranging from translation to free redaction, such as those of Bernardo Tasso, Baldi, Marot, Boscán. A multitude of readers knew the story through the letters in the *Heroides*. In England there were countless allusions to the tale, but no English translation of Musaeus except one that Abraham Fleming said he had published.[11] In 1592 Abraham Fraunce remarked that "Leander and Heroes loue is in euery mans mouth," and proceeded to draw, as Fulgentius had done a thousand years before, the allegorical lesson that the extinguishing of Hero's torch means the decay of lust, and "Leander tossed with the colde storme of old age, is at last drowned." [12] This is not quite Marlowe's reading of the tale.

A few parallels that have been observed between Marlowe and Tasso, Marot, and Boscán, are weak and negligible. He depended mainly of course upon Musaeus (probably in a Greek-Latin edition), but the original contains about three hundred and forty lines, the English fragment over eight hundred. Marlowe omits a number of things, such

[7] Entered on October 22, 1593 (*Stat. Reg.*, ed. Arber, II, 639). Edwards is noticed in the Appendix, under 1595.

[8] See the Appendix, under 1596.

[9] Lee, *Life of Shakespeare* (New York, 1929) p. 142, note.

[10] Lee, *Elizabethan Sonnets*, II, 292. In addition to the above items, Nashe's *Jack Wilton* (1594) possibly borrowed the description of Hero's extraordinary buskins: see *H. and L.*, i. 31 ff.; *Works of Nashe*, ed. McKerrow, II, 283–84. (Cf. Sidney's *Arcadia*, ed. Feuillerat, 1912, p. 92; Browne, *Brit. Past.*, Bk. ii, Song 3, ll. 504 ff.; Drayton's *Minor Poems*, ed. C. Brett, p. 175, ll. 249 ff.) See the "stolne remnants" from Marlowe in Matthew's poem in *Every Man in his Humour* (Herford and Simpson, *Ben Jonson*, III, 249, 365).

[11] See the Appendix, under 1577.

[12] *Third part of the Countesse of Pembrokes Ivychurch*, p. 46. Fraunce, by the way, quotes from Boscán's version.

as the business of the torch, and adds a great many—the long descriptions of Hero, Leander, the temple; the episode of Mercury, the country maid, and Cupid; the first meeting of the lovers in the tower; the account of Leander's behavior in Abydos, and his swim. Everything drawn from Musaeus is much expanded, especially the enamorment and the ensuing dialogue, and the union of the lovers.

When one turns from Musaeus to Marlowe one is conscious of a not always agreeable sophistication of the story. A main reason, Ovidian influence, will be noticed later. A possible minor one might be found in the half-prurient tone that characterizes Greek romances and a good many Renaissance pastorals. Leander's ignorance of the rites of love reminds one of the idyllic innocence of Daphnis.[13] Some lines in the description of Leander's swim might have been inspired by Greek romances, such as that of Achilles Tatius, but perhaps there is no need of going so far afield for an element in Greek civilization which the Italian Renaissance had made its own. The general influence of these romances upon the sensuous and pictorial elements in Renaissance literature has already been observed, and their pictures of physical and artistic beauty sometimes suggest Marlowe's opulent brush.[14]

Much that is remote in spirit from Musaeus may be traced to the *Amores* of Ovid, which Marlowe had translated without any loss of warmth. In addition to the development of Ovidian suggestions,

[13] *Daphnis and Chloe* was translated by Angel Day in 1587, from the French of Amyot. See the reprint by Joseph Jacobs (London, 1890), pp. 33–34, 135. Day, however, following Amyot's example, omits the somewhat protracted business of Daphnis' erotic curiosity.

[14] A couple of specimens may be quoted:

"Hir lockes dispersed on hir shoulders, in colour like the burnisht yellow of the finest gold, made hir to appeare as one of the nymphs, whom Iupiter erst fauored, or Apollo with ardent flames whilom eagerly pursued." *Daphnis and Chloe,* p. 20.

"The virgin sitting upon his back, not after the maner of horsmen, but both her legs being fitly laid downe on his right side, with her left hand held his horne . . . her breast to her privy parts was attired with a vaile of lawne, the rest of her body was covered with a purple mantle, all the other parts were to be seene, save there where her garments covered . . . her tender brests seemed to swel, throgh the midle of which went down a faire narrow way most pleasant & delightfull to the beholders: with one hand did she holde his horne, with the other his taile, but yet so that the attire of her head covered with a scarf cast over her shoulders, was held on fast against the force of the wind, which did so beat on her bosom, that every where it seemed to swell. She thus sitting on the bull, was caried like a shippe, her scarfe serving in stead of a sayle. Round about the bull Dolphins floted about, and sported at their loves in such sort, as that you would thinke, you saw their verie motions drawne." Achilles Tatius, *Clitophon and Leucippe,* trans. William Burton, 1597, ed. S. Gaselee and H. F. B. Brett-Smith (Blackwell, Oxford, 1923), p. 3; and see page xxx.

There is no need of recording here a number of miscellaneous details that Marlowe might have borrowed from various sources. (See Mr. Martin's notes and my note in *P. M. L. A.,* XLIV, 760 ff.) For Hero's second reception of Leander (ii. 235 ff.) one need not seek models—Ovid and Marlowe's imagination were enough—but, if only as a confirmation of the feminine psychology, one might refer to the story of Jupiter and Danae in Caxton's *Recuyell* (ed. Sommer, I, 129). Cf. Harington's *Orlando Furioso,* first published in 1591 (ed. 1607, p. 238, st. 58–59).

something over two dozen lines are more or less made up of verbal reminiscences.[15] Most of these are found in the speeches of Leander; others, drawn from Ovid's most candid accounts of amorous afternoons, contribute to the final picture of Hero "all naked to his sight displayd." There is no need of emphasizing the Ovidian character of Leander's wooing and its fruition, and the Greek maiden of Musaeus does not emerge unsullied from association with Corinna. Further, in contrast with Marlowe's detailed story of two meetings and a delayed climax, Musaeus has a reticent account of one. Taking the physical ardors and satisfaction for granted, the Greek poet, with the tragic issue in mind, concentrates on the pathos of a furtive union that lacks the wedding rites hallowed by tradition. His lovers are so truly in love that there is simple acceptance on both sides, yet their helplessness and their approaching fate are suggested by the darkness of the lonely tower, the absence of processional torches and nuptial hymns. Though Marlowe's treatment of young love rises above the level of a casual encounter with Corinna, it would seem, as I have said, to leave small room for tragic consequences.

The episode of Mercury and the country maid is quite Ovidian in spirit, recalling as it does the many tales of amorous gods. In the Ovidian tradition too, though with the added glow of Renaissance painting, are the abundant mythological decorations. While Musaeus has only one epithet for the temple, Marlowe lets himself go in this purple patch:

> So faire a church as this, had Venus none,
> The wals were of discoloured Iasper stone,
> Wherein was Proteus carued, and o'rehead,
> A liuelie vine of greene sea agget spread;
> Where by one hand, light headed Bacchus hoong,
> And with the other, wine from grapes out wroong.
> Of Christall shining faire the pauement was,
> The towne of Sestos cal'd it Venus glasse.
> There might you see the gods in sundrie shapes,
> Committing headdie ryots, incest, rapes:
> For know, that underneath this radiant floure
> Was Danaes statue in a brazen tower,
> Ioue slylie stealing from his sisters bed,
> To dallie with Idalian Ganimed,
> And for his loue Europa bellowing loud,
> And tumbling with the Rainbow in a cloud:
> Blood-quaffing Mars heauing the yron net,
> Which limping Vulcan and his Cyclops set:

[15] The passages are quoted in *P. M. L. A.*. XLIV, 760 ff.

Loue kindling fire, to burne such townes as Troy,
Syluanus weeping for the louely boy
That now is turn'd into a Cypres tree,
Under whose shade the Wood-gods loue to bee.

Such set pieces of mythological painting are conventional, as we have
seen, in medieval pictures of temples and courts of love, but Marlowe's
treatment is not Chaucer's. He is making use of at least two passages in
the *Metamorphoses* that Spenser also adapted—the pictures of Jove's
amours woven into Arachne's web, and the description of the palace of
the sun [16]—although these are only a starting point. Marlowe's vivid
glow and energy outdo Ovid.[17]

Although we cannot survey the classical matter in Marlowe's plays,
the foregoing sketch of Ovidian elements in *Hero and Leander* may
permit a glance at the great speech of Faustus uttered when he has one
bare hour to live. "He prays that this final hour may be but

A year, a month, a week, a natural day,
That Faustus may repent, and save his soul.
O lente, lente currite noctis equi.

Here too his mind goes back to the past; he is quoting Ovid, the prayer
of a lover in his mistress's arms that the horses of the chariot of the night
may move slowly across the sky. There is a grim irony in the application
of it here; it is the agonized cry of the sensualist who had claimed Helen
for his paramour." [18] But time will not stand still. There comes the
overwhelming vision of Christ's blood streaming in the firmament, and
as his fear and torment increase Faustus calls upon mountains and hills
to fall upon him and hide him from the heavy wrath of God. He is
quoting again, not Ovid this time, but the Bible. While one cannot
properly compare works of different scope and intention, yet there is a
scale of values, and those who entertain Swinburnian sentiments toward
Hero and Leander might, after reading *Doctor Faustus*, recognize the
gulf between major and minor poetry.

The Greek poem, as Symonds said, unites classic form with the warm
autumnal tint of decadence.[19] It is a miniature epic, admirably propor-

---

[16] *Metam.* vi. 103 ff., ii. 1 ff.

[17] The Leander-Hero epistles in the *Heroides* also afforded some hints, such as the
rather absurd allusion to an interchange of letters, and certain details for the long and
florid account of Leander's swim. From the same source evidently comes Hero's nurse, who
is barely mentioned in Musaeus (*Her.* xix. 25, 45). For other similarities in detail, cf.
Marlowe, ii. 150 ff., and *Her.* xviii. 47–48, 53; Marlowe, ii. 205, and *Her.* xviii. 49;
Marlowe, ii. 206, and *Her.* xviii. 84.

[18] Percy Simpson, "Marlowe's *Tragical History of Doctor Faustus," Essays and Studies
by Members of the English Association,* XIV (1929), 26.

[19] *Studies of the Greek Poets* (ed. 1893), II, 346–47.

tioned, without superfluous details. There is scarcely a jarring note; characters, setting, motives, are in harmony. The story is not told with classic bareness of style, yet, compared with Marlowe's version, it seems almost Sophoclean, and its relative simplicity and naturalness are its strength. It is highly pictorial, but the pictures have the plastic clarity of figures on a Grecian urn, figures of young lovers remembered from an antique world, at once sculptural and timeless, human and of yesterday. What one feels is the beauty and pathos of the story as a story.

Among the virtues of Renaissance writing form is not generally reckoned, and the formless unrestraint of Marlowe's poem one might think obvious if so much critical opinion had not spoken otherwise. Swinburne set the fashion, in his eulogy of a work that "stands out alone amid all the wide and wild poetic wealth of its teeming and turbulent age, as might a small shrine of Parian sculpture amid the rank splendour of a tropic jungle." [20] Mr. Elton, comparing the fragment with Drayton's *Endimion and Phœbe,* praises "the lucid glow, as of a burning alabaster lamp of Greek design, that fills *Hero and Leander;* there alone was the secret of satisfying form, pure amid its richness." [21] More recently Miss Ellis-Fermor, in her sympathetic and sensitive study of Marlowe, writes of "added gravity of form," of "Hellenic security and repose in the mood," and again of "Hellenic repose, security, and formal excellence." Miss Ellis-Fermor also remarks that "heavy ornament and rich irrelevant imagery conceal for a while the slenderness and the ephemeral quality of the emotions." [22] How heavy ornament and rich irrelevant imagery contribute to Hellenic formal excellence does not appear. If Musaeus reminds one of a Grecian urn, not a little of Marlowe is suggestive of Cellini's saltcellars, and to speak of form is to speak of what is not. Ovid was a brilliant maker of pictures, as Marlowe and his fellows well knew; it was not always remembered that he was in the main a swift and straightforward story-teller. *Hero and Leander,* it might be said, is like *The Eve of St. Agnes,* narrative poetry of a kind that makes its own laws, but Marlowe lacks Keats's sustained perfection of detail, his perfect harmony of tone. He does surprise by a fine excess, yet he was an Elizabethan, and his excess is frequently cloying.

Marlowe seems resolved to gather up all the pictorial conventions that tradition supplied and excel all predecessors in the luxuriant handling of them. When he describes Hero's dress, including the singing buskins, he forgets that he is writing about a young woman, he is showing what rich effects an unrestrained pen can create. Musaeus, as we observed,

---

[20] Introduction to Chapman's *Poems and Minor Translations* (1875), p. lix.
[21] *Michael Drayton* (1905), p. 63.   [22] *Christopher Marlowe* (1927), pp. 124–139.

bestows one adjective upon the temple; Marlowe gives an exuberant series of mythological pictures. A hundred lines are occupied with a somewhat incoherent tale of Mercury, Cupid, and the Destinies; it is quite irrelevant, but furnishes occasion for more sensuousness.

In general Marlowe's crowding images are drawn from art and fancy rather than nature. The fact itself is not damaging, the meretricious character of many images is. We do not like the incessant conceits; Cupid turns Hero's tears into pearls and winds them on his arm, Neptune's mace returns to strike the hand that threw it. One exceptional and vivid little scene from nature is this:

> Far from the towne (where all is whist and still,
> Saue that the sea playing on yellow sand,
> Sends foorth a ratling murmure to the land . . .

But such lines provoke the question why, in the long account of Leander's swim, there is such a lack of feeling for the sea. Though the passage has its beautiful bits, the general impression is of Leander gliding over waves of mythological tapestry. The human values of the story suffer from the cumulative effect of artifice in description and narrative. They suffer also from the excess of rhetorical speech-making. Leander's plea is so long and subtle that one forgets, because Marlowe himself does, that he is a flesh-and-blood lover; he becomes the mouthpiece for the *suasoria* of a naturalistic philosopher of love. Thus for all the picture-making we seldom really see the lovers—indeed, despite the prevailing sensuousness we are not sure that they have bodies and faces—and for all the expression of feeling we seldom really feel with them. We have to turn to Musaeus for the dignity, humanity, and pathos of the story.

Anachronisms never troubled an Elizabethan poet, and, in plays of vivid characterization, they do not trouble us. But when, along with slight and shadowy characters, we have sixteenth-century dress and manners introduced into a Greek story, the total effect is discordant. Marlowe's Greek maiden does not need to wear gloves, for neither sun nor wind would injure her hands. Her admirers, finding their love scorned, write sharp satires. She faints, and, revived by a kiss, "away she trips." Leaving the temple, she drops "her painted fanne of curled plumes," [23] "thinking to traine Leander therewithall."

[23] Cf. Peele, *Arraignment of Paris* (Bullen, I, 12):

> Fair Venus of sweet violets in blue,
> With other flowers infixed for change of hue;
> Her plumes, her pendants, bracelets, and her rings,
> Her dainty fan, and twenty other things,
> Her lusty mantle waving in the wind,
> And every part in colour and in kind.

> He being a nouice, knew not what she meant,
> But stayd, and after her a letter sent,
> Which ioyfull Hero answerd in such sort,
> As he had hope to scale the beauteous fort,
> Wherein the liberall graces lock'd their wealth . . .

As M. Chabalier says, it is obvious that Marlowe, writing in the spirit of his time, gives to the idyll of Hero and Leander the character of an affair of gallantry between a gentleman and lady of the court.

This external impression of artifice and unreality is heightened by the inconsistent behavior of the hero and heroine. In the lines just quoted Leander, for all his amatory lore, shows himself a novice.[24] Though a master of Ovid's *Amores* and a learned enemy of virginity, the young man, at the first meeting in the tower,

> Long dallying with Hero, nothing saw
> That might delight him more, yet he suspected
> Some amorous rites or other were neglected.

He is supposedly a strong and bold swimmer, but many of the descriptive lines have a taint of effeminacy. Hero's diverse qualities are likewise hard to reconcile. The Hero of Musaeus is really virginal, and she is overcome by nature rather than persuasion. Marlowe's Hero is at times an artless virgin, at times—as we have seen in the business of fainting and dropping a fan—a sophisticated coquette. The first enamorment (lines 158–98) is admirably simple and direct in feeling; then Leander's casuistry begins and feeling is obscured. Between passages which show Hero's newborn love, in spite of religious and maidenly scruples, achieving an innocent avowal, come these lines of hers:

> A dwarfish beldame beares me companie,
> That hops about the chamber where I lie,
> And spends the night (that might be better spent)
> In vaine discourse, and apish merriment.

The parenthetical phrase belongs to Mrs. Pinchwife rather than Hero; Marlowe has forgotten his character and cannot resist inserting a sentiment of his own. The addition of Ovidian wine to the crystal water of Musaeus is not altogether fortunate. Hero and Leander are different persons at different times, because the author wishes to run the whole gamut of erotic emotions, from reverent adoration to voluptuous abandonment—somewhat as Beaumont and Fletcher disregard consistency

---

[24] The mingled boldness and shyness of the Leander of Musaeus is natural, not exaggerated.

of character in order to extract the maximum of theatrical effect from every situation.

Hero and Leander is often linked with *Romeo and Juliet* as a story of pure and ardent love finding a pure and ardent consummation.[25] But there are essential differences in conception and treatment. Shakespeare's lovers, like those in the Greek poem, are consistent, natural, healthy. Their love, not of course because it enjoys benefit of clergy, is deep, intense, complete. The love Marlowe represents is satisfying on its own level, but it does not go beyond a rapturous exaltation of the senses, the kind of experience from which the mature Donne turned away. Marlowe's preoccupation with the primary phases of love makes the emotional world of his poem infinitely smaller and poorer than that of Shakespeare's play. Nor is he conscious of any lack; there is no striving for the

> One thought, one grace, one woonder at the least,
> Which into words no vertue can digest.

In Musaeus and in *Romeo and Juliet,* moreover, the theme is treated with complete sincerity and pity, and the reader's emotions are simple, direct, homogeneous. Marlowe has no such emotional integrity. Preserving at times the sincerity and pity which the subject demands, he brings into the poem almost mocking comments. He can write thus:

> And like a planet, moouing seuerall waies,
> At one selfe instant, she poore soule assaies,
> Louing, not to loue at all, and euerie part
> Stroue to resist the motions of her hart.
> And hands so pure, so innocent, nay such,
> As might haue made heauen stoope to haue a touch,
> Did she uphold to Venus . . .

And then he can laugh at Hero's confusion and perplexity, and her latest actions, inspired by mingled eagerness and fear, are treated with half-cynical acknowledgment of the power and cruelty of Cupid:

[25] The veteran disintegrator, Mr. J. M. Robertson, has even argued that *Hero and Leander* "bears marks of being partly developed from poetic matter in *Romeo and Juliet* which there is reason to regard as of Marlowe's own drafting. On that view, Marlowe in his poem has made effective use of ideas that had served him in drama" (*Problems of the Shakespeare Sonnets,* 1926, p. 128). Mr. Robertson's case is presented in his *Shakespeare Canon,* Part III (London, 1925), pp. 165 ff. The case consists of parallels which are either Elizabethan commonplaces or applicable to any love story, as I showed in a note in *P. Q.,* IX, 396 ff. The degree of the critic's haste can be measured from the fact that he finds a recollection of the play in

> Where both deliberat, the loue is slight,
> Who euer lov'd, that lov'd not at first sight?

And yet Mr. Robertson has read *As You Like It.* He reaffirms these views in his *Marlowe* (London, 1931), pp. 134 ff.

> Loue is not ful of pittie (as men say)
> But deaffe and cruell, where he meanes to pray.[26]

The account of Leander's inexperience is partly sensuous, partly ironical. There is mirth of a sort in the tale of Mercury. Such touches of irony or bitterness are doubtless not too serious, as Miss Ellis-Fermor says, but they are there, and their slight yet recognizably acidulous taste does act as "a cooling card."

If passion is for the most part inadequately represented it is nevertheless intended to be consuming; the outer world of order and convention fades away, for each lover is the other's world. The powers Marlowe recognizes are beauty and love. In being beautiful and in loving Hero and Leander fulfill the law of their nature, the one law that is supreme. They themselves are not responsible.

> It lies not in our power to loue, or hate,
> For will in us is ouer-rul'd by fate.

But though fate is thus invoked as the cause of love, the conception of fate as foredooming lovers, which is so essential to the story, Marlowe scarcely does more than play with. There are slight hints in the first sestiad (which we forget in the intoxication of the second), but in general, instead of the ever present consciousness of tragic destiny that Shakespeare gives us, or Chaucer in *Troilus,* we have the mingled conceits and satire of the tale of Cupid, and briefer but not less trivial allusions to the part played by the gods.

Although the poem celebrates the union of two inexperienced lovers the philosophy of love, expressed and implied, is in accord with the doctrines of Renaissance naturalism. Leander pleads for chaste love, not the plurality of loves of many fellow rebels, but he uses the stock arguments in attacking conventional notions of virtue, honor, virginity, as sterile and negative:

> This idoll which you terme *Virginitie,*
> Is neither essence subiect to the eie,
> No, nor to any one exterior sence,
> Nor hath it any place of residence,
> Nor is't of earth or mold celestiall,
> Or capable of any forme at all.
> Of that which hath no being doe not boast,
> Things that are not at all are neuer lost.
> Men foolishly doe call it vertuous,

---

[26] Cf. *Pastor Fido,* iii. 6, ed. Brognoligo, p. 106. The lines are thus rendered by Fanshawe (ed. 1676, p. 99):

> [Love] . . . is at first
> Weak and raw, but when 'tis nurst,
> Fierce and cruel.

What vertue is it that is borne with us?
Much lesse can honour bee ascrib'd thereto,
Honour is purchac'd by the deedes wee do.
Beleeue me Hero, honour is not wone,
Untill some honourable deed be done.

The positive, realistic spirit of the Renaissance, which in politics is called Machiavellian, becomes in the sphere of sexual morality an antipathy to traditional restraints, to anything that curbs the impulses of nature. Many Elizabethan writers give expression to it, but usually in order to add triumphant counter-arguments.[27] It crackles, along with other ingredients, in the pregnant pot of Donne, who, like Jean de Meung and many successors, celebrated the Arcadian license of the golden age when no one suffered from Christian monogamy and monotony.

Who e'r rigg'd faire ship to lie in harbors,
And not to seeke new lands, or not to deale withall?
Or built faire houses, set trees, and arbors,
Only to lock up, or else to let them fall?
Good is not good, unlesse
A thousand it possesse,
But doth wast with greedinesse.

The youthful Donne's seriousness is mingled with wit. Not so Leander's, which echoes Ovid, but adds a note of high romantic eloquence:

A stately builded ship, wel rig'd and tall,
The Ocean maketh more maiesticall:
Why vowest thou then to liue in Sestos here,

[27] In Daniel's *Complaint of Rosamond* (1592) "a seeming Matrone, yet a sinfull monster" uses the customary arguments to work upon the heroine (*Poems*, etc., ed. A. C. Sprague, p. 47, ll. 267 ff.):

Pleasure is felt, opinion but conceau'd,
Honor, a thing without us, not our owne . . .

The debate is a common theme in pastorals. See the opening pages of Tasso's *Aminta*, or these passages from Guarini's *Pastor Fido* (ed. Brognoligo, pp. 19, 31; trans. Fanshawe, pp. 13, 26):

For as the Iron, of it self too rough,
And of a harsh unmalleable stuff,
Softned with fire, and gentler metal, strength
From weakness gathers, and becomes at length
Fit for the noblest use: so hearts untam'd,
(Which their own stifness often breaks) enflam'd
With generous Love, and with his sweets allay'd,
Are clearer, apter for great Actions made . . .
What's beauty (tell me) if not view'd? or view'd,
If not pursu'd? or if pursu'd, pursu'd
By one alone? Where Lovers frequent are,
It is a sign the party lov'd is rare,
Glorious and bright.

Some other examples of naturalistic arguments more or less akin to Leander's are: Seneca, *Hippolytus*, ll. 435 ff.; Pettie's *Petite Pallace*, "Germanicus and Agrippina"; Sidney's *Arcadia*, ed. Feuillerat (1912), pp. 402-10; Gabriel Harvey, *Letter-Book*, ed.

Who on Loues seas more glorious wouldst appeare?
Like untun'd golden strings all women are,
Which long time lie untoucht, will harshly iarre.

This, and much more, is not the speech of a simple Greek youth to a
simple maiden, but the rhetoric of an emancipated young poet of the
Italian Renaissance who tramples underfoot the puritan, bourgeois
standards professed by his countrymen. And the Elizabethan *enfant
terrible* did not live down his *Poems and Ballads* in the elderly and
suburban decorum of Putney. *Hero and Leander* is, in Swinburnian
phrase, a love song of earth. The poet who dramatized his thirst for
knowledge and power had also before him the vision of Helen,[28] and in
Hero and Leander he showed the same egoism, on a smaller stage,
seeking and enjoying possession of beautiful bodies and beautiful things.

With intoxicating rhythms and pictures in one's ear and eye one
cannot draw up a profit-and-loss account of virtues and defects. The
latter have been given rather disproportionate space partly because they
are ignored or minimized in the conventional eulogies, partly because
Hero and Leander, the best Elizabethan poem of its kind, shows so
clearly the fundamental weaknesses of the whole genre. But the faults
are mainly those of the age, the beauties are Marlowe's own, and they
are obvious to anyone whose senses are not dead. Marlowe's energy
divine makes the poem read as if it had been written at a breath.
Thronging images are poured out with the prodigality that marks a
master who has no need to husband a slender stock. Everything in the
poem, good or bad, is tinglingly alive.

But far aboue the loueliest Hero shin'd,
And stole away th' inchaunted gazers mind,
For like Sea-nimphs inueigling harmony,
So was her beautie to the standers by.
Nor that night-wandring pale and watrie starre

Scott, pp. 86–87; Warner, *Albion's England,* bk. v, c. 24 (1589), Chalmers, IV, 565
(quoted in *P. M. L. A.,* XLIV, 762); *The Faerie Queene,* II. vi. 15, and elsewhere; Drayton,
Heroical Epistles (see below, page 164); S. Brandon, *The Virtuous Octavia,* 1598, Malone
Society Reprints, ll. 891 ff. (Brandon seems to have some echoes of Sidney); Heywood,
Troia Britanica (1609), canto 2, st. 53–54 (see below, page 189). Of course the theme is
often touched by the sonneteers.
   [28] The vision remains no less dazzling though a source has been suggested, Lucian's
Dialogues of the Dead, xviii (trans. Fowler, I, 137):
   Hermes. This skull is Helen.
   Menippus. And for this a thousand ships carried warriors from every part of Greece . . .
The parallel was pointed out by Mr. F. Tupper, *M. L. N.,* XXI, 76; and Mr. E. H. W.
Meyerstein, *T. L. S.,* March 22, 1928, p. 221.
   I might add the quite irrelevant query whether the famous "pampered jades of Asia"
might have been sired by Golding's "pampred Jades of Thrace" (ed. Rouse, p. 186, l. 238).

(When yawning dragons draw her thirling carre
From Latmus mount up to the glomie skie,
Where crown'd with blazing light and maiestie,
She proudly sits) more ouer-rules the flood,
Than she the hearts of those that neere her stood.

But quotation can only suggest a quality which pervades and vivifies the whole.

Marlowe's unique magic is best appreciated if one thinks of the mythological poems which had been written during the preceding generation. Mythological allusion, moreover, had been used copiously but seldom with distinction. Marlowe, to a degree which perhaps no poet except Keats has excelled, made classical myths his own. Shelley could live in a myth, but his mythological beings were all air or water, his Pan was not rude and shaggy. Marlowe really sees Diana in the sky, and under the sea sweet singing mermaids sporting with their loves, and on the earth goat-footed satyrs and up-starting fauns. Such things are not merely bookish allusions taken out of Ovid. Further, Marlowe, like Spenser, invents myths of his own. Too often they are bad conceits, but sometimes they are not:

Hero the faire,
Whom young Apollo courted for her haire,
And offred as a dower his burning throne,
Where she should sit for men to gaze upon.

The tasteless conceits in fact are inseparable from Marlowe's peculiar gifts. His imagination inhabits a brave new world, in which it is bliss to be alive, and to be young is very heaven; his vision is not merely fresh but extravagant. He must sing of the body electric with an untamed splendor of the senses and of language. When he pillages Ovid to describe the beauty of his lovers he combines literary sophistication with a kind of primitive spontaneity.[29]

If the indescribable beauty of bodies and things compels the use of mythological parallels, for indescribable emotions Marlowe resorts, a few times, to the very opposite kind of figure, the scientific and "meta-

[29] To mention a detail of mythology, the drowning of Narcissus (i. 74) is unclassical, but the tradition goes back to the Middle Ages (*Histoire littéraire de la France*, XXIX, 499). Some random references are these: Villon, *Ballade contre les mesdisans de la France;* Lydgate, *Reson and Sensuallyte* (E. E. T. S., ll. 3850, 4258); *Handful of Pleasant Delights,* ed. Rollins, pp. 29 ff.; John Clapham's Latin *Narcissus* (1591); *Albion's England,* bk. ix, c. 46 (Chalmers, IV, 609); Lodge, *Phillis* (1593), Sonnet xxxiv; *Phœnix Nest,* ed. Rollins, pp. 81, 91. Lodge and one of the *Phœnix Nest* authors were translating Ronsard (Marty-Laveaux, I, 12); see Rollins, p. 181. Shakespeare's allusions to Narcissus' drowning (*V. and A.,* l. 161; *Luc.,* l. 265) might have been suggested by Marlowe or the general un-Ovidian tradition.

physical." [30] One such image has been quoted already—Hero, with conflicting emotions in her soul, is "like a planet, moouing seuerall waies" —and it is one of the most memorable parts of the poem. However vivid the mythological pictures, they seem merely pictures when set beside a couple of lines in which, for a moment, a metaphysical image gives an intensity and depth of emotion that is nowhere else approached:

> She trembling stroue, this strife of hers (like that
> Which made the world) another world begat
> Of unknowne ioy.

The last hundred lines of the poem certainly carry sensuous rapture above the fleshlincss of the *Amores,* yet, as one comes on the words quoted, in the midst of a tissue of Ovidian motives and sensations, one wonders what miracle Marlowe might have achieved if he had been able to approach Musaeus directly, to create and sustain the note of simple and genuine passion. But when one thinks of what even Elizabethan poetry would be without *Hero and Leander,* perhaps the fragment is miracle enough as it is.

[30] Miss Elizabeth Holmes has called attention to the presence of metaphysical imagery in *Hero and Leander* as well as in Elizabethan drama (*Aspects of Elizabethan Imagery,* 1929, pp. 22 ff.).

CHAPTER SEVEN

SHAKESPEARE : *VENUS AND ADONIS* AND *THE RAPE OF LUCRECE*

SWINBURNE declared in his emphatic way that *Hero and Leander* was a model of what a young poet should write on such a subject, *Venus and Adonis* a model of what he should not write. Certainly Shakespeare's poem, though parts of it still yield pleasure, is not, like Marlowe's, a living thing. Yet in such a chronicle as this poems which exerted the influence of Shakespeare's two narratives have an important place, and their historical interest does not depend upon the name of their author. Contemporary readers had a different perspective from ours; they ranked *Hero and Leander* and *Venus and Adonis* in the same category as spicy amorous poems. And, historically, those two are the twin peaks of the Ovidian tradition in England. In this chapter we must try to sum up both the conventional and the original qualities of Shakespeare's work, and as briefly as possible, for everything that can be said about these poems has been said, said many times, with that fearless disregard of repetition which is characteristic of Shakespearean scholarship.

I. *VENUS AND ADONIS*

Venus and Adonis was entered in April, 1593, and published shortly afterward. There is no need of considering the old theory that the poem had been written years before, since there is no evidence in favor of such a speculation, and very much evidence against it. The obvious facts are that the mythological poem was beginning to be fashionable and that the young playwright, in a theatrical off-season, decided to advance himself by using the new recipe.

There is no reason to think that Shakespeare borrowed from any Italian source. The citations of Sir Sidney Lee and others only help to show, what is important enough in itself, that certain motives and methods of treatment were common property among Renaissance poets. It is hardly necessary to ransack continental authors to find a source for the sunny atmosphere of *Venus and Adonis,* or for such a conceit as the boar's wanting merely to kiss the youth, which was a commonplace of

139

sixteenth-century verse.[1] Nor, in order to explain Venus' apostrophe to Death, does one need to invoke the obscure name of Tarchagnota.[2]
Shakespeare's appropriation, if direct, of Ronsard's lines,

> Les Muses lierent un iour
> De chaisnes de roses, Amour,[3]

does stimulate one to look further, especially in Ronsard's version of the story of Adonis. This is quite different in conception from Shakespeare's, but there is, as Lee observed, a similarity in tone and temper, though perhaps no more than natural coincidence.[4]

The chief items in Shakespeare's debt to Ovidian material are set forth in every edition of the poems and may be briefly summarized. From the tenth book of the *Metamorphoses* he takes the central figures and something of the general background; from the eighth book the description of the boar, which reveals verbal echoes of Golding.[5] Since the Adonis of Ovid and common tradition is not a reluctant lover, it has generally and reasonably been assumed that Shakespeare partly modeled his characters on the wanton and dominating Salmacis and the shy young Hermaphroditus, as these appear in Ovid's fourth book.[6] The somewhat similar story of Narcissus and Echo may also have been in the poet's mind; but more will be said of Adonis a little later. This rapid outline gives an exaggerated notion of the actual amount of matter taken over from Ovid, for, in proportion to the length of Shakespeare's poem, it is really slight.

[1] The conceit had lately appeared in English in the.*Six Idillia* of 1588 (see above, page 55). It occurs also in a French translation by Saint-Gelais (*Œuvres*, Paris, 1873, I, 127) and in Latin in *Adonis Theocriti, ex Gallico Sangelasii* (Gruter, *Delitiae C. Poetarum Gallorum*, Part II, Sec. 1, p. 470); and in Minturno's *De Adoni ab apro interempto* (Gruter, *Delitiae CC. Italorum Poetarum*, II, 924).

[2] *Venus and Adonis*, etc., ed. Lee (1905), p. 27.

[3] These lines had already been cited and turned into English by that indefatigable borrower, Thomas Watson (*Poems*, ed. Arber, Sonnet lxxxiii, p. 119):

> The Muses not long since intrapping Loue
> In chaines of roases linked all araye.

Shakespeare's much finer phrase, "Leading him prisoner in a red-rose chain" (l. 110), admirably suggests the tone of a mass of amatory and mythological verse of the Renaissance. For Ronsard's poem see *Œuvres*, ed. Marty-Laveaux, II, 360; and Lee, *French Renaissance in England*, p. 221.

[4] *Œuvres*, IV, 26 ff. Passages illustrating the similarity are collected in my note in *P. Q.*, VI, 300; one is quoted below, page 141, note 8. Lee's parallels with other French poets seem quite fanciful.

[5] This useful boar also contributed, apparently, to Spenser's dragon (L. Rick, *Ovids Metamorphosen*, p. 58), though Mr. Whitney Wells has shown the dragon's kinship with medieval monsters (*M. L. N.*, XLI, 1926, 143 ff.).

[6] On the resemblances between Adonis and Hermaphroditus see Pooler's edition of the poems, pp. xxxi–xxxii.

A few not insignificant details of probable Ovidian coloring may be added. When we read

> Look, how a bright star shooteth from the sky,
> So glides he in the night from Venus' eye,

we may be justifiably content to praise a vivid original image. But we may also remember these lines from Golding's second book:

> But Phaeton (fire yet blasing stil among his yellow haire)
> Shot headlong downe, and glid along the Region of the Ayre
> Like to [a] Starre in Winter nightes (the wether cleare and fayre),

or this,

> There glyding from the sky a starre streyght downe too ground was sent.[7]

There may be a similar mingling of common observation and bookish or pictorial reminiscence in the description of Venus running:

> And as she runs, the bushes in the way
> Some catch her by the neck, some kiss her face,
> Some twine about her thigh to make her stay . . .

There is a hint of this in Ovid's first book, in the words of Apollo to the fleeing Daphne, and more than a hint in the picture offered to Christopher Sly:

> Or Daphne roaming through a thorny wood,
> Scratching her legs that one shall swear she bleeds;
> And at that sight shall sad Apollo weep,
> So workmanly the blood and tears are drawn.[8]

The most attractive passage of any length in *Venus and Adonis* is the account of the hunted hare, a very English vignette in this conventional Arcadia. Reading it we may say, with Bagehot, that we know Shakespeare had been after a hare. But recollections of Warwickshire seem to be mixed with recollections of Ovid. Poor Wat in desperation

> sometime sorteth with a herd of deer;
> Danger deviseth shifts; wit waits on fear.

---

[7] Golding, ed. Rouse, p. 49, ll. 404–06; p. 294, l. 978; *V. and A.*, ll. 815–16. See above, page 53, note.

[8] *Taming of the Shrew*, Induction, ii. 59 ff. Cf. Ronsard's poem on Adonis (*Œuvres*, IV, 34):

> Furieuse d'esprit, criant à haute vois,
> Ie veux escheuellée errer parmy les bois,
> Pieds nuds, estomac nud: ie veux que ma poitrine
> Se laisse esgrafiner à toute dure espine,
> Ie veux que les chardons me deschirent la peau.

Of course the idea is in Bion.

Ovid, describing the pursuit of Daphne by Apollo, has an elaborate simile of a hare and hound, which ends with a typical Ovidian line, *Sic deus et virgo est, hic spe celer, illa timore.*[9] Shakespeare's phrase is an evident attempt to rival in English the antithetical brevity of the Latin.[10]

This particular example suggests the importance of Ovid as one source of a conspicuous element in the style of *Venus and Adonis,* that is, the antithetical pattern of lines and phrases. Here are some of the more obvious instances in the first fifty lines:

> Hunting he lov'd, but love he laugh'd to scorn.
> Saith that the world hath ending with thy life.
> But rather famish them amid their plenty.
> Ten kisses short as one, one long as twenty.
> He red for shame, but frosty in desire.
> Backward she push'd him, as she would be thrust,
> And govern'd him in strength, though not in lust.

It is hardly too much to say that the whole fabric of the poem is woven of antitheses, as if Shakespeare had fallen in love with one of Ovid's tricks and worked it to death. The central antithesis of subject, between the warm goddess and the cold youth, is reflected in line after line that breaks more or less clearly into two parts containing opposed ideas. The use of the antithetical formula is marked enough in narrative and descriptive passages; it is, as one would expect, still more persistent in the speeches. The effect is somewhat as if a clever young writer of prose had resolved to outdo Mr. Chesterton. One must allow of course for the Petrarchan and euphuistic delight in logical and verbal antitheses, but eager first-hand imitation of Ovid evidently counted a good deal. When one compares *Venus and Adonis* with the work of Lodge and Spenser it is plain that, while Shakespeare exploits Italianate conventions, his taut style is different in texture from the smooth velvet of Italianate verse.[11]

[9] *Metam.* i. 539; cf. Golding (p. 34, ll. 659–60):
> So farde Apollo and the Mayde: hope made Apollo swift,
> And feare did make the Mayden fleete devising how to shift.

[10] With *V. and A.,* ll. 681 ff. and 703 ff., compare Golding's lines about the hound of Cephalus (pp. 156–57, ll. 1014–17):
> And like a wilie Foxe he runnes not forth directly out,
> Nor makes a windlasse over all the champion fieldes about,
> But doubling and indenting still avoydes his enmies lips.

See also Pooler's notes on the Shakespearean lines.

[11] This poem, like the plays, shows that Shakespeare was familiar with both Ovid's Latin and Golding's English. A select list of discussions of Shakespeare and Ovid is given

To say that *Venus and Adonis* reveals hardly a trace of direct foreign influence is not of course to say that apart from Ovidian elements it is an original poem. Even in the plays Shakespeare was seldom an innovator; his way was to accept the current fashion and excel in it. His first narrative poem, naturally, is almost wholly conventional, an exhaustive collection of traditional motives and devices, though he appropriates them, and plies his nimble wit in embroidering them, with as much zest as if they were his own jerks of invention. Shakespeare breathed the same air as other men, and his scent for popular formulas was unusually keen and prophetic. The luxuriant Italianate manner had been naturalized in England, and no immediate foreign contacts were necessary. Not only was every poetical device at hand, there was also Elizabethan fiction. If in Shakespeare's poems action bears to rhetoric much the same proportion as bread to sack in Falstaff's bill, we may remember the technique of Pettie, Lyly, and Greene in their prose tales.

Shakespeare's representation of a chaste youth solicited by an amorous woman had precedents not only in Ovid but in the pastoral tradition derived partly from Ovid. The vain pursuit of a woman by a man or of a man by a woman was, as we have seen in connection with Lodge, the stock situation of the Italian pastoral. The conventions had now become familiar in English, and *Venus and Adonis,* like the other mythological poems, makes use of them (though it stands somewhat apart on account of its more direct imitation of Ovidian style). There must be an obstacle somewhere in such stories of love; if Adonis were as willing as Barkis, and Venus equally laconic, what would become of the poem? As for Shakespeare's choice of the more piquant of the two standard situations, it offered some obvious advantages. Since it appears virtually certain that he had read *Hero and Leander,* he might have felt as Rossetti did about *The Raven*—that, as Poe had said all that could be said on one aspect of the theme, *The Blessed Damozel* would take the other side. Anyone who knew Leander's plea could hardly avoid the conviction that the subject must be freshened by reversal of the parts.

For the particular conception of a reluctant Adonis there were suggestions at hand also. There is a faint hint of initial coyness in the Adonis of Spenser:

in the bibliography to this chapter. In apparent ignorance of all these (except Pooler) and others, Mr. E. I. Fripp recently set out to prove what everyone knows, that Shakespeare was acquainted with the text of Ovid as well as with Golding (*Shakespeare Studies,* 1930). Anyhow Mr. Fripp's breathless catalogue of phrases proves little one way or the other, for the ostensible thesis is hardly touched; and, while no one doubts that Shakespeare absorbed much of his mythology directly from Ovid, most of Mr. Fripp's items are Elizabethan commonplaces.

Then with what sleights and sweet allurements she
Entyst the Boy, as well that art she knew,
And wooed him her Paramoure to be.

Further, Spenser's picture of Venus watching Adonis bathe suggests a mild combination of the story with that of Salmacis and Hermaphroditus.[12] Less vague are two songs of Greene's quoted by all the editors, which show that the notion of a chaste Adonis was current; they appear in *Perimedes the Blacke-smithe* (1588) and *Never Too Late* (1590). Marlowe's allusion to Venus and "proud Adonis" is sufficiently different from Shakespeare's conception to suggest independent use of a non-classical variant. Thus Shakespeare had only to look about him to find hints for a cold Adonis.[13]

Shakespeare was obviously indebted to Lodge's languidly pretty *Glaucus and Scilla,* both in the central theme and in details, such as the popular sixain stanza and the likewise popular "echo" device. Lodge's purple patch on Venus and Adonis, which was quoted above, is enough to indicate not only the degree to which Shakespeare caught the Italianate style, but the extent of his rhetorical originality and vigor. In all points, form as well as detail, Shakespeare greatly bettered his instruction.[14]

Shakespeare doubtless knew at least two treatments of Adonis in Spenser; a few lines from one passage have already been quoted. Spenser's half-symbolic adaptation of the myth in the sixth canto of the third book is quite remote from Shakespeare's, for Shakespeare's attitude toward his material is simply that of a Renaissance Ovid; his Venus and Adonis are symbolic only in the sense that they and everything connected with them are manifestations of physical beauty. The pictorial warmth and richness of Spenser's work in general must have affected Shakespeare, as such qualities affected most poets of the day, but *Venus and Adonis* has a distinct hardness and precision of line which is not Spenserian. Whatever Italian Shakespeare picked up, he does not, even at his most

[12] *F. Q.*, III. i. 35-36.
[13] Adlington's *Golden Asse* (ed. Seccombe, 1913, p. 48) has the phrase "as the proude yonge man Adonis who was torne by a Bore"; the epithet does not seem to be the common one for Adonis. There is a hint of a chaste Adonis in Servius on *Ecl.* x. 18 (ed. Thilo and Hagen, III. i, pp. 121-22). It will be remembered that the Venus of Lyly's *Sapho and Phao* (1584) is decidedly aggressive.

For later combinations of Venus and Adonis with Salmacis and Hermaphroditus (*Taming of the Shrew,* Induction, ii. 52-55; *Passionate Pilgrim*), it is enough to refer to some discussions in editions of Shakespeare's poems, such as those of Pooler (pp. xxx-xxxi), Carleton Brown (pp. xxi ff.), Feuillerat (pp. 185-86); and Chambers, *William Shakespeare,* I, 547-48. Constable's poem is mentioned in the Appendix, under 1600.

[14] Pooler, pp. xvi-xvii, gives the chief parallels between Shakespeare and Lodge.

florid, write like Spenser and others to whom the soft fluidity of Italian
verse was both more familiar and more congenial.[15]

The influence of Marlowe the dramatist upon Shakespeare was so
strong that it affected the structure, characterization, and style of some
of the earlier plays. The influence of *Hero and Leander* upon *Venus and
Adonis,* however, is both obvious and superficial. Some apparent resemblances are only characteristics of the mythological genre. What
seem to be demonstrable borrowings, though numerous, are mainly
incidental and external, and Shakespeare, for good or ill, subdues them to
his own style and mode of treatment. Many passages in the Marlowesque
plays one might assign to Marlowe; there are few bits of *Venus and
Adonis* that could be mistaken for quotations from *Hero and Leander*.

Conceits of course everyone delighted in, but Shakespeare's, especially
those of the myth-making sort, sometimes resemble Marlowe's. Mythological allusions were also common property, and Shakespeare, like his
fellows, took them indifferently from Ovid and from modern sources.[16]
Since Shakespeare's plays are full of mythological allusions,[17] and since
these were a conventional element in the mythological poem as established

---

[15] Spenser's *Astrophel* was published in 1595, though probably written some years
earlier. The passage on Adonis (ll. 151 ff.) is somewhat akin to Shakespeare, but still
closer to Lodge and continental imitations of Bion.

　　Another luxuriant handling of the story appears in Fraunce's *Third part of the Countesse
of Pembrokes Ivychurch* (1592). Since the book is rare I may quote some lines:

> Sometimes downe by a well with Adonis sweetly she sitteth,
> And on Adonis face in well-spring louely she looketh,
> And then Adonis lipps with her owne lipps kindely she kisseth.
> Rolling tongue, moyst mouth with her owne mouth all to be sucking,
> Mouth and tong and lipps, with Ioues drinck Nectar abounding.
> Sometimes, louely records for Adonis sake, she reciteth;
> How Læander dyde, as he swamme to the bewtiful Hero,
> How great Alcides was brought from a club to a distaffe . . .

> Sometimes unto the shade of a braunched beech she repaireth,
> Where sweete bubling brooke with streames of siluer aboundeth,
> And faire-feathred birde on tree-top cherefuly chirpeth;
> There her voyce, which makes eu'n Ioue himselfe to be ioying,
> Unto the waters fall, and birds chirpe ioyfuly tuning.

Venus is here presented as the wooer. In particular one may compare the fourth and fifth
lines of the quotation with *V. and A.,* ll. 541 ff., and l. 572, "Such nectar from his lips she
had not suck'd"—which, to be sure, is not beyond Shakespeare's unaided imagination.
One may note, with the same reservation, Shakespeare's "Ten kisses short as one, one
long as twenty" (l. 22), and Fraunce's

> Thinking euery howre to be two, and two to be twenty,
> Til she beheld her boy . . .

[16] For instance, though Shakespeare knew Ovid so well, he was content to take over,
perhaps from Marlowe, the non-Ovidian drowning of Narcissus. See above, page 137.

[17] In addition to the older discussions of mythology in the plays there are the brief but
suggestive remarks of Mr. George H. W. Rylands in his *Words and Poetry* (1928), pp.
87 ff., 135 ff.

by Lodge and Marlowe, it may be observed that such allusions in *Venus and Adonis* are relatively scanty and unadorned. If in this respect Shakespeare departed from the convention he was evidently following Lodge and Marlowe—and Ovid—when he scattered aphorisms and epigrams through an erotic poem. The amorous arguments of Venus recall Leander's and those of the *Sonnets,* where the theme of procreation is decidedly more pertinent than in the mouth of the undomestic goddess.[18]

The differences between Marlowe and Shakespeare are no less obvious, and more important, than the resemblances. Hero and Leander, despite Marlowe's inconsistencies of characterization and excess of decoration, win our sympathy; there is warmth and something of natural passion. Shakespeare, dealing with an unattractive pair who are more remote from humanity, fiddles on the strings of sensuality without feeling or awakening any such sympathy, without even being robustly sensual. Marlowe has too many merely pretty lines, but generally he is strong, masculine, swift; Shakespeare is much more content with prettiness, and the poem, though far from languid, is sicklied o'er with effeminacy. Many lines in *Hero and Leander* glow with a beauty that might be called haunting if the word were not overworn; the reader of *Venus and Adonis* is chiefly impressed by the astonishing skill of phrase and rhythm—

> Which bred more beauty in his angry eyes.
>
> Leading him prisoner in a red-rose chain.
>
> Full gently now she takes him by the hand,
> A lily prison'd in a gaol of snow.

But when one thinks of "Love's not Time's fool," not to mention the plays, one is made aware of the fatal lack of emotion. Finally it is noteworthy, in a poem which is a tissue of bookish conventions, that

---

[18] J. M. Robertson, *Problems of the Shakespeare Sonnets*, p. 126. It does not seem necessary to enter into the question whether *Venus and Adonis* was an exhortation to Southampton to marry. As a piece of advice it is at any rate more roundabout than, say, the "Solemnization of Matrimony." Mr. Rylands (p. 131) makes the rather odd comment: "The argument of *Venus and Adonis* is the argument of the third book of *The Faërie Queene.*

> Seeds spring from seeds, and beauty breedeth beauty,
> Thou wast begot; to get it is thy duty."

However positive Spenser's conception of virtue, the relation between his book of Chastity and *Venus and Adonis* is not readily apparent.

Parallels between *Hero and Leander* and Shakespeare are recorded in various editions, e.g., Pooler (pp. xxii ff.); C. Brown (Tudor ed., p. x, and notes). See Lee, "Ovid and Shakespeare's Sonnets," *Elizabethan and Other Essays* (Oxford, 1929); Alden's edition of the *Sonnets;* Janet G. Scott, *Les sonnets élisabéthains* (Paris, 1929), pp. 259 ff.

Shakespeare's best bits of imagery are fresh pictures of nature. Marlowe's images are almost wholly a fusion of art, literature, and imagination.

Incongruity of costume we have already observed as a normal element of mythological poems as well as other types of Renaissance writing, and Shakespeare of course does not depart from the mode. When Venus approaches Adonis and "heaveth up his hat," and at other times, we have a suspicion that we are witnessing an Arcadian encounter between a scantily clad Maid of Honor and, say, the Earl of Southampton in a rare moment of satiety.[19] Indeed if one considers the opportunities offered by Shakespeare's subject, and the popularity of voluptuous anatomical catalogues, in which even the sober Sidney and philosophic Chapman indulged, Shakespeare's neglect of "the nude" is somewhat remarkable. In this respect he is less sensuous than Marlowe the pagan or Spenser the moralist. We have here another instance in which Shakespeare is closer to Ovid—the Ovid of the *Metamorphoses,* that is—than to the Italianate fashion.[20]

The Shakespeare of the mature plays is greatest perhaps in his power over words; he uses language as if it were his own creation and he alone understood its infinite capacities. What is missing in these poems—and in the early plays—is just that faculty, that genius for packing a world of meaning into a phrase. In the poems there is hardly a trace of such concentration and suggestion; the words mean what they say, and that is not much. (One remembers that in the fifteenth chapter of *Biographia Literaria* Coleridge, undertaking to elucidate "the specific symptoms of poetic power," strangely chose these poems for "critical analysis.") Only a few times in *Venus and Adonis* is there a slight break in the flat, two-dimensional surface, when the poet works in a natural image from his own observation, the dive-dapper, the snail, the gentle lark, the dew-bedabbled hare, and such fresh glimpses of something real, welcome as they are, heighten the total effect of artifice. In them, however, we do have a faint promise of the real Shakespeare, the poet who can see and feel and communicate what he sees and feels. On the other hand the

[19] In his first *Elizabethan Journal* (London, 1928, pp. xii, 236) Mr. G. B. Harrison gives a reproduction of a tapestry that depicts Venus and Adonis in the dress of the period, and remarks: "This, rather than the more fleshly kind of painting, was the Elizabethan conception of Venus. The connection between tapestry pictures and such narrative poems as *Venus and Adonis* and *Hero and Leander* is close." Cf. the quotation from Peele, above, page 131.

[20] There are to be sure such lines as 233 ff., which are sensual enough, but their indirectness is far from the set description. In fact a graduate student, a not unintelligent young woman, once quoted them in all good faith in a paper on "Description of Nature in *Venus and Adonis.*" Ll. 397 ff. have been related to the poem in *The Phœnix Nest* cited above, page 72.

auctioneer's description of the horse, which, since Hazlitt, has so often been put beside the passage on the hounds in the *Midsummer Night's Dream,* shows the difference between the minute, self-defeating realism of the tyro and the swift, suggestive strokes of the master. The horse embodies all the good points prescribed in Elizabethan treatises on the animal, and remains a catalogue; we see, hear, touch, and smell the hounds.

The living things described in the poem are not all creatures of the English countryside. We know that the man who wrote of the lark ascending, or of "poor Wat," had been in the fields as well as in his study. We know that the same man fully shared the taste of his age when we read this:

> To see his face the lion walk'd along
> Behind some hedge, because he would not fear him;
> To recreate himself when he hath sung,
> The tiger would be tame and gently hear him;
> If he had spoke, the wolf would leave his prey,
> And never fright the silly lamb that day.
>
> When he beheld his shadow in the brook,
> The fishes spread on it their golden gills . . .

Even if such a string of fancies be half humorous—and Venus' lamentation is not especially merry—it reminds us that Shakespeare not only laughed at euphuism but practiced it with some relish. The poem everywhere shows that its author lavished artistic labor upon it, in a sense put himself into it, yet perhaps nothing proves more clearly what a circumscribed self it was than the fact that the creator of this polite lion behind an English hedge was shortly to create another kind of polite lion for Snug the joiner. But every age, our own included, has its stylistic tricks which lose their charm for posterity.

The Elizabethans generally anticipated Wilde in believing that nothing succeeds like excess, and if we dislike their rhetorical extravagance it is after all no great price to pay for their unique virtues. Their exuberant excesses were the natural overflow of tremendous energy in an era of uncertain taste and an intoxicated delight in words. In the plays Shakespeare never entirely outgrew his love of rhetoric, though his critical powers ripened with his other faculties and enabled him to satirize flamboyance. In *Venus and Adonis* he seems quite satisfied and happy in seriously exploiting the popular conceits, decoration, rhetorical wooing, rhetorical declamation. In the speeches of Venus we have the arguments of an Ovidian lover combined with the strained fancies of a sonneteer, moral aphorisms, and, even from Adonis when he finds his tongue, some of the paradoxes on the nature of love so dear to Elizabethan writers,[21] all worked out with an inexhaustible ingenuity that compels a kind of admiration. The poem is indeed a bible for lovers. To quote one allusion out of many, a character in a play of 1640 longs for "the book of *Venus and Adonis* to court my mistress by."[22] And when speaking of rhetoric one must notice Venus' apostrophe to Death. It is thoroughly of the Renaissance; it is also thoroughly medieval.[23]

If *Venus and Adonis* were wholly bookish, a piece of pure tapestry, all would be well, in a limited sense. But for an orgy of the senses it is too unreal, for a decorative pseudo-classic picture it has too much homely realism. We observed somewhat similar discords in *Hero and Leander*, but in the cooler, shallower, more deliberate *Venus and Adonis* the effect of artifice is much greater. *Hero and Leander* exists more fully in a poetic world of its own, and its author's passion for beauty partly reconciles inharmonious elements. With such distinctions Elizabethans were not greatly concerned. Shakespeare was wholly successful in what he set out to do, and it is only a posterity for whom the poem was not written that asks "Was it worth doing?"[24] Since at the moment the poetic shibboleth is a line of Donne, the answer is not in doubt, yet Shakespeare, at the age of twenty-nine and thirty, chose to write not merely one unsatisfactory classical poem but two. At any rate his cultivation of these expansive and empty pieces did not prevent his studding the plays with allusions of often concentrated and suggestive beauty.

II. *THE RAPE OF LUCRECE*

Having produced an erotic poem much to the taste of Southampton and the emancipated in general, Shakespeare, with easy nonchalance, paid his debt to morality and the non-emancipated by celebrating, in the following year, the most famous of all martyrs of chastity. Although *Lucrece* contains few indications of intense feeling in the author, when he comes later to conjure up the sinister specters of night no image is more vivid in his memory than that of Tarquin's ravishing stride. However, the poem seems to be quite as deliberate a literary exercise as

[21] For these paradoxes see ll. 649 ff., 793 ff., 1137 ff. Since almost every Elizabethan indulged in at least one such series it is needless to give references. Miss Jeffery comments on the habit (*John Lyly*, pp. 82, 123).

[22] Pupillus in Lewis Sharpe's *The Noble Stranger*.

[23] Cf. the address to Death in the *Philomena* (above, page 13).

[24] One need only mention Mr. H. T. S. Forrest's *The Original "Venus and Adonis"* (London, 1930). The author, in his disintegrating loyalty to Shakespeare, tries to show that the bad parts of the poem are the work of an interpolator or interpolators.

Venus and Adonis, and the reversal of the theme and the graver style need not imply anything in the way of apology. Almost any Elizabethan could write a sensuous mythological poem once; he could hardly do it twice. *Lucrece* is not a sensuous mythological poem, and, if less attractive than its predecessor, it is in some respects much more ambitious.

As before Shakespeare greatly embellishes the original tale. Here he seems to have followed Livy in the main, with supplementary details from Ovid and others.[25] A number of details point to knowledge of Chaucer's story in the *Legend of Good Women,* such as Tarquin's definite threat to kill one of Lucrece's slaves and not merely a slave, and the carrying of her body to Rome. There are perhaps verbal reminiscences in the words "stalk" and "dishevelled." Lucrece's golden hair and the simile of the wolf and the lamb are found in Ovid, Chaucer, and Gower. In Chaucer—and Gower—Lucrece swoons, though not in the classical sources.[26] The brief reflections in Chaucer on Tarquin's violation of chivalry might have suggested a text for the long debate in Shakespeare.

In addition to elaboration of the story proper there are the Trojan scenes in the painting which the distraught Lucrece was able to study so minutely. The classical model for the episode was Aeneas' scrutiny of the pictures in Dido's palace, and the Shakespearean description is based on the second book of the *Aeneid.* We have, however, such un-Virgilian details as these:

[25] Livy, i. 57–59; Ovid, *Fasti,* ii. 685 ff. For a convenient summary of the items see Feuillerat's edition of the poems, page 177. Fuller discussions of the sources are given in various editions, e.g., those of Pooler and Lee; and see Ewig, *Anglia,* XXII, 1 ff., 343 ff., 393 ff.

Livy and Ovid Shakespeare evidently read in Latin, and it has commonly been said that he did not use Painter's paraphrase of Livy's story. In the poem itself I observe only one hint to the contrary; while Livy (c. 59) has *Brutus castigator lacrimarum atque inertium querellarum,* Painter's phrase is "childishe lamentacions," and Shakespeare (ll. 1825, 1829) has "such childish humour" and "lamentations." The prose argument, however, offers more evidence. Here Lucrece "dispatcheth messengers, one to Rome for her father, and another to the camp for Collatine." Ovid has only the word *evocat* (ll. 815–16), and Livy (c. 58) has *eundem nuntium.* Chaucer and Gower say nothing of two messengers. Painter writes: "Lucrece sent a post to Rome to her father, and an other to Ardea to her husbande." Bandello speaks of two messengers, but there is no reason to think that Shakespeare knew his version. (W. Marschall gives not very cogent parallels to prove that Shakespeare used Bandello; see *Anglia,* LIII, 1929, pp. 102–22.) In Shakespeare's poem there is only one messenger. There are in the argument a few other possible traces of Painter, for example, Shakespeare's "late in the night . . . amongst her maids," and Painter's "late in the night . . . amonges her maydes." While using Livy's text for the poem, Shakespeare might have turned to the convenient Painter for the argument.

[26] Cf. Chaucer, ll. 1815–18; Gower, *C.A.,* vii. 4986–89; Shakespeare, ll. 1261–67. Gower is commonly ruled out of the list of sources (see Pooler, p. lvi), but one slight detail may be mentioned. In Shakespeare (l. 170) Tarquin, having risen from bed, sets forth "Throwing his mantle rudely o'er his arm." There seems to be no such action in any version except Gower's (ll. 4964–65):

> And thanne upon himself he caste
> A mantell . . .

Here one man's hand lean'd on another's head,
His nose being shadow'd by his neighbour's ear;
Here one being throng'd bears back, all boll'n and red;
Another smother'd, seems to pelt and swear . . .

A combination of separate incidents in one picture was of course traditional in poetry; the shields of Achilles and Aeneas (the latter of which Sackville had imitated) were illustrious precedents. But the multitude of scenes that Lucrece described, along with such concrete pictorial items as those just quoted, lend color to Sir Sidney Colvin's conjecture that Shakespeare had in mind one of the common tapestries depicting the Trojan story.[27]

The sources so far mentioned have to do more with plot and detail than with the general mode of treatment, and that, as scholars have long recognized, owes much to Daniel's *Complaint of Rosamond* (1592).[28] The story of Lucrece could not very well be told in the manner of *Venus and Adonis,* and for a tragedy of guilt and innocence and sorrow Shakespeare found a partial model outside the mythological convention. *Lucrece* belongs with *Rosamond* in the category of "complaints." Both poems are in rhyme royal, which was regarded by Elizabethan critics as especially suited to serious themes. The opening lines of *Rosamond* indicate the poem's relation to the *Mirror for Magistrates* and the medieval tradition:

Out from the horror of infernall deepes,
My poore afflicted ghost comes heere to plaine it . . .[29]

Rosamond tells how she, a virtuous maiden, was corrupted by "a seeming Matrone," the character of whose arguments we noticed already in

[27] "The Sack of Troy in Shakespeare's 'Lucrece' and in Some Fifteenth-Century Drawings and Tapestries," *A Book of Homage to Shakespeare* (1916), pp. 88 ff. Cf. W. Marschall, "Das Troja-Gemälde in Shakespeares „Lucrece,'" *Anglia,* LIV (1930), 83–96; and M. F. Thorp, *P.M.L.A.,* XLVI (1931), 687 ff.
    While there is a clear connection, whether satirical or not, between the player's speech in *Hamlet* and Marlowe's *Dido* (see Brooke's edition of *Dido,* page 160), it has not, I think, been noticed that *Dido* is related to the Trojan scenes in *Lucrece.* Several phrases have to do with Sinon:
    Dido (p. 154, l. 144): A man compact of craft and perjury. Cf. *Aen.* ii. 195.
    Lucrece (l. 1517): False-creeping craft and perjury.
    Dido (p. 155, l. 153): Phrygian shepherds. Cf. *Luc.,* l. 1502; *Aen.* ii. 58–59.
    Dido (l. 161): O, th' enchanting words of that base slave.
    Luc. (l. 1521): whose enchanting story.
    In *Dido* (p. 159, l. 242) Pyrrhus in killing Priam is described as "treading upon his breast," a detail not in Virgil. In *Lucrece* (l. 1449) Priam's body "bleeding under Pyrrhus' proud foot lies."
    On the whole question see Else von Schaubert, "Die Stelle vom „Rauhen Pyrrhus" (Hamlet II, 2, 460–551) in ihrem Verhältnis zu Marlowe-Nashes „Dido," zu Seneca, etc.," *Anglia,* LIII (1929), 374–439.
[28] See especially Pooler, p. xlviii.
[29] *Samuel Daniel: Poems,* etc., ed. A. C. Sprague (1930), p. 39.

connection with Leander's.[30] Rosamond's detailed analysis of the inner conflict that preceded her surrender to Henry, and her moralizing on the consequences of sin, gave an obvious cue for Shakespeare's psychological handling of his story. One particular incident Shakespeare turned to account. Rosamond describes a casket sent to her by her lover; the pictures engraved on it, showing the suffering victims of amorous Neptune and Jove, forecast her own sorrows, as Paris and Sinon and the Trojan scenes remind Lucrece of hers. In execution the poem represents the middle level of the well-languaged but somewhat prosaic Daniel; it is much simpler and quieter in style than Shakespeare's piece, which is scored for the brasses rather than the wood winds.[31]

Lucrece differs from *Venus and Adonis* in attempting to deal dramatically and realistically with a tragic situation involving two "historical" persons. The versions of the story that Shakespeare knew are very brief compared with his eighteen hundred and fifty-five lines, and, while the action is spun out as much as possible, the great additions are the long passages of dramatic or rhetorical moralizing. He does try to enter into the feelings of the characters, though his love of rhetoric runs away with his sense of drama. The conflict in Tarquin's mind when he sets out for Lucrece's room occupies nearly two hundred lines of soliloquy and description; like the villains of the plays he leaves nothing unsaid in the way of self-condemnation. Lucrece, when awakened, marshals orderly arguments in about eighty lines. Later, after a few hundred lines of rhetoric, she exclaims, with justice:

> In vain I rail at Opportunity,
> At Time, at Tarquin, and uncheerful Night . . .

Declamation roars while passion sleeps. The description of the Trojan scenes and Lucrece's reflections thereupon involve a further smoke of words, to the extent of about two hundred lines.

Dramatic realism is likewise defeated by the incessant conceits. Shakespeare does not, as Spenser sometimes does, treat rape as a decorative theme, but his handling, in trying to be both serious and decorative, falls between two stools. When Tarquin arrives on his evil

---

[30] See above, page 135.

[31] Daniel in turn seems to have been inspired by *Lucrece* to amplify and heighten rhetoric in his own poem. See the long addition made in the revised version of 1594 (Sprague, pp. 198 ff., especially ll. 99 ff., 113 ff.).

Various minor obligations to other contemporaries need not be recorded, though some are mentioned later. Shakespeare again derives ornamental details from *Hero and Leander*, but, the tone of the poem being so different, they are of no great account.

errand, three stanzas are given up to the "silent war of lilies and of
roses" in the face of his hostess:

> This heraldry in Lucrece' face was seen,
> Argu'd by beauty's red and virtue's white:
> Of either's colour was the other queen,
> Proving from world's minority their right:
> Yet their ambition makes them still to fight;
>   The sovereignty of either being so great,
>   That oft they interchange each other's seat.

Granting of course that the conceited style was instinctive with most
Elizabethans as it cannot be with us, one discerns in this baffling tissue
of ingenuities only a clever brain, not a quickened pulse. So too when
Tarquin gazes at his prospective victim we have such a conceit as this,
in Marlowe's worst vein:

> Her lily hand her rosy cheek lies under,
> Cozening the pillow of a lawful kiss;
> Who, therefore angry, seems to part in sunder,
> Swelling on either side to want his bliss.

As often in the early plays, the author has quite forgotten the situation;
he is holding the subject at arm's length, turning it round, saying as
much as he can about every side of it.

Almost every line gives evidence of a self-conscious pride in rhetorical
skill. The antithetical pattern of *Venus and Adonis* appears again.
Shakespeare rejoices in matching Ovid:

> Quid, victor, gaudes? haec te victoria perdet.
> A captive victor that hath lost in gain.

A Tarquin who "justly thus controls his thoughts unjust" is too cool,
his creator too epigrammatic, for the matter in hand; one thinks of the
equally strained phrase of Tennyson, "And faith unfaithful kept him
falsely true."

In addition to the usual gnomic lines[32] we have an extraordinary
profusion of proverbs, singly and in series, after the style of the euphuists
in verse and prose. *Venus and Adonis* had its heaped-up illustrations,
but the quantity of them in *Lucrece* helps to give the poem an old-
fashioned air. Says Tarquin to Lucrece, in words feverish with desire:

[32] Not being versed in Baconian literature, I do not know if an obviously Baconian line
(353) has been observed: "Thoughts are but dreams till their effects be tried." Cf. *Of Great
Place:* "For good thoughts (though God accept them) yet towards men are little better
than good dreams, except they be put in act."

> I see what crosses my attempt will bring;
> I know what thorns the growing rose defends;
> I think the honey guarded with a sting . . .

And, justly controlling her just thoughts, Lucrece replies:

> Mud not the fountain that gave drink to thee;
> Mar not the thing that cannot be amended;
> End thy ill aim before thy shoot be ended;
> He is no woodman that doth bend his bow
> To strike a poor unseasonable doe.

Accompanied by such antiphonal wisdom vice loses half its evil by losing all its grossness.

The mere bulk of Lucrece's declamation after the event demands that something be said of it. Having tried his hand at oratory in *Venus and Adonis,* Shakespeare liked it well enough to provide Lucrece with a whole series of apostrophes. They have undeniable force, but the effect is like that of Senecan declamation, like an explosion in a vacuum. The apostrophe to Time may have been inspired by contemporary poets, but it has a literary pedigree that goes back to Ovid's *Tristia.*[33] The apostrophe to Night is likewise conventional in style and subject matter, but it bears a special resemblance to a speech that Spenser puts in the mouth of Arthur.[34] Sir Sidney Lee remarked that Lucrece's address to Opportunity "seems an original device of Shakespeare." The matter at least is proverbial; in fact most of it is contained or suggested in the comment on *Nosce tempus* in Taverner's *Proverbes or Adagies, gathered out of the Chiliades of Erasmus.*[35] This trick of apostrophe, inherited from the more rhetorical Roman writers, was one of the most important devices of rhetoric in the Middle Ages, and Lucrece's declamations are of obvious medieval flavor.[36]

In technique *Lucrece* is nearer to Chaucer's *Troilus* than to Ovid, though it has nothing of Chaucer's irony, emotion, and depth. With all

[33] *Luc.,* ll. 939 ff.; *Tristia,* IV. vi. 1 ff. See Watson, Sonnets xlvii, lxxvii, and Giles Fletcher, *Licia,* Sonnet xxviii.

[34] *Luc.,* ll. 764 ff.; *F. Q.,* III. iv. 55–59. The details are given in *P. Q.,* VI, 301. Cf. Drayton, *Ideas Mirrour* (1594), Sonnet xlv. In Chaucer's *Troilus and Criseyde* (iii. 1429 ff., 1450 ff.) are apostrophes to night and day, for which both Ovid and Boccaccio have been suggested as sources (E. F. Shannon, *Chaucer and the Roman Poets,* pp. 133 ff.). See below, page 201, notes 5 and 6.

[35] Ed. 1552, fol. xxiv. The comment is quoted in *P. Q.,* VI, 302. Cf. Spenser's Occasion (*F. Q.,* II. iv. 4). Spenser's painfully didactic personification, which is as old as Phaedrus, is born of the same habit of mind as Shakespeare's apostrophe.

[36] "Third in importance among the devices of amplification may be placed apostrophe, with its rhetorical colours *exclamatio, conduplicatio, subiectio,* and *dubitatio.* It would be difficult to exaggerate the importance of apostrophe in medieval literature. Addresses to persons living or dead, present or absent, to personified abstractions, and even to inanimate objects are to be found in almost every composition with any pretensions to style from the

its Renaissance trappings it is thoroughly in the medieval tradition. On the other hand, with its undramatic drama, its endless rhetorical digressions, it reads at times like an unconscious burlesque of Elizabethan plays. There are a few really dramatic touches, such as parts of Tarquin's behavior, and especially the sympathetic maid and the "sour-fac'd groom." This "homely villein," who, summoned to act as Lucrece's messenger, "curtsies to her low," receives only a few phrases, but he is almost as real a person as either of the principals. These various bits are slighter and paler than the pictures of the lark and the hare in *Venus and Adonis*, but they are similarly out of key. They introduce an air of truth and actuality into a would-be dramatic but quite bookish poem, and they are too few to do more than heighten the artificial unreality of all the rest. For all its seriousness of theme and intention *Lucrece* is as soulless as the earlier poem, and much more wearisome.

Thus for a modern reader it remains a museum piece. Both it and *Venus and Adonis* lack the headlong poetic vitality of *Hero and Leander;* they lack also the charm and sweetness of most of Drayton's *Endimion and Phœbe*. But there is no doubt that the rising dramatist knew what the public wanted; we may recall the familiar words of that useful index of taste, Francis Meres. *Venus and Adonis,* said the more exacting Gabriel Harvey, pleased the younger sort, *Lucrece* (and *Hamlet!*) the wiser sort. Both poems were abundantly praised; it is not every poet who can contrive to be both the Swinburne and the Patmore of his generation. But, from the testimony of editions and allusions, the wiser sort, as usual, appear to have been a minority, and for the next generation at least *Venus and Adonis* was linked with *Hero and Leander* as the amorist's *vade mecum,* equally popular in study, boudoir, and brothel.

eleventh century onward; and a special form, the *Complainte,* developed into one of the most widely cultivated types of literature." J. M. Manly, "Chaucer and the Rhetoricians," *Proceedings of the British Academy,* XII (1926), p. 104.

With the speeches of Lucrece compare those of the ravished woman in Nashe's *Jack Wilton* (ed. McKerrow, II, 293–94).

CHAPTER EIGHT

DRAYTON: GILES AND PHINEAS FLETCHER: WILLIAM BROWNE

I. MICHAEL DRAYTON

DRAYTON'S *Endimion and Phœbe* (1595) was not reprinted, apart from excerpts in *England's Parnassus,* until the third quarter of the nineteenth century, and no popular edition was available until 1925.[1] Thus belatedly was rescued a poem which was in the anomalous situation of having been read only by a handful of specialists and yet thought worthy of a page in the *Cambridge History of English Literature.*[2] Skeptics for whom this last item is an imperfect guarantee of merit can test critical opinions for themselves. The poem has a further interest in that a strong case has been made out for Keats's use of its main theme in *Endymion.*

Surveying Drayton's voluminous output, from the unreadable *Harmony of the Church* (1591) to the lovely *Muses Elizium* (1630), one may grant that he seldom sings because he must. Yet this most industrious of poets took up one fashion after another, eclogues, sonnets, mythological poems, historical chronicle, heroic ballad, fairy poetry, and the rest, and he gained respectable rank in all forms, unique excellence in some. His writing mirrors the poetic history of a whole period. His first work, as Fuller said of Sternhold and Hopkins, contains more of Jordan than of Helicon, while his last has the charm and lightness, if not the flawless detail, of Herrick. And between these he had done all manner of good things; even *Polyolbion* has rewards for the well-girt reader.

The strength of *Endimion and Phœbe* does not lie in its narrative structure. Indeed most mythological poems recall Bayes's exclamation, "Plot stand still! why, what a devil is the plot good for, but to bring in fine things?" Yet Drayton has a story. Endymion is a devout servant of the goddess, who returns his love, though she has not yet confessed it. In the guise of a mere nymph she appears to him at the river side and makes love. Loyal to his goddess the youth rejects her, and prefers to go on fishing. The supposed nymph again pleads in vain, then returns

---

[1] Ed. J. W. Hebel.　　　　　　　[2] IV, 180.

to Latmus. But now Endymion, overcome in spite of himself, feels a
new passion. At night, sitting near his flock, he utters an amorous plaint.
With the dawn Phoebe glides down from her crystal chair, "longing to
see her sweet Endimion." She finds him asleep, and after her nymphs
have danced in, with garlands, and danced out again, she wakens him.
Endymion, "not knowing yet great Phœbe this should be," tells of his
ardent love. Phoebe now pretends to be coy, but after further protestations
from her lover she reveals her identity, and avows that she has long
loved him. Wrapping him in a fiery mantle she carries him through the
air, so that he learns the mysteries of the heavens. Set down on earth
again, Endymion is endowed with new powers and finds all nature
ready to serve him. The rest of the poem describes the gorgeous
mythological pageantry that attends his wedding and deification—not
without further discourses on the trinal triplicities of the heavenly
hierarchy. Then Endymion is transported to Latmus to remain, "ever
beautifull and yong," the goddess' paramour.

The various disquisitions on the heavenly mysteries with which the
narrative is interlarded, and which a modern reader is inclined to skip,
have a real relation to the main theme. For Drayton stands quite apart
from the fleshly school in his conception, although he writes in the
decorative manner. He pictures no erotic delights, and chooses a subject
that allegorical interpreters had long understood as a symbol of high
contemplation.[3] As Mr. Hebel says, Drayton "presents in concrete story
the 'way of love' of traditional Platonism. Endimion reluctantly comes
to love material beauty in Phœbe disguised, whom he supposes to be a
nymph 'of fayre *Floras* trayne,' only to discover to his happiness that the
nymph is absolute beauty, Phœbe herself. Then, just as the Platonist is
led on by love for beauty, Endimion is whisked away to the heavens
where Phœbe imparts to him the 'heavenly secrets.' Thus love has

> impt the wings of his desire,
> And kindled him, with this cœlestiall fire." [4]

Platonism was such common property that it is needless to seek a

[3] Cf. Fulgentius, ii. 19; Natalis Comes, iv. 8. Drayton might have got most of his titles
for Diana (p. 43) from Comes (iii. 15–18; iv. 1). The opening glosses on Chapman's
Hymnus in Cynthiam (nearly all of the glosses on the poem are derived from Comes) give
six of the titles. A passage (based on Comes) near the end of Chapman's poem sets forth
the Platonic conception of Endymion and Diana (*Poems and Minor Translations*, 1875,
p. 16).

[4] Cf. Spenser, *Hymne of Heavenly Beautie*, ll. 134 ff.:
> Thence gathering plumes of perfect speculation,
> To impe the wings of thy high flying mynd,
> Mount up aloft through heauenly contemplation,
> From this darke world, whose damps the soule do blynd . . .

definite source for Drayton's ideas, but one may illustrate them by glancing at a versifier who enjoyed extraordinary popularity in England for two generations, Du Bartas. In 1584 King James published his translation of *Uranie,* and from that date onward almost every other year witnessed further renderings.[5] Drayton dedicated his *Moyses* (1604) to Du Bartas and his English translator, though Upham remarks that at that time he possibly knew both original and translation chiefly by repute; in some later work there is evidence of knowledge. But he might have known Du Bartas as early as 1594–95; so conscientious and idealistic a writer as Drayton, and one so sensitive to changes in poetic taste, would surely not be backward in welcoming such a remarkable portent. At any rate it is permissible to observe some similarities without offering them as arguments for influence.

The story of Endymion and Diana, as traditionally Platonized, virtually endows Diana with the attributes of Urania. In *Uranie* the goddess appears, like Drayton's Phoebe, in an azure mantle; we have planetary lore, and the suggestion of a journey above the poles to learn heavenly secrets and absorb the divine fire of poesy.[6] There are frequent resemblances between Drayton and portions of the "first week" of Du Bartas,[7] both in descriptive details and in the abundant matter on such topics as the zodiac, the nature of the elements, the relations of Phoebus and Phoebe, the influence of the planets and the moon in particular, the aspirations of the flesh-imprisoned soul toward heavenly truth, voyages through the air in quest of these cosmic secrets.[8] While such ideas were not novel, the mention of Du Bartas at least emphasizes the change of spirit that Drayton wrought in his mythological poem; one would not look in the Protestant epic for illustrations of *Hero and Leander* and *Venus and Adonis.*

Since Drayton was an inveterate imitator it might be expected that he had some model for his central device, Phoebe's appearing in disguise as a rival to herself. But no source has been found, and I have come upon

[5] See the table in Upham, *French Influence in English Literature,* p. 152.

[6] See Arber's reprint of *The Essayes of a Prentise* for King James's translation and the French original, or *Works of Joshua Sylvester,* ed. Grosart, II, 3. Sylvester's version was apparently first published in 1605.

The Urania of Du Bartas and the Platonized Phoebe of Drayton are sisters, or at least cousins, of Spenser's "Sapience." The medieval character of Phoebe's habiliments may be illustrated by comparison of Drayton (pp. 44–45) with Alanus de Insulis, *The Complaint of Nature* (trans. D. M. Moffat, New York, 1908, pp. 7 ff.).

[7] The dates of various sections of Sylvester's version defy the bibliographer, "yet partial translations by him began appearing in print that same year [1591], and by his own statement these pieces existed in fragmentary form long before they were printed as a collected whole" (Upham, p. 157).

[8] For these aërial journeys cf. Drayton, pp. 36–39, and Sylvester, ed. Grosart, I, 31, ll. 409 ff.; 79, ll. 842 ff.

nothing more than hints of a similar situation.[9] One is in an Italian poem, *L'Endimione,* by Francesco Ellio, though in general this piece is different from Drayton's.[10] Diana, inspired by Venus and Cupid with love for Endymion, and much disturbed in consequence, descends to Latmus. Laying aside her divine splendor she appears as a nymph with purple buskins and hair adorned with myrtle. She gazes at Endymion as he sleeps, and talks of her love until he awakes. In language modeled on the much-imitated meeting of Venus and Aeneas, Endymion asks if she is nymph or goddess, and how she came there. Diana avows her love, and then her divinity.

Further, there is the Homeric *Hymn to Aphrodite,* which tells how the goddess of love, who controlled even the gods, conceived a passion, through the agency of Zeus, for the mortal youth, Anchises. She appeared to him as a nymph, and did not reveal her identity until their union was consummated. Both these stories stop short of Drayton's plot. There is always the possibility, though it does violence to scholarly instincts, that Drayton himself "thought of Mr. Pickwick."

Instead of reviewing one another's works Elizabethan poets, with their deficient ethical sense, indulged in imitation or plagiarism, and no more than other men could Drayton ignore the existence of *Hero and Leander* and *Venus and Adonis.*[11] Indeed he had given testimony of his appreciation already. In *Peirs Gaveston* there are several certain imitations of *Venus and Adonis*—the earliest known—and a possible reminiscence of *Hero and Leander.*[12] Though Drayton did not in

[9] The Platonic possibilities of Lyly's play involve two distinct persons, Tellus and Cynthia.
[10] The only text I have seen is that in G. Bidelli, *Gl'idillij di diversi ingegni illustri* (Milan, 1618); whether Ellio's poem had appeared before I do not know.
[11] While Drayton does not mention Marlowe and Shakespeare he honors Lodge with an over-generous tribute. The influence of *Glaucus and Scilla* had been swallowed up in that of its greater successors, and it is hard to isolate any special proofs of it in *Endimion and Phœbe.* The dance of the nymphs, though a common device, may be related to a similar incident in Lodge, and perhaps Endymion's change of heart was derived from Lodge also (Hebel, p. xi). Phoebe's assertion (p. 16) that she was "Begot by Pan on Isis sacred flood" recalls the scene of Lodge's poem, "nere to Isis floud." The description of the Muses as "heaven-inspired Babes of memorie" (p. 47) evidently comes from another poem of Lodge's in the *Scilla* volume, *In commendation of a solitarie life,*

See where the babes of memorie are laid
Under the shadow of Apollos tree.

Cf. *Britannia's Pastorals* (Bk. i, Song 5, l. 283): "O come, ye blessed imps of Memory."
[12] J. W. Hebel, *M. L. N.,* XLI, 248–50. *Peirs Gaveston* was entered on December 3, 1593, and "evidently published soon after."
The thirty-eighth sonnet of *Ideas Mirrour* (1594) has these lines:

If chaste and pure deuotion of my youth,
Or glorie of my Aprill-springing yeeres,
Unfained loue in naked simple truth . . .

The phrasing, however, is as close to Marlowe's *Ovid* as to *Hero and Leander* (*Works of Marlowe,* ed. Brooke: *H. and L.,* i. 207–08; *Elegies,* i. 3, ll. 5–6, 13–14). Cf. *The Faithful Shepherdess,* II. iv. 9–10.

Endimion and Phœbe include Marlowe among his teachers, he made ample recompense many years later, in the briefest and best eulogy the poet has ever received. In those famous lines the memory of Marlowe raises Drayton's writing above its normal level, and his inspiration is potent in *Endimion and Phœbe*. There are obvious borrowings, like this:

> The shag-haird Satyrs Mountain-climing race,
> Have been made tame by gazing in his face.
> For this boyes love, the water-Nymphs have wept
> Stealing oft times to kisse him whilst he slept:
> And tasting once the Nectar of his breath,
> Surfet with sweet, and languish unto death . . .[13]

Throughout the poem, except in the learned parts, are equally clear echoes or imitations of Marlowe's mythological conceits, descriptive details, gnomic lines. The sensuous pictures of Endymion and Phoebe would not be what they are but for Leander and Hero. The similarity in style, however, only emphasizes the difference in spirit between the two poems. The love which in Marlowe is final, the sweet fruition of an earthly crown, in Drayton is the first step toward the mystical apprehension of truth. But Drayton was no mystic, and the heavenly secrets prove less memorable than the lovers' ecstasy.

More important than actual imitation of Marlowe is the pervasive influence that gives "air and fire" to long stretches of original writing, that inspires the creation of more purely sensuous beauty than Drayton ever achieved again. More than one passage might have come out of *Hero and Leander,* and it would be severe to dismiss such things as merely derivative, for not every poet can write like Marlowe by taking thought.

> She layd Endimion on a grassy bed,
> With sommers Arras ritchly over-spred,
> Where from her sacred Mantion next above,
> She might descend and sport her with her love,
> Which thirty yeeres the Sheepheards safely kept,
> Who in her bosom soft and soundly slept;
> Yet as a dreame he thought the tyme not long,
> Remayning ever beautifull and yong,
> And what in vision there to him be fell,
> My weary Muse some other time shall tell.

"This," says Mr. Elton, very moderately, "is nearer the manner of the dead shepherd than much of the *Endymion* of Keats."[14] Drayton's loving study of Marlowe is evident not only in substance and style, but also in rhythm. Instead of using the sixain of Lodge and Shakespeare

[13] P. 12.   [14] *Michael Drayton* (1905), p. 65.

he follows Marlowe in electing the couplet, and his handling of it, as extracts will already have suggested, is close to Marlowe's. If Drayton's lines do not attain the impetuous rush of their model they are sufficiently swift, strong, fluent, and varied in movement, equally remote from the rocking-horse couplets of the eighteenth century and from the wayward meanderings of Hunt and the youthful Keats.

The influence of *Venus and Adonis* is less significant and appears mainly in Phoebe's wooing of the reluctant Endymion. But even here the spirit of Drayton's work is different, for Phoebe's vein of badinage sets her apart from the rather feverish Venus.[15]

Drayton pays tribute to Spenser, and with reason. But in discussing a genre devoted to sensuous word-painting one cannot readily isolate special influences. Some of Phoebe's speeches to Endymion remind one of Spenser as well as of Shakespeare.[16] Further, while Marlowe has almost no natural scenery, and Shakespeare has a few bits of fresh observation, Drayton indulges in luxuriant landscapes in which literary convention and the authentic countryside are pleasantly mixed. Only quotations, for which there is no space, would make clear how his Elizabethan gusto gives charm to his catalogues of pastoral properties, and how he appropriates and embroiders Spenser. The picture of Mount Latmus is closely modeled on the Gardens of Adonis, with further details from the Bower of Bliss.[17]

By this time, having indicated the nature if not the full extent of Drayton's borrowings from others, one may ask if the poet had any capital of his own. The answer of almost any reader must be that he had a good deal. For though the mythological poem in its very nature is highly "literary," *Endimion and Phœbe* as a whole has a distinct character

[15] One may wonder if the odor of unsanctity which clung to Marlowe's name, and which quickly attached itself to *Venus and Adonis*, deterred the more chaste and idealistic Drayton from mentioning these creditors in his postscript and thereby formally linking his Platonic poem with the two notorious erotic pieces.

[16] *E. and P.*, pp. 19–20; *V. and A.*, ll. 1093 ff. (quoted above, p. 148); *F. Q.*, I. vi. 24–26.

[17] *F. Q.*, III. vi. 42–45, and II. xii. 71. This last bit of Spenser is of course adapted from Tasso.

Since Drayton has two tree-lists (pages 10, 20), and since we meet the convention elsewhere, I might make a catalogue of tree-lists somewhat fuller than any I have seen: Ennius, *Annales* (ed. Vahlen, 1903, ll. 187–91; ed. E. M. Steuart, 1925, bk. vi, frag. 9, p. 26); Virgil, *Culex*, l. 123; *Georg.* ii. 12, 65, 442; *Aen.* vi. 179; Ovid, *Metam.* x. 86; Seneca, *Oed.* 532; Lucan, *Phars.* iii. 440; Statius, *Theb.* vi. 90; Claudian, *De Raptu Proserp.* ii. 107; Joseph of Exeter, *Bellum Troianum*, i. 505 (see above, page 9); *Roman de la Rose*, ll. 1338 ff. (1355 ff. in Chaucerian version); Boccaccio, *Teseide*, xi. 22–24; Chaucer, *Parl. Foules*, 176 (based on Joseph of Exeter), and Knight's Tale, A 2920–24; Tasso, *G. L.*, iii. 75; Sidney, *Arcadia* (original version), ed. Feuillerat (1926), pp. 83–84; Spenser, *F. Q.*, I. i. 8–9 (based on Ovid and Chaucer; see above, page 108); Robert Chester, *Loves Martyr*, ed. Grosart, pp. 95–96; *Works of Joshua Sylvester*, ed. Grosart, I, 45; Hugh Holland, *Pancharis* (see the Appendix, under 1603); William Browne,

which is not that of Marlowe or even Spenser. The characters remain phantoms, and, in such a cool silvery tale, we are content that they should. There is no disconcerting admixture of sophistication or realism in the treatment of Drayton's Platonic lovers. The poem certainly does not possess intensity, yet it accomplishes what it sets out to do with charm and color and sweetness.

With much that is conventional the mythological background combines numerous bits of pastoral description which, to be sure, are partly conventional also, but are partly fresh and English. Sprays of roses and sweet eglantine; the nightingale, ousel and mavis caroling, the joyful lark stretching her wing, the cock playing "hunts-up" for the day star; the shepherd singing, piping a roundelay, fishing by a river side; dew falling upon flowers and pastures; fountains bubbling over silver sand—such things make a pastoral scene that is more than bookish.[18] We hear of the good old game of barley-break, played by satyrs on Latmus; of sports on shearing day; of shepherds telling stories—an Ovidian story in particular—as they sit by their folds; of naked fairies dancing the "heydegies." The mixture is at least as much English as mythological, but the youthful world of the poem has a harmony of its own.

Of course *Endimion and Phœbe,* like most poems of the kind, is rather too facile, and, if not invertebrate, has not a back strong enough to bear the load of Drayton's beloved "nines and threes," the business of the celestial hierarchies inherited from Dionysius the Areopagite. Nor do such stout bags of astrological ballast facilitate the ascent to the Platonic heaven. But, as we often have occasion to remember, even the greatest Elizabethans are subject to what for us are lapses in taste and literary tact; they display a medieval readiness to tell all they know up to the date of publication, and poets as well as prose men do not hesitate to incorporate footnotes in the text.[19]

Drayton showed originality chiefly in abandoning half-realistic

Britannia's Pastorals, Bk. i, Song 2, l. 353; Patrick Hannay, *The Nightingale (Minor Caroline Poets,* ed. Saintsbury, I, 622; see the Appendix, under 1622); W. Basse, Eclogue ix (ed. Bond, pp. 253–54).

Such lists are naturally more or less alike, and Drayton knew more than one, from Spenser's backward. But it may be remarked that his Larix and Teda (p. 20) are in the *Hypnerotomachia* (trans. of 1592, pp. 77, 239, in reprint of 1890); and cf. Sylvester, *loc. cit.*

By way of a botanical conclusion to this note it may be added that "lunary," which Drayton mentions (page 12), occurs repeatedly in Lyly, in *Endimion* and elsewhere.

[18] For a random bit of pastoral-mythological extravagance, the promise to turn sheep's fleece into gold, cf. Drayton, p. 19, and Peele's *Arraignment of Paris* (Bullen, I, 28–29).

[19] Cf. Gabriel Harvey: "Other commend Chawcer, & Lidgate for their witt, pleasant veine, varietie of poetical discourse, & all humanitie: I specially note their Astronomie, philosophie, & other parts of profound or cunning art. Wherein few of their time were more exactly learned. It is not sufficient for poets, to be superficial humanists: but they

eroticism for idealistic symbolism. Poets could hardly go beyond *Hero and Leander* or *Venus and Adonis,* they could only imitate, and they did. But if that type of mythological poem had become sterile, the symbolic was not. Though the minor writers of the next generation tried to work the vein of Marlowe and Shakespeare, modern poets have generally been of Drayton's mind.

We do not know why *Endimion and Phœbe* was not reprinted. Drayton did, unhappily, rewrite the poem and published the new version in 1606 as *The Man in the Moone.* It is about half as long as the original and not half so good. The piece opens with a shepherd feast in honor of Pan—a suggestion that Keats turned to account. After the festival the shepherds call on one of their number to while away the time by telling a story in the moonlight. The story is that of Endymion and Phoebe.

One large addition is a description of the pictures on Phoebe's mantle, which occupies over seventy lines; it was perhaps inspired by Chapman's lines on Hero's wondrous robe, though Drayton's realistic picture of the stormy sea and the inland birds is quite different.[20] Hero's buskins may be responsible for the similar tasteless extravagance of Phoebe's equipment. The central idea of Drayton's earlier piece, Phoebe's appearing as a nymph and winning Endymion's love away from herself, is dropped. Instead the goddess merely visits the youth and gives him a long account of her life and divine powers; the planetary lore is not dropped, though it is somewhat altered. Endymion finally becomes the man in the moon and accompanies Phoebe on her celestial circuit. The rest of the poem, about forty lines, is given up to rather clumsy satire; the man in the moon sees the doings of men on earth which remain hidden from their fellows. The poem is dull, with little left of the charm of the first version, but it is, as Mr. Hebel remarks, "one of the interesting examples of Drayton's quick change from the Spenserian to the Jacobean manner." The mood of Lodge, Marlowe, and Shakespeare was mainly serious, though Marlowe's digression on Cupid and the destinies, with its somewhat incoherent satirical strokes, anticipated the later style. After about 1600 there is an obviously growing taste for humor or satire in the treatment of mythology, and such qualities, when they appear, generally deflate Elizabethan rhetoric. The older tradition continued to attract the majority, but even the mythological poem could not escape the realistic tendencies, especially conspicuous in the drama, which marked the turn of the century.

must be exquisite artists, & curious uniuersal schollers" (*Gabriel Harvey's Marginalia,* ed. G. C. M. Smith, pp. 160–61).
[20] Chalmers, *English Poets,* IV, 418–19. See page 207, below.

A few words may be added concerning some other works of Drayton's, first of all *England's Heroical Epistles* (1597), his most popular production. These pairs of letters exchanged between famous lovers, Rosamond and Henry, Queen Isabel and Mortimer, and the rest, are of course modeled on the *Heroides*. The influence of Ovid appears not only in the general conception but also in the rhetorical, somewhat declamatory style, and in turns and antitheses which, along with the neat closed couplets, suggest a later age.[21] To the example of Ovid also may perhaps be attributed the restrained handling of mythological allusions, which are mostly sparing of sensuous decoration. A few reminiscences of Marlowe and Shakespeare occur. Here, for instance, are some familiar lines of *Hero and Leander* converted into an Augustan couplet:

> Thus still we strive, yet overcome at length,
> For men want mercy, and poor women strength.[22]

The orthodox naturalistic arguments against chastity are employed in the epistle of John to Matilda (and in the *Legend of Matilda*). King Henry writing to Rosamond echoes the words of Venus to Adonis:

> If I were feeble, rheumatic, or cold,
> These were true signs that I were waxed old . . .
> The tent my bed, no pillow but the ground.[23]

But such items are significant mainly in emphasizing how far Drayton has moved from the Italianate manner.[24]

One last poem may be mentioned, *The Quest of Cynthia* (1627), which marks still another stage in Drayton's treatment of myth.[25] The style and details are Elizabethan—at least once he echoes *Endimion and*

[21] For example, these two bits:
> Punish my fault, or pity mine estate;
> Read them for love, if not for love for hate . . .
> Put on with boldness, and put back with fears.

On the general subject, see G. P. Shannon, *The Heroic Couplet in the Sixteenth and Early Seventeenth Centuries, with Special Reference to the Influence of Ovid and the Latin Elegiac Distich, Stanford University Abstracts of Dissertations* (1926–27), pp. 127 ff.

[22] Chalmers, IV, 91. Marlowe's lines are ii. 286–96. Drayton alludes to Hero and Leander on page 92.

[23] See *V. and A.*, ll. 108, 133 ff.

[24] The Italianate manner appears in the catalogue of mythological pictures in the Tower of Mortimer which is one of the oases in *The Barons' Wars* (1603). Here are Phoebus clipping Hyacinth, Io gazing at herself in the water, Mercury sporting with Hebe, etc. (Chalmers, IV, 51–52).

Polyolbion, with its innumerable nymphs, we must pass by, though we may remember Drayton's fond cherishing, in the first Song and elsewhere, of the legend of Brute, "which now the envious world doth slander for a dream." The envious world, in the person of the learned Selden, amiably proceeded, in the Illustrations to the poem, to demolish "the Arcadian deduction of our British monarchy."

[25] *Drayton's Minor Poems,* ed. C. Brett (1907), p. 144; Chalmers, p. 162.

Phœbe[26]—but the spirit is not. To borrow the suggestive summary of M. Legouis, the poet

se montre suivant la déesse à travers les campagnes dans lesquelles ses pas divins ont laissé des traces charmantes, mille fleurettes épanouies sous ses pieds. Il arrive enfin jusqu'à elle et ils décident de vivre ensemble une vie d'amour et d'innocence. Cynthie symbolise ici la nature. C'est déjà un thème lakiste, mais revêtu de fantaisie élisabéthaine.[27]

II. GILES AND PHINEAS FLETCHER

A marked characteristic of the later English Renaissance, especially notable in Spenser, is the mingling, in entire good faith, of religious earnestness and pagan sensuousness. When we reach Milton we find the same essential elements, combined, however, in very different proportions, and pagan opulence is decidedly subdued. Of the transition from the tone of Spenser to that of Milton no poem is more typical than Giles Fletcher's *Christ's Victorie and Triumph* (1610). The very title of that uneven but often beautiful work indicates a shift of emphasis; here we have set forth, not the attributes of a Renaissance gentleman, from holiness to courtesy, but only the Christian story of redemption. Yet the cross is almost hidden behind the luxuriant draperies; the path to Calvary is roses, roses, all the way. Medieval theology is presented in Italianate style.

But the sumptuousness is not wholly Italianate, it too is partly medieval. Here is one stanza from the long description of Mercy:

> Her upper garment was a silken lawne,
> With needle-woorke richly embroidered,
> Which she her selfe with her owne hand had drawne,
> And all the world therein had pourtrayed,
> With threads, so fresh, and lively coloured,
>   That seem'd the world she newe created thear,
>   And the mistaken eye would rashly swear
> The silken trees did growe, and the beasts living wear.[28]

[26] *Quest of Cynthia:*
> As when she from the water came,
>   Where first she touch'd the molde,
> In balls the people made the same
>   For Pomander, and solde.

Cf. *E. and P.*, p. 17:
> The place wherein my bare feete touch the mold,
> Made up in balls, for Pomander is sold.

[27] E. Legouis & L. Cazamian, *Histoire de la littérature anglaise* (Paris, 1925), p. 293. On Drayton's *Muses Elizium*, which perhaps ought properly to be noticed here, see below, page 223.

[28] *Poetical Works*, ed. F. S. Boas, I, 31, st. 53.

The first line seems to echo a line in Marlowe's description of Hero, and the last lines suggest Ovid's story of Arachne or the many imitations of it. We meet so many elaborately attired divinities and especially so many garments with embroidered pictures that, whatever their differences, they have a family resemblance—we may remember Marlowe's Hero, the embroidered mantle of Chapman's Hero, the resplendent goddess of Drayton's *Endimion and Phœbe,* and the mantle described in *The Man in the Moone*—but Fletcher's Mercy is closest perhaps to Nature in Alanus de Insulis, an author to whom he might have been led by Chaucer or, more probably, by the reference in Spenser's *Mutability.*[29]

Fletcher's Christ in the wilderness might be another Leander or Endymion, Narcissus or Hermaphroditus, with his black hair in short curls, and "His cheekes as snowie apples, sop't in wine."[30] Such a Christ may well attract mythological allusions. Like Golding and others before him Fletcher finds that "obscure fables of the Gentiles" embodied biblical truth:

> Who doth not see drown'd in Deucalions name,
> (When earth his men, and sea had lost his shore)
> Old Noah; and in Nisus lock, the fame
> Of Sampson yet alive; and long before
> In Phaethons, mine owne fall I deplore:
> But he that conquer'd hell, to fetch againe
> His virgin widowe, by a serpent slaine,
> Another Orpheus was then dreaming poets feigne.[31]

Only in the all-reconciling imagination of the Renaissance could "the second Adam" become a second Orpheus.

Of the general influence of Spenser upon Fletcher nothing needs to be said here, since the subject is familiar enough, and some particular imitations are obvious; for instance, the Bower of Vain-Delight is

[29] H. M. Belden, "Alanus de Insulis, Giles Fletcher, and the 'Mutabilitie' Cantos," *S. P.,* XXVI, 131 ff. Mr. Belden also argues plausibly for the general influence of *Mutability* on Fletcher's case presented in the court of heaven. Whether or not there is influence, there is an interesting contrast; Spenser's vehicle is a mythological story, with the Titaness Mutability as plaintiff, while Fletcher is religious rather than philosophical and has such figures of medieval allegory as Justice, Mercy, Repentance, Faith. Cf. Courthope, *History of English Poetry,* III, 126, 134.

As for the figure of Mercy and her mantle, Mr. Belden's argument for Alanus seems probable enough, but he does not take account of the descriptive convention, of which some modern instances are given above.

[30] P. 42, st. 8, 11. The simile is not novel, of course, but one may compare some lines about Hermaphroditus as they appear in Golding (ed. Rouse, p. 90, ll. 405–06):

> For in his face the colour fresh appeared like the same
> That is in Apples which doe hang upon the Sunnie side.

Cf. *The Purple Island* (Boas, II, 169, st. 84).

[31] P. 59, st. 7. Gavin Douglas speaks of Christ as "that hevinlie Orpheus" (Smart, II, 18, ll. 9–10).

modeled on the Bower of Bliss.[32] Of their mingling of medieval allegory with Renaissance paganism some illustrations have been given, and Fletcher, incidentally, is more medieval than his master. One more characteristic combination cannot be passed over. We noticed before the unconscious ease with which Spenser linked in a double simile the Mount of Olives and the mount of the Muses. We need not then be astonished at Fletcher's picture of Christ's ascent into heaven:

> The rest, that yet amazed stood belowe,
> With eyes cast up, as greedie to be fed,
> And hands upheld, themselves to ground did throwe,
> So when the Trojan boy was ravished,
> As through th' Idalian woods they saie he fled,
>   His aged Gardians stood all dismai'd,
>   Some least he should have fallen back afraid,
> And some their hasty vowes, and timely prayers said.

> Tosse up your heads ye everlasting gates,
> And let the Prince of glorie enter in . . .[33]

Christ and Ganymede!

In 1628 appeared a mythological poem entitled *Brittain's Ida*, with the name of Spenser on the title-page. The virtually conclusive internal evidence in favor of Phineas Fletcher's authorship was confirmed some years ago by Miss Seaton's discovery of a manuscript containing *Brittain's Ida*, under the better and presumably correct title *Venus and Anchises*, along with five other pieces known to be Fletcher's and a hitherto unknown *Epithalamium*.[34] Since *Venus and Anchises* is one of the more attractive exemplars of the Spenser-Marlowe-Shakespeare tradition, it is satisfactory to have it definitely established in the Fletcher canon. The date of composition is uncertain.[35]

Fletcher was not the only Jacobean cleric whose "looser merriment"

[32] P. 49, st. 39 ff.

[33] P. 78, st. 14–15. Cf. *Faerie Queene*, III. xi. 34. The sensuous expression of religious feeling in the first half of the seventeenth century needs no illustration. It is enough to recall the name of Crashaw, or, as a less familiar instance, Benlowes' very Italianate description of Theophila, "the soul"(*Minor Caroline Poets*, I, 355).

[34] *Venus and Anchises*, etc., ed. E. Seaton, 1926.

[35] It is safe to assume with Miss Seaton that so voluptuous a poem was written before Fletcher commenced his ministry (about 1616), and Miss Seaton (page xxxix, note 2) would date it "probably soon after 1603." Something can be said for a later date. Adolescent eroticism was not in that period confined to a man's early twenties. Miss Seaton observes that most of Fletcher's poetry centers around 1610, at any rate belongs to the decade 1605–15; further, she shows that the quite warm *Epithalamium*, which she regards as more mature work ("probably before 1611"), "has closer correspondences with *Venus and Anchises* than with any other poem." In addition to these general considerations, which are not unfavorable to a later date than Miss Seaton's, the first line of the third stanza seems a probable echo of a line in Spenser's *Mutability* (1609). Spenser (vi. 36) has "Of Arlo-hill (Who knowes not Arlo-hill?)"; Fletcher says "In Ida vale (whoe knowes not Ida vale?)." Such repetition of a name was a not uncommon device (cf. *Shep. Cal., August*, l. 141),

proved embarrassing. The mythological mode encouraged an erotic warmth which even a free-spoken age did not associate with the cloth, and a respectable country parson might be quite ready in 1628 to let the attribution to Spenser pass unchallenged.[36] Whatever his later qualms Fletcher felt none in writing the poem; it is an untroubled banquet of sense. The opening stanzas tell us that the young poet Thirsil, sitting beside the Cam, began to sing of "fayre Eliza." The poem proper occupies fifty-nine eight-line stanzas, and is only a series of voluptuous pictures. Anchises, since he is most familiar to us in Virgil, we think of as an epic parallel to Mr. Wemmick's Aged Parent; here, naturally, he is a youth, and his beauty and pastimes are described at length. One day, tired of hunting, he wanders in the grove of Venus. Hearing music come from a bower, he creeps up to it, and beholds Venus, whose bodily beauties are catalogued, in the traditional manner, in about a hundred lines. Fainting with delight, Anchises sinks down, and Venus, awakened, revives and comforts him. Not at all offended by his evident adoration, the goddess equips him with bow and quiver like another Love. He utters his passion in solitary laments. But when opportunity prompts a more open declaration, and he entreats a kiss, his gracious divinity leads the novice on to a happy consummation. Anchises now lives in joy, but he is one of those who kiss and tell, and Jove sends his lightning. The poet, says the final stanza—for again we have the old personal note—would not blab if he received such favors from his love.

The union of Venus and Anchises is treated, as we have noticed in connection with Drayton, in the Homeric *Hymn to Aphrodite*. Fletcher takes over little except the names. Anchises is mentioned as "a lowlie swaine," "not noblie borne," but otherwise the original story, with its epic dignity and restraint, is forgotten. Motives, character, situation, are altered in accordance with the Italianate convention.

By this time, indeed earlier, the "lacteall path" of that convention was too well worn to leave very distinct traces of individual influences, apart from actual verbal clues. In style, contrasted with the onward movement and energy of Marlowe and Shakespeare, the softness of Fletcher's "sugered streames" is nearer to that of Spenser, or even Lodge. *Venus and Anchises* has more virility than *Glaucus and Scilla,* but Fletcher,

but I do not recall examples of the formula's being used with place names. We have just noticed Giles Fletcher's probable borrowing from *Mutability* in a poem published in 1610. Of course both brothers might have read Spenser in manuscript. But it is not impossible that *Venus and Anchises* was written in 1609–10.

[36] There may be an acknowledgment of the poem, along with a farewell to the scenes and the writings of his youth, in the last lines of *Non invisa Cano*. See Miss Seaton, pp. xxiii, xxix, xxxi, 32, and Mr. Boas' edition, II, xxi, note.

like Lodge, has a notable relish for feminine endings (especially those in
ing), and, like Lodge also, he places his mythological tale in a personal
framework. The poem is full of conceits and antitheses which are more
akin to those of the Elizabethan Petrarchists than to Ovid's. Miss Seaton
records a number of parallels with Sidney's *Arcadia,* and one may add
that, however conventional the anatomical catalogue, Fletcher's description of Venus bears some resemblances to Zelmane's song in praise of
Philoclea.[37]

Fletcher with his economical habits offers an especially good illustration
of the close affinity between the pastoral and the mythological poem.
As Miss Seaton observes, the seventh eclogue, "though less directly
personal in subject, is in tone and treatment so close to *Brittain's Ida* as to
read almost like a first draft of its descriptive passages," and the third
"also has close correspondences with the long poem." [38] For instance,
Fletcher divides between Mira and Stella of the eclogues a good many
of the bodily beauties (and metaphors) that appear in the picture of
Venus.[39] For Fletcher as for many predecessors the pastoral and mythological worlds were identical, and the artificial tone, setting, themes, and
pretty diction appropriate to one kind of writing were equally appropriate
to the other.[40]

The general situation of Venus and Anchises bears some obvious
resemblance to that of Venus and Adonis, though the bashfulness of
Anchises is caused by lack of confidence rather than lack of ardor, and
it soon disappears. Anchises is a shepherd, but also, like Adonis, a huntsman who pursues the hart and the tusked boar. Like some Ovidian youths
he disdains the attentions of affectionate nymphs. Fletcher's Venus, like
Shakespeare's, is the wooer, but she has no need of Shakespearean
eloquence. In teasing Anchises for asking too little she displays, moreover,
a slight but sufficient degree of humor, and her tone of banter, like that of
Drayton's Phoebe rather than the rhetoric of Shakespeare's tempestuous
and perspiring goddess, helps to keep the poem's fleshliness wholesome.
There are incidental traces of *Hero and Leander*.[41] The chief item is

[37] *Arcadia,* ed. Feuillerat (1912), pp. 218 ff. Miss Seaton (page 106) notices one parallel,
but there are others. Koeppel (*Anglia,* XI, 362) quoted Tasso in connection with stanza 28.
[38] P. xli.
[39] Cf. Boas, II, xvii, 217, and Seaton, st. 21, 23, 27, 28.
[40] One might quote Chapman's fine eulogy of *The Faithful Shepherdess,* which, he says,
Renews the golden world, and holds through all
The holy laws of homely Pastoral,
Where flowers, and founts, and nymphs, and semi-gods,
And all the Graces find their old abodes.
[41] Cf. "His lovelie limbs . . . Were made for playe" (st. 4), and Marlowe, i. 88;
"Night is Loues holyday" (st. 12), and Marlowe, i. 191. The idea of this last phrase was of

Fletcher's use of a titbit for the erotic palate, Leander's ignorance of what might follow kisses.[42]

The "garden of delight," where Anchises discovers Venus in her bower, we have visited before, and the song that Anchises hears is on a not unfamiliar text:

> Then while thy time affordes thee time & leasure
> Enioye while yet thow mayst thy life's sweet pleasure.

Whether the scene is taken directly from Tasso[43] or from Spenser's imitations of Tasso, or from both, does not greatly matter. The differences, however, are significant. Tasso's picture is highly sensuous, but Armida is a wicked enchantress to be shunned. The episodes of Phaedria and Acrasia's Bower of Bliss, in both of which we have a similar setting and lyrics, are of course, the second especially, among Spenser's most purple passages;[44] but the knight of temperance breaks away from the wanton lady of the lake and destroys Acrasia's bower. Fletcher uses the same material in order to conduct his hero, not without envy, to the acme of sensual delight.

When a poet has gone on a moral holiday and created a piece of voluptuous tapestry, one need not shake a moralistic finger. At the same time such a poem as Fletcher's provides a fair test for readers who find all or most of Spenser in his picture-making and are skeptical of his didactic seriousness. *Venus and Anchises,* considered simply as poetical writing, is inferior to the Spenserian cantos, yet not so much inferior that they cannot be compared. In point of sensuousness they are pretty much on a level, but *Venus and Anchises,* however pleasant a concoction, is, after all, empty, and Spenser is not. Fletcher's cake is all icing.

One illustration of Fletcher's flexibility of mind (as well as economy) cannot be passed over. He has no less than four versions of Boethius' tale of Orpheus and Eurydice.[45] The paraphrase in *A Father's Testament* is the closest to Boethius, and the last lines are these:

course common. Further, cf. "Too foolish is the man that starves to feed his treasure" (st. 16), and Marlowe, i. 243.

[42] St. 56, 59. Cf. Marlowe, ii. 61 ff., 68–71.

[43] Koeppel, *Anglia,* XI, 361–62.

[44] *F. Q.,* II. vi and xii. The songs occur at vi. 15 and xii. 74 respectively. One of Spenser's most Spenserian lines in the song of the mermaids (II. xii. 32) is this: "Here may thy storme-bet vessell safely ride." In Fletcher (st. 58), Anchises, having boldly entered "Loves highway," goes further and at length arrives "Where safe from storme the love beate vessell rides."

[45] One is a chorus to the fourth act of *Sicelides.* Another, in the fifth canto of *The Purple Island,* follows a discourse on the tongue and its office. A third appears among *Poeticall Miscellanies.* The fourth is mentioned in the text. See *Works,* ed. Boas, I, 246; II, 66 ff.; II, 243–44; II, 336–37; and see remarks and notes, II, viii, xii, 364, 366.

This Fable looks to thee, who tir'd with night
Desir'st to draw thy soul to life, and light
On that Eternal Sun set, fasten, fix thy sight.

If you turn back on hellish Shades to pore,
Thou ever losest what thou wan'st before:
Thy soul more barr'd from Heav'n, in hell implunged more.[46]

The versions in *The Purple Island* and the *Poeticall Miscellanies* end on a similar note. Not so the chorus in the *Sicelides;* indeed one asks what Boethius is doing in that galley, in a labyrinth of pastoral love affairs. This is the conclusion, not quite in harmony with Boethius:

Thus since love hath wonne the field,
Heaven and Hell, to Earth must yeeld,
Blest soule that dyest in loves sweete sound,
That lost in love in love art found.
If but a true-loves joy thou once doe prove,
Thou wilt not love to live, unlesse thou live to love.

This last line (with its suggestion of the *Pervigilium Veneris*) is also the last line of the song that lures Anchises to the bower of Venus.[47]

We shall not linger over *The Purple Island,* which, though it appeared in 1633, was written earlier.[48] Inspired by one of Spenser's most painfully humorless and instructive cantos, and by Sylvester,[49] it dresses medieval conceptions in the colors of the Renaissance. Even in the midst of his anatomical explorations Fletcher sometimes remembers that he is a poet, but the mythology shares the general characteristics already indicated; what is central and all-sufficing in *Venus and Anchises* is here peripheral and decorative. The conclusion of the poem, an epithalamium on the union of Christ and the church, is an especially good example of the way in which the devout ardors of both the Fletchers received, quite naturally, the most sensuous expression. It is not the least medieval of their qualities, though it can be found in religious poetry of all ages.

[46] Cf. Boethius, *De Consolatione Philosophiae,* ed. A. A Forti Scuto and G. D. Smith (1925), bk. iii, met. 12:

Vos haec fabula respicit
quicumque in superum diem mentem ducere quaeritis.
Nam qui tartareum in specus uictus lumina flexerit,
quidquid praecipuum trahit perdit, dum uidet inferos.

[47] The *Sicelides* as a whole I pass by, partly because I am not dealing with drama, and partly because I find it unreadable. It involves Ovidian and kindred stories, more or less modified, such as that of Glaucus, Circe, and Scylla. Some episodes appear to be related to Browne's *Britannia's Pastorals* (Boas, p. xviii, note 1).

[48] Miss Seaton (page xl, note) supposes that it was "begun about the same time as *Christ's Victorie and Triumph,* published in 1610 (cf. Canto i, st. 59)." Cf. Boas, II, vii.

[49] Upham, *French Influence,* pp. 199–201.

III. WILLIAM BROWNE

The pastoral poetry of William Browne, so easy to read and so easy to forget, has its mild and individual charm, but it concerns us because it embodies some general tendencies in the use of mythology which pass from the age of Spenser to the age of Milton. Whereas poets of the breadth and depth of Spenser and Milton re-create tradition, a writer of Browne's slender talent only reflects it. I am speaking of course of his mythological incidents and allusions, in which he follows the Renaissance tradition, and in general it is not these but the more original and attractive parts of his work that sustain his poetic reputation.

The first book of *Britannia's Pastorals* appeared in 1613, when Browne was presumably twenty-two, and the second book in 1616.[50] The plot makes that of *The Faerie Queene* appear neat and compact, and I shall not try to follow its mazes; it is not Browne's main concern. Of the endless episodes involving shepherds and nymphs a number can be called mythological, but the motives had been handled so often in Renaissance pastorals, foreign or English, that their original character is obscured. For instance, the shepherds Remond and Doridon are in search of Fida, who has vanished; they come upon blood—of a hind— and see the collar of Fida's companion, and Remond is sure that Fida has been slain. It is the situation of Pyramus and Thisbe, but Browne is thinking less of Ovid than of Spenser's story of Florimell,[51] and perhaps *Aminta*.

In the third Song of the second book is the half-Spenserian, half-Ovidian tale of two streams, Walla and Browne's beloved Tavy. Tavy, waiting for Walla, is deaf to the solicitations of other nymphs; after singing in her honor he learns that she has been pursued by a satyr. We are told of the pursuit and of Walla's prayer to Diana; when the satyr follows her into the cave where she has sought refuge she prays again, to the nymph Ina, to transform her into any shape. She is changed into a spring, which drowns the satyr, and flows to join her lover. Tavy arrives, to hear of her fate and to grieve. The story is a mosaic of pastoral and mythological themes and conventions.[52]

In addition to such more or less mythological tales there are endless decorative allusions. Like Spenser, Browne is fond of stating the time of day in this manner:

---

[50] Quotations are from the edition in the Muses' Library. The fullest discussion of Browne, which I have made use of, is that of F. W. Moorman (1897).

[51] *F. Q.*, III. vii–viii; Browne, Bk. ii, Song 2, ll. 349 ff.

[52] "The metamorphosis of Arethusa pursued by Alpheus, of Ambra by Ombrone, of the nymphs by the satyrs of the *Salices*, or as frescoed on the temple of Pales in the *Arcadia*,

> Now great Hyperion left his golden throne
> That on the dancing waves in glory shone,
> For whose declining on the western shore
> The oriental hills black mantles wore . . .

But Spenser might not approve of the conceit. Browne is given rather more than Spenser to the ornamental periphrasis; Hippolytus is "he whose chastity made him a star." We have a good deal of "fiery Titan," "radiant Phoebus," and the rest of the mythological slang which tells us that the bookish view of nature is established, and which, of course, appears in most writing of the time, including Shakespeare's plays, but the character of Browne's material makes it conspicuous in him. In similar style he writes not only of honest sheep but of "fleecy train" and "bleating charge," of the sea and also of the "liquid plain." Homely observation and bookishness may be mingled in the same picture, and the genuine exposes the counterfeit. Yet the bookish elements are by no means all counterfeit or disagreeable:

> This swain, entreated by the mirthful rout,
> That with entwined arms lay round about
> The tree 'gainst which he lean'd, (so have I seen
> Tom Piper stand upon our village green,
> Back'd with the May-pole, whilst a jocund crew
> In gentle motion circularly threw
> Themselves about him), to his fairest ring
> Thus 'gan in numbers well according sing:

> Venus by Adonis' side
> Crying kiss'd, and kissing cried,
> Wrung her hands and tore her hair
> For Adonis dying there.[53]

The lyric takes us back to the songs of Greene, though Browne is lighter and more sophisticated in tone.

In describing persons Browne makes abundant use of mythological parallels and conceits, fanciful and extravagant in the Elizabethan manner. Phoebus looked on the bright eyes of Walla

the loves of Mulla and Mollana in Spenser, and the mythological impersonations of the *Polyolbion*, find, as it were, a meeting-place in Browne's lay of Walla" (W. W. Greg, *Pastoral Poetry and Pastoral Drama*, p. 137).

While one constantly meets Ovidian themes more or less disguised by the pastoral convention, Browne does occasionally recount a classical myth without changing the names. The story of Cephalus and Procris receives two dozen lines (toward the end of the fourth Song in the first book). The last three hundred lines of the fragmentary third book are devoted to Cupid and Psyche. Reminiscences of Adlington show that Browne had a text before him, but of course he wandered from the original tale. He added a pastoral episode, and a description of Psyche's beauties which alone fills a third of the piece. The story has hardly got under way when it ends with the suggestion that Psyche's loveliness is painted with "Caelia" in mind.

[53] Bk. ii, Song 2, ll. 95 ff.

And by their radiance was the god struck blind,
That clean awry th' ecliptic then he stripp'd
And from the milky way his horses whipp'd;
So that the Eastern world to fear begun
Some stranger drove the chariot of the sun.[54]

Mythological comparisons are used singly and in series. Now and then
the effect is happy; more often, since Browne lacks Marlowe's gift of
phrase, it is little better than boyish pedantry. Sometimes there are
verbal echoes of Marlowe; for instance the four lines on Leander's
dangling tresses and the golden fleece are twice imitated, the heady
wine of the original becoming somewhat pale and diluted.[55]

Browne imitates other motives and devices that Marlowe had made
popular, arguments against virginity,[56] gnomic lines,[57] myth-making.[58]
The influence of Marlowe of course cannot always be isolated from
that of Marlowe's disciples. The following passage might be said to be
compounded, with variations, from *Hero and Leander, Venus and
Adonis,* and *Endimion and Phœbe:*

Narcissus' change sure Ovid clean mistook,
He died not looking in a crystal brook,
But (as those which in emulation gaze)
He pin'd to death by looking on this face.
When he stood fishing by some river's brim,
The fish would leap, more for a sight of him
Than for the fly. The eagle, highest bred,
Was taking him once up for Ganymede.
The shag-hair'd satyrs, and the tripping fawns,
With all the troop that frolic on the lawns,
Would come and gaze on him, as who should say
They had not seen his like this many a day.
Yea, Venus knew no difference 'twixt these twain,
Save Adon was a hunter, this a swain.[59]

These lines, and thirty more that continue the formula, are, in
substance, diction, rhythm, closer to Drayton than to anyone else. The
lavishly "conceited" description of Walla, part of which has been quoted,
is likewise in the vein of Drayton. Indeed Drayton is for Browne "our

[54] Bk. ii, Song 3, ll. 800 ff.
[55] Bk. i, Song 1, ll. 255 ff., 481 ff.
[56] Bk. i, Song 1, ll. 634 ff.; Song 2, ll. 570 ff.; Bk. ii, Song 3, ll. 939 ff.
[57] Bk. i, Song 1, ll. 77–78; Song 3, ll. 289–90; and *passim.* One example may be quoted:
"True loue is mute, and oft amazed stands" (Marlowe, i. 186); "But love surpriz'd the
hart, the tongue is dumbe" (Drayton, *E. and P.,* p. 20); "Love often makes the speech's
organs mute" (Browne, Bk. i, Song 2, l. 549).
[58] For example, Bk. i, Song 2, ll. 411 ff. (see just below); Bk. ii, Song 1, ll. 211 ff.;
and see the lines about Walla quoted above.
[59] Bk. i, Song 2, ll. 411 ff.

second Ovid." His soft, flowing sweetness was more congenial than the energy of Marlowe; congenial too were Drayton's idealism and his combination of pastoral, mythological, patriotic, and fairy lore. But such generalities call up the greater name of Spenser, whom Browne loved especially to praise, and among whose disciples he is regularly listed. Some Spenserian qualities in Browne's treatment of mythology we have noticed, and the influence of Spenser is often merged with that of a fellow Spenserian like Drayton.

Browne's references and quotations show his considerable learning. He cites not merely the ancient authors commonly read, but some of the less familiar, such as Apollonius Rhodius, Pausanias, Silius Italicus.[60] The chief classical influence is that of Ovid. The adaptation of Ovidian tales to pastoral uses has been touched on already. The allegorical figure of Limos, in the second book, is mainly compounded out of Ovid's *jejuna Fames* and Erysichthon, and the episode perhaps owes something to Dante.[61] There are many Ovidian details as well. No poet of the time knew country life better than Browne, or took more pleasure in describing what he saw with his own eyes, yet he testifies to the power of literary tradition when he paraphrases the elaborate simile of hare and hound that occurs in the tale of Apollo and Daphne[62]—the simile that Shakespeare remembered in his picture of poor Wat.

Browne's elaborate account of the golden age necessarily embodies many of the features sanctified by Ovid and his numerous successors, but he has less familiar details too. His people are not vegetarians, and instead of idleness we have "Labour the salad that their stomachs bred." The customary praise of rural innocence and simplicity leads to satire on modern extravagance, and, what is more novel, to praise of communism, an idea drawn apparently from Don Quixote's discourse to the goat-herds.[63] But for a number of the less traditional details Browne seems to be chiefly indebted to Chaucer's *Former Age.*

The mention of Chaucer reminds us of Browne's unusual knowledge of medieval literature; his special interest in Occleve is well known. Both

---

[60] Without casting unjust slurs upon Browne's scholarship one may illustrate the way in which abstruse erudition could travel about. For the Fates as sisters of Pan Browne cites "Pronapis in suo Protocosmo" (Bk. ii, Song 4, l. 888). Abraham Fraunce had quoted the same authority for a full account of creation and the birth of Pan, the Fates, and other deities, and he took it all from Leo Hebraeus. See the Appendix, under 1592.

[61] Moorman, pp. 52–55. On Lyly's use of the Ovidian episode and probably Boccaccio also, see V. M. Jeffery, *John Lyly,* pp. 87–88.

[62] Bk. ii, Song 3, ll. 1133 ff. It may be added that our country dweller, unlike his illustrious and skeptical namesake, accepts the tradition concerning the legs of the badger (Bk. i, Song 4, ll. 91 ff.).

[63] Bk. ii, Song 3, l. 425; *Don Quixote,* bk. ii, c. 3. Shelton's translation appeared in 1612. See Moorman, pp. 59 ff.

directly and as a Spenserian he has affinities with medieval allegory and satire. Then, although he knows Camden and Selden, he is too proud of the glories of Elizabethan England to pass over the story of "mighty Brute" and "the brave issue of the Trojan line." [64] He praises Robert of Gloucester, and other early bards who had sung of Brute,

> Striving in spite of all the mists of eld,
> To have his story more authentic held.[65]

And, though he quotes Homer in Greek, he tells of a nymph who meets Thetis singing a lay that she had learned from "a skilful swain," Joseph of Exeter.[66]

With the best of Browne's work, the fresh and loving observation of rural scenes and manners, we have not been much concerned; we have rather, not quite fairly, been indicating unhealthy symptoms of pseudo-classicism. But it is not insignificant that a writer of Browne's quality, an ancestor of a long line of genuine poets of nature, should so readily take the literary coloring of the Renaissance pastoral. Sometimes he looks at nature and man for himself, still oftener he looks through a mythological haze. The results of the latter process are as yet seldom unpleasant, but mythology is on the way to becoming a nuisance.

Browne's classicism is of the external kind and quite impure. He is half medieval in his mixtures of classical and unclassical matter, in his rather wooden allegory, in the nature of his satire, in his wayward narrative style. In these respects, and in his combination of moral serious-ness and sensuousness, he is of course a Spenserian. Though less warm and luxuriant than Spenser, Browne can enjoy pictorial beauty for its own sake, as, for example, in the well-known lines on the maiden undressing which caught the eye of a greater artist. Or, again like a mild Spenser, he can present temptation with more pretty paganism than Miltonic severity would allow, as when a nymph tries to seduce Tavy from his loyalty to Walla.[67] But neither seriousness nor sensuousness in Browne has much vitality.

---

[64] Bk. ii, Song 1, ll. 93, 105. Browne quotes "Galf. Monum."
[65] Bk. ii, Song 4, ll. 241–42.
[66] Bk. ii, Song 3, l. 628. The reader is directed to Selden's notes on *Polyolbion*.
[67] Bk. ii, Song 3, ll. 953 ff.

CHAPTER NINE

MINOR WRITERS

THE line of more or less Spenserian poets discussed in the last chapter has anticipated chronology, and we must return to the period following *Hero and Leander* and *Venus and Adonis*. Those two poems, along with the general influence of Spenser, had established the popularity of the Italianate mythological narrative, the Renaissance epyllion, and young men who were in the movement eagerly worked the new vein. As in our day *Eminent Victorians* and *Queen Victoria* virtually banished the two-volume official Life, so the sensuous and pictorial manner conquered the bald and moral,[1] and it was a tune which, like that of satirical portraiture, every warbler soon had by heart.

The two best minor poems in the new convention, *Endimion and Phœbe* and *Venus and Anchises,* have already been noticed, and the present chronicle is of rather small beer. Indeed an unfriendly critic, observing the brief prime and the protracted decadence of the Renaissance genre, might say with Rosalind, "You'll be rotten ere you be half ripe, and that's the right virtue of the medlar." For signs of quick-coming decay were visible even in *Hero and Leander* and *Venus and Adonis,* fresh and youthful in many ways as those poems were. But a number of minor writers justify attention because of either modest poetical merit or historical interest. Of course only a select few can be mentioned here.[2] In addition to poems of the new style, such as Marston's dubious *Metamorphosis of Pygmalion's Image,* the *Salmacis and Hermaphroditus* ascribed to Beaumont, and Barksted's *Mirrha,* we shall take account of some other authors, Davies, Heywood, Basse, and Bosworth, who must be labeled miscellaneous.

I. JOHN MARSTON

Between 1593 and 1598 appeared about fifteen mythological poems of various kinds, most of them touched with Italianate coloring, and some, like those of "T. H.," Barnfield, Drayton, Thomas Edwards, following closely the style of the acknowledged masters. A mythological tale being

[1] A goodly number of old-fashioned poetasters remained unconquerable, as the Appendix testifies.
[2] For a full record of imitations of Marlowe or Shakespeare or both see the index. The series begins with the recently discovered *Oenone and Paris* of 1594, written by one "T. H."

the fashionable exercise for a young man who wished to commence author, the most unlikely persons tried their hand at it. One of these was John Marston. *The Metamorphosis of Pygmalion's Image* was published, along with "certain satires," in 1598.

In prefatory verses "To his Mistress" the poet declares

> My wanton muse lasciviously doth sing
> Of sportive love, of lovely dallying,

and he proceeds, in the manner of so many earlier amatory pieces, to identify himself with Pygmalion, at least to the extent of hoping for a similar consummation.[3] The poem itself is written in the popular sixain stanza. Only the beginning and end are at all close to Ovid, and the embellishments are largely of the kind promised in the verses quoted. The statue is made in the second stanza, and many stanzas are devoted to Pygmalion's raptures of admiration. Bodily beauties are itemized with conventional completeness, and the ensuing dalliance is described with more than conventional detail. The poem has something of the smoothness that is characteristic of the genre, but is quite lacking in charm or beauty.

There is perhaps less interest in the piece itself than in the question of the author's motive. Following the narrative are lines in the crabbed style of the satires, "The Author in praise of his precedent Poem," which repudiate any serious intention in

> The Salaminian titillations,
> Which tickle up our lewd Priapians.
> Is not my pen complete? Are not my lines
> Right in the swaggering humour of these times?

In the sixth satire of *The Scourge of Villanie* Marston gives a good many lines to *Pygmalion's Image,* maintaining that it was written as a burlesque:

> Curio, know'st my sprite?
> Yet deem'st that in sad seriousness I write
> Such nasty stuff as is *Pygmalion?*

Scholars in general have not accepted this declaration "in sad seriousness."[4] I am inclined to believe it. Mr. Allen, who is not, remarks that "we feel that he himself while writing was never emotionally carried away; the poem is always cold and intellectual." Cold and intellectual sensuality is certainly favorable to the notion of satire. The authorities of

[3] *Works of Marston,* ed. Bullen, III, 251 ff.
[4] E.g., Grosart, Bullen, Winckler (*John Marston's litterarische Anfänge,* 1903, p. 38); Morse Allen, *The Satire of John Marston,* 1920, pp. 88 ff. Marston's poem is referred to as a satire by Mr. G. Kitchin, though he does not discuss it (*Survey of Burlesque and Parody in English,* 1931, p. x).

London, like modern scholars, did not perceive an adequate satirical intention, but it has always been the fate of irony to be misunderstood; one might invoke the somewhat greater names of Defoe, Swift, Burke. Besides, Marston had a heavy hand, and a burlesque of erotic poetry needs a light touch. The extravagances of the sonneteering craze had been laughed at in Davies' *Gulling Sonnets,* and to a literary aspirant of strongly satirical bent the vogue of the sensuous mythological poem might well seem to invite an ironic piece of studied excess.[5]

But there are more than general reasons for accepting Marston's statements. If one comes to the poem after *Hero and Leander* or *Venus and Adonis* one perceives a real difference in tone. There are bits of satire, about papists and busk-points, which are echoed in the formal satires.[6] There is an undercurrent of mockery and jocularity that runs from the prefatory verses "To his Mistress" through the poem itself. To cite only an instance or two:

> And therefore, ladies, think that they ne'er love you,
> Who do not unto more than kissing move you . . .

> And now, O now, he finds how he is graced
> By his own work! Tut! women will relent
> When as they find such moving blandishment.[7]

There is no space for illustrating further a quality that seems evident enough. It may be said that Marston's indecency is hardly that of a reforming satirist. But, as his satires show, Marston, like many another censor of society, derived a vicarious gratification from detailed accounts of the vices he attacked, and, as I have said, he had a heavy hand.

A burlesque would naturally glance at the most popular poems of the type. Mr. Allen observes that Marston later hinted, without actually asserting, "that the *Pygmalion* contained definite hits at contemporary poetry. These have been sought for, of course vainly, by modern critics." [8] But the echoes of Marlowe seem fairly audible. To quote only the head and tail pieces, in "To his Mistress" we have this:

> Thy favours, like Promethean sacred fire,
> In dead and dull conceit can life inspire.

Marlowe had written

> Whose liuely heat like fire from heauen fet,
> Would animate grosse clay, and higher set
> The drooping thoughts of base declining soules.

---

[5] In the opening lines of his second satire Marston apparently refers to the poem when he speaks of having "even now lisp'd like an amorist," and of being himself "not immaculate." But the former phrase does not necessarily disprove a satirical purpose, and the latter is too vague to have any force.
[6] Cf. pp. 254-55, 357.   [7] Ll. 119-20, 172-74.   [8] P. 92.

In "The Author in praise of his precedent Poem" Marston asks

> Do not I flatter, call her wondrous fair,
> Virtuous, divine, most debonair?

Marlowe's oft-echoed lines are these:

> But you are faire (aye me) so wondrous faire,
> So yoong, so gentle, and so debonaire.

Marston more than once sneers at lovers who pule "Aye me." [9] There are other more or less evident allusions to *Hero and Leander,* or echoes of its phrasing, which may be thought sufficient to prove a satirical purpose, but they are too numerous to be quoted.[10]

II. FRANCIS BEAUMONT (?): *SALMACIS AND HERMAPHRODITUS*

Salmacis and Hermaphroditus (1602) was published anonymously at first, but in editions of 1640 and later the name of Francis Beaumont was attached to it. Our knowledge of booksellers' methods, the fact that Beaumont must have been eighteen or thereabouts, and differences in style and temper between this poem and the dramatist's undisputed writings, have generally inclined scholars to think that Beaumont was not the author. On the other hand it has been argued that the piece is not beyond the capacity of a precocious Elizabethan young man, that it shows characteristics of Beaumont's mature style which, though not

[9] *Scourge,* vi. 18; viii. 33, 52. Cf. Drayton's sonnet "To the Reader," 1599 (ed. Brett, p. 28). In Marston's second satire in the same book there is a very palpable hit at Marlowe:

> Here Jove's lust-pander, Maia's juggling son,
> In clown's disguise, doth after milkmaids run.

[10] The more tangible correspondences are these:

MARSTON	MARLOWE
L. 19	ii. 317, 324
Ll. 38–39	i. 21–22
Ll. 78, 80, 84, 91 (on the dumbness of the statue)	i. 186 (and Hero's prolonged silence)
Ll. 117–18	ii. 51 ff.
Ll. 134–35	i. 299 ff.
L. 149	ii. 153
L. 155	ii. 248
Ll. 219–20	ii. 255–57, ii. 67 ff.

There are not many tangible links between *Pygmalion* and *Venus and Adonis.* Pygmalion's protracted dalliance and the statue's silence remind one of the relations between Shakespeare's pair (cf. Marston's "dull image," l. 78, the couplet quoted above from "To his Mistress," and "image dull and dead," *V. and A.,* l. 212). There is a fairly clear echo in the epilogue, though one need not take Labeo as Shakespeare:

> So Labeo did complain his love was stone,
> Obdurate, flinty, so relentless none.

Cf. *V. and A.,* ll. 199–200. See Chambers, *William Shakespeare,* II, 195.

For notes on Marston's poem in relation to Shakespeare's plays, see Root, *Classical Mythology in Shakespeare,* p. 103; C. Winckler, *Englische Studien,* XXXIII (1904), 216; C. Fries, *ibid.,* XXXIV, 445; H. Carrington Lancaster, *S. P.,* XXIX (1932), 233.

marked, may be set over against the alleged differences. The mythological poem of the age was to a large degree *sui generis,* and if *Hero and Leander* and *Venus and Adonis* were anonymous one might hesitate to assign them to the authors of *Doctor Faustus* and *Hamlet. Salmacis and Hermaphroditus* is superior to most of its fellows in the Marlowe-Shakespeare tradition, and one would like to identify the writer, but the evidence is vague and not conclusive either for or against Beaumont.[11]

"My wanton lines doe treate of amorous loue," the poet begins, and the promise is amply fulfilled. Skipping fancy expands the Ovidian tale to something over nine hundred lines. Diana, we learn, had resolved to slay the youth whose attractions kept her nymphs from hunting, but she herself fell a victim, and instead of an arrow she bestowed a kiss.

> Then the boy ran; for (some say) had he stayd,
> Diana had no longer bene a mayd.

Further mythological inventions are employed to describe his beauty. Ovid's account of the lad's explorations is paraphrased, but the poet breaks off to indulge in a long and luscious account of Salmacis. She was loved by Jove, who promised to make her a star, but Salmacis-Pamela would not yield until her suitor gained the consent of Astraea. Jove then sought Astraea's court, which was not unlike that of Elizabeth:

> But there was such busie rout before,
> Some seruing men, and some promooters bee,
> That he could passe no foote without a fee;
> But as he goes, he reaches out his hands,
> And payes each one in order as he stands;
> And still, as he was paying those before,
> Some slipt againe betwixt him and the dore.

Jove finds Venus pleading against Vulcan, and, after he has won Astraea's consent to the elevation of Salmacis, he is overtaken by Venus, who urges him to bring no more wantons to heaven. Unsuccessful, Venus, by her own unfailing method, persuades Vulcan to refuse to supply Jove with thunderbolts, and the two go to Jove's palace and threaten him until he agrees to give up Salmacis, though he makes her twice as beautiful as before.

The poet returns to Ovid, but not for long. A mere chance encounter between hero and heroine is not enough, the gods must take a hand. Bacchus saw and loved the nymph, but Apollo

[11] Quotations are from the text in the *Shakespeare Society's Papers,* III (1847), 98 ff. The poem is also in Chalmers, VI, 210 ff. To mention only two discussions, G. C. Macaulay opposed the attribution to Beaumont (*Francis Beaumont,* London, 1883, pp. 21, 197 ff.), while Mr. Gayley considers the case against Beaumont not proven (*Beaumont the Dramatist,* New York, 1914, pp. 38 ff.).

> kept her from the sweets of Bacchus bed,
> And 'gainst her wil he sau'd her maiden-head.

Bacchus complained to Mercury (whose character and functions are described) and Mercury stole the wheels from Apollo's chariot. Apollo offered to show Salmacis the most beautiful youth that ever was if she would obtain the wheels again . . . But it is needless to go through the whole piece. The conclusion, though freely handled, is necessarily closer to Ovid.

The probability that the author did not use a foreign redaction of Ovid is perhaps strengthened by the fact that, although he does not often follow the Ovidian story, he reproduces phrases from Golding. *Venus and Adonis* doubtless influenced the choice of subject and to some degree the general tone, but there is very little specific borrowing; the most obvious bit occurs in the amorous pleading of Salmacis.

Much stronger is the influence of Marlowe, as it is in most of these poems. Those three purple patches in the first part of *Hero and Leander*, the descriptions of the maiden, the youth, and the temple, are clearly imitated. Indeed the picture of Astraea's throne is almost plain theft:

> Then she descended from her stately throne,
> Which seat was builded all of iasper stone,
> And o're the seat was paynted all aboue,
> The wanton unseene stealths of amorous Joue.
> There might a man behold the naked pride
> Of louely Venus in the vale of Ide . . .[12]

Then in the episode of Bacchus and Salmacis there are parallels, partly verbal, with both the meeting of Hero and Leander in the temple and the incident of Mercury and the country maid; this last item may also have suggested the bargain between Apollo and the nymph. The amorous arguments of Salmacis are conventional, of course, but it was Marlowe who had chiefly made them so, and enough of Marlowe's phrasing is echoed to leave no doubt. In short, there are few pages which do not show the stamp of Marlowe, in mythological descriptions, conceits, invented episodes, gnomic lines.[13]

The poem is written with fluent ease. In spite of the excessive play of fancy and memory the narrative is clear and rapid. There is no straining

[12] P. 107. Marlowe's lines on the temple are quoted above, page 128.
[13] To mention some items of probably more remote origin, the business of Venus and Vulcan recalls Venus' persuading Vulcan to make arms for Aeneas. The author may have known Homer; at any rate he knew "the rosie fingred morne." The incident of Bacchus and Salmacis may have been adapted from the story of Bacchus and Ariadne. Finally, although there were accounts of deities in current handbooks and elsewhere, the description of Mercury (pp. 114–15) suggests a partial paraphrase of Horace's tenth ode.

after effect. Epithets are mostly conventional, but quite adequate for the plane on which the story is conceived, and the imagery, though luxuriant, is always definite. The writer works the voluptuous vein with relish, of course, but he is not at all possessed by his theme. His cool, genial detachment appears in occasional touches of humor. For a further instance, one couplet, in the account of the story told by Jove to Astraea, pleasantly vivifies the amiable and elderly rake:

> But a faire Nymph was bathing when he waked,
> (Here sigh'd great Joue, and after brought forth) nak'd.[14]

III. WILLIAM BARKSTED

A mythological poem less lively than *Salmacis and Hermaphroditus,* but not without some gleams of poetry, was the *Mirrha* (1607) of William Barksted, the actor.[15] Ovid tells the story of Myrrha's passion for her father in two hundred and twenty lines; Barksted's version runs to almost nine hundred, and not only the general texture but the added episodes illustrate his debt to the popular models.

After some stanzas on Orpheus and his power of song we are told that the lovely and innocent Myrrha, a servant of Vesta, was one of a number of maidens who gathered to hear Orpheus sing. The bard falls in love with Myrrha and urges his suit, while she appeals to her vows of virginity. This romantic and un-Ovidian incident occupies more than a hundred lines. The story proper then follows Ovid, apart from details and an episode or two.[16] To mention another item, which is a reminder of the close relations between the mythological narrative and the pastoral, Myrrha has an encounter with a satyr, and Diana, angry at the profanation of her grove, transforms the satyr into a poplar, which hangs down its head for the loss of Myrrha. The conclusion of the story, except for the length of Myrrha's final prayer, is Ovidian.

Phrases scattered through the Ovidian portions of the poem show Barksted's dependence on Golding. The commendatory verses of Robert Glover allude to *Venus and Adonis,* and Barksted himself, in declining to carry his tale beyond the birth of Adonis, ends with a compliment to Shakespeare. The popularity of Shakespeare's poem had suggested a

---

[14] P. 108.

[15] Ed. Grosart, 1876. The full title is *Mirrha The Mother of Adonis: or Lustes Prodegies.* See *Metam.* x. 298 ff.

[16] For example, Myrrha carries on a sort of dialogue with her father's picture. Further, near the end of the tale a myth of Hebe is introduced; Jove's handmaiden had spilled nectar in heaven and it fell down, enriching Panchaia "with odorous smell." Cf. the end of E. K.'s gloss on Spenser's eclogue for November. Though the handbooks tell of Hebe's falling while she waited on Jove, I have not noticed a source for the spilling of nectar.

related theme, and Barksted frequently imitates the phrasing and rhythms.

But, though *Mirrha* is commonly referred to as one of the progeny of *Venus and Adonis,* Barksted's chief debt is to Marlowe. The enamorment of Orpheus and Myrrha is closely modeled on the meeting of Hero and Leander, as even my brief outline will have indicated, and the fact is made doubly sure by such lines as these:

> My heart is the true index of my tongue.
> And by my naked wordes you may discouer,
> I am not traded like a common Louer . . .

> With this, she turnd her blushing head aside,
> & vail'd her face with lawne, not half so white . . .

The decorative digression on Hebe recalls Marlowe's incident of Mercury and the country maid; indeed Barksted has it in mind when he writes "Women are enuious, where they long for nectar." Marlowe's trick of the ætiological conceit was learned by Barksted as well as by others:

> Then blusht he [the sun] first, and backward would
> ha fled
> And euer since in rising hee's still red.

Aphoristic or gnomic lines, like mythological conceits, by this time were a trick of the trade, and every imitation of Marlowe and Shakespeare had made them commoner; Barksted of course has his share of them.[17]

Although Barksted borrows and imitates so freely, and in general falls far below his masters, he has a few lines that neither Marlowe nor Shakespeare would have disowned. For instance, he probably remembered Shakespeare's line about the boar—"His eyes like glow-worms shine when he doth fret" [18]—but he amplified and improved the image:

> As glow wormes adde a tincture to the night,
> Glimmering in pallid fire, upon some greene,
> mixt with the dew, so did her eyes appeare.

That fine phrase, "glimmering in pallid fire," indeed describes the reflection, in Barksted and some other small poets, of the Elizabethan glow and voluptuousness of style.[19] And Barksted would be less obscure if he had written more lines like these:

[17] Barksted's *Hiren* (1611), which tells the story, taken probably from Painter, of Mahomet and his fair captive, lies outside of our range. It also reveals some traces of Marlowe and Shakespeare.

[18] Cf. Lyly, *The Woman in the Moone* (Bond, III, 271):
> And yet as bright as Glow wormes in the night,
> With which the morning decks her louers hayre.

[19] Gosse, *Jacobean Poets* (New York, 1894), p. 112.

Night like a masque was entred heauens greate hall
with thousand torches ushering the way.

The personifying habit fostered by mythology was not always a vice.[20]

Before going on to two late representatives of the Ovidian tradition, James Shirley and Cowley, we may look at the less readily definable work of Davies, Heywood, Basse, and Bosworth. If Richard Brathwait's poetical quality at all corresponded to the bulk of his mythological writing he would demand consideration here also, but as it is I hesitate to release him from the cave of dullness; the curious, if such there be, will find brief notices there—in the Appendix, that is—from 1611 onward.

IV. SIR JOHN DAVIES

Mythology has appeared in many strange guises, but perhaps few stranger than the "suddaine, rash, half-capreol" of Sir John Davies' wit, *Orchestra, or A Poeme of Dauncing* (1596). When Homer sang of Ulysses and Penelope, he forgot, it seems, "one thing most worthy his eternall song," the courtly love proffered to the queen by "Antinous

[20] These last lines also occur near the end of Marston's *Insatiate Countess* (ed. Bullen, III, 243), which is thought to have been revamped by Barksted. One may be allowed to add that a line of English verse can hardly fail of rhetorical effect if it has "thousand" as the second and third syllables. Thus Golding rises (ed. Rouse, p. 92, ll. 544–45):

A thousand wayes, a thousand gates that alwayes open stand,
This Citie hath.

And this bit of Ovid recalls the famous lines which show that Nat Lee was not always mad or bad (*Oedipus*, Act V; *Works*, 1722, I, 343):

Thou Coward yet
Art living, canst not, wilt not find the Road
To the great Palace of magnificent Death;
Tho thousand Ways lead to his thousand Doors,
Which Day and Night are still unbarr'd for all.

Another item of interest in connection with *Mirrha* is the fact that one stanza echoes some lines in *Measure for Measure*:

And like as, when some suddaine extasie,
seiseth the nature of a sicklie man,
When hee's discernd to swoune, straite by and by
folke to his helpe confusedly haue ran,
And seeking with their art to fetch him backe:
so many throng, that he the ayre doth lacke.

Cf. *M. for M.*, II. iv. 25 ff. In the Cambridge edition of the play (pp. 132, 118) Mr. Dover Wilson, without alluding to Barksted, observes that ll. 25–30, "which have been generally taken as a complimentary reference to King James's hatred of crowds, read like a later addition."

I have not seen three eclogues by Lewis Machin which were appended to *Mirrha;* two of them dealt with Apollo and Hyacinth, in the approved idyllic-erotic manner (see W. W. Greg, *Pastoral Poetry and Pastoral Drama*, p. 116). To Barksted has been attributed a poem of 1617, a "tragicall narration of Virginias death," which was added to a version of Juvenal's tenth satire "as an illustration of the preceding reflections on the curse of beauty" (R. W. Bond, *Works of W. Basse*, p. xlii; see Brydges, *Restituta*, I, 41; H. R. Palmer, pp. 66–67). I have not seen the piece.

that fresh and iolly knight." [21] This story Davies' light and graceful muse is called upon to tell.

On a festive evening in the palace, when Phemius recites tales of Troy, and Penelope, endowed by Pallas with new beauty, comes in to hear him, Antinous asks her to dance. Her avowed ignorance of the art leads Antinous to commence a long discourse on dancing, which— like Browne's quincunx—appears to be the central principle of the universe. Creation itself, the distribution of the four elements "by Loue's perswasion," are part of the eternal rhythm. The conventional Platonism of these stanzas reminds one of the opening lines of a poem published in the same year, Spenser's first *Hymn;* one is reminded too, as the dance of planets and elements proceeds, of the arguments of Spenser's Titaness, Mutability. Earth alone stands still, though some say it is the earth that moves.[22] Flowers wave in the wind, birds skip from bough to bough, everything in the world is dancing—"Learne then to daunce, you that are Princes borne."

Mythology contributes all manner of examples, at least when reinterpreted. Whatever lewd wits may say, the net that held Venus and Mars together was only the embrace of dancers. But for dancing and the sound of timbrels the infant Jove would have perished. Proteus—as Lucian had said—was a versatile dancer. Caeneus and Tiresias, who were reputed to have changed their sex, sometimes took the woman's part in dancing. Did Venus change herself to a fish? No, she "did daunce with slyding easines." Dancing, in short, is

> The faire caracter of the World's consent,
> The Heau'ns true figure and th' Earth's ornament.

Penelope ventures to cite instances to the contrary, but Antinous goes on to praise "that true Loue which Dauncing did inuent" in Platonic language:

> Life's life it is, and cordiall to the heart,
> And of our better part, the better part.

He longs to convince her, and in answer to his prayei Love appears, with a mirror, the sight of which fills Penelope with winged thoughts—for Vulcan had wrought in it

> Our glorious English Courts diuine image,
> As it should be in this our Golden Age.

Orchestra illustrates the readiness with which a man of the Renaissance

---

[21] *Complete Poems of Sir John Davies,* ed. Grosart (1876), I, 161 ff. The poem was entered in 1594. Bullen notices Davies' borrowings from Lucian (*Some Longer Elizabethan Poems,* pp. vii–ix).
[22] St. 51.

turned to mythology for the embellishment of serious as well as fanciful ideas. *Nosce Teipsum* (1599) is of course wholly serious. Neither *Orchestra* nor the *Epigrams* nor the early misadventures of the genial but choleric lawyer would prepare us for one of the few elaborate philosophical poems in English. With Davies' ideas, and his debts to Primaudaye and Mornay, we are not concerned, but we may notice that even in a treatise on the soul and immortality he does not abandon myth.

Some of his adaptations are traditional, others perhaps original. "Fond fruitlesse curiositie" seeks "in bookes prophane . . . for knowledge hid."

> What is this knowledge but the sky-stolne fire,
> For which the thiefe still chain'd in ice doth sit?
> And which the poore rude Satyre did admire,
> And needs would kisse but burnt his lips with it.[23]

Io, transformed into a cow, was horrified at the sight of herself in the water; so man's soul, when its innocence is spotted with sin, cannot bear to contemplate itself.[24] But it is needless to enumerate examples. The allegorical allusions, in a poem of such a character, have a degree of subtlety lacking in Golding and his predecessors, yet they belong to the same tradition.

V. THOMAS HEYWOOD

The sheer industry of Thomas Heywood appalls a faint-hearted modern reader. As if it were not enough, according to his own famous statement, to have had either an entire hand, or at the least a main finger, in over two hundred plays, he produced monstrous non-dramatic works the mere transcription of which would, one might think, occupy a life of penal servitude.[25]

In 1609 appeared *Troia Britanica,* a poem of about thirteen thousand lines, mainly in the *ottava rima* that Harington and Fairfax had made

[23] *Poems,* I, 17.
[24] *Ibid.,* I, 21.
[25] One need only mention Heywood's formal translations of the *Ars Amatoria* and *De Remedio Amoris.* The former went through at least eight editions, the last appearing in 1705; the version of the *De Remedio* seems to have been lost, or at any rate not identified. While the translation is not distinguished, it shows, along with Heywood's letters of Paris and Helen—and one may add Drayton's *Heroical Epistles*—the importance of Ovidian elegiacs in molding the closed couplet.

Heywood charged one Austin—justly, it would appear—with feloniously appropriating his translations. See the Appendix, under "H. A.," 1613, and the article by Mr. A. M. Clark there cited. See also Mr. Clark's "A Bibliography of Thomas Heywood," *Oxford Bibliographical Society Proceedings and Papers,* Vol. I, Part 2 (1925), pp. 97 ff. For critical comments on the works of Heywood noticed here, see Mr. Clark's *Thomas Heywood* (1931).

Heywood had more than his share of trials at the hands of pirates. To the third edition (1612) of *The Passionate Pilgrim* Jaggard, who had published *Troia Britanica,* added from that work the Ovidian epistles of Paris and Helen and passages from the other Ovidian translations which Heywood had incorporated in his notes.

popular. Apart from episodical digressions, the subject matter of the "xvii. seuerall Cantons" is chiefly the story of Troy, from the time of chaos and creation to the fall of the city; the last two cantos bring Brute to England and chronicle the English kings down to James. The title and scope of the book are significant enough, and its medieval character is further illustrated in Heywood's choice and handling of sources.[26]

The dedication mentions Homer and Virgil as authorities, but one's anticipations of classical orthodoxy are not altogether fulfilled, since not much use is made of either. The fifteenth canto follows the Virgilian account of the fall of Troy, though un-Virgilian details are included. The *Iliad* seems to contribute a few bits, such as the death of Patroclus and Thetis' procuring new arms for Achilles. The treatment of this last incident shows Heywood's eclectic method. The visit of Thetis to Hephaestus is Homeric, her speech is not; she returns to Achilles with a helmet, gorget, "vaunt-brace," and other pieces; the description of the shield, much briefer than in Homer, retains a few items, names the signs of the zodiac, and, instead of the matchless vignettes of scenes of peace and war, gives allegorical figures of the seasons.[27]

Some knowledge of Homer does not necessitate the abjuring of Dares. "The description of the Troians be according to Dares the Troian, who liued in the warres of Troy, and writ their utter subuersion." [28] Indeed, as the example of Warner might lead one to expect, Heywood's main source is Caxton's *Recuyell,* though he does not emphasize the fact; like medieval authors, he prefers ancient names. Throughout the book he offers a bewildering array of authorities; how many are taken over from other compilations one cannot inquire. Thus in his opening pages on the creation, where Caxton fails him, Heywood invokes such various opinions as those of Thales, Moses, Polydore Vergil, Hesiod, Pherecrates, Trismegistus, Marsilio Ficino, Tibullus, to mention only a few.[29]

The source next in importance to Caxton is Ovid. Heywood's ninth and tenth cantos are largely taken up with translations of the epistles of Paris and Helen. In the notes especially are incorporated passages translated from the *Ars Amatoria,* such as the tales of Cephalus and Procris and Bacchus and Ariadne. Incidents like the quarrel between

[26] See J. S. P. Tatlock, "The Siege of Troy in Elizabethan Literature," *P. M. L. A.,* XXX, 683 ff.

[27] Canto xiii, pp. 339 ff.

[28] Pp. 192–93. But the account (pp. 175 ff.) of Priam and his family is much more detailed than in Dares (c. 12), and seems to be taken, along with the ascription to Dares, from Caxton (ed. Sommer, pp. 543–44). Dictys is also cited (e.g., p. 333).

[29] An instance may be given of the circuitous route by which knowledge traveled. In the thirteenth canto (p. 333) Hector and Ajax interchange as gifts a sword and a girdle; the sword became the instrument of Ajax' suicide, the girdle was used to tie Hector's body to Achilles' chariot. Although Heywood has a quotation from Aeschylus (in Latin), and one

Ajax and Ulysses, and many details, come from the *Metamorphoses;*
yet the story of Callisto, as we have observed, elaborates the vivacious
realism of Warner.[30] Nothing can be said of Heywood's other sources,
for he ranges far and wide, but it may be added that his account of a
feast given in Troy to the Greeks is indebted to Greene's *Euphues his
Censure to Philautus.*

Troia Britanica is obviously a medieval chronicle, not an epic, but it is
quite readable. Heywood is an adequate story-teller, and his digressions
and topical allusions are not dull. Thus in the fourth canto remarks on
the birth of Venus lead, very logically, through stanzas on religious sects
to the character of the Brownist or puritan whose

> phrase is, Verily; By yea and nay,
> In faith, in truth, good neighbor, or good brother,
> And when he borrowes mony, nere will pay.

Modern heroes, Howard, Grey, Norris, Sidney, and others are celebrated
as equal to the Greeks and Trojans. Jason and Hercules took Troy as
Drake and Essex took "Cales." Ancient villains have also modern
parallels; as a prelude to Sinon's betrayal of Troy, we hear of Dr. Parry,
Babington, Guy Fawkes. Finally, for a specimen of Heywood's poetical
quality we might take from a passage about the Gorgons some lines on
the idea of people all over the earth being suddenly turned to stone.
We have here, not Keats's bold lover, to be sure, but still something like
poetry:

> Another digging as the Queene came by,
> Stoopes stil with one Hand boue the other placst,
> The right foot fixt, the left aduanced hie
> To driue the dull Spade in, another facst
> the Gorgon-monster, as his loue past by,
> Who spreads his amorous armes t'infould her wast:
> and smiling in her face, his Image stands,
> Laughing with halfe-shut eyes, & broad-spread hands.[31]

Heywood, like Boccaccio, based his hopes of fame not so much on his
imaginative creations as on his encyclopedic compilations of historical
and biographical anecdote. It is hard to think of any story about

from Euripides (Greek and Latin), such things are almost certainly taken from handbooks,
and he would be quite unlikely to know the *Ajax* of Sophocles (ll. 661, 817, 1029). But he
would have found the facts about the gifts in Hyginus (*Fab.* 112); Servius (on *Aen.* iv.
496); or in Whitney's *Choice of Emblemes* (1586), p. 37.

[30] See above, page 65; Heywood, pp. 36 ff. Heywood provides Jupiter with the conventional arguments against virginity. Cf. Warner, bk. v, c. 24 (Chalmers, IV, 565; the passage
is quoted in *P.M.L.A.,* XLIV, 762); Marlowe, Shakespeare, and others. On the use of
these arguments in the Jupiter-Callisto episode in *The Golden Age,* see R. G. Martin,
M.L.N., XXXIII (1918), 23 ff., though Martin does not take account of Warner.

[31] Canto v, p. 111.

women, good or bad, divine or human, that Heywood omitted from
Γυναικεῖον.[32] From planning to printing the work occupied seventeen
weeks, says Heywood; well might he exclaim *Laus Deo!* It was modeled
on the collections of ancients like Valerius Maximus and Aelian, and the
numerous miscellanies of the Renaissance. However much Heywood
took directly from such favorites as Ovid and Plutarch, he took still more
from preceding compilers, especially Ravisius Textor.[33]

To return, for a moment, to Heywood's verse, *Pleasant Dialogues and
Dramma's* (1637) contained, in dramatic form, a few selections from
Erasmus' *Colloquies,* Ravisius Textor, the *Metamorphoses,* and fifteen of
Lucian's mythological dialogues.[34] The work as a whole is decidedly
heavy, but the Ovidian episodes of Jupiter and Io, Apollo and Daphne, are
treated with some original touches in the vein of pastoral masques. Heywood is a too pedestrian and loosely girt Landor to achieve "Hellenics." [35]

VI. WILLIAM BASSE

William Basse is remembered chiefly for his epitaph on Shakespeare.
He wrote pastorals which pleasantly mingle fresh rural impressions with
Ovidian myth, and his mythological fancies received elaborately playful
expression in *Urania. The Woman in the Moone.*[36] Although Basse is
grouped with disciples of Spenser, this poem belongs rather with
miscellaneous works. It was first dedicated to Prince Henry, who died in
1612, and, in the opinion of Basse's editor, was written some years before
that date. A doubtful earlier limit might be found in the second stanza:

> For when Endymion once in Latmos slept
> The Moone (some say) came downe and kis'd him there,

[32] Γυναικεῖον *or Nine Bookes of Various History Concerninge Women* (1624). See
Clark, *Thomas Heywood,* pp. 91 ff.; and R. G. Martin, "A Critical Study of Thomas
Heywood's *Gunaikeion,*" *S. P.,* XX, 160 ff. Martin shows (pp. 180 ff.) that Heywood "had
at best but a distant bowing acquaintance" with Greek. Greek authors are regularly quoted
in Latin.

[33] In his *Exemplary Lives* (1640) Heywood chose nine female worthies to parallel the
traditional nine—Deborah, Judith, Esther, Boadicea, Penthesilea, Artemisia, "Elphleda,"
wife of Æthelred of Mercia, Margaret, wife of Henry VI, and Elizabeth. Around these
were grouped countless other tales of famous women, for such a compiler must needs be
thrifty. A loose adaptation of this book, called *Female Excellency,* was issued in 1688 by
Nathaniel Crouch; see Louis B. Wright, *R. E. S.,* IV (1928), 137.

[34] Reprinted by W. Bang, *Materialien* (1903). Heywood had drawn upon Lucian before
(Martin, p. 167; Clark, *Thomas Heywood,* pp. 157–59).

[35] Heywood of course was not unaware of Spenser, Marlowe, and Shakespeare; the last
two are praised in the roll call of poets in the *Hierarchie of the Blessed Angells* (a eulogy of
Spenser is quoted by F. F. Covington, *M. L. N.,* XLI, 1926, 386–87). Mr. Clark (p. 56)
has rightly called attention to Spenserian influence in *Troia Britanica.* For some echoes of
Venus and Adonis in Heywood see R. G. Martin, *M. L. N.,* XXXIII, 23 ff. In *Pleasant
Dialogues* we have at least one trace of Marlowe—"Women by nature are ambitious"—
though the idea had become proverbial (p. 159, l. 5359; *H. and L.,* i. 428). But the influence
of Shakespeare and Marlowe seems very slight.

[36] *Poetical Works,* ed. R. W. Bond (1893), pp. 267 ff.

Erronious Fame reports that she hath kept
Him euer since within her spotlesse Sphere.
And of this falshood, so profusely blowne,
The generall tale of Man i' th' Moone is growne.

While the tale was common, and the allusion is vague, the lines do
suggest Drayton's *The Man in the Moone* (1606), which, as a partly
satirical treatment of the myth of Cynthia, might have helped to inspire
Basse.[37]

Urania offers a new theory about the face in the moon. Disgusted with
sinful humanity Jove sends down to earth as investigators "two handsome
youthfull Gods." These envoys, carefully observing "ioyes, woes, wants,
wealthes, sinnes, service," find themselves in Ethiopia, then inhabited by
people "white & fayre." Being entertained by the loveliest woman in the
land, the two gods, disguised as mortals, fall in love with her, and make
rapid progress in courtship. Jove's commission is forgotten, though they
have visited all nations except

some base Americans
That know not Ioue, and Ioue cares not to know.

Their hostess loves them equally, and bestows her favors without
prejudice. When the two lovers, to forward their suit, reveal their divinity, the crafty woman extracts from them the secret which enables
them to reach heaven, a place she has longed to see. She mounts on
unfamiliar wings.

Her sprawling heeles, in stead of wonted molde
Kick Cedars tops.

The young gods pursue her, but in vain,

For in this Charme did such a vertue lye,
Those that could fastest speake, could fastest flye.

Passing celestial sentinels with their "harquebushes," she arrives in the
Olympian hall. Jove summons an assembly to decide what shall be done
with the interloper, since this female Tomlinson is "nor fit for heau'n
nor (from heau'n) fit for earth." It is settled that she shall lodge in the
moon.[38]

Cynthia is more annoyed at being saddled with a companion than she
had been at the slanderous tale of there being a man in the moon, but
she bows to Jove's desire. In a rage, however, she dashes around her

[37] Might the choice of Ethiopia for his scene have been suggested by Jonson's *Masque of
Blackness* (1605)? And see below for a possible reference to *Mutability* (1609).
[38] This disturbing invasion of heaven by a woman might have been inspired, humorous
though it is, by the enterprise of the Titaness in Spenser's *Mutability*—which itself has

circuit at great speed, outstripping the other planetary gods, and

> Rattles her tedious guest, to make her bones
> And well knit joynts to totter in her skin,
> To turne her maw or shake th' ambitious dame
> Downe from her seate to earth from whence she came.

The tedious guest, unperturbed, sits in the moon's windows, "Dressing her dainty browes from Morne to Noone." The exasperation of Cynthia leads her to exercise her divine powers in various ways upon all terrestrial things, especially upon women, whom she afflicts

> With fancyes, frenzies, lunacyes, with strange
> Feares, fashions, factions, furyes, & affections . . .[39]

Yet, since Basse would not be a misogynist, his mildly satirical extravaganza ends with praise of womanly virtues.

Following the narrative comes a piece of over eighty lines, "This Story Morallized," which Mr. Bond, from its style, supposed to be a later addition.[40] A friend, says the author, demanded allegory, since fictions without a moral are mere fables. Here as elsewhere Basse seems to be skeptical, but he consents to expound a moral. The woman, "Mind," sought celestial knowledge; her deserting the gods who helped her showed ingratitude; their passion typified the supremacy of love . . . But Basse's heart seems to have been mainly in the telling of his tale. He may not have genius, but he has geniality, a quality not too common in mythological poems to be despised.

There is much more narrative than picture-making, and descriptions, instead of being warm and luscious, are in the cooler style of Drayton. The transition from the Elizabethan to the Jacobean manner is most obvious in the prevailing mock-heroic and satirical tone, though the satire is only a flavor. The passion for beauty, the intoxication of the senses, which inspired poems so various as *Hero and Leander, Venus and Adonis, Ovid's Banquet of Sense,* has given way, even in poets writing partly in the older vein, to an attitude of ironic and humorous detachment. Since, however, we read the earlier poems and do not read the later ones, the change is not entirely a gain.

touches of something like humor. And these lines (page 294) seem a not improbable allusion to Spenser's work:

> They saw that she was none of Titan's race
> Who by pretence of eldership layd clayme
> And title to expulsed Saturne's place;
> For they long since by Ioue were overcame . . .

[39] The influence of Lyly's *The Woman in the Moone* is obvious here (*Works,* ed. Bond, III, 287–88; see also p. 237).

[40] At the beginning of the third canto the woman is said to represent "Mind," though her lively adventures somewhat obscure the symbolism.

VII. WILLIAM BOSWORTH

A chapter much concerned with the influence of *Hero and Leander* cannot pass by the exuberant *Arcadius and Sepha* of William Bosworth. Though written apparently in 1626, when the author was nineteen, the poem did not reach print until 1651.[41]

One can hardly even summarize this wayward romance of sixty-four pages, for the chief story, of the love of Arcadius and Sepha, is not always lucid, and there are five or six inset tales of some length. Sepha falls in love at the first sight of the gallant Arcadius and yearns for a return of affection. On her way to a temple she encounters a band of satyrs and fauns who dance around her as their queen. One of these tells a story of Bacchus and Diana: Bacchus proposes to build in a region frequented by Diana, and in the battle which ensues between the two divinities the maiden Antigone is killed.

There follows—according to the chronology of events it should precede—the story of Haemon and Antigone. A reader who expects something Sophoclean is quickly undeceived. Haemon, stricken by Cupid, sees and loves the sleeping Antigone, who, awakened, first prays to Diana and then arranges to meet Haemon the next night. But she is killed and he, keeping tryst, writes an elegy and kills himself on her tomb. His blood is turned into a columbine, his body to a marble statue.

Sepha, whom we may have forgotten, goes on her way to the temple, and Arcadius rides by her without a word; one cannot help thinking of Lavinia and Aeneas in the *Roman d' Eneas*. She reads on Diana's altar

> Those that Idalia's wanton garments wear,
> No Sacrifices for me must prepare.

She faints. Then comes a story of Eramio and Amissa. In the second book Sepha revives, at the embrace of Arcadius, and as they walk home together he tells the story of Sappho and Phaon. Sepha is offended by her lover's allusion to "Venus' pleasures" and goes to her tower, but when she sees him below, apparently dead, she runs out and kisses him. Arcadius revives, Sepha avows her ardent love—not without a prudential reference to Hymen—and Arcadius goes home elated.

We are now reminded of the original narrator, Epimenides, and he tells of the love of Delithason and Verista, a story which Verista, dying, told to him. Then Epimenides, coming upon two knights in combat, had gone away with the survivor, Arcadius. The two were entertained by Sepha in her tower. A jealous suitor attacked the wedding party and Arcadius was killed. Sepha, after fleeing into a wood, returned to find

⁴¹ Saintsbury, *Minor Caroline Poets*, II, 523 ff.

her lover dead. She killed herself, and the ever helpful Epimenides cremated both bodies; a phoenix arose from the ashes of the star-crossed lovers. Finishing his tale, Epimenides dies.

Even this outline suggests some influences which Bosworth's editor, "R. C.," indicates in his preface—Ovid, Marlowe, Sidney. To the first are indebted "the high, the fluent, and the pathetic discourses of his lovers," and the metamorphoses. "The strength of his fancy, and the shadowing of it in words, he taketh from Mr. Marlow in his *Hero and Leander* . . . You shall find our Author everywhere in this imitation." "The weaving of one story into another" Bosworth had learned from Sidney. And "his making the end of one verse to be the frequent beginning of the other, (besides the art of the trope) was the labour and delight of Mr. Edmund Spencer." Ralegh and Sir Kenelm Digby, says R. C., called Spenser the English Virgil, and in these devices Bosworth imitated both the ancient and the modern poet.

R. C. indicates some aspects of Ovidian influence, and there are others, both in situations and in details. But classical figures may, as in medieval romance, become quite unrecognizable. Here are some lines concerning an old lover of Sappho's, as reported by Arcadius, who is himself the son of Capaneus, one of the seven against Thebes:

> This done, I saw a knight of courage bold,
> Cloth'd all in argent armour, strip'd with gold . . .
> . . . . "Discourteous knight," he said,
> "Dost not repent thee that thou hast betray'd
> That honour'd lady?" [42]

The young poet, whether in the main plot or the inset tales, does not really try to create a mythological world. Classical and mythological figures are introduced into a pastoral and romantic Arcadia, to become bright threads in a fanciful decorative pattern. The author enjoys writing pretty words about pretty things, and denatured characters from ancient story are among the prettiest things available.

The influence of *Hero and Leander,* as R. C. says, is everywhere. One could cite many passages that testify to a study of Marlowe both loving and inadequate, but this will serve to illustrate the difference between, as it were, an Elizabethan Keats and Leigh Hunt:

> Then to the altar went he, where he pray'd,
> While Sepha, overcome with passion, said,
> So loud that he might hear, "Were I the saint
> To whom he prays, sure I would hear his plaint." [43]

[42] P. 577.   [43] P. 570. Cf. Marlowe, i. 177 ff.

Spenser was more than a model of style. Sepha and the satyrs, for example, remind us of Una; but what in Spenser has allegorical significance is in Bosworth only another ornamental episode. So too, as a young man in love with poetry, he responds to the romantic and sensuous elements in the *Arcadia,* not to the serious and didactic. Finally, the poem may be linked, though not in the way of "influence," with *Glaucus and Scilla,* for, despite its length and intricacies, it is in structure a personal love-complaint; we learn the fact at the beginning, and completely forget it until the end. Although the poem is so largely a mosaic of imitations, the author's Elizabethan enthusiasms give it enough freshness and charm to carry one through a single reading at least.[44]

VIII. JAMES SHIRLEY

In 1646 Shirley published *Narcissus, or, The Self-Lover,* a poem that had been entered in 1618.[45] Although he was born in 1596 Shirley is often spoken of as the last Elizabethan dramatist, and *Narcissus* was one of the last specimens of the conventional Elizabethan mythological poem.

The Ovidian story is expanded to the length of about a hundred and thirty six-line stanzas. The incidents are not essentially altered, except that Echo, through the compassion of Juno, is endowed with a voice, and she makes fluent and passionate use of it. The amplification is all in the way of descriptive detail and speeches; a third of the poem consists of dialogue and soliloquy. The Shakespearean epithet in the first line— "Fair Echo, rise, sick-thoughted nymph, awake"[46]—announces a debt to *Venus and Adonis* that increases as the poem proceeds. Shirley makes a good deal of Narcissus as a huntsman, like Adonis, and, as usual, the most obvious imitation is in the woman's wooing of the man. There are abundant conceits in the vein of Shakespeare and his fellows. The customary gnomic lines are lacking. Hitherto we have found that almost any poem that bore traces of *Venus and Adonis* revealed the stronger influence of *Hero and Leander. Narcissus* is an exception, for it seems to contain no suggestion of Marlowe, though there is an echo of the lyric which, along with *Hero and Leander,* sustained his reputation in the seventeenth century.[47]

The poem is smooth and fluent, but the mannerisms of *Venus and*

[44] I may mention inevitable but insignificant allusions to *Venus and Adonis,* pp. 533, 569.
[45] Of the 1618 edition no copy has survived. For the text see Dyce's edition of Shirley (1833), VI, 463 ff.
[46] Cf. *V. and A.,* l. 5.
[47] P. 478: Yet these but shadows of the mirth we'll prove,
If thou wilt stay, and be thy Echo's love.

Adonis without its impetuous verve had been staled by custom. While there are no special felicities, here is a stanza that begins well:

> No portion of a bird's forsaken nest
> Fell from the boughs to interrupt the calm;
> No wither'd leaf did in his fall molest
> The stillness of it, smooth as settled balm,
> But crystal less transparent: such a mirror,
> So form'd, could only shew disdain his error.

One may remember that the man who commenced his career with this thin and facile Elizabethan piece did not abandon Ovid. Over a generation later came *The Contention of Ajax and Ulysses,* with the great lyric on a deeper but still Elizabethan note.

IX. ABRAHAM COWLEY

While a mythological poem had long been for young authors the correct door through which to enter the literary world, no one made his début at quite so early an age as Abraham Cowley. His *Tragicall Historie of Pyramus and Thisbe* was first published in 1633, but it had been written five years before, when the author was ten years old.[48] If less ambitious and sophisticated than the "novels of the nursery and poems of the pram" which the twentieth century has witnessed, Cowley's poem is precocious enough—not to mention the more elaborate romance, *Constantia and Philetus,* composed at the mature age of twelve.

In addition to a lyric and an epitaph, of eight lines each, *Pyramus and Thisbe* contains thirty-five stanzas of rather odd form (*abaabb*). The lyric, which Thisbe sings while waiting under the mulberry tree, and the epitaph, are original ventures. Otherwise the story is a free redaction of Ovid, and the treatment shows some acquaintance with the conventions of the mythological genre. There is not much in the pictorial manner, but we have the conceits and gnomic lines so popular in this kind of writing. Near the beginning Cowley introduces an un-Ovidian motive; Venus, envying the lovers' beauty, has Cupid transfix them with his darts.[49]

A schoolboy's verses usually possess the merit of indicating his favorite authors. We have Cowley's testimony to his early love of Spenser, but there is hardly anything clearly Spenserian in this piece.[50] There

[48] *Essays, Plays and Sundry Verses,* ed. A. R. Waller (1906), pp. 31 ff.
[49] Such a motive is not uncommon in mythological poems, but it may be observed that Dunstan Gale made use of it in his long poem on Pyramus and Thisbe. See the Appendix, under 1596.
[50] Commenting upon the prosody Mr. A. H. Thompson remarks that "Spenser's successors, rather than Spenser himself, appear to have been Cowley's model" (*Cambridge History of English Literature,* VII, 62). See A. H. Nethercot, *Abraham Cowley* (New York, 1931), pp. 10–11.

is a reference to *Venus and Adonis* in *Constantia and Philetus,* and
probably Cowley knew the poem when he wrote his *Tragicall Historie.*
Such lines as these seem to have a Shakespearean ring:

> Thus Beautie is by Beauties meanes undone,
> Striving to close these eyes that make her bright.[51]

Cowley may well have read Ovid in Latin, but he was more familiar
with Golding than perhaps his "very loving Master" of Westminster
would have thought desirable. In fact he sometimes follows Golding
when Golding does not follow Ovid.[52]

It is not unfitting that this chapter should end, allegorically as it were,
with the Ovidian exercise, the belated Elizabethan imitation, of a small
boy, and that boy Abraham Cowley. The mythological poem of the
Renaissance was an unconscionable time a-dying, and, with very few
exceptions, it did not attract the important poets of the early seventeenth
century. Marlowe had carried the Ovidian and Italianate tradition as
far as it could go, and most of his successors could only try to imitate
his incidents, his rich mythological descriptions, his rhetorical tricks.
They followed Marlowe and Shakespeare rather than Drayton, who,
whatever his faults, had inaugurated a kind of poem more fruitful and
less easily exhausted than the merely erotic and decorative minor epic.

Yet these minor epics were only one manifestation of the mythological
impulse, and if we think not merely of them but of allusions in almost
the whole body of Elizabethan poetry, from Shakespeare and Spenser
down, we shall not underestimate the beauties that the Ovidian tradition
carried with it. Whether of gold or gilt, there they are, a sumptuous
tapestry. On the other hand, while it is quite unfair to judge of a tradition
from one brief illustration of one particular vice, a single example will
remind us of certain weaknesses, of the leveling tendencies, which could
develop within the Renaissance convention. Here are three generations
of a popular conceit:

> I sawe Phœbus thrust out his golden hedde,
>   upon her to gaze:
> But when he sawe, how broade her beames did spredde,
>   it did him amaze.
> He blusht to see another Sunne belowe,
> Ne durst againe his fyrye face out showe:

---

[51] More definite, though the figure itself is common, is the resemblance between Cowley's
"Like as a Bird which in a Net is tane" (st. 4) and Shakespeare's "Look! how a bird lies
tangled in a net" (l. 67).

[52] Golding and Cowley speak of Thisbe's not looking back as she runs away; both render
alto pulvere as "subtle sand"; in both Thisbe beats her breast and tears her golden hair,
while in Ovid she does not beat her breast and her hair is not golden.

Some details also suggest that Cowley may have known Brathwait's long tale of
Pyramus and Thisbe (see the Appendix, under 1615).

Let him, if he dare,
His brightnesse compare
With hers, to haue the ouerthrowe.[53]

At which the Sunne his glorious face did hide,
  Each Planet pulleth in his golden head,
The other stars out of the heauens glide:
  And Cynthia from her siluer Palace fled,
The night is robbed of her wonted light,
  Each thing turn'd dark that formerly was bright.[54]

And, though the shady gloom
Had given day her room,
  The sun himself withheld his wonted speed;
And hid his head for shame,
As his inferior flame
  The new-enlighten'd world no more should need:
He saw a greater sun appear
Than his bright throne or burning axletree could bear.

Granted that the three extracts may be ranked in a foreordained order, do they show the differences in quality that one might expect to find among Spenser, an anonymous scribbler, and Milton? To abuse the old phrase again, one touch of Renaissance nature makes the whole world kin.

The stream of Ovidian tradition dried up, for the main current of poetry had been moving along a deeper channel. When the young Cowley was writing his romantic little tales a revolt against the normal Elizabethan spirit and style, a revolt starting from Chapman and Donne, had been in progress for over a generation, and a generation later Cowley himself was to be regarded as the high priest of the new cult. But we may remember that metaphysical poetry also expired, and that the Ovidian mythology of the Renaissance was to be revived and invested with altogether new splendor by Milton. So sinks the day-star in the ocean bed . . .

[53] Spenser, *Shep. Cal., April.*
[54] *The Scourge of Venus* (1613), ed. Grosart, p. 30. The poem goes under the initials "H. A.," but the author is unknown. See the Appendix, and above, page 187, note 25.

CHAPTER TEN

CHAPMAN

IF ANY proof were needed that the classic artist is born and not made it might be found in the work of George Chapman. A man of vigorous and independent mind and character, with a high and serious conception of the function and craft of poetry, endowed with more than a spark of the true poetic fire, and, finally, possessed by a religious adoration for Homer—such a man, one might think, would stand forth as a modern embodiment of authentic classicism. Yet Chapman has been a byword for every kind of Elizabethan vice of thought and expression.[1] Of late, however, critics, following eagerly where Mr. Eliot leads, have been praising him, sometimes apparently reading him. He is taking rank as a metaphysical poet of the first importance; and since he has not been conveniently anthologized there is perhaps less danger than in the case of Donne that his vogue will become an uncritical cult.

The mere possession—one hesitates to say "exposition"—of a philosophy of life and literature is not in itself enough to set Chapman apart from his fellows; we have happily got beyond the notion that the Elizabethans were eternal children. Chapman's ethical ideas sometimes approach Spenser's, his faith in culture sometimes reminds us of Daniel, but his style is equally remote from the warm, melodious fluidity of the one and the pure, rational soberness of the other. What distinguishes Chapman, and Donne, as metaphysical poets is, in Mr. Eliot's pregnant words, "a direct sensuous apprehension of thought, or a re-creation of thought into feeling." [2] Donne's work, though circulating privately, had more influence than Chapman's, but Chapman's published poems were the first open revolt against orthodox or conventional canons of Elizabethan taste. The limitations of our subject forbid any attempt at a

[1] For a compendious account of a reader's first sensations one cannot do better than quote Swinburne, though Swinburne also praised Chapman well. He speaks of the shock given to one's taste by the poet's "crabbed and bombastic verbiage, the tortuous and pedantic obscurity, the rigidity and the laxity of a style which moves as it were with a stiff shuffle, at once formal and shambling; which breaks bounds with a limping gait, and plays truant from all rule without any of the grace of freedom; wanders beyond law and straggles out of order at the halting pace of age and gravity, and in the garb of a schoolmaster plays the pranks of a schoolboy with a ponderous and lumbaginous license of movement, at once rheumatic and erratic" (Introduction to *Poems and Minor Translations*, 1875, p. xxi).
[2] *Homage to John Dryden*, p. 29.

rounded estimate of Chapman, and perhaps compel attention mainly to his weaknesses, which recent critics incline to minimize or ignore, but these are at any rate the weaknesses of gnarled and knotted muscles, not of flaccidity and anæmia. Who touches Chapman touches a man, though an uncouth one, a brine-encrusted Odysseus over whom Athene has not yet shed her luminous grace.

In 1594 appeared *The Shadow of Night,* comprising a *Hymnus in Noctem* and a *Hymnus in Cynthiam,* with prose glosses appended. The first paragraph of the dedication to Matthew Roydon indicates the prevailing character of Chapman's mythology:

It is an exceeding rapture of delight in the deep search of knowledge . . . that maketh men manfully indure the extremes incident to that Herculean labour: from flints must the Gorgonean fount be smitten. Men must be shod by Mercury, girt with Saturn's adamantine sword, take the shield from Pallas, the helm from Pluto, and have the eyes of Græa (as Hesiodus arms Perseus against Medusa) before they can cut off the viperous head of benumbing ignorance, or subdue their monstrous affections to most beautiful judgment.

The allusions, and their significance, Chapman takes from Natalis Comes.[3] Wisdom, he proceeds, is not easily wooed and won, nor does she stoop to the profane rabble—no Renaissance poet is more disdainful of the vulgar than Chapman—but visits only those who approach her "with invocation, fasting, watching; yea, not without having drops of their souls like an heavenly familiar." The words recall a famous utterance of Milton's, with a difference.[4] This arduous ideal, which Chapman never wearied of proclaiming, is set forth in these early Hymns with an enthusiasm that leaves few lucid intervals in the tangle of allegory and allusion. Yet beauty does peep through the blanket of the dark.

Grasping our golden bough, which will prove to be M. Schoell, we

---

[3] This chapter is constantly indebted to M. Schoell's *Études sur l'humanisme continental en Angleterre* (1926). For the item in question see page 179; and Comes, vii. 11 and 12.
[4] See page 270 below. One might recall too Milton's prayer to

> my celestial patroness, who deigns
> Her nightly visitation unimplored,
> And dictates to me slumbering, or inspires
> Easy . . .

but the parallel grows remote.

Chapman's "heavenly familiar" reminds one too of the Shakespearean interest of these poems, and of Chapman's evident dislike of Ovidian eroticism. He may be the rival poet of the *Sonnets,* the cloudy preacher whose nocturnal visitations seem to draw Shakespeare's good-natured chaff (Sonnet lxxxvi):

> He, nor that affable familiar ghost
> Which nightly gulls him with intelligence . . .

These lines are surely—if anything can be sure in that Cave of Despair—a return for an

plunge into the shadows. To begin with a bit of arithmetic, these two
Hymns, of over nine hundred lines, contain matter taken from Natalis
Comes which fills about two hundred, and almost all of the learned
glosses are from the same source. Chapman thinks of the day as the
nurse of evil, an idea that leads to satire, and of the night as the
mysterious source of good and spiritual strength; the conception, so
different from the rhetorical denunciation of night that we met in
Shakespeare and Spenser,[5] is correspondingly more difficult to render.
To mention only one element of confusion, Chapman distinguishes
between the creative aspect of night and "this horrid step-dame, blindness
of the mind," which he compares to a Gorgon.[6] The Calydonian boars
that ravage the fields represent the chaos which followed the reign of
order. Amalthea, who befriended Jove and was translated to heaven, is
an example of virtue rewarded. The ship of the Argonauts was also
placed among the stars because it carried the heroes to and from Colchis.
The story of Orpheus reveals the power of wisdom in civilizing men.

> And that in calming the infernal kind,
> To wit, the perturbations of his mind,
> And bringing his Eurydice from hell
> (Which justice signifies) is proved well.
> But if in right's observance any man
> Look back, with boldness less than Orphean,
> Soon falls he to the hell from whence he rose.[7]

"The golden chain of Homer's high device," Chapman continues,

> Ambition is, or cursed avarice,
> Which all gods haling being tied to Jove,
> Him from his settled height could never move.[8]

apparent rebuke of Shakespeare in Chapman's second Hymn. Chapman, singing the praises
of his Cynthia, "the forces of the mind," breaks off with what seems a clear allusion to the
pocula Castalia of the Ovidian motto prefixed to *Venus and Adonis:*

> Presume not then ye flesh-confounded souls,
> That cannot bear the full Castalian bowls,
> Which sever mounting spirits from the senses,
> To look in this deep fount for thy pretences.

The change from "ye" to "thy" may be thought to indicate a not wholly general object of
censure. Chapman's lines read like the protest of a mystic and moralist against a leader of
the fleshly school. Ll. 375–76 of the first Hymn may be glanced at in *Love's Labour's Lost,*
IV. iii. 346–47 (Boas, *Marlowe and His Circle,* p. 91; Chambers, *William Shakespeare,* I,
247, 335, 568). Chambers is dubious about Chapman as the rival poet.

   [5] See above, page 154, and note 6 below.

   [6] The idea of the "night of mind" is taken from Comes, iii. 12 (Schoell, p. 180). Spenser
may have used the same passage in Comes (Lemmi, *P. Q.,* VIII, 275).

   [7] Schoell, pp. 34–35. Cf. Phineas Fletcher's version of Boethius, page 171 above.

   [8] In Chapman's *Tragedy of Caesar and Pompey* (IV. v. 128 ff.) the golden chain
"becomes in Cato's argument for immortality and freedom a symbol of the power and
tenacity of the soul" (Elizabeth Holmes, *Aspects of Elizabethan Imagery,* p. 78).

These are some of the mythological allusions in the first Hymn, and they all come from Natalis Comes,[9] not, however, in their first simplicity, but colored by their passage through Chapman's prismatic mind. The glosses, as I have mentioned, are likewise taken from Comes, though he is named only once. In any case the borrowed matter suited Chapman's theory and practice of poetry, the enforcing of moral ideas with novel figures and applications. His consciousness of himself as a rebel addressing a chosen few appears again in the last paragraph of the gloss. He will not labor to justify his innovations, they must justify themselves to such as understand them; "for the rest, God help them, I cannot do as others, make day seem a lighter woman than she is, by painting her."

The *Hymnus in Cynthiam,* which is complementary to the first piece, continues to shadow forth the oppositions between day and night, sun and moon, vice and virtue, sense and reason, confusion and order, with all Chapman's love of personification, and with much borrowing from Comes. The dominant idea, quite un-Elizabethan, is the primitive mystery, the vast fecundity, of night. Both poems, or the two parts of one poem, have a pattern of emotion and association, not of daylight logic; they are, as Miss Spens observes in an excellent essay, a dream-fugue.[10] The longest unit is an allegorical tale of the nymph Euthimya, created by Cynthia, who is transformed to a panther and pursued by hounds; we are given a list of the hounds' names, derived from Comes' story of Actaeon. The hounds pursue the nymph vainly during the day, encountering hard obstacles, but at night the goddess blows retreat, and there is peace. Thus the poet's thoughts pursue poetry, and, baffled in the daytime, win peace and inspiration with darkness.[11]

Leaving the myth wrapped in the shadow of night Chapman soon devotes a dozen lines to an account, taken from Comes, of the temple of Ephesus. Comes, who seldom neglects to attach a moral, fails him here, and he expounds an allegory of his own, exhorting "Elysian ladies" to

> Build Cynthia's temple in your virtuous parts,
> Let every jewel be a virtue's glass.

He returns to Comes for the meaning of Ganymede's translation to the skies:

> His beauty was it, not the body's pride,
> That made him great Aquarius stellified.
> And that mind most is beautiful and high,

[9] Schoell, pp. 180 ff.

[10] "Chapman's Ethical Thought," *Essays and Studies by Members of the English Association,* XI (1925), 161. Cf. E. Holmes, pp. 80 ff.

[11] So Miss Spens interprets the tale (page 166). It would be more in harmony with the orthodox moralization of Actaeon (see above, page 71)—and, as regards Chapman, the

And nearest comes to a Divinity,
That furtherest is from spot of Earth's delight,
Pleasures that lose their substance with their sight,
Such one, Saturnius ravisheth to love,
And fills the cup of all content to Jove.

It helps us to measure both Chapman's moral earnestness and his tortured
and eccentric style if we recall the same sentiment in a poet who at his
best combined seriousness and wit with classic clarity:

Earth cannot shew so brave a Sight
As when a single Soul does fence
The Batteries of alluring Sense,
And Heaven views it with delight.

But the effect of the whole poem lies in suggestion and symbol rather
than in the more definite and particular allegories. It is far from a good
poem, yet it adds a poetic province to one's consciousness. Chapman's
conception is, in a way, the exact opposite of Plato's myth of the cave.
Instead of mounting from the contemplation of vain shadows to the
dazzling light of day and reality, one is borne along on a deep and
turbid stream of creation which, far below the realm of the sun, moves
toward the immense and fertile womb of night.

Ovid's Banquet of Sense (1595) is also addressed to the sympathetic
Roydon, and the dedication is a more elaborate and reasoned manifesto
of Chapman's poetical ideals. He hates the profane multitude, and
consecrates his "strange poems to those searching spirits, whom learning
hath made noble, and nobility sacred." Poetry should not be "as pervial
as oratory," or, one might add, as most Elizabethan writing (except
Donne's). True poetry, true clearness, comes not from the easy presentation of an easy subject, but from the adequate rendering of a complex
and difficult one. Deliberate and wanton obscurity is "pedantical and
childish; but where it shroudeth itself in the heart of his subject, uttered
with fitness of figure and expressive epithets, with that darkness will I
still labour to be shadowed." [12]

The extraordinary poem can best be outlined by means of Chapman's
argument:

Ovid, newly enamoured of Julia, daughter to Octavius
Augustus Cæsar, after by him called Corinna, secretly conveyed
himself into a garden of the Emperor's court, in an arbour whereof Corinna was bathing, playing upon her lute and singing;

fact of orthodoxy may be an argument against the notion—to take the hounds as the
"monstrous affections," the irrational senses and emotions, which day, the time of evil,
starts into activity, to disturb the poetic soul, and which, at night, are subdued. The
narrative details seem on any view to involve allegorical inconsistencies; they may be the
tangential footnotes which Chapman cannot help putting into his text.
[12] See Schoell, p. 60; George Williamson, *The Donne Tradition* (1930), pp. 60 ff.

204 MYTHOLOGY AND THE RENAISSANCE TRADITION

204 MYTHOLOGY AND THE RENAISSANCE TRADITION

Auditus.   which Ovid overhearing was exceedingly pleased with the sweetness of her voice, and to himself uttered the comfort he conceived in his sense of Hearing.

Olfactus.   Then the odours she used in her bath breathing a rich savour, he expressed the joy he felt in his sense of Smelling.

Visus.   Thus growing more deeply enamoured in great contentment with himself, he ventures to see her in the pride of her nakedness; which doing by stealth, he discovered the comfort he conceived in Seeing, and the glory of her beauty.

Gustus.   Not yet satisfied, he useth all his art to make known his being there without her offence; or, being necessarily offended, to appease her, which done, he entreats a kiss, to serve for satisfaction of his Taste, which he obtains.

Tactus.   Then proceeds he to entreaty for the fifth sense, and there is interrupted.[13]

One might expect another *Venus and Adonis* or *Venus and Anchises,* but Chapman's poem is more of a treatise than a debauch. He starts from a point beyond where *Venus and Adonis* leaves off. Various as were the uses of classic story, no one but Chapman could have woven an abstruse and subtle treatment of the sublimation of the senses into a series of pictures marked by a voluptuousness at once lavish and dry. Like Spenser, Chapman has both a fear of the senses that compels a desire to master them, and also, as a poet, a fervent belief that the senses, bestowed by nature, by God, are a means through which man may rise above himself to a vision of ideal beauty. But whereas Spenser allows sense to have its way, and then reins it in with reason or conscience, in Chapman sense is analytical and logic becomes sensuous. Even Donne, who can be Platonic and sensual and scholastic, is rarely all three at the same time.[14] As an aesthetic essay the poem is unique in more than one way, and it must embody the only appearance in literature of Julia or Corinna as ideal beauty, and of Ovid as a worshiper thereof. Julia is a world away from Drayton's Platonized Phoebe.

Both Donne and Chapman, though it is not fashionable to say so, wrote a good deal of intolerable stuff. Chapman does not at his best come home to our business and bosoms as Donne frequently does; his

[13] M. Schoell seems to have overlooked Chapman's apparent debt to his favorite, Ficino. See Ficino's discussion of "Ratio, Visus, Auditus, Olfactus, Gustus, & Tactus," in *Comm. in Convivium* (*Omnia Divini Platonis Opera,* Lyons, 1548), v. 2, and cf. i. 4.

[14] Some lines in the poem recall a famous bit of Donne. Chapman writes (page 30):

> The sense is given us to excite the mind,
> And that can never be by sense excited,
> But first the sense must her contentment mind [find?],
> We therefore must procure the sense delighted,
> That so the soul may use her faculty.

Here Chapman is more logical than imaginative, and one misses the sudden lift that comes with Donne's "Else a great Prince in prison lies."

inspiration, more esoteric and abstruse than normal and human, often stirs historical interest more than living sympathy. But he too offers a reward to the persevering, in a fusion of qualities akin to Donne's. It is perhaps heretical to suggest that Chapman is most satisfying, not when he is most subtle, but when his metaphysical strings have just been touched into vibration, when the rich imagery of ordinary Elizabethan writing is quickened by a peculiar intensity. There are such phrases in these bits:

> In a loose robe of tinsel forth she came,
> Nothing but it betwixt her nakedness
> And envious light. The downward-burning flame
> Of her rich hair did threaten new access
> Of venturous Phaeton to scorch the fields . . .[15]

> O Beauty, how attractive is thy power!
> For as the life's heat clings about the heart,
> So all men's hungry eyes do haunt thy bower.
> Reigning in Greece, Troy swam to thee in Art,
> Removed to Troy, Greece follow'd thee in fears . . .

> Herewith she rose like the autumnal star,
> Fresh burnish'd in the lofty ocean flood,
> That darts his glorious influence more far
> Than any lamp of bright Olympus' brood . . .

Chapman published his continuation of *Hero and Leander* in 1598. He confesses in his dedication to Lady Walsingham that he has been "drawne by strange instigation to employ some of my serious time in so trifeling a subiect, which yet made the first Author, diuine Musæus, eternall." Several times he uses the apologetic words "trifling" or "trifle," but, in respect of bulk at least, the reader is soon undeceived, as he is after Chaucer's promise of "a litel thing in prose." The continuation extends to over fifteen hundred and fifty lines.

Chapman begins with an assurance of something "more graue and hie," and his stern Muse will have none of the moral laxity that Marlowe glorified. That part of him which is an artist, a lover of life, tells how Leander, "Lord of his desires," throws into the Hellespont "his Hero-handled bodie." The awkward moralist reports that

> The God of gold of purpose guilt his lims,
> That this word guilt, including double sence,

---

[15] P. 23. The last lines of the next stanza, when Corinna casts off her robe, are these:
> Or as when Venus strived for sovereign sway
> Of charmful beauty in young Troy's desire,
> So stood Corinna, vanishing her 'tire.

The lines may or may not be an echo of Marlowe's "Where Venus in her naked glory stroue . . ." "Charmful" is at any rate unhappily flat compared with the full radiance of "naked glory," and Marlowe's other pictorial words.

> The double guilt of his Incontinence,
> Might be exprest . . .

There follows a sermon on the text

> Joy grauen in sence, like snow in water wasts;
> Without preserue of vertue nothing lasts.[16]

Part of it comes from Plutarch's *Amatorius*.[17]

While, at home, Leander revels in memories of Hero, of how "on his breasts warme sea she sideling swims," [18] divine music pierces his ear, and through the roof, with many-colored lights, descends the Goddess Ceremony, leading Religion. After the exposition of much involved symbolism we have a speech from the goddess which convinces Leander of his sin in the "plaine neglect of Nuptiall rites," a sin that he resolves to atone for at once. In Musaeus the personal integrity of the lovers is full justification, as, though to a less degree, it is in Marlowe; Chapman's introduction into a poetic world of everyday conventions, however disguised, does suggest, in Katherine Mansfield's phrase, "taking up that magical poem and putting it into a bodice and skirt." [19] Yet Chapman's seriousness, here and elsewhere in his work, is not quite that of a mere precisian.

Before analyzing Hero's emotions Chapman takes one of those flights that compensate for many tortured trivialities, and his rather prosaic repudiation of Marlowe's attitude is less memorable than the lines in which he sends a winged message to the dead poet's "free soule":

> Then thou most strangely-intellectuall fire,
> That proper to my soule hast power t'inspire
> Her burning faculties, and with the wings
> Of thy unspheared flame visitst the springs
> Of spirits immortall . . .[20]

We come then to

> Sweet Hero left upon her bed alone,
> Her maidenhead, her vowes, Leander gone.

[16] Cf. *Hymnus in Cynthiam*, ll. 401–03 (ed. 1875, p. 15). Quotations from *Hero and Leander* are from the text in Mr. Brooke's edition of Marlowe's works, pp. 513 ff.

[17] Schoell, p. 225.

[18] Since echoes of Chapman in other poets are not common I might quote a possible one from the extraordinary Nathaniel Whiting (*Minor Caroline Poets*, III, 550):

> Long since did Hellespont gulp in Leander,
> When he presumed on naked breast to wander.

There is another reference to the story (and to *Venus and Adonis*) in the same writer (page 452).

[19] *Letters* (London, 1928), II, 106.

[20] The meaning of the whole passage is not entirely clear. The legend that Marlowe asked Chapman to finish his poem, a legend sufficiently incredible anyhow, was finally exploded by the discovery of the circumstances of Marlowe's death. And, as Mr. Boas remarks

She is besieged by "new come thoughts" as Cadiz was by princely Essex—Chapman's irrelevance is incurable. She reflects, with scientific help from Plutarch,[21] on the contrast between her outer semblance and her inner knowledge. In sorrow over broken vows she puts on a black robe; her feelings becoming more intense, she strews the floor with her hair and tears her mantle. She swoons, and revives to encourage herself with a great deal of casuistry:

> Had I not yeelded, slaine my selfe I had.
> Hero Leander is, Leander Hero.

She and Chapman finally reach a compromise:

> Beautie in heauen and earth this grace doth win,
> It supples rigor, and it lessens sin.

The last lines of the sestiad, after a tissue of ratiocination too subtle to admit emotion, end with a warm simplicity worthy of Juliet:

> Deare place, I kisse thee, and doe welcome thee,
> As from Leander euer sent to mee.

The fourth sestiad opens with a description of Hero's priestly garments. The scarf alone takes nearly a hundred lines, for in it are embroidered not only Leander but allegorical scenes—a fisherman stung by a serpent, two foxes robbing a girl who sings instead of watching her vine [22]— which "shew what death was hid in loues disguise." "Proceed we now with Heros sacrifice," says the poet, but soon makes a digression of some eighty lines concerning Leander's picture and the lessons it teaches, lessons more in the vein of Marlowe than of our moralistic Chapman—

> that what her hart
> Did greatest hold in her selfe greatest part,
> That she did make her god; and t'was lesse nought
> To leaue gods in profession and in thought,
> Than in her loue and life: for therein lies
> Most of her duties, and their dignities;
> And raile the brain-bald world at what it will,
> Thats the grand Atheisme that raignes in it still.

(*Marlowe and His Circle,* page 68), in his dedication to Lady Walsingham Chapman says nothing about personal intercourse with Marlowe. The words already quoted—"drawne by strange instigation"—together with the lines in the poem, imply the notion of "some telepathic agency, inciting him to complete *Hero and Leander*" (T. Brooke, *Life of Marlowe,* 1930, p. 79); see also Mr. Martin's *Marlowe's Poems,* page 12, and notes. Mr. J. M. Robertson takes the expression "soules darke ofspring" to refer to *The Shadow of Night* (*Problems of the Shakespeare Sonnets,* pp. 231 ff.), but thereby raises unnecessary difficulties. Chapman's theory of poetry makes the phrase applicable to any one of his works.
  [21] Ll. 238 ff. See Schoell, pp. 225–26.
  [22] Both scenes are adapted from the description of the engraved bowl in the first idyll of Theocritus. The illusion to "Arachnean ditties" suggests recollection of the Ovidian web,

So Hero resolves on dissimulation, and we are assured that her sin was nothing compared with "those foule faults other Priests are in."

Hero begins the sacrifice, but Venus appears with her swans and rebukes her. The swan "Leucote," provided with a voice by "the Goddesse Ecte," speaks up in Hero's defense. Fire from Venus' eyes kindles the sacrifice, and from the flame is created the maiden "Eronusis" or Dissimulation, a new and useful deity for maids and men. Venus departs, to the accompaniment of more unexpected mythology.

As if enough action had not already been invented, the fifth sestiad announces that

> Day doubles her accustomd date,
> As loth the night, incenst by fate,
> Should wrack our louers.

This long day Chapman undertakes to fill. Hero, "to shorten time with merriment," sends for two lovers, Alcmane and Mya, whom she had hitherto refused to marry. The wedding feast takes place, and in comes the nymph Teras. There follows the tale of Teras, about Hymen's winning of his bride, in nearly four hundred lines.[23] It is told with relative clarity and straightforwardness. The hero and heroine of the tale are duly married, and the symbolism involved is partly taken from Plutarch's *Quaestiones Romanae*.[24] The tale ends with a lyrical epithalamium that shows Chapman at his best:

> Come, come deare night, Loues Mart of kisses,
> Sweet close of his ambitious line,
> The fruitfull summer of his blisses,
> Loues glorie doth in darknes shine.
> O come soft rest of Cares, come night,
> Come naked vertues only tire,
> The reaped haruest of the light,
> Bound up in sheaues of sacred fire.

Elizabethan and metaphysical strength is refined by the clear flame of Catullus.[25] Teras goes away, amid sinister omens, and we have another ingenuous apology for the episode; since trouble awaits Hero, "I use digressions thus t'encrease the day."

In the sixth sestiad the kindly swan, Leucote, gains the consent of the

and other details recall the shield of Achilles. Chapman published his translation of that part of Homer in 1598.

[23] Chapman probably read the story in Servius (on *Aen.* iv. 99; i. 651), but it appears elsewhere, e.g., in Boccaccio, *De Genealogia Deorum*, bk. v; Cartari, *Imagines Deorum* (section on Juno). The part played by the busybody "Adolesche," and her metamorphosis into a parrot, are perhaps Chapman's invention.

[24] Schoell, pp. 226–27.

[25] Catullus, lxii. See J. B. Emperor, *The Catullian Influence in English Lyric Poetry, ca. 1600–1650* (1928), p. 43. The lines quoted are not among the specific parallels with Catullus.

Fates to restrain the winds, but the Fates are treacherous. Hero prepares
her torch; "Her Torch and Hero, figure shew and vertue." At Abydos
cattle are being slain for the marriage feast, and happy Leander does not
know that he is as far short of his supposed felicity as a London gallant;
the parallel leads on to a satirical sketch of "an affectate traveller" and
further parallels. Such a passage, at such a point in the story, is an
astonishing prelude to tragedy. But the conclusion, which makes some
necessary use of the Greek poem, rises above its conceits and moral
comments to a pitch of genuine feeling. The lovers then undergo an
Ovidian metamorphosis.

  This work of Chapman's has been outlined at some length because,
though regularly printed with Marlowe's fragment, it is by nearly all
readers regularly skipped. But no outline gives a notion of the amount
of alien material thrown into it. Marlowe's eight hundred and eighteen
lines carry the story as far as the two hundred and eighty-first line of
Musaeus; Chapman's portion, of nearly sixteen hundred lines, corresponds to the remaining sixty-two lines of Greek. That Chapman is not
a born narrator has been plain enough. We have noticed also the
intrusion at the beginning of didactic morality, and though, as Chapman
falls under the spell of Hero's fated beauty, this seems to wear off, it
really does not. The tale of Teras is not a mere ornament, it shows
ardent love governed by decorum and arriving at a moral consummation;
and of course there are countless brief moral observations. The result of
Chapman's ethical, argumentative, mythological, and other preoccupa-
tions is that Hero and Leander as characters soon cease to exist. After
being abstractions for many hundreds of lines, despite occasional moments of vividness, they cannot at the end come to life sufficiently
for us to feel greatly moved by their fate. In comparison with Chapman,
at least, Marlowe's fragment seems a miracle of elemental simplicity of
conception and treatment. But the faults of Chapman are not accidental.
The poem is fully in accord with his theory, already encountered, that
poetry should convey moral ideas, not in a bald, didactic manner, but
indirectly, through novel figures, comparisons, symbols.[26] And certainly
one is always conscious of a strong and original mind at work. Only
Donne could be imagined as invoking these similes, to describe Hero in
her black robe:

> No forme was seene, where forme held all her sight:
> But like an Embrion that saw neuer light:
> Or like a scorched statue made a cole
> With three-wingd lightning: or a wretched soule
> Muffled with endles darknes, she did sit.

[26] See Schoell, *passim,* and especially page 88.

Yet there is a very frequent failure to fuse the image or emotion and the thought, and, as regards the whole poem, there is an obvious lack of architectonic power. Too often the centrality of Chapman's poetic purpose is frustrated by the eccentric, tangential quality of his intellect, which appears in his conceits, myth-making, abstract images, mysterious or occult symbols, Neo-Platonizing, and his abundance of queer and strained diction. In him as in later poets of wit the desire to compel attention overreaches itself.

We may break the order of chronology to say a word here of Chapman's translation of Musaeus, which appeared in 1616. The dedication, addressed to Inigo Jones, has the customary references to modern barbarism and the taste of the few elect. Speaking modestly, "to the commune reader," of "that partly excellent Poem of Master Marlowe's" and his own translation, he declares that "the Works are in nothing alike; a different character being held through both the style, matter, and invention." He accepts the tradition, not yet banished by scholarship, that Musaeus "lived in the time of Orpheus." His notes show that as usual he had a Latin version as well as the Greek before him; even the text gives evidence of the help Chapman derived from the lexicon of Scapula (a work based on the great *Thesaurus* of Estienne).[27]

Chapman's English is faithful in the main, though his characteristic turns of thought and phrase alter the texture a good deal. Musaeus describes Leander thus:

Then came upon him astonishment, audacity, trembling, shame; in his heart he trembled, and shame seized him at having been made captive: yet he marvelled at the faultless form, and love kept shame away; then manfully by love's guidance he embraced audacity, and gently stepped and stood before the girl.[28]

And this is Chapman:

> Amaze then took him, Impudence and Shame
> Made earthquakes in him with their frost and flame.
> His heart betwixt them toss'd, till Reverence
> Took all these prisoners in him; and from thence
> Her matchless beauty, with astonishment,
> Increased his bands: till aguish Love, that lent
> Shame and Observance, licensed their remove;
> And, wisely liking impudence in love,
> Silent he went . . .

Simplicity is almost beyond Chapman's reach. So we have instead of "as if angry," "put on anger's cloak"; instead of "my rich parents," "The noblesse of my birth-right's either friend." Leander, says Musaeus, returned home "unsatisfied with a whole night of love"; Chapman strikes out a conceit that finely justifies itself—Leander "breathed insatiate of the absent Sun." But in general Chapman's alterations of phrasing are for the worse; the examples illustrate his introduction of irrelevant and top-heavy metaphors and personifications into a narrative that demands clarity and directness.

The same processes are exhibited on a large scale in Chapman's translation of Homer. Many a reader, led by Keats to the "pure serene" of Chapman, has been repelled by the smoke of conceited pedantry that obscures his very genuine fire and energy. No one ever loved Homer more ardently and jealously than Chapman, and no one could be, at times, less Homeric. The voice, quite often, is the voice of Jacob, the flesh is the flesh of Esau. Extended consideration of the *Homer* does not come into our plan, but a glance at its unclassical qualities will help to round out this sketch.

There is no need of repeating Arnold's analysis of those qualities, but we may borrow one of his briefer illustrations. Out of this simple line of Homer, ἔσσεται ἧμαρ ὅτ' ἄν ποτ' ὀλώλῃ Ἴλιος ἱρὴ, Chapman makes this:

And such a stormy day shall come (in mind and soul I know)
When sacred Troy shall shed her towers, for tears of overthrow.

As Arnold says, Homer is "tormented"; Chapman cannot forbear to interpose a play of thought between his object and its expression. Not only does he make Homer conceited and metaphysical in style, he introduces sometimes a moral and didactic element, by simply depositing lumps of alien matter in the text. M. Schoell has demonstrated that Chapman's critical comments owed much to Spondanus (Jean de Sponde), whose edition of Homer he used, and that his other great prop in his Homeric labors was the lexicon of Scapula. Let us take one illustration, the episode of Nausicaa:

Thus she spake, and called to her maidens of the fair tresses: "Halt, my maidens, whither flee ye at the sight of a man? Ye surely do not take him for an enemy? That mortal breathes not, and never will be born, who shall come with war to the land of the Phaeacians, for they are very dear to the gods . . ."

On the word ἀνὴρ (*Odyssey*, vi. 201) Chapman has this note:

Ἀνήρ, *virili animo præditus, fortis, magnanimus.* Nor are those affirmed to be men, *qui servile quidpiam et abjectum faciunt, vel, facere sustinent:* according to this of Herodotus in Poly. πολλοὶ μὲν ἄνθρωποι εἶεν, ὀλίγοι δ' ἄνδρες. Many men's forms sustain, but few are men.

The note is part of Scapula's note. More astonishing is Chapman's version of the Homeric passage:

> Thus, passing him, she to the virgins went,
> And said: 'Give stay both to your feet and fright.
> Why thus disperse ye for a man's mere sight?
> Esteem you him a Cyclop, that long since
> Made use to prey upon our citizens?
> This man no moist man is (nor watrish thing,
> That's ever flitting, ever ravishing
> All it can compass; and, like it, doth range
> In rape of women, never staid in change).
> This man is truly manly, wise and staid,
> In soul more rich the more to sense decay'd,
> Who nor will do, nor suffer to be done,
> Acts lewd and abject; nor can such a one
> Greet the Phæacians with a mind envíous,
> Dear to the Gods they are, and he is pious . . . ' [29]

This little sermon in eight lines inserted in the simple speech of Nausicaa, and quite foreign to Homer, is the commentary of Estienne and Scapula, which Chapman is not content to borrow for his notes but also weaves into his text! Elizabethan freedom in translation could hardly go further —and yet Chapman has a mystical reverence for Homer. He is also a poet, however, and does not always fall short of his divine original; Odysseus is cast up on shore weary and spent, for "the sea had soakt his heart through." Such a phrase counterbalances a score of sermons and conceits.

The last work of Chapman's that demands attention is a performance extraordinary in more ways than one, the *Andromeda Liberata* of 1614. In the first place it is a little disconcerting to find our grave and high-minded moralist celebrating the virtues of that precious pair, the Earl of Somerset and the Countess of Essex, whose marriage, with its train of intrigue and murder and executions, was the scandal of the age. The long Epistle Dedicatory, which paraphrases Plutarch's *Moralia*[30] in several places, sets forth Chapman's usual doctrine of poetry and the soul, reason and sense, with much praise of the two embodiments of virtue whom he addresses, who have been assailed by slanderous tongues. The poem itself, of well over six hundred lines, tells the story of Perseus and Andromeda; of course the noble earl is the gallant rescuer and "this matchless virgin," Andromeda, is Lady Frances (one recalls the dubious findings of the jury of matrons impaneled in the case). The third of the *dramatis personae* is "the monstrous beast, the ravenous multitude." The piece begins by denouncing "ungodly vulgars," then celebrates

[29] *Odysseys of Homer* (Temple Classics), vi. 306–20; Schoell, pp. 153 ff.
[30] Schoell, pp. 234 ff.

"all-creating, all-preserving Love." There follows a long description of Andromeda taken in part from Natalis Comes.[31] Next is a diatribe, partly adapted from Plutarch, against those whose evil minds, seeking evil, befoul the good. We then come to an account of Perseus which, like so much of Chapman, is both mystical and misty.

> The mind a spirit is, and call'd the glass
> In which we see God; and corporeal grace
> The mirror is, in which we see the mind.

This tenet of Renaissance Platonism is worked out at length. To the "form" of Perseus "his mind fit answer made" in sixty-one obscure lines, on the text "Beauty breeds love, love consummates a man." This whole passage, comprising the description of Perseus as a sort of god of love, and the speech of his "mind," is a paraphrase of two chapters of the fifth discourse (that of Agathon) in Ficino's *Commentarium in Convivium*.[32] The attributes of Perseus are those given by Marsupini, who takes the part of Agathon, to Love. The lines on the power of the planet Venus over Mars are taken from the second of the two chapters.

Perseus speaks at length on the nature of love, and on the "interchange" or reciprocity that subsists between "true lovers." That is, the woman beloved should return her lover's passion and yield to his embraces, otherwise she prevents the birth of children and is worse than a homicide, for "divine worth doth in generation shine." These specimens of amatory casuistry are taken from the eighth chapter of the second discourse (Pausanias, as interpreted by Antonio) in Ficino. As M. Schoell says:

On peut imaginer combien surprenante semblable exhortation, issue du cerveau délirant d'un théologien encore médiéval, peut nous apparaître, ainsi placée dans la bouche d'un héros de la mythologie grecque! Mais Chapman ne s'est pas embarrassé de vains scrupules. Il a tout simplement traduit et incorporé le morceau, sans nous donner la moindre indication de source.[33]

Altogether Chapman's treatment of the myth, quite apart from its connection with Somerset and his wife, is remote from, say, Ariosto's adaptation, yet both are of the Renaissance.[34]

[31] Schoell, pp. 195–96.
[32] Chapman (ed. 1875), pp. 188–89, from "Perseus of Love's own form" to the end of the ensuing speech. See Schoell, pp. 14 ff.
[33] P. 14.
[34] See above, page 70, for a reference to the allegorical interpretation of the myth derived by Harington from Leo Hebraeus.
A word may be added about the ill success of the poet's tribute to the royal favorite and the "innocent and spotless virgin." More tactful men than Chapman might have blundered, in treating such a theme at such a time, and he, having in his "innocency" used expressions which had been misapplied, felt moved to write a "justification" in prose and verse. "Bound to a barren rock" was infelicitous, whether with regard to Somerset or the notorious charges against Essex. No less suggestive was the word "homicide"; there was (or soon was to be) in London too much whispering about homicide of a kind less theoretical than Chapman's. On the whole a quaint incident!

In Chapman's work as a whole medieval and modern elements are especially difficult to distinguish. His contempt for the unlettered mob and his faith in culture are both proclaimed with more than Renaissance fervor. His knowledge of classical literature goes beyond medieval limits, and he has some first-hand acquaintance with Greek. In many respects, more apparent in the plays, his mind reveals the secular, mundane interests, the conception of *virtù,* the realistic curiosity about life, that belong to the Renaissance. The metaphysical quality of his thought and style, which looks both backward and forward, has already been touched upon.

On the other hand we recall his exceptionally large use of secondhand erudition, his allegorical interpretation of mythology and of the classics generally,[35] a didactic conception of poetry held with unusual strictness. Chapman draws fruitful lessons of Stoicism and decorum and rationalism from Seneca, Cicero, Plutarch. But much of the substance and mode of his thought comes from the very different Ficino and Natalis Comes— Ficino, who worshiped Plato and almost made a burlesque of Platonism; Comes, who for all his learning is of the company of Fulgentius and Berchorius. Indeed the sixteenth-century mind was at once a museum and a world's fair, exhibiting the oldest and the newest intellectual acquisitions in paradoxical confusion.

Along with Chapman's allegorical mythology goes a distaste for Ovidian decoration and Ovidian rhetoric, which, though dear to his contemporaries, seem shallow to him. Marlowe and Shakespeare might use the myth of Narcissus as a bit of poetic ornament or as a warning to enjoy the April of youth and love. Chapman, after Ficino, takes Narcissus' self-love as an example of the way in which the soul is softened and

> rapt (as with a storm)
> With flatteries of our base corporeal form
> (Which is her shadow) that she quite forsakes
> Her proper noblesse, and for nothing takes
> The beauties that for her love, thou putt'st on,
> In torments rarefied far past the Sun.[36]

---

[35] To preceding illustrations should be added these words from the dedication of his *Odyssey* to Somerset:

"And that your Lordship may in his face take view of his mind, the first word of his Iliads is μῆνιν, wrath; the first word of his Odysseys, ἄνδρα, man; contracting in either word his each work's proposition. In one, predominant perturbation; in the other, over-ruling wisdom: in one, the body's fervour and fashion of outward fortitude to all possible height of heroical action; in the other, the mind's inward, constant and unconquered empire; unbroken, unaltered, with any most insolent and tyrannous infliction."

This at least is a worthy conception of Homer.

[36] *Hymn to Christ upon the Cross* (p. 146); Schoell, pp. 7–8. The passage in Ficino had inspired some lines in the *Narcissus* of 1560 (see above, page 49).

There are not many lines of religious poetry more memorable than these last two.

Obviously the classics did not teach Chapman anything of clarity, selection, form, restraint. He had enough knowledge of ancient literature to profit, if his mind had been attuned to them, by the great exemplars of "fullness in the concise and depth in the clear." But his powerful and individual mind was more medieval than classical. As Swinburne said, he "enters the serene temples and handles the holy vessels of Hellenic art with the stride and the grasp of a high-handed and high-minded barbarian." (It is perhaps permissible to remember that there is a touch of the Goth in the great Ben.) But, despite mental and stylistic vagaries, Chapman is more truly humanistic than many who have received the epithet. Without disowning the senses, of which he is such a curious explorer, and with full admiration for the complete personality, he insists upon law for man and law for thing, upon the necessity of man's dominion over experience, over the restless animal within. His ideal is secular and humanistic, not ascetic or pagan, and it is bound up with learning and culture.[37]

Chapman's obscurity is partly deliberate and temperamental, and it is partly due to the miscellaneous borrowing of materials not easily fused. Besides, Chapman is wrestling continually with difficult problems of the inner life—problems that leave Marlowe's "atheism" the talk of a clever schoolboy—with the relations of a trinity that roughly corresponds to the body, brain, and spirit of one of the most subtle of modern poets. But, with a full desire to appreciate Chapman and his significance, one may demur when a critic writes that it would "be difficult to exaggerate the wealth of possibilities that came into existence with Chapman's individual poetry; but after Chapman came Milton, destroying this indigenous growth." [38] Possibilities there are, yet Chapman is so uneven that no poem is good as a whole. He does frequently fuse thought and emotion. Even more frequently what appears to be metaphysical poetry results from Chapman's failure to remove the cumbrous scaffolding, the débris of bricks and mortar, that remain from his wasteful operations. A happy phrase of Mr. Chesterton's is true of Chapman: "An utterance of Browning is often like a strange animal walking backwards, who flourishes his tail with such energy that everyone takes it for his head." That Milton might have learned from Chapman and Donne is true, but he could have taught them much more.

[37] See especially *The Tears of Peace,* which, in comparison with *Musophilus,* hardly receives its due.
[38] Herbert Read, *Reason and Romanticism* (1926), p. 42.

CHAPTER ELEVEN

LYRICAL VERSE

SOME mythological conventions in lyrics of the first two-thirds of Elizabeth's reign have already been described. To turn to the period from about 1589 to the death of Milton and contemplate the immense body of lyrical verse, with the thousand or two mythological allusions embedded therein, is to recall Psyche's task of separating the seeds; and the parallel is not a casual one, for a good deal of the mythology is without distinction. In the absence of Psyche's supernatural aid we may be content with a brief sketch, especially since allusions in lyrical or short poems in general reflect the changing fashions that are more fully recorded in other chapters.

The amatory formula so popular among the courtly makers in Tottel's *Miscellany* and its successors did not become extinct in the seventeenth century, but it underwent some alterations. An anonymous poet in 1606 begins a complaint:

> The Queen of Paphos, Erycine,
> In heart did rose-cheeked Adon love . . .[1]

The piece is not notable, though its ease and lightness tell of a general advance in poetic expression; *Venus and Adonis* furnishes the theme, and an epithet that Shakespeare and Marlowe had made current. But while the older lyrics on this pattern left the poet prostrate and disconsolate, our lover remains cool and sensible:

> Hence, groaning sighs! mirth be my friend!
> Before my life, my love shall end.

We leap forward to Waller's *The Story of Phœbus and Daphne, Applied,* and find him, his suit rejected, comforting himself in this manner:

> Like Phœbus thus, acquiring unsought praise,
> He catched at love, and filled his arm with bays.[2]

The conceit, drawn from Marino, appears also in Stanley and Ayres.[3]

---

[1] J. Bartlet, *A Book of Airs* (Norman Ault, *Elizabethan Lyrics*, p. 374).

[2] *Poems* (Muses' Library), I, 52.

[3] Marino, *Lira,* parte prima, *Trasformazione di Dafne in Lauro.* For Stanley and Ayres, see M. Praz, *M. L. R.,* XX, 283, 426, and below, page 237. Cf. the lines quoted from Marvell's *The Garden,* page 228 below.

The name of Ayres brings us full circle, for another piece of his, which is not much longer than the title, takes us back to the Elizabethans—*Compares the Troubles which he has undergone for Cynthia's Love, to the Labours of Hercules*. We are not surprised to find that it is translated from Guarini.[4]

While seventeenth-century lyrists could still, like the Tudor poets, make serious and plaintive applications of myth, though with an added elegance and sophistication,[5] verses written on the old formula generally shared in the movement away from the Petrarchan pose toward a more courtly and robust gallantry, or more purely bookish compliment.

The majority of love poems did not follow this particular pattern, but they were studded with brief allusions and comparisons. The sonneteers worked mythology to death; we may leave them alone. The same spirit of extravagant idealism gave birth to such poems as Greene's *Samela,* the subject of which is likened to Diana, Arethusa, Aurora, Thetis, Venus, Juno, Pallas.[6] Greene can be pedantic, but here "he touches the brink of perfection in his own kind, in an atmosphere as clear and stainless as early morning in a garden." [7] The apt phrase suggests the special quality of Elizabethan mythology at its best, and such a quality in the nature of things could not survive.

Herrick was very much of an Elizabethan, but his mythological allusions underwent the same strict and loving scrutiny that tested every syllable of his verse; the Roman poets, in their lighter moods, had entered into his being. *The Description of a Woman,* one of the last of the voluptuous Renaissance catalogues, is distinguished from its Elizabethan predecessors only by more conscious and delicate craftsmanship. In general Herrick's mythological allusions are elegant, attractive, poetic, yet in their context they become less mythological.

> The passive Aire such odour then assum'd,
> As when to Jove Great Juno goes perfum'd.[8]

The occasion is "Julia's unlacing her self," and though the reference may add a Junoesque cubit to Julia's stature, the queen of heaven loses some regality. When Leander drowned, Love sat on a rock and "Wept as he'd drowne the Hellespont." [9] In common mythology the milk of Juno created the Milky Way; Herrick prefers the smaller and daintier myth, that the breast of Venus, under the fingers of Cupid, yielded the milk

[4] Saintsbury, *Minor Caroline Poets,* II, 341; Praz, p. 429.
[5] Cf. Drummond's madrigal "Like the Idalian queen . . ." (Ault, page 462), which ends with a conceit taken from Marino (*Works of Drummond,* ed. Kastner, I, 188).
[6] Ault, p. 125.
[7] Elizabeth Holmes, *Aspects of Elizabethan Imagery,* p. 18.
[8] *Works.* ed. Moorman, p. 157.   [9] *Ibid.,* p. 42.

which made the lilies white.[10] Stories of Jove's amours become less
Olympian when told among maids under a tree, with talk of brides,
posies for rings, and gloves and ribbons.[11] Indeed one title would suggest
the character of myth when it is painted into Herrick's exquisite
miniatures, *The Parcæ, or, Three dainty Destinies.* To read Herrick
after Marlowe or Spenser is to turn from the Italian painters to Watteau.

When myths are used to decorate the scenes and the loves of artificial
lyrics they are likely to become polite and sophisticated. The great
mythological themes are avoided by the lyrists, or else divested of their
greatness. In the whole body of lyrical verse Cupid exceeds all other
deities in the frequency of his appearance—his nearest rival is his mother
—and under the dominion of the blind bow-boy goddesses become
nymphs or pretty mistresses, the gods elegant shepherds or admiring
courtiers. We seldom meet such a conception of Cupid as animates
Jonson's famous stanza:

> At his sight the sun hath turned,
> Neptune in the waters burned;
> Hell hath felt a greater heat;
> Jove himself forsook his seat:
> From the centre to the sky,
> Are his trophies reared high.[12]

Whether the association of myths with trivial themes is satisfying or
not depends, like everything else, upon the poet. No one is likely to
quarrel with Herrick, or with such lines as these by William Strode,
from one of the three or four most popular lyrics of the seventeenth
century:

> I saw fair Chloris walk alone,
> Whilst feathered rain came softly down,
> And Jove descended from his tower
> To court her in a silver shower.[13]

But when, as in the often charming Randolph, or the seldom charming
Waller, a classical education runs to seed in trite or absurdly extravagant
allusions, mythology becomes merely the capitalized slang of courtly
gallantry.[14] The vice was not unknown to the Roman love poets, but the
allusions in Ovid's *Amores* have ironic or mock-heroic touches, and,
though the very Alexandrian Propertius is stuffed with mythology, no
amount of otiose ornament can cool the Propertian fire.[15]

[10] *Ibid.,* p. 74.
[11] *Ibid.,* p. 215.
[12] *Masques and Entertainments,* ed. H. Morley (1890), p. 91.
[13] Ault, *Seventeenth Century Lyrics,* pp. viii, 81.
[14] See Thorn-Drury's complaint, *Poems of Thomas Randolph* (1929), p. xxiv.
[15] In speaking of the slightness of more or less mythological lyrics one must remember
that often they are real lyrics, that they may take a mythological name as a theme for

Of course there are some notable examples of the serious or even didactic use of mythology in lyrical poems of our period. I can quote only the beginning and end of a piece perhaps by Ralegh:

> Praisd be Dianas faire and harmles light,
> Praisd be the dewes, wherwith she moists the ground;
> Praisd be hir beames, the glorie of the night,
> Praisd be hir powre, by which all powres abound . . .
>
> Time weares hir not, she doth his chariot guide,
> Mortalitie belowe hir orbe is plaste,
> By hir the vertue of the starrs downe slide,
> In hir is vertues perfect image cast.
>
> A knowledge pure it is hir worth to kno,
> With Circes let them dwell that thinke not so.[16]

One might almost call such a poem—even if Diana be related to Elizabeth—a Renaissance parallel to the hymn of St. Francis.

Among the few good poems which inherit the didactic sobriety of Tudor humanism one of the finest is Daniel's *Ulysses and the Siren* (1605).[17] The improvement made on the poetic inheritance can be measured if one turns back to *Beware of Sirens* in *The Paradise of Dainty Devices*.[18] Daniel's poem, being Daniel's, creates its effect, not by winged words and rich overtones, but by moral elevation and straightforward purity of style. The story of Ulysses and the sirens, like that of Circe, had its didactic implications in Homer, and was accepted allegorically by Cicero and Horace.[19] Daniel's lyrical statement of the rival claims of slothful ease and honorable toil recalls Belphoebe's answer to Bragga-docchio and other eulogies of heroic effort in Renaissance literature. But Daniel's siren is no voluptuous Spenserian temptress, she is rather a disembodied attitude of mind, and her language is, so to speak, as manly as that of Ulysses.

Elizabethan lyrics and their still more delicate progeny seldom carried any weight of personal emotion or felt any obligation to interpret life.

musical variations, as, for instance, in *When Orpheus sweetly did complain* (*Poetical Works of William Strode*, ed. B. Dobell, London, 1907, p. 1; *Parnassus Biceps*, ed. G. Thorn-Drury, London, 1927, p. 100). William Cartwright, Orinda's "Prince of Phansie," has a piece of over one hundred lines, a complaint called *Ariadne deserted by Theseus*, which, after Catullus and Ovid, is not very satisfactory, but it may have been better when set to the music of Henry Lawes. See R. C. Goffin, *Life and Poems of William Cartwright* (Cambridge University Press, 1918), pp. 59 ff., 190; J. B. Emperor, *Catullian Influence*, pp. 72–73; Masson, *Poetical Works of John Milton* (1874), III, 476–77.

[16] *Poems of Sir Walter Ralegh*, ed. A. M. C. Latham (London, 1929), p. 111. See *The Phœnix Nest*, ed. Rollins (1931), pp. 77, 166.

[17] Ault, *Elizabethan Lyrics*, p. 358.

[18] Ed. Rollins, p. 63. Master Bew quickly leaves Ulysses for his real subject, the sirens of the moment—"Thei sigh, thei sobb, thei prate, thei praie . . ."

[19] Cicero, *De Finibus*, v. 18; Horace, *Epistles*, i. 2. 23. See above, page 101, note 26. See also Fulgentius, ii. 11.

Their beauty or their prettiness was sufficient cause for existence, and the spirit of such verse was naturally unfavorable to any very significant use of mythology. For that reason one poem, or some lines of one poem, must be singled out as a rare embodiment of intense feeling, in words of simple and dazzling felicity:

> Brightness falls from the air;
> Queens have died young and fair;
> Dust hath closed Helen's eye:
> I am sick, I must die.
> *Lord, have mercy on us!*

The lines were quoted at the beginning of this book, but no excuse is needed for quoting them again. Our interest here is first in the intuitive craftsmanship, the way in which the statement of the universal theme closes in by degrees from the general to the particular, from the transiency of earthly beauty to the death, long ago, of the most beautiful of women. And, in the second place, what is the source of such feeling? Not the classicism of the Renaissance, certainly, but the *Ubi sunt* of the Middle Ages, the spirit of Villon's *Ballade,* of Donne's meditation on eternity and the little lives of all the powerful kings and all the beautiful queens of this world.

Most of the wealth of Elizabethan song is the happy product of exuberant if not always happy life, and it is not easy to find anything comparable to Nashe's poem. One might quote Campion:

> When thou must home to shades of underground,
> And there arrived, a new admirèd guest,
> The beauteous spirits do ingirt thee round,
> White Iope, blithe Helen and the rest . . .[20]

But the promise of these Roman lines, with their special echo of Propertius, is not fulfilled; the poem ends with a trivial Petrarchan conceit. Perhaps as near an approach to Nashe as there is would be the medieval-metaphysical lines of Benlowes:

> Death's serjeant soon thy courted Helens must
> Attach, whose eyes, now orbs of lust,
> The worms shall feed on, till they crumble into dust.[21]

But Nashe is at once classical and romantic; Benlowes is odd.

We have had in other chapters sufficient intimations that the mythologizing of nature was well under way in the Elizabethan period. Phoebus, hot Titan, Aurora, sad Philomel, were in constant demand, and they continued to be for many generations. But the novelties of every

[20] Ault, p. 313. For Nashe's poem see *ibid.,* p. 174.　　[21] *Minor Caroline Poets,* I, 427.

age—not least our own—quickly become clichés, and allusions which in the eighteenth century seem frigid and pedantic may, in the sixteenth and early seventeenth, have a pleasant color, spontaneity, and pastoral sweetness. Not always, to be sure. This is Bartholomew Griffin's unique picture of the dawn:

> So soon as peeping Lucifer, Aurora's star,
> The sky with golden periwigs doth spangle.[22]

Pedantry in the earlier period is likely to have a touch of the eccentric, as when the bookish Drummond makes birds into "Amphions of the Trees." [23] Or, remembering the pure beauty of Spenser and Milton, we may contrast with it the slight oddity of Cleveland's athletic suggestions:

> The sluggish morne as yet undrest,
> My Phillis brake from out her East;
> As if shee'd made a match to run
> With Venus, Usher to the sun.[24]

Even bookish poets had their share of that heady quality which carried Elizabethans to both heights and depths. Drummond begins a poem with a tissue of conventional mythology, and before he ends can write with the almost too violent splendor of Francis Thompson:

> Night like a drunkard reels
> Beyond the hills to shun his flaming wheels.[25]

Though the figure is borrowed it is given a larger imaginative quality; Shakespeare's is vivid, but has just a hint of a tipsy pedestrian. Such lines remind one that personification is one of the richest elements in Elizabethan poetry, and that it is almost inseparable from the mythological instinct. It is needless to quote familiar examples, from "Night's candles are burnt out" to "While the still Morn went out with sandals gray."

Nature for the Elizabethans and their successors was no mystical or mysterious spirit, beneficent or ruthless, but a mixture in varying degrees of a conventional and ideal Arcadia with the more real but no less attractive sights and sounds of the English countryside. Mythologized

---

[22] Lee, *Elizabethan Sonnets,* II, 288. But one need not blame mythology. Cf. Sylvester (ed. Grosart, I, 124, l. 187): "And perriwig with wool the balde-pate Woods." See Lee, *French Renaissance in England,* pp. 336, 346.

[23] Kastner, I, 21. Nightingales are "the Pandionian birds" (page 46).

[24] Grierson, *Metaphysical Lyrics and Poems,* p. 47. For quotations from Spenser and Milton, see above, page 95, and below, page 259.

[25] Ault, pp. 462–63. Cf. *Romeo and Juliet,* II. iii. 3–4:

> And flecked darkness like a drunkard reels
> From forth day's path and Titan's fiery wheels.

pictures of such a world may have their own congruity, and a relish for
Dick the shepherd blowing his nail, or Breton's black-haired coney, is
not incompatible with admiration for the cool, clear, monumental beauty
of "Queen and huntress, chaste and fair." Though Elizabethan vitality
gave way to a more desiccated mythologizing, some men continued to
see through Elizabethan eyes, and the older tradition might enable a
middling poet like Cotton to rise above himself:

> Now Phœbus is gone down to sleep
> In cold embraces of the deep,
> And Night's pavilion in the sky,
> (Crown'd with a starry canopy)
> Erected stands, whence the pale Moon
> Steals out to her Endymion . . .[26]

The mythologizing of nature is not quite the same as the naturalizing
of mythology, and the latter, which is the healthier instinct, is responsible
for much of the most attractive verse of the period, both dramatic and
non-dramatic. Whatever foreign influences, ancient or modern, contributed in the way of motives or polished workmanship, the native
pastoral tradition (like the native drama) was strong enough to
undergo refinement without losing its own color and sap. Lyrical poems
which were subdued by mythology we do not read; those that subdued
mythology everyone knows. In the former category might be placed, for
example, Spenser's eclogue for March, which hardly succeeds in acclima-
tizing Cupid.

But we need not linger over failures when there is an embarrassing
wealth of charming specimens.

> Pan's Syrinx was a girl indeed,
> Though now she's turned into a reed,

sings Lyly, and it is Pan's pipe that stirs the feet of

> Cross-gartered swains and dairy girls,
> With faces smug and round as pearls.[27]

Diana is quite at home in rural England. One thinks of Greene's picture
of a white-legged and not too austere goddess with her taffeta cassock
tucked above her knee, or of a tuneful moralizer in *England's Helicon*:

> Hey downe a downe did Dian sing,
>   amongst her Virgins sitting:
> Then loue there is no vainer thing . . .[28]

---

[26] *Poems of Charles Cotton*, ed. J. Beresford, p. 101.
[27] Ault, p. 123. In Caxton's *Methamorphose*, by the way, we have Pan, in his contest
with Apollo, "vauntynge hyme of the horne-pype of Cornewaylle."
[28] Ed. H. Macdonald (1925), p. 123. For Greene's lyric, see *ibid.*, pp. 117–18.

In more serious mood, and with the delicate and deliberate precision of
diction and movement that mark the disciplined classicist, there is
Campion's familiar

> Hark, all you ladies that do sleep!
> The fairy queen Proserpina
> Bids you awake, and pity them that weep.[29]

The infinite gradations in the process of Anglicizing myths are
illustrated in the almost infinite number of translations and imitations
of Anacreontic pieces, Greek idylls, and similar things, variations on the
hue and cry after Cupid, Cupid stung by a bee . . . Italian and French
models count more than ancient as a rule, but the pastoral-mythological
lyric of the Renaissance is essentially international, and only a slight
coloring is needed to make it seem English.[30] As examples of the wide
range of treatment we might take Giles Fletcher's *Dialogue betwixt two
Sea Nymphs, Doris and Galatea, concerning Polyphemus,* which is
derived from Lucian,[31] and the most popular lyric of the age, Marlowe's
Passionate Shepherd. This we think of as the fine flower of Elizabethan
pastoral song, yet the invitation to love goes back ultimately to the
Ovidian and Theocritean story of Polyphemus and Galatea.[32] Naturali-
zation of a mythological theme could hardly be carried further. Or one
might mention a different kind of example from Caroline days; Sidney
Godolphin gives an English tone to the myth of Cephalus and Procris
by altering the names and making it into a pastoral "ballet." [33]

No poet is more English than Drayton, and in his *Muses Elizium* he
domesticates mythology with an abundance of realism both homely and
dainty.

Olympus and Parnassus seem to have poured forth their people, if we listen
to their names only, upon the pages of his Elysium. But whatever they may be
called, the most unmistakable English men and maids, hale and buxom,
blithe and frolic, discover themselves in the faces and forms that bear these
classic labels and attributes. Venus and Cupid, trespassing furtively in the
Elysium from which they have been sternly excluded, become a merry English
wife and her 'little lad'; they take ferry, and she chats gaily with the ferry-

[29] Ault, p. 151.
[30] See above, page 115, note 74. The *Complaint of the Satyres against the Nymphes,*
which formed part of the "Entertainment at Harefield" given before the queen in 1602,
is not exactly English, yet one would not suppose it to be taken from Cinthio (V. M.
Jeffery, *M. L. R.,* XIX, 56 ff.).
[31] *Elizabethan Sonnets,* II, 63. While professing to translate from Lucian, Fletcher does
not say that he is making use of the expanded Latin version of Johannes Secundus
(D. Crane, *Johannes Secundus,* Leipsic, 1931, p. 53).
[32] R. S. Forsythe, "*The Passionate Shepherd;* and English Poetry," *P.M.L.A.,* XL,
692 ff.
[33] *Poems,* ed. Dighton (1931), p. 15; *Minor Caroline Poets,* II, 242.

man, who marvels at the 'little dapper elf,' 'half bird half boy,' and finds it passing strange 'to have a child have wings to fly, and yet want eyes to see.' Drayton, in some sense the 'brave heroic mind' *par excellence* among all the Elizabethans, dared these incongruities with impunity, such is the charm of the English freshness and homeliness which his magic throws upon the most exotic figures.[34]

It is one evidence of the strength and originality of Jonson's classicism that his lyrical poems, which owe so much to the classics, in the main— apart from songs in the masques—avoid the mythology of his contemporaries. So too in that astonishing phenomenon of his late years, *The Sad Shepherd,* the scene and persons are English, and there is hardly an allusion to mythology or anything ancient—for Jonson will not here, like Drayton, mix two worlds—yet the piece is inconceivable without the mythological tradition.[35]

So far we have been concerned with representatives of the main stream of Elizabethan verse. We turn now to an equally brief sketch of the metaphysical movement in relation to mythology, and shall here follow poets rather than species of poetry. The whole body of Donne's work contains much more mythological allusion than one remembers at first, yet his best-known pieces have hardly any. (Apart from specific debts, which are not lacking, Donne's love poems in their intensity are closer to Catullus and some other ancients than are those of his fellow lyrists with their more obvious classicism.) Instead of diffuse Italianate word-painting we have in Donne's mythology the stamp of his special qualities, wit, realism, ratiocination, learning, concentration of feeling and expression, sometimes deliberate harshness and ugliness. What his contemporaries would spread over a page he puts into a line and a half:

> And to make blinde men see,
> What things gods are, I say they' are like to thee.[36]

When the soul in its progress mounts through the planets,

> Hee that charm'd Argus eyes, sweet Mercury,
> Workes not on her, who now is growne all eye.[37]

The first line might occur in any Elizabethan poet, but not the second. Donne can make use of Phoebus, but what one remembers is "Busie old foole, unruly Sunne." Venus is not the lover of Adonis, she is the patroness of "Loves sweetest Part, Variety." Orthodox poets might treat Cupid as the sportive god of love in idleness, or even rail at him with

---

[34] Herford and Simpson, *Ben Jonson,* II, 230.
[35] *Ibid.* We may remember that Jonson wrote a long poem on Proserpine which was destroyed by fire.
[36] *Poems,* ed. Grierson, I, 124.   [37] I, 257.

affected anger, but they did not entangle him in such nets of witty or passionate reasoning as Donne creates.

He does sometimes echo the love poems of Ovid, but he is no Renaissance Ovidian in style. His most outspoken poems are perhaps less titillating to average senses than several passages in Spenser the moralist. For Donne's fleshliness is at once too intense and too intellectualized to spend itself in voluptuous painting of the body; his mind rather than his eye is at work. The Elizabethan Ovidians inclined to be, in Donne's phrase, all eye, and if we could imagine Donne's eighteenth and nineteenth elegies as written by one of them, the poems would be a series of mythological pictures.

His abstinence from, or perversion of, mythological allusions implies of course a deliberate revolt against this as against other conventions. The significance of that revolt was described once for all in Carew's familiar lines, some of which bear directly upon the matter in hand. Now that Donne is gone, says Carew, other poets

> will recall the goodly exiled train
> Of gods and goddesses, which in thy just reign
> Was banish'd nobler poems; now with these,
> The silenc'd tales i' th' Metamorphoses,
> Shall stuff their lines, and swell the windy page,
> Till verse, refined by thee in this last age,
> Turn ballad-rhyme, or those old idols be
> Adored again with new apostacy.[38]

It was time for revolt, but Carew is naturally biased. Whatever the vices of the Renaissance tradition, it produced a body of poetry that needs no defense. If we are rash enough to read, say, *England's Helicon* at a sitting, we may turn to Donne for something craggy to break our minds upon; but a continuous spell of Donne may also, if one dare to say it, breed a taste for *England's Helicon*. At any rate the monarch of wit did react powerfully against the idealistic and idyllic mythology of the Elizabethan lyrists, and for the consequences we may take a brief glance at some of his more or less metaphysical descendants.

In the first place, there is much less mythology in lyrics of the seventeenth century than in those of the sixteenth. If we take Mr. Ault's two anthologies as a standard, remembering that they are divided at 1620, not 1600, we find that the allusions in the second volume are only about half as numerous as they are in the first.[39] In Mr. Grierson's

[38] *Poems* (Muses' Library), p. 102.
[39] This rough estimate leaves out, in the second volume (pp. 246–49), a catalogue of some two score deities, a very racy and jolly piece, but awkward for the statistician. See below, page 229.

anthology of metaphysical poetry mythology is very scarce; it occurs
mainly in poems or poets not genuinely metaphysical, such as Milton's
Nativity and Randolph. Much metaphysical verse, to be sure, is religious,
but Spenser, the Fletchers, Milton, could use mythology freely in didactic
or religious poems. George Herbert, when he wrote Latin in the humanistic tradition, scattered classical references abundantly; his English
poems, written under the influence of Donne, are almost wholly free
from them.[40]

In spite of his praise of Donne's independence of Renaissance classicism,
Carew himself found his master's laws too hard. He is not above
mythological conceits; a fly that gets into his mistress' eye is scorched
and drowned, and falls like Phaethon.[41] *On Sight of a Gentlewoman's
Face in the Water* has only one explicit allusion, but the tissue of imagery
is essentially mythological. We have room for only the last two stanzas:

> But if the envious nymphs shall fear
>   Their beauties will be scorn'd,
> And hire the ruder winds to tear
>   That face which you adorn'd,
>
> Then rage and foam amain, that we
>   Their malice may despise;
> When from your froth we soon shall see
>   A second Venus rise.[42]

Carew's style is far less realistic than Donne's, and here the symmetry
of the logical and rhythmic pattern, the rhetorical energy, the artistic
remoteness of the imagery, achieve a kind of dignity which makes a
trivial theme worthy of the concluding allusion. So too in the opening
lines of Carew's most smoothly perfect lyric the name of Jove just serves
to take us out of our world into the world of pure art.

A Rapture, so clearly inspired by Donne, is partly metaphysical, partly
Ovidian. Among the allusions to Venus' doves, Danae, Lucrece, Lais,
Penelope, we may take this, as a notable example of pastoral mythology
quickened and strengthened by a new mode of feeling and thinking:

> Daphne hath broke her bark, and that swift foot
> Which th' angry gods had fasten'd with a root
> To the fix'd earth, doth now unfetter'd run
> To meet th' embraces of the youthful Sun.
> She hangs upon him like his Delphic lyre;
> Her kisses blow the old, and breathe new fire . . .[43]

Mythology is not very important in Crashaw, but one passage may
be quoted, since it forms part of one of his most illuminating figures.

[40] George Williamson, *The Donne Tradition* (1930), p. 109.
[41] *Poems,* p. 52.   [42] P. 140.   [43] P. 74.

In persuading the Countess of Denbigh to resolution in religion he
speaks of the perversity of the soul that fights against its own instincts:

> What fatall, yet fantastick, bands
> Keep The free Heart from it's own hands!
> So when the year takes cold, we see
> Poor waters their owne prisoners be.
> Fetter'd, & lockt up fast they ly
> In a sad selfe-captiuity.
> The' astonisht nymphs their flood's strange fate deplore,
> To see themselues their own seuerer shore.[44]

The simile of the water elucidates a difficult idea, but the nymphs are less
essential; in fact the addition of a mythological image is a touch of that
decorative excess to which Crashaw was always liable. At any rate the
nymphs are very distant relations of the large sisterhood of *Polyolbion*.

Recent criticism, in praising the metaphysical fusion of thought and
feeling, has been inclined to overlook or minimize the innumerable
instances, in both Donne and his followers, of imperfect fusion, of
writing that is simply undisciplined eccentricity and extravagance. Even
mythological allusions can be odd and tormented. Crashaw describes a
musician

> Trembling as when Appollo's golden haires
> Are fan'd and frizled, in the wanton ayres
> Of his owne breath . . .[45]

With the lines on Daphne quoted from Carew compare the ingenuity
that contrived the opening stanza of Cowley's *Ode upon Dr. Harvey*:

> Coy Nature, (which remain'd, though aged grown,
> A Beauteous virgin still, injoy'd by none,
>   Nor seen unveil'd by any one)
> When Harveys violent passion she did see,
> Began to tremble, and to flee,
> Took Sanctuary like Daphne in a tree;
> There Daphnes lover stop't, and thought it much
>   The very Leaves of her to touch,
> But Harvey our Apollo, stopt not so,
> Into the Bark, and root he after her did goe . . .[46]

The mythological parallel is worked out in all its demented intricacies
for two dozen lines more. It was indeed time for Dryden. Yet Cowley's
On the Death of Mr. William Hervey is almost wholly free from
mythology, and is one of the genuine elegies in English.

Marvell, to take a last example, is at his best a poet who combines the
metaphysical range and subtlety of thought and feeling with classical

[44] *Poems*, ed. L. C. Martin, p. 237.
[45] *Ibid.*, p. 152.
[46] *Poems*, ed. A. R. Waller (1905), p. 416.

economy, clarity, and precision of style, who draws strength and beauty
from liberal puritanism and the sensuous tradition of the Renaissance.
His occasional mythological allusions are not fully representative of his
powers, but they have their arresting individual note:

> So weeps the wounded Balsome: so
> The holy Frankincense doth flow.
> The brotherless Heliades
> Melt in such Amber Tears as these.[47]

In *The Garden* the decorative mythology of the Elizabethan pastoral is
handled with swift lightness, and given larger suggestions:

> When we have run our Passions heat,
> Love hither makes his best retreat.
> The Gods, that mortal Beauty chase,
> Still in a Tree did end their race.
> Apollo hunted Daphne so,
> Only that She might Laurel grow.
> And Pan did after Syrinx speed,
> Not as a Nymph, but for a Reed.

When in *The Gallery* the poet invites Clora to view his soul and the
paintings there, he offers a picture of Italianate opulence but quite
un-Italianate brevity and surprise:

> But, on the other side, th'art drawn
> Like to Aurora in the Dawn;
> When in the East she slumb'ring lyes,
> And stretches out her milky Thighs . . .

Finally, there is no better example of pregnant metaphysical suggestion
made concrete and vivid by the mythological tradition than this:

> But at my back I alwaies hear
> Times winged Charriot hurrying near . . .

The lines are also a reminder that this sketch must be cut short, since
we cannot, like Harvey, penetrate bark and root. Mythology in poetry
owed much to the metaphysical movement. The flood of indiscriminate
allusion and merely sensuous picture-making was checked. Such things
ceased to be satisfying, even in lyrical verse, and mythological allusions,
becoming fewer, became more concentrated and significant. Pictorial
luxuriance was burned out by intellectual subtlety; the best poets as a
rule declared war on the adjective and death to the optic nerve. There
was a general tightening of sinews. When lyrics became the vehicle for
complex philosophic conceptions of the universe and man's place in it,
the Elizabethan manner was gone beyond recall. Even after the impulse

---

[47] *The Nymph complaining for the death of her Faun* (*Poems*, ed. Margoliouth, I, 24).

had spent itself it left its mark on poets not especially philosophic. It was not merely the classical or the Renaissance Cupid that caught the fancy of Sedley and Mrs. Behn:

> Love still has something of the sea
> From whence his mother rose ...

> Love in fantastic triumph sat,
> Whilst bleeding hearts around him flowed ...

Unhappily the lyrical mythology which passed into the eighteenth century was that of the main Renaissance tradition, devitalized, bookish, and bad.

This chapter, like the book itself, must end with an anticlimax, for in lyrics as well as other kinds of verse the humorous treatment of mythology becomes quite noteworthy in the third quarter of the seventeenth century. Cleveland's *Mark Antony* (which has a Gilbertian last stanza) describes rustic dalliance, and the nymph's "amber tresses" make on the lover's arm a bracelet

> Gaudier than Juno wears when as she graces
> Jove with embraces more stately than warm.[48]

A quite infectious gayety inspired *The Hunting of the Gods* in the *Westminster Drollery* (1672). No serious poetical directory of Olympus rattles along at such a pace:

> To see club-footed old Mulciber booted,
> And Pan promoted on Chiron's mare;
> Proud Faunus pouted, and Aeolus shouted,
> And Momus flouted, but followed the hare.[49]

The same collection contains a piece, *The Moon's Love*, that is far removed from Drayton; Phoebus (or perhaps "the Day") appears in waistcoat of red, and as for the Moon—

> Such changes of thought in her chastity wrought,
> That thus she besought the boy:
> 'O tarry and marry the starry Diana
> That will be thy gem and joy!'[50]

Finally, we might take it as an allegorical piece of literary history that the mythology which appears in the *Covent Garden Drollery* (1672) is mostly concentrated in *Mad Tom of Bedlam*.[51] Not here does Vulcan fall from morn to noon, from noon to dewy eve—

> Mars with his Weapon laid about,
> But limping Vulcan had the Gout ...

[48] Ault, *Seventeenth Century Lyrics*, p. 196.
[49] *Ibid.*, p. 248. The poem was written *ca.* 1650 (?). [50] *Ibid.*, p. 368.
[51] Ed. G. Thorn-Drury (London, 1928), pp. 41 ff. See the editor's note, p. 138.

CHAPTER TWELVE

TRANSLATORS

THE study of formal translations is a huge subject by itself and one that cannot be treated in such a volume as this. But from the multitude of translations in the seventeenth century this chapter selects a few that may serve to illustrate some general tendencies in the treatment of myth and in poetic style, the changes in taste which lead from Chapman's *Homer* to Pope's, from the Elizabethan Phillida and Corydon to the Augustan Strephon and Chloe.

The Elizabethan translators as a rule thought more of matter than of manner.[1] But some of the later Elizabethans and Jacobeans began to concern themselves a little with the principles of translation, with the rights and the obligations of a translator. As the seventeenth century advanced and translators grew both more self-conscious and more confident in matters of technique, the theory of literal translation was increasingly condemned—not that it had ever been extensively practiced. Denham and Cowley may stand as representatives of the prevailing view, though the former, as Dryden said, "advised more liberty than he took himself." The theory of translation is of course as relative as any other question of taste—witness the diverse character of the classic English versions of Homer—and the style that is one age's meat is another's poison. Drayton extols Sandys' translation of Ovid as superior in sweetness and grace to the original; Dryden declares that all or most of Ovid's poetic quality evaporated in Sandys' pedantic lines.[2] The obvious retort, and the true one, is that both were wrong.

The motives and aims of translators in the last three-quarters of the seventeenth century moved further and further from the patriotic and didactic ideals of the Elizabethans. England and the English language no longer needed apology in comparison with foreign achievement. Then, instead of the relative homogeneity of Elizabethan social and cultural standards we have a reading public broken up into groups marked off from one another by differences in birth, breeding, politics,

---

[1] On the theory of translation in the seventeenth century see F. R. Amos, *Early Theories of Translation* (1920), cc. 3–4, and J. E. Spingarn, *Critical Essays of the Seventeenth Century*, I, xlviii ff.

[2] Drayton, *Epistle to Reynolds*, ll. 157 ff.; Dryden, Dedication to *Examen Poeticum* (*Poems of Dryden*, Oxford, 1913, pp. 425–26). Dryden makes some amends in the preface to the *Fables*.

religion; instead of the Elizabethan effort to spread enlightenment by popularization of the classics we have translators appealing to a select class of educated readers who are the arbiters of taste. As the accompaniment of more sophisticated scholarship there is a more conscious attempt to appreciate and render the special quality of an author—although neoclassic translations, from Ovid or Homer, Horace or Virgil, seem to us to have a good deal of family likeness. Translation comes to be a gentleman's accomplishment, and, as such, confined mainly to Latin poetry; it is a specimen of polite learning, and of skill in English versification.[3]

The reaction against Elizabethan and metaphysical waywardness and irregularity made translation from the classics a welcome instrument of discipline. To the nineteenth century that refining process seemed to have destroyed the soul of poetry.

"It cannot be denied," Johnson ends, after weighing Waller piece by piece and finding him light currency, "that he added something to our elegance of diction, and something to our propriety of thought." How important this end seemed may be judged from the amount of the sacrifice that was cheerfully made to reach it. By the time it was fully attained the jettison of poetry had been so great that in the eyes of a new reaction a century later it seemed there was nothing left worth saving: "Is Pope," people began to ask, "a poet at all?" [4]

To the achievement of correctness the translating activity of the seventeenth century contributed not a little. Its object, as Mr. Mackail says, was to make the English language into a complete vehicle of poetical expression, and to unite English poetry with the main European tradition. The few translators discussed in this chapter belong to a transitional phase, and show the refining process going on. First of all we may notice a representative of the old tradition, of post-Elizabethan style decorative, vigorous, uneven, "unrefined."

I. SHAKERLEY MARMION

No myth has been retold in English more elaborately than that of Cupid and Psyche, and the roll of poetic paraphrases opens not unworthily with the work of a man whose name alone is seductive. Readers who have lost their way in *Pharonnida* and the other labyrinthine romances which wind through the volumes of Mr. Saintsbury's *Minor Caroline Poets* may begin Marmion's *Legend of Cupid and Psyche*

[3] And thus we arrive at Mr. Beerbohm's "Statesman of Olden Time, making without wish for emolument a flat but faithful version of the Georgics, in English hexameters"—a generic portrait true in everything but the last word.
[4] J. W. Mackail, "Sir Richard Fanshawe," *Studies of English Poets* (1926), p. 44. At present the writing of Dryden and Pope is in no danger of being undervalued.

(1637) with the initial assurance that the poet relied more upon Apuleius than his own invention.

Embroidery of course there is, but Marmion's version is not, like William Morris', oppressively luxuriant and sweet. At the beginning he amplifies the description of Psyche's beauty, not with the aid of the beloved catalogue, but, in what was also a Renaissance fashion, by invoking extravagant parallels.[5] Mythological conceits in general vary from a few lines to a page or more; we have inserted even a version of the ever popular "hue and cry after Cupid." In the Ovidian tradition of the Renaissance is the needlework on Cupid's quiver, though the picture-making is more restrained than in Marlowe or Spenser:

> Next Venus and Adonis, sad with pain,
> The one of love, the other of disdain:
> There Jove in all his borrow'd shapes was dress'd,
> His thefts and his adulteries express'd,
> As emblems of Love's triumph; and these were
> Drawn with such lively colours, men would swear,
> That Leda lay within a perfect bower,
> And Danaë's golden streams were a true shower.[6]

Marmion's additions are not usually extensive enough to impede greatly the course of the story, and his narrative manner is clear, fluent, effortless. Bridges' version of the myth is beautiful, much more exquisitely finished than Marmion's, but it is not wholly free from the sophisticated simplicity that calls attention to itself. Marmion evidently had before him the prose of Adlington as well as the Latin of Apuleius, and the fact reminds us that his language has Elizabethan color and richness. To say that his taste is uncertain is only to say that he is a poet of the early seventeenth century. The most generous of editors has a sad footnote on the lines,

> Night and her husband came, and now the sport
> Of Venus ended, he began to snort.

When her nocturnal bridegroom flew away in anger, Psyche "hung, as an appendix of his flight." But the general texture is smooth and attractive. By the light of the lamp one can see

> The god of Love himself, Cupid the fair,
> Lie sweetly sleeping in his golden hair.

And there is the phrase that awakens Mr. Saintsbury's enthusiasm, in Psyche's despairing outcry against Venus:

> What darkness can protect me? what disguise
> Hide me from her inevitable eyes?[7]

[5] *Minor Caroline Poets*, II, 11.   [6] P. 29.   [7] P. 44. See also Saintsbury's introduction.

But Marmion merely had the wisdom—though not everyone would have had it—to render literally the words of Apuleius, *Veneris inevitabiles oculos.*[8]

II. TRANSLATORS OF VIRGIL

Marmion, along with such men as Digges and Reynolds,[9] may stand as representative inheritors of the Elizabethan tradition, by virtue of their poetic style, their mode of handling their authors, and their allegorical interests or professions. For the sake of a compact illustration of the change from the post-Elizabethan to the Augustan manner we may consider briefly two versions of the fourth book of the *Aeneid.* They are the work of two of the most engaging figures of the period, Sir Richard Fanshawe (1608–66) and Sidney Godolphin (1610–43). Fanshawe's was written about 1639–40,[10] Godolphin's doubtless near the same time, yet the two pieces seem to belong to different generations. It is not merely that Fanshawe uses the Spenserian stanza, Godolphin the heroic couplet; there is a real difference in taste. Even if Godolphin's work passed under the smoothing hand of Waller, it will still serve our purpose.[11]

Like all other translators these two fail to render the subtleties of Virgilian style, but the work of Godolphin is respectable, that of Fanshawe is often something more. The opening lines are as characteristic as any. This is Fanshawe:

> But she who Love long since had swallowed down,
> Melts with hid fire; her wound doth inward weep:
> The man's much worth, his nation's much renown
> Runs in her mind: his looks and words are deep
> Fixt in her breast: care weans her eyes from sleep.[12]

[8] The translator does not neglect the allegory. Most of the exposition is a paraphrase of Fulgentius, whether at first hand or not, and the argument, except for a phrase or two, follows the narrative given by Fulgentius. Marmion's pleasure in story-telling does not seem to be much affected by his sense of "more deep and weighty mysteries."

[9] See the Appendix, under 1617, 1628, 1632.

[10] *The Fourth Book of Virgil's Aeneid on the Loves of Dido and Aeneas,* ed. A. L. Irvine (1924). It was published in 1648.

[11] *The Passion of Dido for Æneas* was published in 1658 as "translated by Edmund Waller and Sidney Godolphin." In the 1664 edition of Waller's poems ll. 455–585 are ascribed to him. The remaining 114 lines of the 699 have not been claimed for either Waller or Godolphin. Mr. Dighton thinks it likely "that Sidney Godolphin translated the whole, and that Waller in preparing the poem for publication reworked the middle section to such an extent that he considered it his own" (*Poems of Sidney Godolphin,* ed. W. Dighton, 1931, pp. xxxix ff.). Waller's work is said to have been done in 1657. How far Waller may have revised the whole one cannot tell.

In connection with the style of Virgilian translations of this period, see the remarks on Denham's work in Mr. T. H. Banks's edition of Denham (Yale University Press, 1928).

[12] At regina gravi iamdudum saucia cura
vulnus alit venis et caeco carpitur igni.
multa viri virtus animo multusque recursat
gentis honos: haerent infixi pectore vultus
verbaque, nec placidam membris dat cura quietem.

Here is plain, strong literalness mixed with strong but gratuitous and irrelevant metaphors such as Chapman so abundantly provides. Godolphin is "correct" and diffuse, and ends with a gratuitous antithesis:

> Meane while the Queene Fanning A secret Fyer
> in her owne brest, revolves her deepe desire
> shee oft reflects upon the princely grace
> of great Eaneas, and that Noble race
> from whence he springs, her wounded fancy feedes
> on his discourse, his high Heroyike deedes
> his wordes, his lookes, her waking thoughts imploy
> and when shee sleepes, shee sees him with more joye,
> but seldome sleepes.

Many phrases illustrate the same qualities. *Degeneres animos timor arguit* Fanshawe is content to render "Fear shows ignoble minds"; "The mortall seede of men acknowledge feare" is Godolphin's inflated rhetoric. In the description of the fateful storm we have the contrast between Fanshawe's uncertain force and Godolphin's Augustan rotundity. The passages are too long for quotation, but they begin thus:

> Meanwhile loud thunder heaven's pavilion tears
> Making a passage for th' ensuing rain . . .

> Meane while the gathering clowdes obscure the Pole
> they flash out Lightnings and in Thunder Role.

"She calls it wedlock, gives her fault an honest name," writes Fanshawe soberly, for *coniugium vocat, hoc praetexit nomine culpam*. Godolphin prefers the grandeur of generality:

> but doeth excuse it with Chast Hymens name
> and lives exposd a theame to various fame.

The refining process is carried further with the picture of Atlas, where Godolphin simply omits the lines that Fanshawe renders thus:

> Thick on his aged back the snow doth lie,
> And down his dravel'd chin pour plenteous springs,
> His beard in icicles grows horribly.[18]

Uncertainty of taste is one part of Fanshawe's heritage. Venus says to Juno:

> And yet, perchance, you lying in his breast
> With a wife's rhetoric may his counsels sway;
> Then break the ice; I'll second the request.

Godolphin, with unusual condensation, has "this in your prayers, who

---

[18] *Aen.* iv. 250–51:

> nix umeros infusa tegit, tum flumina mento
> praecipitant senis, et glacie riget horrida barba.

are his wife doeth lie." The best passage in Fanshawe's whole book is followed by a painfully Elizabethan rendering of

> Talibus orabat, talisque miserrima fletus
> fertque refertque soror.

He writes:

> This Dido spake. The sad ambassadress
> Carries her tears, and brings them back again
> (As brackish tides post from and to the main).

While Godolphin generally maintains a level of decorous ·evenness, Fanshawe rises with some power to the height of Dido's passion. Thus Godolphin (whose third line is almost in the other's manner):

> I'le follow thee, bee present in thy paine,
> and when cold earth shall this mixt frame devide
> my Ghost shall lacquey by thy frighted side,
> thou dearely shalt repent, the newse of this
> shall overtake my soule, and give it blisse.

Fanshawe's version is free, but his Dido speaks like a Fury:

> For when cold death shall part with dreary swoon
> My soul and flesh, my ghost, where'er thou be,
> Shall haunt thee with dim torch, and light thee down
> To thy dark conscience: I'll be Hell to thee,
> And this glad news will make Hell Heav'n to me.[14]

Best of all, for sustained dramatic vividness, is Dido's speech to Anna.[15]

Waller's section is too little distinguishable from Godolphin's to require special comment, but his rendering of one bit may be compared with Fanshawe's.

> . . . with that word
> he cutts the cable with his shyning sword,
> through all the Navy doeth like Ardor raigne
> the[y] quitt the shoare, and rush into the Maine
> plac'd on their Barks, the lusty Trojans sweepe
> Neptunes smooth face, and cleave the yeelding deepe.[16]

The effect is of a most orderly tumult; and the first half of the last line is rather a petrified metaphor than a mythological conceit. Fanshawe's Trojans are really in a hurry:

> This said, whipt out his lightning sword, and strook
> The fastening ropes. Like zeal his pattern bred

---

[14] *Aen.* iv. 384 ff.

[15] *Aen.* iv. 420 ff. The passage is quoted in Mr. Mackail's essay on Fanshawe (*Studies of English Poets*, p. 51).

[16] Dighton, pp. 54–55. Cf. *Aen.* iv. 579–83. Only the last line need be quoted: *adnixi torquent spumas et caerula verrunt.*

> In all. They snatch'd, they ran, the shores forsook,
> Their sails like wings over the waves were spread:
> They comb'd with oars great Neptune's curled head.

The vividness is a trifle marred by the last line, which out-Chapmans Chapman. But such things are only occasional lapses.

On the significance of Fanshawe's work I cannot do better than quote Mr. Mackail's comments regarding one passage:

> But it shows a gentleman's scholarship to perfection; for combined dignity and sweetness it is, I think, unsurpassed by what any other rendering of Virgil into English has achieved . . . There are traces still left here of the Elizabethan rhetoric, and of the post-Elizabethan mannerism; but both are becoming subdued and civilised, while still possessing the glowing colour and melodious phrasing of that great school of poetry. Just a little more, and Fanshawe would have attained what he and all his contemporaries were feeling after, the secret of a style which will never be obsolete.

III. STANLEY : SHERBURNE : AYRES

Something may be said of a few minor poets united partly by personal ties, partly by the range of their translating activities. The most original writer of the group, and the germinal force in the matter of translation, was Thomas Stanley. He appears in some respects as a belated Eliza-bethan, though more scholarly and more "smooth and genteel"—to borrow the phrase of Anthony à Wood—and it is significant that in youth he was taught by William Fairfax, son of the translator of Tasso. With Stanley's original lyrics we need not linger,[17] but the scope of his translations reveals both his Greek scholarship and his unusual knowledge of Italian, Spanish, and French poetry of the sixteenth and seventeenth centuries.

The volume of 1651 contained *Anacreon. Bion. Moschus. Kisses, by Secundus. Cupid Crucified, by Ausonius. Venus Vigils, Incerto Authore.* Nearly one hundred pages following these translations were devoted to notes or "excitations," which contained also some illustrative versions from Ronsard, Marino, and others. A third section comprised translations thus listed on a separate title-page: *Sylvia's Park, by Theophile. Acanthus Complaint, by Tristan. Oronta, by Preti. Echo, by Marino. Loves Embassy, by Boscan. The Solitude, by Gongora.* At the end of the volume came the prose version of Pico's *Platonick Discourse upon Love.*

The list of titles, ancient and modern, is briefer than comment would

---

[17] These, and a number of brief versions from continental poets, are given in Saintsbury's *Minor Caroline Poets*, III, 95 ff. For Stanley's modern sources see M. Praz, "Stanley, Sherburne and Ayres as Translators and Imitators of Italian, Spanish and French Poets,"

be, and it indicates Stanley's taste for delicately carved cherry stones. The mythology that appears in the English reflects the familiar characteristics of the originals. Within his range Stanley is an easy and elegant translator. His versions of the ancients are faithful enough; as regards the moderns, "unlike other translators Stanley almost constantly condenses his model." [18] In one piece of twelve lines, *Apollo and Daphne,* he combines conceits drawn from poems by Garcilaso de la Vega and Marino. This is the Marinesque ending:

> And though the conquest which he sought he miss'd,
> . With that triumphant spoil adorns his brow.
> Thus this disdainful maid his aim deceives:
> Where he expected fruit he gathers leaves. [19]

From Stanley one may turn to his friend Sir Edward Sherburne (1618–1702), who was likewise a prolific translator from the classical and modern languages. After the death of the king whom he had served, Sherburne spent some time in reading French and Italian poets, profiting from Stanley's acquaintance with continental literature. But while Stanley's stronger individuality found expression in some original work (not to mention the *History of Philosophy*), Sherburne "is purely a translator," with hardly anything original to his credit. [20] Two of his longer translations, however, are of interest in connection with the mythological poem and also with the influence of translation in refining poetic style.

With occasional slight omissions and expansions Sherburne's *Salmacis* is a close paraphrase of Preti's *La Salmace,* and Preti had taken the usual liberties with Ovid. [21] Almost everything in Ovid's tale is adorned with fanciful and pictorial detail except, oddly enough, the account of the nymph's ecstatic embracing of Hermaphroditus. At the beginning Ovid's few lines about the boy's history are elaborated into a tissue of pretty mythological inventions. The Augustans would hardly have approved of this picture of a mountain:

> So far above the clouds his head doth rise
> That his green locks no summer dripping spies

M. L. R., XX, 280 ff.; and H. Thomas, "Three Translators of Góngora," *Revue hispanique,* XLVIII, 180 ff. The latter prints copious extracts from both Stanley and his originals.
[18] Praz, p. 281.
[19] *Minor Caroline Poets,* III, 128–29; Praz, p. 283. See above, page 216.
The myth of Europa, by the way, seems to have especially attracted Stanley. For his references to a number of versions see Thomas, pp. 191, 228–29, and Praz, p. 287.
[20] Praz, p. 290.
[21] *Salmacis, Lyrian & Sylvia, Forsaken Lydia, The Rape of Helen,* etc., London, 1651. Sherburne is reprinted, with some omissions, in Chalmers, Vol. VI; since the original volume is not now accessible my quotations are made from Chalmers.

With rain, his face no winter does behold
Mask'd with a snowy muffler 'gainst the cold.[22]

The translation of Colluthus, following the Greek, does not exhibit the conceits which the Ovidian tale owed to Preti. Some bits of description recall such poems as *Endimion and Phœbe*. The picture of Paris, if less beautiful than Tennyson's, is also less artificial:

> Low as his knee a mountain goat's rough hide
> Hung from his shoulders, flagging by his side:
> In's hand a neatherd's goad: such to the eye
> (As slowly to his pipe's soft melody
> He moves) appear'd the gentle Phrygian swain,
> Tuning on's reed a sweet, though rural strain.

Sherburne's oxen emit a bovine odor:

> His oxen, cloy'd with the rank grass, were laid,
> Stretching their fat sides in the cooler shade . . .

By way of measuring Sherburne's position we might observe how, in the eighteenth century, the oxen have learned deportment and become gentlemanlike:

> The herd full fed the fertile grass refrain,
> And scatter'd lay reclin'd upon the plain.[23]

Sherburne's couplets are smooth enough, but not quite regular. His diction in general retains a good deal of the older juice and sweetness, even though here and there, to mix metaphors, it reveals, if not a cloven hoof, just the tip of a patent leather shoe. But, from comparison with most translators of the eighteenth century, Sherburne, like many of his fellows, emerges without loss. Apart from any question of individual talent, they had a better medium at their disposal. It might be uncertain, it might be subject to Elizabethan lapses in taste, or even show traces of Augustan poetic diction, but it was not a uniformly glossy picture postcard.[24]

This sketch may be rounded out with a word concerning Philip Ayres (1638–1712), though his *Lyric Poems* were published as late as 1687, because he is related through his work, if not personally, with Stanley

---

[22] Incidentally, the conclusion of the piece makes use of the personal motive which we have often met. Amintas tells the story to coy Iole,

> Then adds: "O thou more fair, in love more cold
> Than he! Heaven yet may make thee mine in spite . . ."

[23] From a version of Colluthus published in 1731 (*The Rape of Helen*, Brit. Mus., 11340. c. 2).

[24] Some of the notes that Sherburne appended to his translation are links with the past. Citing Fulgentius, he interprets the marriage of Peleus and Thetis as the union of earth and water. Dictys Cretensis is mentioned more than once.

and Sherburne.[25] Two of Ayres's poems have been mentioned already,[26] and there is no need of adding much here, since his almost wholly lyrical pieces are drawn from the same general range of authors translated by his predecessors.[27] Mr. Saintsbury has remarked upon his fondness for Greek—"the small Greek poets," as Ayres calls them—at a time when Latin was becoming more predominant than ever; and the same critic emphasizes Ayres's conservatism, his loyalty to "the tastes, the traditions, the style even to some extent, of the reign of Charles I."

In *Endymion and Diana,* however, Ayres was far from loyal to the monster-spawning tradition of the earlier period, for the poem contains but thirteen eight-line stanzas, and, as the editor observes, is "the shortest of our 'Heroic' poems, but complete enough in its miniature." [28] For that virtue we may thank Alessandro Tassoni, whom Ayres duly acknowledges as his source. In conception the little piece is remote from Drayton or Keats. While Endymion sleeps on a bed of flowers, with Cupids playing around him, Diana comes and sees him. His beauty overcomes her virgin modesty, and she fondles him until he wakens. When he starts up she holds him back, and consents to his demand for a place in heaven. After a night of pleasure the goddess wishes she had not wasted so much time in hunting. The polished prettiness of the poem recalls the mythological paintings of the seventeenth century.

[25] M. Praz, *M. L. R.,* XX, 419 ff.; H. Thomas, *Rev. hisp.,* XLVIII, 243 ff., 311 ff. Ayres is reprinted in Saintsbury, II, 265 ff.

[26] Pp. 216–17 above.

[27] To mention one lyric on a classical theme, Mr. Thomas (p. 251) observes that *Leander drowned* was modeled on Garcilaso de la Vega's imitation of Martial. Cf. Praz, p. 429.

[28] Saintsbury, II, 285. See Praz, p. 424.

CHAPTER THIRTEEN

ALLEGORY AND ANTI-PAGAN SENTIMENT IN THE SEVENTEENTH CENTURY

I

B Y THIS time allegory may seem to have become a King Charles's head in our Memorial, but a record of the treatment of mythology would be very incomplete if it left out of account the continued flourishing of allegorical ideas in the seventeenth, even in the eighteenth, century. Although some great and less great names appear in the list of orthodox believers, the story, as the seventeenth century advances, is one of decline and fall. What in the Elizabethan age had been orthodoxy, sometimes genuine, sometimes not, dwindles by degrees into a heterodoxy cherished by persons of slightly queer notions, Platonists and such. Yet the skeptical and scientific movement was very slow in undermining the allegorical tradition, and we may assemble enough testimonies to outline the gradual dissolution of the venerable doctrine. The result might cheer the ardent lover of truth, but it was more than coincidence that the decline of the allegorical and didactic conception of myth was accompanied by the loss of imaginative and spiritual values in poetry.

While Bacon labored to emancipate his age from medieval ways of thought he was so imperfectly emancipated himself that posterity is in doubt whether to call him medieval or modern. He is one of the conspicuous instances of the phenomenon we have often noticed, that Renaissance minds are (though free from vulgarity) like luxurious houses of the newly rich, with rooms incongruously furnished in the style of many periods. No room in the spacious mind of Bacon is more significant for our purpose than the *De Sapientia Veterum* (1609), a book expounding the allegorical meaning of thirty-one characters or stories from classical mythology.[1] In his preface Bacon manifests a little uneasiness when he anticipates the possible charge that he is entertaining himself with a toy, but he proceeds to argue on traditional grounds for allegory concealed in 'fable. If the ancients did not write thus with conscious purpose at any rate they were lucky in falling "upon matter which gives occasion to such worthy contemplations."

[1] *Works*, ed. Spedding (Boston, 1860), XIII, 75 ff. Cf. Bacon's discussion of "poesy parabolical" (Spingarn, *Critical Essays of the Seventeenth Century*, I, 7 ff.).

Bacon then expounds the myths, under such titles as "Cassandra, or Plainness of Speech"; "Narcissus, or Self-Love"; "Endymion, or the Favourite"; "Sphinx, or Science" . . . Outwardly, and often inwardly, the method is that of a thousand, or two thousand, years earlier, and it is true that Bacon "wasted much time and ingenuity in showing that some mute inglorious Newton has hidden the true principles of Natural Philosophy in the story of *Pan,* and that some pre-historic Clausewitz has embedded the rules of military strategy in that of *Perseus and Medusa."* [2] But the approach is not wholly medieval.

The story of Cassandra and Apollo "seems to have been devised in reproof of unreasonable and unprofitable liberty in giving advice and admonition." The story of Typhon has to do with the variable fortunes of kings and rebellions against them. Narcissus, of course, represents self-love, but with a Baconian difference; the victim is averse to public business, and, secluding himself with a circle of admiring "echoes," he grows besotted and weak, fading away like flowers. The fates of Actaeon and Pentheus deal respectively with "the secrets of princes" [3] and "the secrets of divinity." Thus if we forget the myth involved we have virtually another series of civil and moral essays, with the same realistic grasp of human nature and affairs, the same practical and utilitarian motives. The interpretations of myth are generally of a corresponding character; in fact we meet some of them in the *Essays, Advancement of Learning,* and elsewhere.

A number of chapters are concerned with science.

Nor need we wonder that Pan's horns touch heaven; since the summits, or universal forms, of nature do in a manner reach up to God; the passage from metaphysic to natural theology being ready and short . . .

With regard to the audacity of Pan in challenging Cupid to fight, it refers to this,—that matter is not without a certain inclination and appetite to dissolve the world and fall back into the ancient chaos; but that the over-swaying concord of things (which is represented by Cupid or Love) restrains its will and effort in that direction and reduces it to order. [4]

Cupid has lost his dominion over the heart; his character and activities have to do with "the natural motion of the atom." Bacon's adaptation of myths to the illustration of his scientific notions sometimes embodies the traditional lore of the mythographers, but a good deal of it seems to be

[2] C. D. Broad, *Philosophy of Francis Bacon* (Cambridge University Press, 1926), pp. 26–27.
[3] Cf. Natalis Comes, *"De Actæone"* (Padua, 1616, p. 546): "Significant præterea deui-tandam esse omnibus curiositatem & earum rerum studium, quæ nihil ad nos pertinent, quoniam multis perniciosa fuit arcanorum consiliorum principum cognitio." See also *ibid.,* vi. 24, p. 354.
[4] Pp. 95, 99. Cf. Natalis Comes, v. 6 (p. 247): "Dicunt illum [Pan] fuisse cum Cupidine colluctatum ab eo victum, quia, ut diximus, amor & litigium principium fuisse rerum naturalium putata sunt."

original. Everywhere too he emphasizes the necessity, in the search for truth, of infinite patience, of single-hearted devotion to the cause. The seeker is Mercury restoring the sinews of Jupiter, Prometheus transmitting the torch of light, Oedipus wresting her secrets from the sphinx.[5] The book was very popular, and not undeservedly. If it was not *L'Esprit des Mythes* it was in a sense *l'esprit sur les mythes*.

Ralegh's *History of the World* (1614) is, as Arnold easily demonstrated, less modern in its attitude than the work of Thucydides, for Ralegh starts from uncritical premises. But the early books of the *History*, with their medley of Hebraic and classical legend and medieval accretion, do not mark their author as behind the times. His view of myth is quite similar to that of George Sandys. Within the prescribed limits he is critical. He constantly relates biblical and classical stories, trying to distinguish between fact and fiction. He accepts allegorized myth, and sometimes quotes Natalis Comes. As an example of rationalizing we might take this interpretation of the amorous activities of Jupiter:

> And of these his several ravishments, betrayings, stealing away of men's wives, daughters, and sons, buying of virgins, and the like, came in all those ancient fables of his transformations into showers of gold, eagles, bulls, birds, and beasts; and of him and by him (in effect) all that rabble of Grecian forgeries.[6]

Robert Burton, who read everything, of course read the mythographers, and he quotes such familiar ones as Fulgentius, Lilius Giraldus, Natalis Comes, Cartari. Lovers, he says,

> become at last *insensati,* void of sense; degenerate into dogs, hogs, asses, brutes; as Jupiter into a Bull, Apuleius an Ass, Lycaon a Wolf, Tereus a Lapwing, Callisto a Bear, Elpenor and Gryllus into Swine by Circe. For what else may we think those ingenious Poets to have shadowed in their witty fictions and Poems, but that a man once given over to his lust (as Fulgentius interprets that of Apuleius, Alciat. of Tereus) is no better than a beast.[7]

In the preface to Γυναικεῖον (1624) Thomas Heywood sets forth conventional opinions about the "misticall sences" of "poeticall fictions," and carries out his principles in treating pagan divinities. A passage on Juno as Air, and the engendering of "creatures, trees and plants," is translated literally from Natalis Comes.[8] In his *Pleasant Dialogues and*

[5] John Nichol, *Francis Bacon* (Philadelphia and Edinburgh, 1889), II, 217.
[6] *History* (1829), bk. i, c. 6, sec. 5 (II, 172–73). For some further items see the chapter on Milton.
[7] *Anatomy of Melancholy* (Bohn's Popular Library), III, 177. Cf. *ibid.*, I, 299, 499, etc., and index (for mythographers).
[8] Heywood, pp. 6–7; Comes, p. 533.

Dramma's (1637), annotating Textor's *Dialogue of Earth and Age,* Heywood takes from Comes, whom he mentions, the notion that Eurydice represents the soul and Orpheus the body.[9]

The greatest repository of allegorized myth in English is the commentary which Sandys added to the 1632 edition of his translation of the *Metamorphoses.*[10] Sandys' list of authorities ranges from Plato to Bacon, and his interpretations, like those of earlier mythographers, are eclectic. Expositions maybe be theological, moral, euhemeristic, scientific. References in the text range from Fulgentius and Lactantius to Copernicus, Galileo, Tycho, and Kepler. Like Ralegh Sandys is critical, within the limits set by his fundamental assumptions. He tries to disentangle fact from fiction, and to relate "history" to biblical matter. The commentary, if one has a taste for that sort of thing, is never dull, and Keats did not find it so.[11] And I think Milton had read it, as footnotes in the following chapter may or may not suggest to the candid reader.

In the same year apparently was published the *Mythomystes* of Henry Reynolds. The essay is, as Mr. Spingarn said,

the chief example in English of the systematic application of Neoplatonism to the interpretation of poetry. Bacon had already indicated the road, but Reynolds follows it into a tropical forest of strange fancies: the Cabalists and Neoplatonists, Philo and Reuchlin, but especially Pico della Mirandola and Alessandro Farra, here find an English voice.[12]

But we cannot plunge into the tropical forest. Nor can we linger with Alexander Ross, to whom a casual couplet of Butler's gave an immortality doubtfully achieved in *Mel Heliconium* and *Mystagogus Poeticus.* Ross, said Addison, had dived deeper into Ovid's design than anyone else, "for he discovers in him the greatest mysteries of the Christian religion, and finds almost in every page some typical representations of the

[9] Ed. W. Bang, *Materialien* (1903), p. 288; Comes, vii. 14, p. 402.

[10] Sandys apparently issued five books in 1621, and the complete text in 1626. In view of the fact that the first work printed in English by Caxton was the *Recuyell,* it is noteworthy—as regards the prestige of our subject matter—that Sandys' *Ovid* seems to have been the first piece of literature achieved in the land of the pilgrims' pride.

For a critical account of Sandys as a translator see *Cambridge History of English Literature,* VII, 50 ff. It is there said, by the way, that Sandys' rendering of the tale of Actaeon gains strength from his finding appropriate equivalents for the names of Actaeon's hounds. It is hardly an accident that some eighteen of the names are the same as Golding's —not that it matters.

[11] See Mr. de Selincourt's edition of Keats, for both parallels from the text of the translation and suggestions of symbolism probably derived from the commentary, which we know he read. In connection with *Hyperion* it may be noticed that Sandys (ed. 1632, p. 27) identifies the giants with ignorance, the gods with virtue.

[12] *Critical Essays of the Seventeenth Century,* I, xxi. See the text, I, 141 ff., and my Appendix, under 1632.

World, the Flesh, and the Devil." [13] A much more important lover of mysteries was Henry More.

By this time the allegorical plant, though of sturdy ancestry, was drooping in the nipping air of reason. In 1674 Rymer declared in his downright way: "And it was the vice of those Times to affect superstitiously the Allegory; and nothing would then be currant without a mystical meaning. We must blame the Italians for debauching great Spencer's judgment . . ." [14] In the year following the very un-mystical Hobbes surveyed Homer with unblinking eyes, and, mainly by negative implications, removed allegory from the field of discussion.[15] Yet the rising tide of rationalism represented by such names did not sweep away all vestiges of traditional opinion. The later history of allegory lies beyond our present limits, but we may remember that Pope's preface to the *Iliad,* following Le Bossu, remarks on the breadth of knowledge embodied in Homer's allegories;[16] that in the essay contributed to the same work Parnell, though snorting at extreme allegorical vagaries, avowed that some rays of truth streamed through the darkness;[17] that Garth's preface to the translation of the *Metamorphoses* done by Dryden and others expounded Ovid's allegories and endorsed the work of Sandys. These are only a few examples. Such interpretations of myth lingered on in volumes like Tooke's *Pantheon,* which Keats read as a boy. The name of Keats reminds us that, so far as poetry is concerned, the distance between allegory and symbolism is not great. In general the best modern treatments of myth, unlike those of the common Renaissance type, have been poems in which more is meant than meets the eye.[18]

II

Although the allegorical theory of poetry had enabled Ovid and some Ovidian poems to take on a protective coloring, the best-known pieces, like Marlowe's and Shakespeare's, laid no claim to hidden moral truth. They were pagan, and it depended upon the reader's upbringing whether the paganism were glorious or wicked. In this section we must glance at

[13] *Miscellaneous Works, In Verse and Prose* (London, 1726), I, 236–37.
[14] Spingarn, II, 168.
[15] *Ibid.,* II, 67 ff. Cf. pp. 54 ff.
[16] See A. F. B. Clark, *Boileau* (1925), p. 247; Austin Warren, *Alexander Pope* (1929), pp. 81, 100–01.
[17] *The Iliad of Homer. Translated by Alexander Pope,* ed. G. Wakefield (London, 1796), I, clxii–clxiii, clxxxiii.
[18] The list of references given above for allegorical doctrine might be expanded indefinitely. To go no further than this book, see in the Appendix: Fraunce, 1592; Brathwait, 1611, 1621; Digges, 1617; Brinsley, 1618; Hall, 1651, 1655; Jones, 1658. Since allegory was last discussed we have encountered such more or less sincere exponents as Basse, Chapman, Marmion.

representatives of the latter persuasion. The moral excesses and aesthetic deficiencies which are commonly associated with the puritan party (or rather parties) of the sixteenth and seventeenth centuries are found of course, with infinite variations of hue and degree, in all ages and countries; indeed one may well be chary of using a word that can be applied alike to Plato and to William Prynne. The so-called puritan reaction to imaginative literature, though always with us, is likely to be especially marked at any time when culture is rapidly broadening down from ignorance to ignorance, through layer after layer of the middle class. It was thus in our period.

In the sixteenth century, as in the fourteenth or the fourth, there were those who appreciated Ovid as a poet, those who compounded for enjoying his tales by attaching a moral, and those who regarded his pagan pantheon as the devil's chapel. Each group might contain puritans. But as the third increased in numbers and shrillness it became more and more expressive of strict puritan sentiment. Ovid, like Shaw's amiable dustman, found himself "up agen middle class morality." Whereas a liberal puritan like Golding could enjoy a moralized Ovid—and Golding's allegories were confined to his prefaces—the increasing majority of illiberal and dismal puritans would have no such compromise. Some of these "painful" servants of God we have listened to already.[19] We noticed also in an early chapter the moralizing habit which, especially during the years 1560–70, devitalized ballads and appended sermons to Ovidian tales; this was one way of preventing the devil from having all the tunes.[20] It failed to satisfy those who were resolved, as Sir Toby might have said, that because they were virtuous there should be no more Cupids and Venuses. Sylvester, though he made occasional use of mythology, prayed

> O! furnish me with an un-vulgar stile,
> That I by this may wain our wanton Ile
> From Ovid's heires, and their un-hallowed spell
> Here charming senses, chaining soules in Hell.[21]

And the popularity of Sylvester's translation in the first half of the seventeenth century is a most significant cultural phenomenon; it was the epic of middle-class Protestantism, and it influenced Milton, even the youthful Dryden.

When in the disreputable suburbs of London theaters rose and flourished like evergreen trees of diabolical knowledge, puritan axes began to be wielded with vigor. One might not have expected mythology to come in for a share of the invective, but not the least vigorous of

[19] Page 70, note 10.   [20] Page 60 above.   [21] Ed. Grosart, I, 99.

Gosson's pages denounce the immoralities of the pagan gods and the wickedness of the poets who write about them:

Whilest they make Cupide triumphe in heauen, and all the gods to marche bounde like miserable captiues, before his charriot, they belie God, and bewitch the reader with bawdie charmes . . .
Thus making gods of them that were brute beastes, in the likenes of men, diuine goddesses of common harlots; they robbe God of his honour, diminishe his authoritie, weaken his might, and turne his seate to a stewes.[22]

Gosson's work is a mere preface compared with the tremendous *Histriomastix* of 1632, and Prynne, by the way, quotes Gosson with approbation. In the general anathema against the stage mythology is included, and the tone is at once more medieval and more puritanical than Gosson's; Prynne's artillery is mostly charged from the early fathers. It is infamous for Christians even to read or hear the names of pagan gods, who were really devils or wicked men or mere fictions, and stories about them, sugared over with art and rhetoric, cool our love for the soul-saving word of God.[23]

Mythology, however, was coming into disfavor with more than puritans. The merely pagan impulses of the Renaissance were exhausted; they had not vitality enough to preserve them from putrefaction. They could still appeal to some genuine poets, but the metaphysical movement brought fresh life to another kind of writing. For an important group thoughts of God and St. Teresa and eternity were replacing Olympus and Venus. Besides, puritanism, for good or ill, had leavened the lump; the slow and not always silent pressure of the middle class was, for a time, purifying literature and taste. Thus by the middle of the century we find a number of the literary men sharing the continental dislike for classical subjects. Whereas the ideal of the Renaissance had been an edifying but more or less secular heroic poem, the great aim now is the Christian epic.

In the preface to *Psyche,* the only part of that work that one can read, Joseph Beaumont declares his hope "That this Book may prompt better Wits to believe, that a Divine Theam is as capable and happy a Subject of Poetical Ornament, as any Pagan or Humane Device whatsoever." [24] Davenant, the unpuritanical loss of whose nose engendered so much delicate wit, made a well-known defense of a Christian subject in the preface to *Gondibert* (1650).[25] Still more significant, as regards the soil

[22] *An Apologie of the Schoole of Abuse* (1579), ed. Arber, pp. 65–68.
[23] Ed. 1633, pp. 28, 79–80.
[24] *Psyche* (London, 1648).
[25] Spingarn, II, 5, 9–10, and *passim.* The movement against paganism in poetry had begun quite early on the continent. One may recall again the case of Tasso (see H. M.

out of which grew Milton's major poems, is Cowley's preface of 1656, especially when we remember that as a child he had been won to poetry by the benign and radiant Spenser, that his first production was an Ovidian tale, and that much of his best mature work was amorous and festive. The devil has reigned over the realm of poetry, says Cowley, and among poets' sins has been the handling of "confused antiquated Dreams of senseless Fables and Metamorphoses." These things "are all but the Cold-meats of the Antients," and nothing is left for modern writers. Anyhow biblical stories are far better than "the obsolete threadbare tales of Thebes and Troy." "Can all the Transformations of the Gods give such copious hints to flourish and expatiate on as the true Miracles of Christ, or of his Prophets and Apostles?" [26] Cowley is far from desiring mere versified Scripture; he remains, whatever be thought of his own effort, an artist. It is partly as an artist too that he feels the exhaustion of the classic themes, though a greater poet might not have had the feeling. At the same time his Christian condemnation of mythology is quite as harsh as the outburst in *Paradise Regained,* and Cowley (who oddly enough was one of Milton's favorite English poets) is not branded a puritan.

Briggs, "Tasso's Theory of Epic Poetry," *M. L. R.,* XXV, 457 ff.). Fairfax introduced into his translation mythological allusions which he did not find in the original (Courthope, *History of English Poetry,* III, 82 ff.). Further, as Herford says, "the fiends of the *Gerusalemme Liberata* are in essence medieval devils disguised under the names and characteristics of the more monstrous figures of Greek myth" ("Dante and Milton," *The Post-War Mind of Germany,* p. 93). See, at the beginning of Tasso's fourth canto, the description of Pluto, with horns, fiery eyes, a mouth emitting blood, "sparks and smells."

[26] Spingarn, II, 88–90. Cf. *Davideis* (*Poems,* ed. Waller, 1905, p. 243):

> Too long the Muses-Land have Heathen bin;
> Their Gods too long were Dev'ils, and Vertues Sin;
> But Thou, Eternal Word, hast call'd forth Me
> Th' Apostle, to convert that World to Thee;
> T'unbind the charms that in slight Fables lie,
> And teach that Truth is truest Poesie.

CHAPTER FOURTEEN

MILTON

What besides God has resolved concerning me I know not, but this at least:
He has instilled into me, if into anyone, a vehement love of the beautiful.
Not with so much labour, as the fables have it, is Ceres said to have sought
her daughter Proserpina as it is my habit day and night to seek for this idea
of the beautiful, as for a certain image of supreme beauty, through all the
forms and faces of things (for many are the shapes of things divine) and to
follow it as it leads me on by some sure traces which I seem to recognize.

Letter to Diodati, 1637.[1]

For Beauty stands
In the admiration only of weak minds
Led captive; cease to admire, and all her plumes
Fall flat, and shrink into a trivial toy,
At every sudden slighting quite abash'd.

Paradise Regained, 1671.

MASSON suggests that Shakespeare and Ben Jonson, as they went
along Bread Street from the Mermaid Tavern, might have passed
a small boy at play whose name was John Milton. It is probable that when
Ben at least quitted his chair and his cup little John Milton had been some
hours in bed, yet the pleasant fancy helps to emphasize the poet's close
relation to the Elizabethans, to remind us that he was born nine years
after the death of Spenser, when *The Tempest* was not yet staged, when
England, if not merry—it never has been that—was still a land of
music and song. Sixty years bring us to a worn champion of freedom,
blind but cheerful, despite chalkstones and frustrated hopes, who
publishes *Paradise Lost* when gentle George Etherege is rousing himself
to produce *She Would If She Could;* and who, in the year of *The
Rehearsal,* offers *Paradise Regained* and *Samson Agonistes* to the polite
censure of the town.

Those sixty years really were, if the daring phrase be permissible, a
period of transition. We have, or think we have, a fairly definite notion of
what we mean by "Elizabethan," and of what we mean by "neoclassic";
what lies between does not invite such easy labels. Among the various
cross-currents in poetry the most important was the metaphysical. But

[1] Masson, *Life,* I, 644–45.

248

from the first Milton moved in the main stream of Renaissance humanism, and he remained closer to Spenser than to any other single poet.
Such a statement, concerning so potent an individuality as Milton's, is
of course only comparative, and it is truer of his ethical thought than of
his poetic expression. The latter is necessarily our chief interest. Yet
Milton's treatment of classical myth does lead us sometimes to the center
of his thought, and he is the last poet until the romantic period of whom
that can be said.

Of the sources, ancient and modern, of Milton's mythology some
account will have to be taken, but with a purpose rather different from
that which governed similar discussions in earlier chapters. Spenser,
Marlowe, Shakespeare, have highly individual styles, yet at times they
reflect the tone of a particular source, such as Ovid. Milton knew Ovid
better than any of these men, but almost from the beginning he wrote
in such a consistently personal idiom that one can very rarely say "This
is like Ovid," or "This is like Homer." Wherever Milton gets his material
the result, except in a few early pieces, is simply John Milton.

Further, the mere extent of Milton's learning inclines one to accept
the advice given to Adam and forbear inquiry. I may summarize the
summary made in Mr. Osgood's standard work:

There are four poets from whom he certainly derived more help than from
any others. These are Homer, Hesiod, Vergil, and Ovid . . . Next in import-
ance to these four sources are Euripides, Pindar, Theocritus, and the *Homeric
Hymns*. With these we may mention also the prose writers, Pausanias and
Apollodorus. Milton has also drawn some of his mythology from Æschylus,
Sophocles, Plato, the *Orphic Hymns,* and Apollonius of Rhodes; from
Herodotus, Plutarch, Pliny, Diodorus, and Strabo; from Horace, Statius,
Claudian, and the tragedies of Seneca. To these we may add, though the
list will be by no means exhaustive, Cicero, Athenæus, Hyginus, Aratus,
Macrobius, Lucretius, and most of the minor poets of the empire.[2]

In other words, and as everyone knows, Milton was steeped in ancient
literature as no English poet before him had been, and in Greek no less
than in Latin. He drank copiously from the sources which Spenser,
with a few exceptions, only sipped, and from many sources that Spenser
did not know. Milton's Latin verse alone shows that as a young man
he had Ovid and Horace and Virgil's minor poems pretty well by heart.
It shows too how critically he knew them, even to the minutiæ of style
and versification. He was, in short, a classical scholar, in both an
extensive and intensive sense that applies to no other poet we have met

---

[2] *The Classical Mythology of Milton's English Poems* (1900), pp. xlii–xliii. This chapter
is everywhere indebted to Mr. Osgood's study of sources, and also to his general discussion,
though I have tried as far as possible to avoid repetition of the latter.

except Ben Jonson, and Milton's critical as well as his creative faculties were aesthetically more keen and delicate than Ben's. The significance of Milton's classical studies in his whole life and work is at once too large and too familiar a subject to be touched in such a sketch as this. It is enough to say that Latin and Greek literature colored everything he was and did, from his syntax to his love of liberty—and his equally strong love of self-discipline and obedience.

One would expect so learned a poet, with all ancient literature at his command, to deal with "authentic" classical mythology, and certainly Milton is not guilty of those innumerable "errors" which in Spenser reveal a much inferior familiarity with original sources, a larger infusion of medievalism, and in general a less scholarly attitude. Milton does now and then invent or adapt a non-classical story, but usually for obvious reasons, as in the genealogies of Melancholy and the Graces in *L'Allegro,* or the parentage of Comus. Commentators who seek to catch Milton in a mistake are generally caught soon or late themselves. Yet his fidelity to ancient sources, though much greater than Spenser's, is only relative, for he was too much a man of the Renaissance to be a classical purist in mythological matters. Indeed his mythology is sometimes more medieval in spirit than Spenser's.

I

Nothing places Milton more clearly in the Renaissance tradition than his attachment to Ovid. Writing to Diodati in 1626 about his own exile from the university, he exclaims: "Would that no heavier blow had fallen on the lamentable bard who was exiled to the land of Tomis. In naught would he then have yielded to Ionian Homer, nor would the first praise be yours, O vanquished Maro." [3] When full allowance is made for boyish enthusiasm, and for the inflated style of Neo-Latin compliments, this is a large claim, larger, no doubt, than its author even then would have soberly supported. Milton knew Ovid through and through, and delighted to imitate him, but, for a young man preparing himself to be a Christian *vates,* other guides than "the smooth elegiac poets" were needed. Yet although in later years Milton's heavenly muse was not on speaking terms with the Roman lover of earth, many Ovidian offerings were still laid on the shrine. For Ovid was not with Milton a mere schoolboy passion—not that schoolboy passions are negligible. Dr. Johnson says: "The books in which his daughter, who used to read to him, represented him as most delighting, after Homer,

[3] *El.* i. 21–24 (W. MacKellar, *The Latin Poems of John Milton,* 1930, pp. 68–69).

which he could almost repeat, were Ovid's *Metamorphoses* and Euripides." [4]

Since Milton's enthusiasm for Ovid is so marked in his Latin verse, we may glance at it for a moment.[5] If we think of Milton's religious self-dedication to the office of poet-priest, of the *Nativity,* of his early pledge to live as ever in his great Task-master's eye, and then turn to gay and mundane pieces in Latin, we may experience a slight shock. Here we have the vagaries of Cupid in springtime, praise of wine as the fuel of poetry, a record of a fair face seen, loved, and never seen again, all in polished elegiacs, rich in mythological allusions and pagan sensuousness.

The shock would be uncritical, of course, because Milton's Latin poems are thoroughly in the humanistic tradition of the Renaissance. Not merely Ovid and Horace but George Buchanan and his kind are Milton's teachers, and in real charm as well as craftsmanship the young student excels most of his countrymen. When one wrote Latin one imitated the Latin poets, perhaps especially the saltier ones, for even the theological humanist's fancy could move easily on pagan as well as Christian levels. So Milton, with no slackening of his high resolves, which indeed are proclaimed in a memorable passage of his Latin verse,[6] can quite naturally and whole-heartedly indulge in pagan manners as well as in pagan idiom. The decent obscurity of a learned language may even permit the revelation of more intimate personal feeling, whether grave or gay, than appears in English poems to be read by all and sundry. But paganism was never more innocent than here, for much of Ovid is left behind. In one poem, celebrating a happily concluded visit from Corinna, Ovid prays *proveniant medii sic mihi saepe dies.*[7] (It was this piece that contributed a good deal to Marlowe's picture of Hero naked before her lover.) Milton echoes the Ovidian phrase—in an elegy on the deceased bishop of Winchester.[8]

As we have noticed before, the mixing of pagan and Christian allusions,

[4] *Lives of the English Poets* (ed. G. B. Hill, Oxford, 1905), I, 154, 158, 199. Cf. Todd, *Life and Writings of Milton* (1809), p. 151; Masson, VI, 754.

[5] No student of Milton needs to be reminded of two essays, of which one has been used here and the other constantly, Mr. Rand's vivacious "Milton in Rustication" (*S. P.,* XIX, 109 ff.), and Mr. Hanford's illuminating "Youth of Milton," *Studies in Shakespeare, Milton, and Donne* (1925). See also E. M. W. Tillyard, *Milton* (1930). Milton's Latin poems are cited from Mr. MacKellar's edition and translation.

[6] *El.* vi. 55 ff.

[7] *Amores,* i. 5. 26.

[8] *El.* iii. 68. Mr. Rand (page 133) mentions another innocent application of a phrase from an Ovidian poem that modern translators commonly leave in Latin (*Am.* iii. 7. 68; Milton, *El.* v. 8).

which we meet constantly in poetry of the Renaissance, began, like most Renaissance fashions, in the Middle Ages. And, as we also saw, the "naïve" medieval mixture persisted in the more decorative art of the Renaissance; though sometimes it became quite self-conscious, thanks to the paganizing habits of the Ciceronians and the virtual necessities of Neo-Latin verse-making. Milton of course observes the rules of the game. Satan is described in terms of Pluto:

> Cum ferus ignifluo regnans Acheronte tyrannus,
> Eumenidum pater, aethereo vagus exul Olympo.[9]

But the much-quoted conclusion of the *Epitaphium Damonis* is illustration enough. The soul of Milton's dearest friend is welcomed into heaven, "and the joyous revels rage under the thyrsus of Zion!"

Moreover Milton's English poems, especially the later ones, are the great examples of both the good and the ill effects of carrying over into English the style and conventions of Latin verse. The allusive circumlocution, the preference for unfamiliar proper names as more sonorous and suggestive than the familiar ones, these and other devices help to give Miltonic verse its peculiar quality of artifice and rhetorical rotundity —not that artifice and rhetoric are unpoetical.

But these are commonplaces, and they have led us away from the particular question of Ovid and Milton. In his first enraptured study and imitation Milton had mastered the complete works, and, while a young Ovidian a generation earlier would have written a mythological tale in English, Milton, writing in Latin, responded chiefly to the amatory poems.[10] He recoiled at all times from the vulgar amorists of his own day, but Ovid was long dead, and his form, language, workmanship, were elegance itself. Yet Ovid's love poems, however valuable in awakening senses and emotions, could never have satisfied more than a part of Milton's mind, and when this phase gave way to higher enthusiasms the *Metamorphoses* remained. The author of that book must have been, after a fashion, a prophet and priest of the wonder and bloom of the world, and, as such, a desirable supplement to Sylvester.[11]

Discussion of Milton's large debt to Ovid must be limited, here and

---

[9] *In Quintum Novembris*, ll. 7–8. Cf. the reference to Tasso above, page 247, note 25; Crashaw (ed. L. C. Martin), pp. 111–12; Giles Fletcher, *Christ's Victorie*, ii. 22 (ed. Boas, I, 45). Fletcher's picture of hell in this stanza, by the way, obviously copies Spenser, *F. Q.*, I. v. 32–33.

[10] In the *Apology for Smectymnuus* (Bohn ed., III, 116–17) Milton gives a slightly idealized account of the motives that inspired both the Roman elegiac poets and his own delight in them. See Hanford, "Youth of Milton," pp. 111 ff.

[11] There is no need of discussing here the case elaborately argued in Mr. H. C. H. Candy's *Some Newly Discovered Stanzas Written by John Milton on Engraved Scenes Illustrating Ovid's Metamorphoses* (London, 1924). Mr. Candy dated the script *ca.* 1623. Mr. C. W. Brodribb showed that the author knew Golding and Sandys (probably the latter's edition of 1632 with the commentary as well as the first edition), and suggested that perhaps

elsewhere, to a few specimens, and specimens of Milton speak for themselves better than comment. On account of both his freedom of handling and his fusing of many sources one seldom, especially in the early poems, finds distinct echoes of Ovid. There is no happier example of that early manner than these lines from *L'Allegro:*

> That Orpheus' self may heave his head
> From golden slumber on a bed
> Of heap'd Elysian flowers, and hear
> Such strains as would have won the ear
> Of Pluto to have quite set free
> His half-regain'd Eurydice.

This is not warmly voluptuous, softly flowing, elaborately pictorial, as when Spenser follows Ovid, but cool, plastic, economical, achieving a sensuous effect with hardly a sensuous word. It might be called Ovidian in its decorative objectivity, but the ideal beauty, the pure and not too glamorous magic (a good share of which lives in the melody), are beyond Ovid. Another instance of free and original re-creation of Ovidian motives, with a similar mixture of firm precision and suggestive generality, is the song of the Lady in *Comus:*

> Sweet Echo, sweetest nymph, that livest unseen
> Within thy airy shell
> By slow Meander's margent green,
> And in the violet-embroider'd vale . . .

It is a long way from such fanciful yet controlled delicacy to the style of the later heroic similes, or even the lines on Orpheus in *Lycidas.*

II

That combination of qualities, imaginative, intellectual, ethical, stylistic, which we sum up in the rather intimidating word "Miltonic," is associated especially with *Paradise Lost.* But the essential elements, in somewhat different proportions, are manifest in the early poems, for Milton's total production, though covering forty-five years, is more of a unit than the work of Chaucer or Spenser or almost any great English poet. His course from the beginning, as both poet and publicist, was as straight as the career of any strong mind can be. The pseudo-Ovidian tone of a sheaf of Latin verse was artificial and transient, though the humanistic tradition left permanent marks upon his English style, and though Ovid's fables—not the love poems—remained attractive to the sense of beauty they had helped to nourish. *L'Allegro* and *Il Penseroso*

Sandys wrote the stanzas (*Notes and Queries,* CXLVII, 1924, 77–78). Mr. Candy's reply (*ibid.,* 122–24) was hardly convincing, as regards his main thesis at least. Metrical arguments are offered also (*ibid.,* CLIX, 1930, 165–67, 189–92).

are the expression of a mood too serene to endure or recur, and they are not typical in spirit of the early Milton, though even in them are revealed the lineaments of an uncommonly serious young man. But *Comus* is, as the event proved, central, and leads on naturally to *Paradise Lost, Paradise Regained,* and *Samson Agonistes.*[12]

Milton's conception of the disciplined life early became and remained his citadel, the fortress from which he sallied out to battle in the field of prose for the right to exercise self-government, the tower in which, under the guidance of Urania, he celebrated the struggles and victories of the resolved soul. While that tower stood apart from the world, new and untried as yet by severe assault, grass and flowers and trees flourished around it, pastoral music was in the air. When it was no longer on the outskirts of life but in the center, when years of warfare had battered its masonry and altered its contours, grass and flowers almost vanished, trees stood gaunt and leafless, there was no music but the trumpet's.

This impromptu allegory embodies the history of Milton's poetic craftsmanship, and the changes are mirrored in his treatment of mythology. In this section we may run through a number of the poems in chronological order, with an eye to Milton's poetic evolution, the continuance in his early work of the Renaissance manner, and the emergence of a more classical style of his own. Of course the movement is not uniform, but the general tendency is clear enough, and familiar enough. Our special purpose, the attempt to view Milton's handling of mythology as the culmination of the Renaissance tradition, will perhaps justify the disproportionate space given to the earlier poems.

Such an outline must consist of a selection of more or less obvious illustrations. There is hardly a late Elizabethan or Jacobean poet who has not been quoted in comments on the earlier, and often the later, work of Milton, with one notable exception already suggested. Both the profounder and the more external qualities of Donne were alien to Milton from the beginning, and even the numerous conceits strewn about his early poems are in the fanciful rather than the metaphysical vein.[13]

To turn to the poems, the *Fair Infant* is, as Mr. Eliot might say, pustular with mythology, despite its sincerity and the occasional beauty of its Elizabethan sweetness or Elizabethan rhetoric. In the first mythological allusion[14] one line approaches the large accent of *Paradise Lost*—"By

[12] Remarks on Milton's consistent development apply of course to central motives and principles, not to particular ideas, many of which were modified.

[13] H. J. C. Grierson, *Cross Currents in English Literature of the 17th Century* (1929), p. 241; G. R. Potter, *P. Q.*, VI, 396–400.

[14] One might notice the veiled reference at the end of the first stanza to Winter's thinking to kiss and killing instead. See above, p. 139, for the conceit about the boar and Adonis, and also *The Purple Island*, c. 5, st. 61.

boisterous rape the Athenian damsel got"—but more typical are these lines:

> For so Apollo, with unweeting hand,
> Whilom did slay his dearly-lovèd mate,
> Young Hyacinth, born on Eurotas' strand,
> Young Hyacinth, the pride of Spartan land;
> But then transform'd him to a purple flower.

Their Elizabethan quality is sufficiently attested by a bit of Spenser

> And all about grew euery sort of flowre,
> To which sad louers were transformd of yore;
> Fresh Hyacinthus, Phœbus paramoure,
> And dearest loue,
> Foolish Narcisse, that likes the watry shore,
> Sad Amaranthus, made a flowre but late,
> Sad Amaranthus, in whose purple gore . . .[15]

In the *Vacation Exercise* (1628) the poet aspires to a theme

> Such as may make thee search thy coffers round,
> Before thou clothe my fancy in fit sound:
> Such where the deep transported mind may soar
> Above the wheeling poles, and at Heaven's door
> Look in, and see each blissful deity
> How he before the thunderous throne doth lie,
> Listening to what unshorn Apollo sings
> To the touch of golden wires, while Hebe brings
> Immortal nectar to her kingly sire.

Milton is adapting the picture given at the end of the first book of the *Iliad*, and the lines have the Miltonic dignity, the Miltonic sense of space, which are lacking in the plaintive bit about Hyacinth. The effect can best be measured by means of another quotation from Spenser:

> There thou them placest in a Paradize
> Of all delight, and ioyous happie rest,
> Where they doe feede on Nectar heauenly wize,
> With Hercules and Hebe, and the rest
> Of Venus dearlings, through her bountie blest,
> And lie like Gods in yuorie beds arayd,
> With rose and lillies ouer them displayd.[16]

It is needless to emphasize the gravity, economy, and coolness of Milton's lines. Though Spenser is in an exalted mood, one suspects that he would not be averse to stealing a kiss from Hebe.

[15] *F. Q.*, III. vi. 45. Cf. *Astrophel* (ll. 7-8):
> Young Astrophel the pride of shepheards praise,
> Young Astrophel the rusticke lasses loue . . .
[16] *Hymne in Honour of Love*, ll. 280 ff. Cf. *Odyssey*, xi. 601 ff.

On the Morning of Christ's Nativity (1629) marks in more than one way the young poet's coming of age. It contains in embryo the mixed elements, classical, medieval, modern, which were to receive full expression in *Paradise Lost*. Not only is Christ Pan—we are used to that —but he is also an infant Hercules who, paradoxically, controls "the damned crew" of pagan divinities. Of the twenty lines beginning "For, if such holy song . . . ," Mr. Osgood remarks, and the summary is true in spirit of a good deal of Milton: "Various sources of details in this passage from the Psalms, the *Iliad*, the Fourth Eclogue of Virgil, and Horace, have been noted by the editors. But the thought as a whole is that in the Fifth Book of the *Divine Institutes* of Lactantius."[17] The stanza on the cessation of oracles—which Keats turned to other uses— seems to be compounded out of authors ranging from Plutarch and Prudentius to Giles Fletcher.[18] From medieval allegory, perhaps by way of Fletcher, we have the four daughters of God, who are destined to appear so often in Milton; one of them, Peace, comes down to earth in the manner of Iris or the Virgilian Mercury, or some figure in a masque.[19] Finally, Milton develops the patristic and medieval doctrine that the pagan gods were demons, a doctrine important in *Paradise Lost*. But delight in handling the names of the gods contributes at least as much as religious emotion to the account of the overthrow of paganism. Indeed if one thinks of the poems of Donne, Herbert, Crashaw, Vaughan, one can hardly regard the *Nativity* as religious at all; however, the conception of Christ, equally remote from the Catholic and the evangelical, was to prove characteristically Miltonic. In its essential unity and crystalclear beauty the poem is beyond the reach of the Fletchers, in spite of conceits which they might have owned. It reveals what was to be Milton's lifelong genius for lavishing inexhaustible imagination, learning, and artistic skill upon the illustration of a few simple ideas.

In *L'Allegro* and *Il Penseroso* Milton comes under the sway of more secular and more lyrical masters. For sources and analogues, general or specific, commentators have cited most Elizabethan and Jacobean poets, and, though such lines as the following are in the best sense original, the

[17] *American Journal of Philology*, XLI, 76 ff.
[18] A. S. Cook, "Notes on Milton's Ode on the Morning of Christ's Nativity," *Transactions of the Connecticut Academy of Arts and Sciences*, XV (1909), 349–51. E. K. had told the story "Great Pan is dead" in his gloss on ͻpenser's eclogue for May. It is also in Sandys' *Relation* (ed. 1627, p. 11). See Osgood, *Classical Mythology*, p. xlvii. One might compare Ralegh's account of the overthrow of paganism, *History*, i. 6. 8 (1829, II, 185). Tasso's *Canzone sopra la Cappella del Presepio* has been cited as a general parallel to Milton's poem.
[19] Cook, pp. 322–24. See Ben Jonson's *Masques* (ed. H. Morley), p. 390; R. L. Ramsay, "Morality Themes in Milton's Poetry," *S.P.*, XV, 133–136; Enid Welsford, *The Court Masque*, pp. 310–11.

names of Jonson and Shakespeare help to explain their dew-washed
purity, the airy delicacy and precision of their mythological invention:

> Or whether (as some sager sing)
> The frolic wind that breathes the spring,
> Zephyr, with Aurora playing,
> As he met her once a-Maying,
> There on beds of violet blue,
> And fresh-blown roses wash'd in dew,
> Fill'd her with thee, a daughter fair,
> So buxom, blithe, and debonair.[20]

Milton's next few lines, with the help of Burton and others, present
an Elizabethan or Jacobean Hebe:

> Nods and Becks, and wreathèd Smiles,
> Such as hang on Hebe's cheek,
> And love to live in dimple sleek.

The Olympian cupbearer is by way of becoming a pastoral nymph.
A quality barely hinted in these lines, and quite agreeably, is more
marked in a passage of *Il Penseroso:*

> Thus, Night, oft see me in thy pale career,
> Till civil-suited Morn appear,
> Not trick'd and frounced, as she was wont
> With the Attic boy to hunt,
> But kerchieft in a comely cloud . . .

"Civil-suited" is less appropriate here than its original is in Juliet's speech:

> Come, civil night,
> Thou sober-suited matron, all in black.

"Trick'd," "frounced," "kerchieft," make Aurora a sort of damsel at a
fête champêtre, a little too politely rustic.[21] Of course everything depends
upon mood and context, and in these poems we expect mythology to be
somewhat domesticated. When Milton writes

[20] See the lyric in Jonson's *Penates* sung by Aurora, Zephyrus, and Flora (*Masques,* ed.
Morley, p. 420), and the lyrical allusions to the same characters, pp. 221, 421. Cf. Campion's
Maske . . . in honour of the Lord Hayes (*Works,* ed. P. Vivian, Oxford, 1909, p. 64).
   Petruchio declares that when Katherine frowns he will say she looks as clear "As
morning roses newly wash'd with dew." The opening chorus of *Pericles* tells of a female
heir "so buxom, blithe, and full of face." Commentators have cited Randolph's "blithe,
buxom, and debonair" (*Aristippus,* in *Works,* ed. Hazlitt, London, 1875, I, 21); see
G. C. M. Smith in *T. L. S.,* January 19, 1922, p. 44.
   Mr. Foster Damon has called attention to the resemblance between the first thirty lines
of *L'Allegro* and the first part of the last satire in Marston's *Scourge of Villanie* (*P. M. L. A.,*
XLII, 1927, 873–74; Marston, ed. Bullen, III, 371). The not improbable relation, which
was observed by Warton, illustrates Milton's ability to extract gold from ore.
[21] Mr. Rylands discusses the "urban" quality of a number of Milton's epithets in *Words
and Poetry,* page 113.

> While Cynthia checks her dragon yoke
> Gently o'er the accustom'd oak,

he does not, like the more primitive Marlowe, really see the goddess and her dragons; he is a bookish young poet who watches the moon glide above a familiar tree near his home and recalls Elizabethan, not classical, allusions to Cynthia.[22]

Nowhere in these serene and lovely poems is there a hint that the classical divinities which help to adorn them are of the tribe of Satan; "yet there was no fear of Jove." Troy is "divine." Country games and dances, the well-trod stage (and the Anglican church service), all are good. Yet the young man's pursuits and studies are not unworthy of one who aspired to be himself a true poem.

The mythology of *L'Allegro* and *Il Penseroso* shows that the waywardness and conceits of the Spenserians have given place to the purer, more classical influence of Jonson. It was Jonson especially who helped Milton to find his own lyric style, to achieve athletic diction and definiteness of line and form without altogether losing Elizabethan opulence. The mythological allusions are often Jonsonian also in their civilized, courtly, masque-like quality. Milton's study of Jonson's masques and lyrics is very apparent in the plot, tone, and details of the *Arcades*.

> This, this is she alone,
> Sitting like a goddess bright
> In the centre of her light.

The first line echoes "This is she, this is she" of Jonson's *The Satyr*,[23] and the second line (which originally read "Seated") recalls "Queen and huntress, chaste and fair." Milton's "glassy, cool, translucent" mythology is much more Jonsonian than Elizabethan.

III

When one begins "Before the starry threshold of Jove's court . . . ," one shrinks from soiling the pure ambrosial weeds of *Comus* with the rank vapors of annotation, but something must be done. Though the two aspects of the poem can hardly be separated, we may postpone the matter of doctrine and allegory and consider here mainly the artistic quality of

[22] Marlowe's lines are quoted above, page 137.
[23] Morley, p. 411; cf. Marston, ed. Bullen, III, 391. With the third stanza of *The Satyr* compare the last lines of Milton's third song. As for the "plot," the discourse of the Genius of the Wood is in the vein of Jonson; Milton's Platonic lines were doubtless suggested by the business of the Genius and the Fates in Jonson's entertainment given at Theobalds in 1607 (Morley, pp. 428 ff.).
Masson dated *Arcades* "not later than the year 1631" (*Poetical Works of John Milton,*

Milton's treatment of myth. We have seen the young poet, with the classics in his head, and Jonson as a further corrective to Elizabethan fluency, richness, and eccentricity, emerging on a *via media* of his own. It is that starry path (*via lactea,* one might say, though not in Phineas Fletcher's sense) which Milton follows with such triumphant originality in *Comus.* Yet there are occasional deviations, for the style now and then recalls the past or anticipates the future. Passages of modified Elizabethan sensuousness may be followed by lines of expository bareness approaching the manner of *Paradise Regained;* we have some Elizabethan or Jacobean conceits,[24] a few traces of turgid Jacobean rhetoric,[25] and some lines of smooth eighteenth-century classicism.[26] The mythology woven into the texture naturally partakes of both the dominant and the occasional qualities.

We have observed that very seldom, even in Milton's earliest poems, is there writing that approaches the sensuous warmth, the soft fluidity, of Spenser. Remembering the stanza in which Spenser united a radiant Phoebus with the sun of the psalmist—and remembering also the conceits about the sun in the *Nativity*—we can measure the cool restraint of Milton when he handles the same combination:

> And the slope sun his upward beam
> Shoots against the dusky pole,
> Pacing toward the other goal
> Of his chamber in the east.[27]

1874, II, 210–211); Grierson puts it in 1630–32 (*Poems of John Milton,* 1925, pp. xiii–xiv). *L'Allegro* and *Il Penseroso* are usually assigned to the beginning of the Horton period, but they may have been written in one of Milton's college vacations.

[24] Cf. ll. 139 ff., and *Venus and Anchises* (ed. Seaton, p. 4):
> The thick-lac'd boughs shutt out the Telltale Sunne.
> For Venus hated his all-blabbing light.

A conceit involving Scylla and Charybdis (ll. 257–59) was apparently suggested by Silius Italicus, xiv. 471–74 (quoted in Osgood, page 76). Milton might perhaps have reached the fourteenth book of such a poet, but he might have remembered the lines from Sandys' *Relation* (ed. 1627, p. 237). Both in the *Relation* (p. 248) and the *Metamorphosis* (ed. 1632, p. 476), Sandys, in translating an epigram, has "fell Charybdis." Todd cites the same phrase in Sylvester.

While speaking of Sandys I may add another item, in connection with *Comus,* ll. 675 ff., where Milton describes the "nepenthes" given to Helen as "to life so friendly." He is recalling the *Odyssey,* iv. 219–30, where the words are φάρμακα μητιόεντα, ἐσθλά. We expect Milton's phrases to be freely original, but, in view of his knowledge of the *Relation,* it may be more than coincidence that Sandys, who quoted part of the Homeric passage, in Latin as usual, rendered *pharmaca utilia bona* by "a friend to life" (page 126).

[25] E.g., ll. 597–99, 603 ff. These last lines are not quite Virgilian (cf. *Aen.* vi. 287 ff.). The "sooty flag" of Acheron comes from Phineas Fletcher's *Apollyonists* (ed. Boas, I, 151, st. 39), and with the two following lines compare Fairfax's *Jerusalem Delivered* (bk. xv, st. 51, ed. H. Morley, 1901, p. 312).

[26] Ll. 984–87. Gray of course registers the fact by his borrowing of "the rosy-bosom'd Hours," for his spring is also "spruce and jocund." Yet Milton's lines follow the magical phrase that sang in Tennyson's head to such romantic effect. See below, page 262.

[27] Ll. 98 ff. Cf. *F. Q.*, I. v. 2 (quoted above, page 95).

That is Milton's more characteristic tone, and even these lines in *L'Allegro* seem luxuriant:

> Right against the eastern gate,
> Where the great sun begins his state,
> Robed in flames and amber light,
> The clouds in thousand liveries dight.[28]

Although a learned scholar, Milton borrows mythological allusions from his immediate predecessors, and, further, he often gives them a didactic application. When he writes that she who is chaste "may pass on with unblench'd majesty," that Diana "set at nought the frivolous bolt of Cupid," he has been thinking of Plato, and of Belphoebe and Britomart, but he has not forgotten "the imperial votaress" who

> passed on,
> In maiden meditation, fancy-free.

When, at the conclusion of the same speech, the Second Brother exclaims that divine philosophy is "musical as is Apollo's lute," he is quoting the un-Platonic Berowne's praise, not of chastity, but of love.[29] And when the Lady declares

> Were it a draught for Juno when she banquets,
> I would not taste thy treasonous offer,

is she not echoing, with some unconscious irony, Jonson's most famous lyric? We do not have the devil citing Scripture, but we do have Comus quoting Sylvester, and combining him with Homer, in a line much too beautiful for a wicked tempter—"Love-darting eyes, or tresses like the morn." Shakespeare's Ariel was content to be Ariel; the Spirit of Milton, after celebrating the mystic marriage of Cupid and Psyche, echoes Ariel, and ends with praise of Virtue.

The actual space that Milton gives to the story of Circe is small, and some details seem to follow Ovid more than Homer.[30] Homer and Ovid, however conscious of didactic implications, were disinterested

---

[28] Cf. *Midsummer Night's Dream*, III. ii. 391: "Even till the eastern gate, all fiery-red . . . ," and Milton's very Elizabethan *Song on May Morning*. See Osgood, page xxxii.

[29] *Love's Labour's Lost*, IV. iii. 342.

[30] See Warton's notes on ll. 252, 637, 651, 815, 880, 981 (and Osgood, page 24). Warton remarked upon the fact that in his sixth Elegy Milton chose to illustrate Homer's poetical character by the *Odyssey* and not by the *Iliad*, and Keightley added "which was quite natural in one who was so fond of Ovid" (MacKellar, p. 232).

Considerations of allegory and dramatic presentation would account for some changes in the classical story, such as the figure of Comus himself, his parentage, the incomplete metamorphosis of the victims of enchantment, and their unconsciousness of degradation. The last two items are found in the *Orlando Furioso*, vi. 60–66 (E. G. Ainsworth, *M. L. N.*, XLVI, 91–92). We need not repeat the facts about the influence of Jonson and others.

story-tellers, Milton is not, and though the myth itself contains the essence
of romance most of that is inevitably strained out in the Miltonic version.
Comus is more romantic than Milton's other work, but its beauty is a
clear, finite beauty, without much strangeness added to it. While the
poem is not romantic in spirit, it is full of romantic details. It could
hardly be otherwise when to such a myth were added, from Spenser,
Shakespeare, Fletcher, and the rest, all manner of pastoral decoration,
magic spells, fairy lore, British legend. As Warburton said, "Though
Milton builds his fable on classick mythology, yet his materials of
magick have more the air of enchantments in the Gothick romances." [31]
But Milton could not, like Spenser, wander delightedly through a
world of enchantment; his classical instincts, the weighty discourses on
virtue, and the formal requirements of the masque, all were a check upon
extravagance. Yet the thread of mythology is more or less colored, like
classical tales in The Faerie Queene, by the partly "Gothick" texture into
which it is woven.

Thus we hear of Circe surrounded by "the Sirens three" and "flowery-
kirtled Naiades." [32] We have water-nymphs with pearled wrists, Sabrina
under the waves and in her chariot, and we owe something to Jonson,
Drayton, and others for such pleasant apparitions. There is the song to
Sabrina which, if not—like "Full fathom five"—of the water watery,
at any rate contrives by means of more or less classical allusions to
divinities of the sea to create an atmosphere and a picture. One says
"more or less classical" because of

> fair Ligea's golden comb,
> Wherewith she sits on diamond rocks
> Sleeking her soft alluring locks.[33]

We have noticed before some hints of "urban" mythology in Milton,
and even romantic bits of Comus may be touched with that quality.
"The pert faeries and the dapper elves," whatever is allowed for a
change of meaning in the words, are not quite a wood-note wild. There
is a clue to this somewhat spruce vein of writing in these lines:

[31] Quoted in Todd (1809), VI, 245.
[32] Homer and Ovid do not give Circe sirens as attendants, but Browne does, and sirens
were welcome in Comus as traditional symbols of fleshly delights. Mr. Osgood has dwelt
upon the distilled charm of "flowery-kirtled Naiades," a Botticellian picture at once definite
and vaguely suggestive (pp. lxvi, 58).
[33] Ovid's Salmacis and Galatea comb their hair, and cf. Georg. iv. 336–37:
> Drymoque Xanthoque Ligeaque Phyllodoceque,
> caesariem effusae nitidam per candida colla.
The gold comb and diamond rocks, as Warton observed, are new allurements for the
unwary.

> . . . and such court guise
> As Mercury did first devise
> With the mincing Dryades
> On the lawns and on the leas.

Milton is thinking of masques, and "mincing" is more suited to dryads of the court than to those of the woods.[34]

Finally, there are sixteen lines which not every reader of Milton knows. There is no better proof of Milton's sense of form than that, after writing such a passage, he could strike it out as superfluous. I can quote only part of it, beginning with four lines which preceded it and which still remain:

> Before the starry threshold of Jove's court
> My mansion is, where those immortal shapes
> Of bright aerial spirits live inspher'd
> In regions mild of calm and serene air
>
> Amidst the Hesperian gardens, on whose banks
> Bedew'd with nectar and celestial songs
> Eternal roses grow and hyacinth
> And fruits of golden rind, on whose fair tree
> The scaly-harness'd dragon ever keeps
> His unenchanted eye . . .[35]

Here, says Mr. Mackail, classical and romantic elements are for a moment in perfect fusion, and he quotes two other passages in *Comus* which deal with the Hesperides. One is the magical phrase already referred to,

> Of Hesperus, and his daughters three
> That sing about the golden tree.

The other is this:

> But Beauty, like the fair Hesperian tree
> Laden with blooming gold, had need the guard
> Of dragon watch with unenchanted eye
> To save her blossoms, and defend her fruit,
> From the rash hand of bold Incontinence.

The central line "gives the concentrated essence of the suppressed

[34] Mr. Osgood (pp. 42, 65) finds only rather vague classical authority for Mercury's dancing with the dryads, and it is not our common conception of him. Cf. Jonson's *Pan's Anniversary* (Morley, p. 336).

> Of Pan we sing, the best of leaders, Pan,
> That leads the Naiads and the Dryads forth;
> And to their dances more than Hermes can.

One is reminded of masques by such lines as *Paradise Lost*, iv. 266 ff.

[35] The whole passage is quoted by Mr. Mackail (*Springs of Helicon*, p. 155), with admirable comments. It occurs on page 10 in the *Facsimile of the Manuscript of Milton's Minor Poems*, ed. W. A. Wright (Cambridge University Press, 1899).

passage," fuses classical and romantic; "the rest is hardening into classicism." One can trace other mythological motives through Milton and find a similar process going on.

Before leaving the opening lines of *Comus,* as we have them now, we may observe that they are an excellent specimen of Milton's combining of pagan and Christian materials in harmonious purity. The speech is a sort of Euripidean prologue, spoken by a guardian angel, about angels and the souls of virtue's servants, who live in Hesperian gardens. The description of the gardens seems to unite traditional accounts of happy isles with the Olympus of the *Odyssey.* "Above the smoke and stir" is a clear echo of Horace's *fumum et opes strepitumque Romae.* And with "sainted seats" we come to the white-robed elders seated round the throne in *Revelation.*[36] But Milton, unlike many Elizabethan borrowers, makes things completely his own.

Such a mixture may serve to lead on to *Lycidas,* about which only a word can be said here. The briefest remarks cannot overlook Dr. Johnson's opinions, which are still to be met in criticism. We do not share his religious scruples, whatever our aesthetic judgment, about the mingling of Christian and pagan figures and ideas. If Milton had written in Latin the poem would appear quite natural along with the earlier elegies and the later *Epitaphium Damonis.* We should not therefore be surprised even when Lycidas is first welcomed into the heaven of *Revelation* and then apostrophized as the genius of the shore. Yet, writing in English, Milton does seem to feel more conscious of mixing alien ideas; the passages on fame and on hireling shepherds are followed by references to "a higher mood" and "the dread voice," although both these themes were conventional in pastoral verse and needed no apology.[37]

We may or may not agree with Johnson that sincere grief does not express itself through pastoral artifice. But the question of the adequacy of Milton's personal sorrow is largely irrelevant; there is no question of the adequacy of poetic emotion. *Lycidas,* which begins and ends with allusions to Milton's poetic career, is not so much a lament for Edward King as it is an impassioned meditation on the death of any young poet, a poem which embodies the doubts and the high hopes, earthly and heavenly, that throng the author's path. Nor, it must be added, does Milton for very long forget himself even in the *Epitaphium Damonis.*

[36] *Rev.* iv. 4.
[37] The thunderous tone of Milton's invective is quite in character, in view of his intense convictions, but it is not so much like Spenser and Mantuan as it is like Dante when he puts into the mouth of St. Peter a denunciation of Boniface (C. H. Herford, "Dante and Milton," *The Post-War Mind of Germany,* p. 83).

Lycidas is in the main one of those lofty inventories that Milton was in the habit of taking at successive stages in his progress. He was too much a man of the Renaissance to reject earthly fame, and in *Lycidas* even his heavenly aspirations wear a half-classical dress. When in *Paradise Regained* Satan, the personification of wrong ambition, praises earthly glory, Christ's answer does not link Phoebus with all-judging Jove.[38]

The charges laid by reason against the pastoral convention, and against *Lycidas* as the supreme English exemplar, admit a wide solution. The poem is more artificial than its Greek originals, for the pastoral had absorbed more and more foreign elements, had moved further and further from any recognizable actuality. Sir Walter Raleigh, with alarm at his own temerity, avowed some uneasiness, which readers of less courage sometimes repress, on the score of fauns and satyrs, Hippotades, Camus, and St. Peter. Robert Bridges, on the other hand, brushing aside Dr. Johnson as an unpoetic mind, maintained that Milton's poetic magic weaves all the apparent artifices into an harmonious whole; even the much-abused dolphins do not sound frigid or artificial in the poem.[39] And there, with the jade's trick of a *de gustibus,* one may or must leave such a question. But perhaps it may be said that *Lycidas* is far removed from Greek writing, that it is thoroughly of the Renaissance, and that, for all its wondrous power, it is less human, less moving, than the invocation to Light or the close of *Samson Agonistes.*

IV

Milton's expressed or implied opinions concerning the nature and the validity of myth demand consideration by themselves. In helping to explain some aspects of his poetic treatment those opinions, in their very inconsistency, make clear the dilemma of a humanist, an heir of the Renaissance tradition, who has solemnly resolved to bring the finest pagan art to the exposition of the loftiest Christian truth.

During Milton's lifetime the allegorical interpretation of mythology was, as we have seen, retreating before the advance of rationalism, although it still numbered some strong adherents. We might expect on the whole to find Milton with the rationalists, yet he has some points of contact with the venerable tradition, especially in *Comus.*[40] The ethical

[38] *P. R.,* iii. 60–62. See J. H. Hanford, "The Temptation Motive in Milton," *S. P.,* XV (1918), 184–85.
[39] "Poetic Diction," *Collected Essays, Papers, etc.* (1928). Raleigh's remarks are in his *Six Essays on Johnson* (1910), pp. 28–29, 150 ff. Cf. W. P. Ker, *Form and Style in Poetry* (London, 1928), p. 122.
[40] There is the concrete fact that Milton owned a copy of *Heraclidis Pontici Allegoriae in Homeri Fabulas.* Allegorized myths are numerous enough in the academic prolusions, but they are rather like pulpit anecdotes and need not imply serious conviction.

core of *Comus* is of course the orthodox allegorical interpretation of the
myth of Circe, which commended itself to Milton as inevitably as it had
to Spenser for the presentation of virtue's triumph over sensuality. The
moralized myth was the example *par excellence* of both the pagan
conflict between reason and appetite and the Christian warfare between
spirit and flesh. It was so universally familiar that the name of Circe had
long been a byword, yet it is no wonder that Milton chose once to put
in mythological dress the theme which occupies the center of his four
major poems. No myth left a deeper or more permanent impress upon
him. At the end of his first Elegy, in which he had praised the beauty of
English damsels, he had taken the magic herb moly as a symbol of the
Christian teaching that governed his conduct.[41] And when in his last
poem Samson achieves victory over the sensual temptation that had
ruined him, the Philistine woman is another embodiment of Circe:

> Thy fair enchanted cup, and warbling charms
> No more on me have power.

Milton's choice of such a subject for a masque was natural, although
masques ordinarily ministered to youth and joy. Jonson had led the
way in combining classic myth and personified abstractions to produce
an edifying spectacle; he had also, as everyone knows, treated the figure
of Comus. But Milton went far beyond Ben in didactic seriousness;
Comus could in no wise be entitled *Pleasure Reconciled to Virtue*. Even
rustic games, which *L'Allegro* happily chronicled, are harshly condemned
in the first words uttered by the Lady. In its conflict between virtue and
vice, with characters representing fixed moral attitudes, *Comus* has
obvious affinities with the medieval tradition, whether exemplified by the
morality play, the *débat,* or Milton's own prolusions.

Many elements entered into the allegory. There was Plato, whom
Milton knew or came to know thoroughly at first hand, unlike his poetic
predecessors and still more unlike contemporary authors ot "Platonics." [42]
Yet the Plato of *Comus* is not quite our Plato. One *locus classicus* must
be quoted:

Thus, from the laureat fraternity of poets, riper years and the ceaseless
round of study and reading led me to the shady spaces of philosophy; but
chiefly to the divine volumes of Plato, and his equal Xenophon: where, if I
should tell ye what I learnt of chastity and love, I mean that which is truly so,
whose charming cup is only virtue, which she bears in her hand to those
who are worthy; (the rest are cheated with a thick intoxicating potion, which

---

[41] Cf. *English Works of Roger Ascham*, ed. Wright, pp. 225–26.
[42] See H. Agar, *Milton and Plato* (1928). The juxtaposition, in *Il Penseroso,* of Plato
and Hermes Trismegistus suggests that Milton's early Platonism could be tinged by Neo-
Platonic tradition. See E. C. Baldwin, *M. L. N.*, XXXIII (1918), 184–85.

a certain sorceress, the abuser of love's name, carries about;) and how the first and chiefest office of love begins and ends in the soul, producing those happy twins of her divine generation, knowledge and virtue.[43]

This is the Plato discerned and not a little altered by the selective instinct of a cultivated puritan of the Renaissance. To quote Herford:

Plato makes the passion even of the noble lover an intoxication, which is the very condition of his acquiring a reach of vision beyond that of cool reason; Milton, consciously or not, alters the whole purport of the thought; with him it is only the sensual lovers who experience the intoxication of passion, and it is from their intoxication precisely that their fatuous delusions spring . . . Milton had the strength and the weakness of his clear rationality; even his loftiest inspirations owed little to the divine unreason which Plato declared to be 'the source of the chiefest blessings among men.' [44]

While this is not Plato's only mood, the general distinction made holds true. *Comus* expounds the Platonic doctrine that reason must govern the irrational elements in the soul, and expresses a Platonic fear of "contagion," but even in echoing the language of the *Phaedo* Milton, in his fear of the flesh, his ascetic fervor, is an Englishman, a Christian, and something of an inexperienced doctrinaire. His permanent view of life as an unceasing moral conflict, of sensuality as, if not the chief of sins, at least a source and symbol of most others, is only partly Platonic and scarcely Greek. Milton's much more rigorous dualism is Pauline, patristic, puritan.[45]

Then there was Spenser, whom Milton, after dallying with the Spenserians, had learned to know as a poet who added beauty to moral allegory and moral idealism. Spenser's partly Platonic treatment of chastity, temperance, sensual temptation, exerted a deep influence upon a nature strongly predisposed to feel it, an influence visible not merely in *Comus* but in the later poems as well. Sir Guyon, however, achieved temperance only with struggles, his appetites had to be resisted up to the end; in *Comus* there is no struggle, no human frailty at all. (It was in *Paradise Lost,* and still more in *Samson Agonistes,* that Milton humanized his great theme.) In his third book Spenser had celebrated the chastity that is not negative and sterile, the love that ennobles and stirs to high endeavor. Of this also there is not much in *Comus.* In Milton generally the love that everywhere kindles Spenser is of slight account, and his praise of wedded love in *Paradise Lost,* compared with Spenser

[43] *Apology for Smectymnuus* (Bohn ed., III, 119).
[44] "Dante and Milton," p. 71. See *Phaedrus* 244a.
[45] See Hanford, "Youth of Milton," p. 149; Tillyard, pp. 374 ff. For the possible influence of Lactantius on the passage about "contagion" (ll. 463 ff.), see K. E. Hartwell, *Lactantius and Milton* (1929), pp. 83 ff.

and Plato, is somewhat practical and domesticated; even when, at the end of the eighth book, Raphael utters some Platonic sentiments, Milton's emphasis is on the dangers of connubial sensuality. In *Comus,* as Herford says, "Milton's Chastity, sublime and exalted as it is, is at bottom a self-regarding virtue." Neither Plato nor Spenser is, like the young Milton, single-minded in his concentration on austere self-control. Further, Milton seems here to conceive of chastity as conferring something like magical powers on its possessor.

Such naturalistic arguments as were poured forth by Leander, with Marlowe's full sympathy, are put in the mouth of Comus, the evil tempter, and uncompromisingly denounced.[46] Milton was not the first to repudiate these doctrines, but in comparison with the Elizabethans he shows here an ungenial strictness. At the same time his vein of Spenserian and Platonic idealism gives an inward glow to his rather dogmatic asceticism and exaltation of not quite reasonable reason. In his presentation of evil Milton does not of course use the nymphs of Tasso and Spenser, but Comus is not as repulsive as he should be. Like Tasso and Spenser—and Jeremy Taylor—Milton, in his degree, cannot help making beautiful the things of sense that he condemns. The cultivated and music-loving Comus is in some ways as close to the author as the Lady or the Elder Brother.

Finally—for we cannot touch the innumerable sources—we may notice some of Sandys' comments on the story of Circe, in the *Ovid* that Milton may have known:

That the upper part of her [Scylla's] body, is feigned to retaine a humane figure, and the lower to be bestiall; intimates how man, a divine creature, endued with wisdome and intelligence, in whose superiour parts, as in a high tower, that immortall spirit resideth, who only of all that hath life erects his lookes unto heaven, can never so degenerate into a beast, as when he giueth himselfe over to the lowe delights of those baser parts of the body, Dogs and Wolues, the blind & saluage fury of concupiscence . . .

Yet Ulysses could not loose his shape with the rest, who being fortifyed by an immortall power, was not subiect to mutation. For the diuine & cœlestiall soule, subsisting through the bounty of the Creator, can by no assault of nature be violated, nor can that bee conuerted into a beast, which so highly participates of reason . . . [Circe's sensual charms] are not to bee resisted,

---

[46] Milton seems to echo Marlowe at times in the speeches of Comus; see Mr. Martin's edition of Marlowe's poems, and below, page 273, note 64. One speech of Comus (ll. 710–42) has been related particularly to the passage in Randolph's *Muses' Looking-Glass* which begins "Nature has been bountiful" (*Works,* ed. Hazlitt, ii. 3, I, 208–09). The play was not printed until 1638, but was probably acted at Cambridge while Milton was there; see G. C. M. Smith, *T. L. S.,* January 19, 1922, p. 44. For references to these naturalistic ideas in Elizabethan poetry, see above, p. 135. Although they soon become commonplaces, Randolph seems now and then to echo Marlowe; see his *Epithalamium to Mr. F. H., A Pastorall Courtship,* and *Upon Love fondly refus'd for Conscience sake.*

but by the diuine assistance, Moly, the guift of Mercury, which signifies temperance . . .

Sandys proceeds to explain

their head strong appetites, which reuolt from the soueraignty of reason (by which wee are onely like unto God, and armed against our depraued affections) nor euer returne into their Country (from whence the soule deriueth her cœlestiall originall) unlesse disinchanted, and cleansed from their former impurity. For as Circes rod, waued ouer their heads from the right side to the left: presents those false and sinister perswasions of pleasure, which so much deformes them: so the reuersion thereof, by discipline, and a view of their owne deformity, restores them to their former beauties.[47]

In addition to the allegory implicit in the fable Milton permits the Attendant Spirit to express a general belief in the doctrine of divine truth concealed in poetic story. But the speech is a dramatic utterance, and it occurs in the only work of Milton's grounded on ancient myth, so that something may be allowed for a special apologia. Further, the terms of the reference, from "sage" and "the heavenly Muse" to the "rifted rocks," suggest that Milton had Spenser especially in mind.[48] Two examples of allegory in detail may be mentioned. The Elder Brother, invoking "the old schools of Greece" on the theme of invincible chastity, finds that virtue symbolized in the bow of Diana and the Gorgon-shield of Minerva.[49] Herford makes the interesting suggestion that the lines on Minerva embody a recollection of Beatrice's passing by in the *Vita Nuova,* and adds that Milton's warrior maid, unlike Beatrice,

---

[47] *Ovid's Metamorphosis* (1632), pp. 475, 480–81. In Sandys' *Relation* (ed. 1627, p. 308) moly is also said to signify temperance. See above, page 265.

   The reversing of Comus' rod and spells has been emphasized as the clearest parallel, so far as the plot is concerned, between *Comus* and the rescue of Amoret (*Comus,* ll. 816 ff.; *F. Q.,* III. xii. 36; Hanford, "Youth of Milton," p. 141). Without discounting Spenserian influence we may observe the last sentence quoted from Sandys, which is his comment on *Metam.* xiv. 300–01, thus rendered in his translation (p. 462):

   Sprinkled with better jüyce, her wand reuerst
   Aboue our crownes, and charmes with charmes disperst.

For Milton's use of Ovid rather than Homer, see above, p. 260, note 30.

[48] Ll. 513 ff. See Osgood, pp. xlix, 23. We recall "the sage and solemn tunes" of chivalric romance, in whose enchantments "more is meant than meets the ear" (*Il Penseroso,* ll. 116–20); the equally obvious Spenserian reference in *Smectymnuus* (Bohn ed., III, 118–19; see Hanford, "Youth of Milton," pp. 136–37); "the sage and serious doctrine of Virginity," *Comus,* ll. 786–87; and the "sage and serious poet Spenser" of *Areopagitica* (Bohn ed., II, 68).

   "Enchanted isles" include Spenser's as well as Homer's and Tasso's, and the rifted rocks, while perhaps partly Virgilian (Osgood, page 23), suggest the cave of Mammon (*F. Q.,* II. vii. 28); as the allusion in *Areopagitica* shows, this canto of Spenser's made a lasting impression on Milton.

[49] Ll. 441 ff. The linking of the two goddesses here, as proof against Cupid, might occur to anyone who knew mythology, but Milton might remember Lucian's *Venus and Cupid* (trans. Fowler, I, 77; see Todd, VI, 316). Jonson, in his *Hue and Cry after Cupid* (Morley, pp. 91–93), quotes Lucian; cf. *Cynthia's Revels,* I. i. Sandys also quotes Lucian concerning Cupid and Diana (*Ovid,* p. 70).

disables rather than ennobles her foes in a manner characteristic of
Milton's "self-regarding" chastity.[50]

At the end of *Comus* allusions to Venus and Adonis and Cupid and
Psyche are woven into a half-mystical allegory, which is preceded by a
warning that the lines are not mere mythological decoration—"List,
mortals, if your ears be true." Spenser had been content with a "scientific"
allegory. Not so Milton. "The pagan image of the love of a mortal
youth for a goddess draws insensibly nearer to the truth in the reversed
symbol of the union of the God of love himself with Psyche, the human
soul, and if Milton's classic taste prevents him from concluding with an
allusion to the Lamb and his eternal bride it is because there is no need."[51]
Later we shall meet Adonis in less celestial company.[52]

There are in *Paradise Lost* a few slight implications of allegory,[53] but
only one passage needs to be quoted here:

> Spot more delicious than those gardens feign'd
> Or of revived Adonis, or renown'd
> Alcinous, host of old Laertes' son,
> Or that, not mystic, where the sapient king
> Held dalliance with his fair Egyptian spouse.[54]

[50] "Dante and Milton," p. 73.

[51] Hanford, "Youth of Milton," p. 152. In addition to *F. Q.*, III. vi, see the quotation
from the *Hymne in Honour of Love*, page 255 above.

[52] The roll call of pagan gods in *Paradise Lost* may remind one also of the noble passage
in *Areopagitica* (Bohn ed., II, 89) in which the dismembered body of "the good Osiris" is
likened to the scattered fragments of the virgin Truth. Miss Seaton suggested that Milton
might have seen and remembered the pictorial representation of the myth of Osiris in the
Vatican (*M. L. R.*, XVII, 168–70). He would doubtless remember that Clement of
Alexandria compared Truth to the body of Pentheus, torn asunder by fanatics (Sandys,
History of Classical Scholarship, I, 324). The story of Osiris is told, for example, in
Plutarch's treatise and in Diodorus Siculus, i. 21; see Ralegh, *History*, ii. 2. 5; Selden,
De Diis Syris, Syntagma i. 4. The personification of Truth recalls Milton's numerous allu-
sions to the four daughters of God; see R. L. Ramsay, *S. P.*, XV, 123 ff.

[53] When Milton writes (ii. 1005, 1051) of the world hanging by a golden chain he has
in mind the golden chain of Homer, and doubtless many later references to it. We have
already noticed that Spenser and Chapman, following Natalis Comes, take the chain as a
symbol of ambition. Milton's allusion has no obvious symbolism, but he may be recollecting
such an interpretation as he had given in the *De Sphaerarum Concentu*, "that Homer
meant the golden chain as a symbol of the chain of connection and design that runs
through the universe" (Verity). See *Milton: Private Correspondence and Academic Exer-
cises*, by Phyllis and E. M. W. Tillyard (Cambridge University Press, 1932), pp. 65, 137.
In addition to Verity's references, cf. Davies, *Nosce Teipsum* (ed. Grosart, 1876, I, 53–54).
Verity cites Ben Jonson, *Masque of Hymen* (Morley, pp. 69–70; cf. also Morley, p. 194);
Ben quotes Macrobius on the symbolism of the chain. With the allusion in Jonson's *Epode*,
cf. Lucian, *Demosthenes* (Fowler, IV, 149).

To mention another item or two in Milton, the "universal Pan" of *P. L.*, iv. 266 is an
echo of the orthodox exposition of the mythographers; for example, see Sandys, *Ovid*,
p. 483. Ll. 499–501 of the fourth book, on Jupiter and Juno, are in harmony with the
conventional interpretaton of Jupiter and Juno as the upper and lower air, but they may
be merely a recollection of Virgil and Homer (Osgood, p. 49). Cf. Fulgentius, i. 2; Natalis
Comes, ii. 1 (Padua, 1616, p. 50).

[54] *P. L.*, ix. 439 ff. See Osgood, p. xlix; Greenlaw, *S. P.*, xiv, 209. Sandys (*Ovid*, p. 452)
speaks of the "Iland famous for the Hortyards of Alcinoë, and wonderfull pregnancy of
the soyle (a fable deriued from the terrestriall Paradice)." Cf. Ralegh, i. 3. 3; i. 4. 1.

Mr. Osgood and others have taken "mystic" here as meaning that Milton is thinking of such a sense as Spenser (or he himself, at the end of *Comus*) had given to the myth of Adonis, and it may be so. But, in that case, why should he label the gardens of Adonis and Alcinous as "feign'd"? And, however famous the gardens of Alcinous, what mystical meaning is connected with them? Besides, in the first book Adonis had been put in the catalogue of false gods. Surely "mystic" means simply "mythical." [55] After mentioning "feign'd" gardens, Milton could not pass from pagan fiction to scriptural fact, as represented by the garden of Solomon, without indicating the difference. Thus in *Paradise Lost* there appears to be no instance of mythology used in a really allegorical way as Milton had used it in the fable and some details of *Comus*. His attitude toward myth had undergone some changes in the interval, and we may proceed to sketch the results, if not the causes.[56]

V

In the previous chapter we noticed the growth, not merely among puritans but, in the seventeenth century, among poets, of a strong sentiment in favor of Christian truth in poetry and opposed to pagan fiction. Reviewing Milton's background and career one might predict his attitude. From the beginning he had with religious seriousness devoted himself to the writing of great poetry. His early choice of Arthurian matter for his heroic poem—and in his hands that theme would have become religious—was abandoned, on account of historical skepticism and other reasons of a negative kind.[57] For positive reasons, one may recall the exalted language of the passages in *The Reason of Church Government* (1642) which set forth the function and the responsibility of the poet-priest. The poet should inculcate virtue, celebrate the power and the works of God, "sing victorious agonies of martyrs and saints, the deeds and triumphs of just and pious nations." Such poetry is above the level of ancient epics, for it is not

to be obtained by the invocation of dame memory and her siren daughters, but by devout prayer to that eternal Spirit, who can enrich with all utterance

---

[55] Miss Lockwood's *Lexicon* gives "mythical." And see Verity.

[56] Before leaving allegory I may mention the climax of *Paradise Regained*. When Satan falls, leaving Christ triumphant, Milton alludes to the combat of Hercules and Antaeus. There is no hint of allegory—indeed the allusion begins with one of Milton's disparaging phrases—but one wonders if he had read Sandys' exposition of the myth (*Ovid*, p. 322; cf. Fulgentius, ii. 7). Hercules is the soul, or prudence; Antaeus the body, or sensual pleasure. Reason must raise the body above the contagion of earthly things. At any rate if Milton had come upon so congenial an account he would not have forgotten it.

[57] See Roberta F. Brinkley, *Arthurian Legend in the Seventeenth Century* (1932), pp. 81, 126 ff.

and knowledge, and sends out his seraphim, with the hallowed fire of his altar, to touch and purify the lips of whom he pleases . . .[58]

It was not quite in these terms that Spenser announced to Ralegh the purpose of *The Faerie Queene.*

More immediate duties impelled Milton to postpone the fulfillment of his task, and when at last he came to write *Paradise Lost* age and experience had deepened still further his sense of the eternal verities, his understanding of what above all demanded utterance in a truly heroic poem. It is wholly natural, then, that at intervals Milton should proclaim that his purpose and his theme—as artist he is humble enough—elevate his work above its ancient models. The opening lines, though echoing classical invocations, are a prayer to the Spirit

> that dost prefer
> Before all temples the upright heart and pure.

Milton intends to soar above the Aonian mount. At the beginning of the third book, though he glances at "blind Mæonides," he is again praying, with thoughts of Zion and sacred song, for the inward light that will enable him to

> see and tell
> Of things invisible to mortal sight.

Passing by the seventh book for the moment, we come to the less exalted and more specific introduction to the ninth, where Milton declares that his argument is "not less but more heroic" than that of the *Iliad, Odyssey, Aeneid,* and poems of "fabled knights in battles feign'd."

When a great poet embarks, with the consciousness of divine guidance, upon the most sacred of themes, for which all his life has been a preparation, it is hardly matter for astonishment or regret that, so far from finding hidden truth in classic myth, he goes out of his way to label it pagan untruth. What is astonishing is that he can make such frequent and splendid use of it in any way; but he is still a poet of the Renaissance.

Before considering the artistic quality of the mythological allusions in Milton's later poems we must take some account of his Christian or puritan scruples.[59] The word "scruple" is hardly adequate for the identification of the fallen angels with the pagan gods. However common

[58] Bohn ed., II, 479–81.
[59] The first conscientious reservation occurs in the youthful *On the Death of a Fair Infant.* In the earlier part of the poem Milton dwells without uneasiness on Aquilo and Hyacinth, but when he mentions Elysian fields he adds "if such there were." The thought of the Christian heaven causes a momentary qualm, yet it is only momentary, for in the next stanza heaven is enveloped in mythological allusions.

this belief, and however convenient for Milton's epic plot, it does not belong to the most modern part of his mind, and we should be surprised to meet it in some other seventeenth-century classicists. At the same time acceptance of the doctrine does not necessarily have puritan implications; it was endorsed by Hooker and Sandys as well as by Gosson and Prynne.[60]

While Milton often alludes to myths without any skeptical comment, he does also often remind us that such tales are fiction:

> The rest were long to tell, though far renown'd,
> The Ionian gods, of Javan's issue held
> Gods, yet confess'd later than Heaven and Earth,
> Their boasted parents: Titan, Heaven's first-born . . .[61]

One cannot pass by the lines about Mulciber,

> and how he fell
> From Heaven they fabled, thrown by angry Jove
> Sheer o'er the crystal battlements: from morn
> To noon he fell, from noon to dewy eve,
> A summer's day; and with the setting sun
> Dropt from the zenith, like a falling star,
> On Lemnos, the Ægæan isle. Thus they relate,
> Erring . . .[62]

Here we have a mythological allusion occurring at the end of a catalogue of false gods, and prefaced and concluded with expressions of hostile disbelief, while the myth itself is told with quite unnecessary richness of detail, and is notable even in Milton for beauty of phrase and sound.

[60] Verity, *Paradise Lost*, II, 382, 516, 604, 672–74; Hooker, *Eccles. Pol.*, i. 4. 3; Sandys, *Ovid*, p. 392 and elsewhere. Cf. Burton, *Anatomy* (Bohn's Popular Library), I, 214 ff.

[61] *P. L.*, i. 507 ff. Miss Hartwell (*Lactantius and Milton*, p. 54) remarks that "this idea of the priority of heaven and earth over the earliest gods is part of the argument against the Greek deities in the first book of Lactantius." Cf. Hesiod, *Theog.*, l. 45. One may quote Ralegh (*History*, i. 8. 5): "True it is that the Greeks had their Janus, but this was not Noah; so had they Ion the son of Xuthus, the son of Deucalion, from whom they draw the Iones, who were indeed the children of Javan, the fourth son of Japhet." Cf. *ibid.*, i. 8. 7.

Miss Hartwell observes (pp. 47 ff., 147, 181–83) that Keightley, Verity, and others have been wrong in charging Milton with an error in alluding to a single Titan, and she records the story of Titan and Saturn, as Milton uses it, in Lactantius, Boccaccio's *De Genealogia Deorum*, Caxton's *Recuyell*. As these names imply, it was quite common. Cf. Warner, *Albion's England*, i. 1–3; Natalis Comes, ii. 1–2 (Padua, 1616, pp. 40, 56–57); Ralegh, *History*, i. 6. 5. Mr. Osgood had pointed out the commentators' errors, and Milton's choice of a patristic version, in *M. L. N.*, XVI, 282–85.

[62] *P. L.*, i. 740 ff. Sandys, as I remarked before, tries both to link biblical and classical stories and to separate truth from fiction. In the *Relation* (ed. 1627, p. 23) he refers to "Lemnos; famous for the fabulous fall of Vulcan." After quoting and translating Homer's lines, he adds: "The Grecians there now inhabiting, do relate

> —(What dares not lying Greece
> In histories insert?)—

that he brake his thigh with a fall from a horse . . ."

It is a case of a clear divorce between artist and theologian. Nor is there perhaps a more remarkable instance of the Miltonic transmutation of Homer; the tale in the *Iliad* is a bit of Homer's divine comedy.[63]

In the prayer that opens the seventh book we have the contrast between Orpheus, the pagan bard, whose mother the Muse could not defend him, and the Christian poet who appeals to the Christianized Urania:

> So fail not thou who thee implores;
> For thou art heavenly, she an empty dream.

"So he says; but in the very act of saying it he has himself returned into that world of dreams, and confessed that he too is an artist, and that his own work is art." [64]

One other passage in *Paradise Lost* may be quoted because it not only speaks of myth as pagan fiction but illustrates the habit of linking myths and scriptural history. In these lines, as Mr. Mackail observed, we hear Milton thinking aloud:

> However, some tradition they dispersed
> Among the heathen of their purchase got,
> And fabled how the Serpent, whom they call'd
> Ophion, with Eurynome, the wide-
> Encroaching Eve perhaps, had first the rule
> Of high Olympus, thence by Saturn driven
> And Ops, ere yet Dictæan Jove was born.[65]

[63] *Il.* i. 586–93. See Tillyard, p. 238.
[64] Mackail, *Springs of Helicon*, p. 180. For a parallel on a lower level one might turn to Sylvester's account of the tree of life in Eden. After naming various famous juices and herbs, such as nectar, ambrosia, the apples of the Hesperides, moly, nepenthe, he proceeds (ed. Grosart, I, 101, ll. 256 ff.):

> No, none of these: these are but forgeries,
> But toyes, but tales, but dreams, deceits, and lies.
> But Thou art true, although our shallow sense
> May honour more, then sound thine Excellence.

Some other passages in Milton that involve expressions of disfavor may be listed briefly: *P. L.*, i. 197–98; ii. 627–28, 921–22; iv. 250–51 (quoted below, page 286); iv. 706; x. 578 ff. (quoted just below); xi. 10 ff. (see below, note 66).
In the fifth book (380 ff.) Eve is said to be

> more lovely fair
> Than wood-nymph, or the fairest goddess feign'd
> Of three that in Mount Ida naked strove.

Is Milton not thinking of that vain amatorious poem *Hero and Leander*—"Where Venus in her naked glory strove"? For other possible echoes of the poem in Milton see above, p. 267, and, in Mr. Martin's edition of Marlowe, the notes on *Hero and Leander*, i. 31, 197, 241, 249, 251, 262, 265, 301, 325, 393.
[65] *P. L.*, x. 578 ff.; Mackail, *Springs of Helicon*, p. 190. Osgood (p. 34) shows that the mythological source is Apollonius Rhodius, *Arg.* i. 503 ff. The story is also told by Natalis Comes (ii. 2, p. 61). Sandys' discussion adds some things that Milton would not find in classical authorities:
"Pherecides the Syrian writes how the Divels were throwne out of heauen by Iupiter (this fall of the Gyants perhaps an allusion to that of the Angells) the chiefe called

Similarly Adam and Eve at prayer recall the "fables old" of a "less ancient" pair, Deucalion and Pyrrha.[66]

In *Paradise Regained* the woody scene where Satan appears to Christ —the kind of place that Milton had delighted to populate with classic divinities—seemed

> to a superstitious eye the haunt
> Of wood-gods and wood-nymphs.[67]

Indeed all of the relatively few allusions to myth in this poem are accompanied by a disparaging phrase, unless they are put in the mouth of Satan, and even he can express Miltonic skepticism. When Belial suggests that Christ be tempted through women, Satan replies that Belial and his lusty crew, "false-titled Sons of God," had been wont before the flood to waylay nymphs.[68] We might expect such sentiments from Milton, but hardly from Satan. He goes on, in the undramatic manner of Elizabethan villains, to pay tribute to Christ's moral strength, and, speaking of the effect of Venus' girdle upon Jove, he adds "so fables tell."

Then, in the fourth book, comes the harsh outburst that makes the most devout Miltonist squirm, especially as it follows upon the eulogy of Athens (put in the mouth of Satan) which seems no less sincere, as it is not less beautiful, than the ode in *Oedipus at Colonus*.[69] One does not enjoy the spectacle of Milton turning and rending the orators, poets, philosophers (even Plato), who had made him a humanist and an artist; nor does the description of the style of ancient poetry leave his own withers unwrung. Yet he would not be Milton if he had not reached this state of mind. Chaucer and Spenser had turned at moments from the world, Milton's mood is deeper and more lasting. They had been religious in their way, but they had not come face to face with God, they had not felt Milton's imperious need of making a decision between human literature and divine revelation.

One may agree with Mr. Kellett that "it was not Milton the classicist, but Milton the medievalist, who made a devil of Apollo," [70] but it is not quite fair to make Milton the solitary scapegoat. Cowley, who has already

Ophioneus, which signifies Serpentine: hauing after made use of that creature to poyson Eue with a false ambition" (*Ovid*, p. 27).

[66] *P. L.*, xi. 10 ff. Sandys discusses the problem of chronology (*Ovid*, p. 31; and see p. 218). Cf. Ralegh, i. 7. 3; ii. 6. 5.

[67] *P. R.*, ii. 296. See Osgood, p. 64.

[68] *P. R.*, ii. 178 ff. Part of the passage is quoted below, p. 284. See Milton's indignant reference to Justin Martyr's story of angels mixing with women and begetting devils (*Prose Works*, Bohn ed., II, 379–80).

[69] *P. R.*, iv. 286 ff. See Tillyard, p. 309.

[70] *Reconsiderations* (Cambridge University Press, 1928), p. 121. See *P. R.*, i. 393 ff., 430 ff. Cf. Browne, *Religio Medici*, ed. Greenhill, pp. 23, 248. Mr. Kellett recognizes the universality of such beliefs in Milton's time.

been quoted in condemnation of mythology, was doubtless not a very
profoundly religious nature, yet he could write thus in one of his best
poems:

> Still the old Heathen Gods in Numbers dwell,
> The Heav'enliest thing on Earth still keeps up Hell.
> Nor have we yet quite purg'd the Christian Land;
> Still Idols here, like Calves at Bethel stand.
> And though Pans Death long since all Oracles broke,
> Yet still in Rhyme the Fiend Apollo spoke.[71]

Can we reconcile Milton's contradictory attitudes toward myth? On
the one hand he declares that myths, properly understood, may embody
truth, and he can use them allegorically. Then, apart from any question
of allegory, there is the obvious delight with which, in all his chief poems
except the last,[72] he lavishes beauty of diction and rhythm upon mythological allusions. On the other hand we have this series of astringent
footnotes, as it were, relegating myth to the level of pagan fiction, not
without gratuitous coldness of manner at best and sometimes with
Hebraic warmth.

Such inconsistencies cannot be altogether reconciled, because they are
part of Milton's Renaissance heritage. They are, as we have seen, writ
large in Spenser, but in him we feel no such sharp edges as we do in
Milton. In temperament as in time Spenser was a complete child of the
Renaissance. M. Legouis has well said of him:

> L'avantage de ces contradictions c'est que sa pensée est large et hospitalière.
> Elle ne procède pas par le retranchement. Elle part de la sensualité pour la
> purifier et l'exalter, non pour la proscrire. Elle n'écarte le spectacle d'aucune
> splendeur, même profane, même licencieuse, quitte à la réprouver après l'avoir
> complaisamment dépeinte. Elle prêche la vertu sans jamais lui sacrifier l'art
> ni la beauté.
>
> Mais elle surprend aujourd'hui parce qu'elle ne paraît avoir aucune con-
> science de ses disparates . . . Tous ces contrastes voisinent dans son œuvre
> comme dans sa vie. Seule son imagination, nous le verrons, réussira à les
> concilier dans son grand poème, mais ils resteront incohérents dans son
> intelligence.[73]

But even the young Milton who for a time imitated Ovid was a
generation removed from the spirit of omnivorous assimilation that
characterized Spenser and his age. Whereas Spenser appears, in spite

---

[71] *On the Death of Mr. Crashaw* (*Poems,* ed. Waller, 1905, p. 48). Sylvester, by the way,
after citing Scaliger and his thirteen languages, praises the "Hebrew tongue, Mother and
Queene of all the rest," but there is also abundant praise of classical and modern writers
(I, 141 ff.).
[72] *Samson Agonistes,* in spite of its material and form, does contain two brief allusions to
classic myth, from the Hebraic standpoint (ll. 148–50, 499–501).
[73] *Edmund Spenser* (Paris, 1923), pp. 216–17.

of himself, to present Christianity and paganism, the moralistic and the sensuous, on almost equal terms, in Milton from the beginning Elizabethan catholicity of feeling, richness and glow of expression, are much more restrained and subdued. Milton never ceased to be a lover of beauty, but from his youth up he had a sense of personal responsibility to God and man that more and more sternly asserted itself in writings which were to be doctrinal to a nation. The twenty years given to public affairs had proved vain, the Restoration had found him a frustrated and angry rebel in a country of slaves, the Hebraic strain evident in early manhood had come, in Milton's writing if not in private life, to dominate other impulses. He could not put away childish things like classic myths, he could not, any more than St. Jerome, forget what was part of himself, but, even while recutting pagan jewels to heighten the luster of their Christian setting, he could sometimes call them childish, even wicked.

Further, as the preceding sketch suggests, some contradictions become less acute when we follow chronology. Milton's poetical use of allegorized myth virtually ends with *Comus;* after that, with hardly any exceptions, he employs unvarnished myth for artistic reasons, but with diminishing gusto and with frequent indications of its untruth. Something also must be allowed for the flexibility of belief not only possible but normal in liberal religious minds of Milton's period. If modern students are left in doubt concerning the degree of Milton's literal acceptance of the Bible, it is no wonder if his attitude toward mythology shows changes and inconsistencies.[74]

Then one must take account of Milton's sense of decorum, "which is the grand masterpiece to observe." In Latin verse, in pastoral and masque, he might accept in a measure the liberties which tradition sanctioned. But in a heroic poem on the greatest of Christian themes, and in its sequel presenting Christ and his grand foe, mythological decoration might well need both pruning and apology. Besides, *Samson Agonistes* is a drama, *Paradise Regained* a drama with poetic stage directions; Spenser or Shakespeare in treating such subjects—if that can be imagined —would have used mythology freely, but not Milton.

Finally, the condemnation implied or expressed in the passages cited is not absolute but relative. Mythological illustrations, Milton says, are not to be taken at the same valuation as the scriptural truths with which they are mingled. If Milton had been a thorough puritan he would not,

[74] Mr. Tillyard (page 223) quotes a passage from *Tetrachordon* in which Milton seems to take quite literally the story of Eve's creation out of Adam's rib. But in *Areopagitica* "the legend of Psyche is mingled with the legend of the Fall and mentioned in exactly the same tone. Milton appears to believe the one legend as implicitly as the other, and yet would anyone suggest that he understood the legend of Psyche as literally true?" See Bohn ed., III, 335; II, 67–68.

in his old age, have listened to readings from his favorite Ovid, Homer, and similar authors.[75]

VI

Whatever Milton's scruples about the use of classic myth in Christian epics, he could not avoid drawing upon it, both tacitly and openly. One must remember Milton's peculiar difficulties. For Homer epic subject and epic material were one and indivisible. In the *Aeneid* they were not; an abstract philosophic theme was cast in an inadequate epic mold. For Milton the gap had widened immeasurably. His theme was still more abstract than Virgil's, and a biblical fable—Adam and Eve in the garden, God in heaven, Satan in hell—cut him off from traditional heroic stuff, from a traditional concrete background, except what had developed in modern treatments of the Fall. So in *Paradise Lost* the fighting is, next to the speeches of the Almighty, Milton's least successful achievement. As his own words show, he felt at least as keenly as we do the risk of dealing with spiritual and ethical ideas on the necessarily concrete plane of the heroic epic.

Milton had then to make bricks without much straw, to put substantial flesh on the merest skeleton of a fable. And where was much of the flesh to come from if not from the great plastic mass of ancient story? There were first of course the conventional epic devices by which the plot could be enlarged. Borrowing chiefly from Virgil, the supreme model of epic decorum, and, like Virgil, giving a new significance to what he borrowed, Milton took over such conventions as the roll call and council of leaders, epic games, the recapitulatory narrative after the plunge *in medias res,* the unfolding of future events, and the rest. With such matters of technique we have nothing to do.

We are concerned with Milton's more or less silent appropriation of classical material wherewith to give his shadowy actors a local habitation and a personality—a name they had already, though sometimes not much more—and to build a solid stage and background. How would the revolt of the angels be conceived? There were the wars of gods and giants and Titans. What would be the dominant qualities of Satan? To the established conception might be added suggestions ranging from Parliamentary leaders to Mephistopheles, and including the divine rebels Prometheus and Typhon. How would Satan and Gabriel confront each

---

[75] In 1679 appeared an imitation of *Paradise Lost* called *Order and Disorder*. The author's first object "was to remove from the Mosaic legend all accretions from heathen fable and philosophy" (C. A. Moore, *M. P.,* XXIV, 1926–27, 321–22). Blackmore's denunciation of pagan mythology is notorious; see A. F. B. Clark, *Boileau,* pp. 308 ff., especially p. 321. Some readers found *Paradise Lost* dangerously pagan. Cf. Addison's censure, *Spectator,* 297.

278 MYTHOLOGY AND THE RENAISSANCE TRADITION

other? Like Turnus and Aeneas in their last combat.[76] What of the character and speech of Satan's lieutenants, such as Belial? Virgil's Drances furnished hints.[77] How would Adam and Eve behave after they had eaten the fruit of knowledge? Somewhat like the wanton Paris and Helen, and Zeus and Hera when the goddess had put on the girdle of Aphrodite.[78] How were the animals created? They broke out of the ground, like the warriors in the tales of Cadmus and Medea.[79] What was the nature of the flood? Ovid was more detailed than *Genesis*. How would God and his Son express themselves? Here, alas, Zeus and his numerous offspring were of small help, and Milton had to fall back upon theology.

These random examples show how the meagerness of the fable was eked out with abundant borrowings from classical literature and classical myth. Such mixing of biblical and pagan stories was of course in harmony with the practice of more prosaic writers on mythology, who had fewer difficulties than a modern student of comparative religion in reconciling variants.[80] In general the tradition permitted one, with due regard to the admixture of pagan fiction, to think of classical myth and biblical history as one great body of material. Milton's identification of fallen angels and pagan deities has been mentioned more than once. And Eden is said to be fairer than

> that Nyseian isle,
> Girt with the river Triton, where old Cham,
> Whom Gentiles Ammon call and Lybian Jove,
> Hid Amalthea, and her florid son,
> Young Bacchus, from his stepdame Rhea's eye.[81]

Cham is Ham, Noah's son, and also Jupiter Ammon.

[76] Mr. A. S. Ferguson showed that the last forty lines of *P. L.* iv are a highly original manipulation of the last three hundred lines of the *Aeneid* (*M. L. R.*, XV, 168–70).

[77] E. C. Baldwin, *J. E. G. P.*, VII, 85–86, on *P. L.*, ii. 108–18, and *Aen.* xi. 336–42.

[78] *P. L.*, ix. 1029 ff.; *Il.* iii. 442, xiv. 315.

[79] *P. L.*, vii. 463–74. J. D. Bruce (*Englische Studien*, XLI, 166 ff.) pointed out a parallel in Apollonius Rhodius (iii. 1354 ff.), whom Milton knew well, and a closer one in the less familiar *Dionysiaca* of Nonnus (iv. 427–40). Ovid (*Metam.* iii. 104 ff., vii. 121 ff.) is not so close to Milton.

[80] One extract from Ralegh will serve to remind us of the method used by him, by Sandys, Reynolds, and others:

"And as Adam was the ancient and first Saturn, Cain the eldest Jupiter, Eva, Rhea, and Noema, or Naamah, the first Venus; so did the fable of the dividing of the world between the three brethren, the sons of Saturn, arise from the true story of the dividing of the earth between the three brethren the sons of Noah: so also was the fiction of those golden apples kept by a dragon taken from the serpent which tempted Evah: so was paradise itself transported out of Asia into Africa, and made the garden of the Hesperides: the prophecies, that Christ should break the serpent's head, and conquer the power of hell, occasioned the fables of Hercules killing the serpent of Hesperides, and descending into hell, and captivating Cerberus . . . ," *History*, i. 6. 4 (II, 167). Cf. *ibid.*, II, 130–31, 163.

[81] *P. L.*, iv. 275 ff. The story of Amalthea is told by Diodorus Siculus, iii. 67–70, and repeated from Diodorus by Ralegh, *History*, i. 6. 5 (II, 175). See Verity (II, 685), who

Although Milton could use mythology lightly and fancifully, as the
Elizabethans had done, and sometimes with uninspired bookishness,
as the neoclassicists did, the best proof of its hold upon him is the fact
that it is often most spontaneous and beautiful when, in his most serious
moods, it is blended with Christian or Hebraic sentiment. There is the
sonnet on his wife, where recollection of his favorite dramatist's heroine
leads on to "purification in the Old Law." Or there is the fusion that
runs through the opening lines of *Paradise Lost*. The muse is the
heavenly muse, the temple is "the oracle of God," and Moses is a Hebrew
Hesiod. In the invocation to Light, though Milton claims superiority to
"the Orphean lyre," the name recalls the myth of Orpheus, and he echoes
Ovid in describing his own spiritual journey:

> Taught by the heavenly Muse to venture down
> The dark descent, and up to re-ascend,
> Though hard and rare.[82]

While St. Luke has Satan quote to Christ the assurance of angelic aid,
there is no such thing in the narrative itself. In Milton, when Christ has
foiled the tempter, angels appear

> Who on their plumy vans received Him soft
> From his uneasy station, and upbore
> As on a floating couch through the blithe air;
> Then in a flowery valley set him down
> On a green bank, and set before him spread
> A table of celestial food . . .

Here as elsewhere in *Paradise Regained* Milton is making use of Giles
Fletcher, though Fletcher's poem is quite medieval and theological,
Milton's humanistic and Protestant, and though the one is as sensuous
as the other is bare. But Milton is also thinking of the airy voyage of
Psyche to her lover's mansion—St. Luke, Apuleius, and Giles Fletcher![83]

does not notice Ralegh. Although Milton knew Diodorus he might, on account of the turn
given to his allusion, have had Ralegh in mind also. A few pages further on Ralegh says:
"But the Egyptians, even after the flood, began (somewhat before this Chaldean Jupiter)
to entitle Cham, the parent of their own Mizraim, Jupiter Chammon, or Hammon" (i. 6. 6).
And a few pages earlier (i. 6. 4) Ralegh speaks of "Mizraim, the son of Cham, who had
learnt the same of Cham, and Cham of his father Noah." Cf. Sandys, *Ovid*, pp. 111, 191–
92; and Osgood, p. 7.

[82] The lines in Ovid (*Metam*. x. 53–55) are rendered by Sandys (page 338) with a free
turn of phrase which might almost seem to prepare them for Milton's use—not that one
needs to invoke Sandys:

> A steepe ascent, dark, thick with fogges, they clime
> Through euerlasting Silence. By this time
> Approach the confines of illustrious Light.

The last phrase renders *telluris margine summae*. Milton has also in mind the journey of
Aeneas under the guidance of the Sibyl (*Aen*. vi. 126–29).

[83] *P. R.*, iv. 583 ff.; Fletcher, ii. 38, 61 (Boas, I, 49, 56).

No poet weaves together more diverse threads into a more original whole than Milton. The passage describing the archangel's voyage to the earth illustrates the way in which scattered materials, held in solution in the well of poetic consciousness, move to their appointed place like the primal elements at the command of Love:

> Down thither prone in flight
> He speeds, and through the vast ethereal sky
> Sails between worlds and worlds, with steady wing
> Now on the polar winds; then with quick fan
> Winnows the buxom air, till, within soar
> Of towering eagles, to all the fowls he seems
> A phœnix, gazed by all, as that sole bird,
> When, to enshrine his reliques in the Sun's
> Bright temple, to Egyptian Thebes he flies.
> At once on the eastern cliff of Paradise
> He lights, and to his proper shape returns,
> A Seraph wing'd. Six wings he wore, to shade
> His lineaments divine: the pair that clad
> Each shoulder broad came mantling o'er his breast
> With regal ornament; the middle pair
> Girt like a starry zone his waist, and round
> Skirted his loins and thighs with downy gold
> And colours dipt in heaven; the third his feet
> Shadow'd from either heel with feather'd mail,
> Sky-tinctured grain. Like Maia's son he stood,
> And shook his plumes, that heavenly fragrance fill'd
> The circuit wide . . .
> Into the blissful field, through groves of myrrh,
> And flowering odours, cassia, nard, and balm,
> A wilderness of sweets . . .[84]

The first line suggests the incident that Milton later mentions, Mercury's speeding down to warn Aeneas to leave Carthage, and Milton remembered too some lines in one of the plays he knew best.[85] Mercury has no such equipment as the angel, and here Milton resorts to Isaiah's account of the three pairs of wings of the seraphim.[86] For the coloring of the wings ancient descriptions of the phoenix supply some details.[87] Neither the Virgilian nor the Shakespearean Mercury shook his plumes

[84] *P. L.*, v. 266 ff.
[85] *Aen.* iv. 238 ff. (and i. 300 ff.); *Hamlet*, III. iv. 58–59. Cf. *Il.* xxiv. 340; *Od.* v. 43.
[86] *Isa.* vi. 2. Cf. *Ezek.* i and x.
[87] See Osgood, p. 69. Miss Hartwell (pp. 123 ff.) discusses accounts of the phoenix in Herodotus, Ovid, Claudian, Pliny, Lactantius, in connection with *Epit. Dam.*, ll. 185–89. I may quote Sandys (*Ovid*, p. 520):

"They say, (saith Pliny) I knowe not whether fabulous or no, that there is but one of that kinde, and hee seldome seene in the world: of the bignesse of an Eagle, glittering about the necke like gold, the rest of his body purple, his azure traine distinguisht with

and scattered heavenly fragrance. The angel Gabriel did, however, not in Tasso but in Fairfax's embroidered version of Tasso:

> On Libanon at first his foot he set,
> And shook his wings with rory May dews wet.[88]

The fragrance suggests that Milton still has the phoenix in mind, a suspicion that is confirmed by the lines following which describe the blissful field. Ovid thus tells of the death of the bird:

> This strew'd with Cassia, Spiknard, precious Balme,
> Bruz'd Cinamon, and Myrrh; thereon she bends
> Her bodie, and her age in odors ends.[89]

And this does not exhaust the literary reminiscences embedded in the very Miltonic lines.

For another example we might take the passage in which the fallen angels are reduced to the size of pygmies

> or faery elves,
> Whose midnight revels, by a forest side
> Or fountain, some belated peasant sees,
> Or dreams he sees, while overhead the moon
> Sits arbitress, and nearer to the Earth
> Wheels her pale course: they, on their mirth and dance
> Intent, with jocund music charm his ear;
> At once with joy and fear his heart rebounds.[90]

A fairy dance is unexpected in *Paradise Lost,* and it is to another of Milton's favorite plays that we turn for suggestions.[91] But one phrase echoes Virgil; Milton remembers the meeting of Dido and Aeneas in the underworld.[92] Then the dance of fairies by a fountain, and Virgil, call up another Virgilian scene which suggests Milton's last line—Dido moving like Diana when she leads the dance, and *Latonae tacitum pertemptant gaudia pectus.*[93] This veiled kind of borrowing is perhaps the most interesting of all. Often it can be felt rather than demonstrated, though now and then a name or revealing phrase gives a definite clue.

rosecolour, and his head adorned with a plumy Coronet: in the rest agreeing with our Author."
[88] Fairfax, bk. i, st. 14 (ed. H. Morley, p. 4). Cf. Tasso:
Pria sul Libano monte ei si ritenne,
E si librò su l'adeguate penne.
See Warton on *Comus,* l. 989.
[89] Sandys, p. 499; *Metam.* xv. 398–400. See Verity's notes, II, 485–88. Cf. Sylvester, ed. Grosart, I, 66.
[90] *P. L.,* i. 781 ff.
[91] *Midsummer Night's Dream,* II. i. 28–29, 141.
[92] *Aen.* vi. 450 ff.
[93] *Aen.* i. 498 ff.; cf. *Od.* vi. 102 ff.

Open and direct mythological allusions were of course prescribed for any heroic poem in the Renaissance tradition. Milton's proper names, mythological, historical, geographical, almost always suggest grandeur, or remoteness, or both, and in doing so help to give the Miltonic world that isolation which is essential to great art. And yet, when we think of what may be called the disembodied quality of Milton's subject, such allusions often achieve at the same time the opposite effect; in a poem depicting heaven and hell and earth and infinite space even bookish associations may relate the unknown and indescribable to the familiar and accepted. Satan, voyaging toward the earth, wins his way through fighting elements.[94] The lines are imaginative and suggestive, but when we come to the names of the Argo and Ulysses our recollections of two voyages more realistic than Satan's add a degree of visual concreteness to our notion of his. Or, again, the appearance of the serpent to Eve is not an everyday incident, and Milton relates it to a body of serpent lore. The creature's physical characteristics are taken almost literally from Virgil.[95] Then we are assured that there has been no serpent

> Lovelier; not those that in Illyria changed
> Hermione and Cadmus, or the god
> In Epidaurus; nor to which transform'd
> Ammonian Jove, or Capitoline, was seen,
> He with Olympias, this with her who bore
> Scipio, the highth of Rome.

Though Milton might not share our skepticism, the list of other famous serpents does lend reality and dignity to Satan.[96]

For a brief survey of the varied uses of myth in the epics we may return to Ovid. With the lines on Orpheus from *L'Allegro,* and the Lady's song from *Comus,* which were quoted above,[97] compare this passage:

[94] *P. L.,* ii. 1010 ff.

[95] *P. L.,* ix. 498–504; *Aen.* v. 84–90.

[96] Milton knew of these various serpents from various sources, but Sandys might have reminded him of them. The story of Aesculapius is in *Metam.* xv. 622 ff. (Sandys, *Ovid,* pp. 504–07). In his comment Sandys quotes Lactantius for the view that this serpent was "the great Divell; called a Serpent in the sacred Scriptures" (page 526). The other two that Milton names Sandys links together (page 319):

"A Serpent was said to haue beene found about Olympia's bed, that night wherein she conceaued with Alexander; which gaue a colour to the claime of his descent from Iupiter. The like the Romans divulged of Scipio Africanus, both reports no doubt but proceeding in part from the Serpents amorous inclination."

Mr. Osgood has shown that Milton had good precedent, in editions of Horace and elsewhere, for using "Hermione" instead of "Harmonia" (*American Journal of Philology,* XLI, 76 ff.). It may be added that "Hermione" is Sandys' regular form, in text and commentary.

[97] Page 253.

Still govern thou my song,
Urania, and fit audience find, though few;
But drive far off the barbarous dissonance
Of Bacchus and his revellers, the race
Of that wild rout that tore the Thracian bard
In Rhodope, where woods and rocks had ears
To rapture, till the savage clamour drown'd
Both harp and voice; nor could the Muse defend
Her son.[98]

The epic allusion is cast in a resonant rhetoric quite different from the lyric melody of the earlier passage, and, so far as a mere allusion can be compared with a narrative, these lines are much closer to Ovid—witness *Threicius vates, vocisque lyraeque, ingens clamor,* and other phrases. Further, the myth is given a symbolic value, since "Bacchus and his revellers" represent an audience neither fit nor few.[99]

When speaking of Milton's compression of a whole Ovidian tale into an epic simile one could not pass by that supreme example in the fourth book:

Not that fair field
Of Enna, where Proserpin gathering flowers,
Herself a fairer flower, by gloomy Dis
Was gather'd, which cost Ceres all that pain
To seek her through the world; nor that sweet grove
Of Daphne by Orontes, and the inspired
Castalian spring, might with this Paradise
Of Eden strive . . .[100]

Whatever Milton leaves out, he contrives a symphonic pattern of musical and suggestive names.[101] Every word, every syllable, is significant, but the secret of the choice, of the arrangement, of the heightened and deepened feeling—"all that pain"—such things are not achieved by Ovidian cleverness. Beside these lines we may set one of Spenser's melodious but casual stanzas, from one of his most luxuriant cantos:

More sweet and holesome, then the plesaunt hill
Of Rhodope, on which the Nimphe, that bore
A gyaunt babe, her selfe for griefe did kill;

[98] *P. L.*, vii. 30 ff. The relation of the passage to Ovid (*Metam.* xi. 1 ff.) was discussed by J. W. Hales (*M. P.*, I, 143).
[99] The phrase "barbarous dissonance" had been used of Comus and his crew (*Comus*, l. 550).
[100] For examples of this favorite Miltonic formula, cf. Giles Fletcher, *Christ's Victorie*, I, 50, st. 40; *F. Q.*, I. xi. 27 (quoted above, page 94); Dante, *Paradiso*, ix. 97 ff. (and *passim*).
[101] These lines, and the whole picture of Eden, illustrate the practice mentioned just above, the use of classical parallels, rich in associations, to describe the indescribable.

> Or the Thessalian Tempe, where of yore
> Fair Daphne Phœbus hart with loue did gore;
> Or Ida, where the Gods lou'd to repaire,
> When euer they their heauenly bowres forlore;
> Or sweet Parnasse, the haunt of Muses faire;
> Or Eden selfe, if ought with Eden mote compaire.[102]

Spenser's crowded, glancing allusions, his particularizing details, are not salient; his epithets—and sacred Eden—slip by unnoticed, while economy and arrangement give a prominence to Milton's which they must live up to (contrast the use of "fair" in the two extracts). Nor have the lines any weight of emotion, though Spenser could hardly write anything without revealing, however faintly, his love of beauty.

Ovid serves for more than direct similes. The experience of Narcissus is woven into Eve's story of the way in which she was led to Adam, though the erotic ardors of an Ovidian youth are replaced by the "sympathy and love" more fitting for our first parent.[103] Christ in battle puts forth only half his strength; so good an Ovidian scholar as Milton could not forget Jove's unhappy visit to Semele.[104] Reminiscences of Ovid may be given a didactic twist. The Milton of the Latin poems had delighted to picture Cupid flitting about on his irresponsible errands. No such Cupid unites Adam and Eve:

> Here Love his golden shafts employs, here lights
> His constant lamp, and waves his purple wings . . .

These lines are the very reverse of Ovid.[105] In the seventh book Milton argues that man's erect posture raises him above other animals and fits him to worship God; it is an Ovidian idea made Christian.[106] In *Paradise Regained* Satan reminds Belial that he and his fellows had been wont to roam the earth

> In valley or green meadow, to waylay
> Some beauty rare, Callisto, Clymene,

---

[102] *F. Q.*, II. xii. 52.   [103] *P. L.*, iv. 460 ff.
[104] *P. L.*, vi. 853–54; *Metam*. iii. 302.
[105] *P. L.*, iv. 763 ff.; *Am.*, iii. 9. 7–9; Osgood, p. 26. Cf. *Epit. Dam.*, ll. 191 ff.
[106] *P. L.*, vii. 505 ff.; *Metam*. i. 76 ff. Miss Hartwell (pp. 75 ff.) shows that the Christian interpretation was a favorite theme of Lactantius, whom Milton knew. But the idea was a commonplace. The Ovidian passage was paraphrased by Barthélemy Aneau in his *Décades;* accompanying the text was the figure of a nude man praying in the midst of a group of animals (J. L. Gerig, *Romanic Review*, IV, 36–37). See Sandys, *Ovid*, p. 25, and the extracts on page 267 above; Chapman, *Hymnus in Noctem*, ll. 123 ff.; Anguillara, *Metamorfosi* (Venice, 1575), p. 12ᵛ.

Some other didactic items may be mentioned here. The figure of Sin is obviously modeled on Scylla, to whom Milton refers, but, as a repellent allegorical personage, she is a sister of Spenser's Error, Phineas Fletcher's Hamartia, and similar medieval horrors. See Verity on

Daphne, or Semele, Antiopa,
Or Amymone, Syrinx, many more,
Too long, then lay'st thy scapes on names adored,
Apollo, Neptune, Jupiter, or Pan,
Satyr, or Faun, or Silvan.[107]

There may be here a recollection of Ovid's list of divine amours, but a number of the names, and the flavor of the passage, perhaps derive from a less tolerant source, Clement of Alexandria.

The similes of the ancient epics had generally been drawn not from myth but from nature and common experience. Such similes we find plentifully in Milton, as in Spenser and others, but the neoclassic fashion, averse to anything "low," favored mythology as the richest and most dignified kind of ornament. The dangers of that fashion Milton did not wholly escape. There are few of his mythological similes and allusions which, in themselves, we should wish away, and yet they are seldom so natural and integral as the Homeric similes are. A brief allusion will serve as well as a longer one.

Comus says:

> But first I must put off
> These my sky-robes, spun out of Iris' woof,
> And take the weeds and likeness of a swain . . .

The reference to Iris, following "sky-robes," is consciously decorative, yet, especially in a masque, appropriate enough. In the eleventh book of *Paradise Lost* Michael is thus described:

> Over his lucid arms
> A military vest of purple flow'd,
> Livelier than Melibœan, or the grain
> Of Sarra, worn by kings and heroes old
> In time of truce; Iris had dipt the woof.

The association of Iris with the archangel's military vest is not one of Milton's happy fusions of Hebraic and Hellenic, and the reference attracts attention to itself as a small but superfluous patch. The richer, half-Elizabethan texture of the earlier poems admitted more decoration than arises naturally out of the increasingly bare style of the epics. Quoting two mythological allusions from the eleventh book Mr. Mackail remarks that "classical ornament, as though he felt this harder manner

P. L., ii. 650; J. S. P. Tatlock, M. L. N., XXI, 239–40; Aen. iii. 426 ff. and Ecl. vi. 74 ff.; Metam. xiv. 59 ff.
  The birth of Sin from the head of Satan is an equally obvious adaptation of the birth of Athene. See P. L., ii. 752 ff.
  [107] P. R., ii. 185 ff.; Osgood, p. 10.

growing on him and wished to give it some artificial counterpoise, is attached rather than organically incorporated." [108] And since Mr. Mackail's comments on the Hesperian gardens of *Comus* were utilized in earlier pages, I may profit by his assembling of three passages on the same theme from *Paradise Lost:*

> Or other worlds they seem'd, or happy isles,
> Like those Hesperian Gardens famed of old,
> Fortunate fields, and groves, and flowery vales,
> Thrice happy isles . . .

> Groves whose rich trees wept odorous gums and ·balm;
> Others whose fruit, burnish'd with golden rind,
> Hung amiable, Hesperian fables true,
> If true, here only, and of delicious taste . . .

> But I can now no more; the parting sun
> Beyond the Earth's green Cape and verdant Isles
> Hesperean sets, my signal to depart.[109]

Thus, says Mr. Mackail, "the imaginative or musical motive passes through successive contractions, shrinking in the last to a mere verbal or musical suggestion, an intangible colour on the language."

Finally, there is in *Paradise Regained* the description of the banquet offered to Christ by Satan, a banquet served by youths fairer than Ganymede or Hylas, and by nymphs of Diana's train and naiads,

> And ladies of the Hesperides, that seem'd
> Fairer than feign'd of old, or fabled since
> Of faery damsels met in forest wide
> By knights of Logres, or of Lyones,
> Lancelot, or Pelleas, or Pellenore.

Here, as often in Spenser, the artist conquers the moralist. The banquet is a symbol of seductive luxury, and Milton's moral purpose justifies the presentation of a sumptuousness that would appeal to human frailty, yet in the very act his youthful love of romance asserts itself. Who, with such chiming syllables in his ear, observes the distinction made between truth and fiction, or recoils as he should from the enemy of all mankind? The poet who allows himself this last vision, half mythological, half medieval, of a Renaissance Arcadia, is looking backward and downward from a bare puritan hill top, but he is still the greatest English artist who has ever touched classic myth.

[108] *P. L.*, xi. 10 ff., 128 ff.; Mackail, p. 177.
[109] *P. L.*, iii. 567; iv. 248; viii. 630; Mackail, pp. 159–60.

CHAPTER FIFTEEN

TRAVESTIES OF CLASSICAL THEMES AND POEMS

A CHRONOLOGICAL sketch of changing tastes in classical matters compels us to employ the art of sinking and descend from Milton to the travesties that litter the second half of the seventeenth century. They may be roughly classified as dull and obscene, and merely dull. Wit is not always absent, but it is likely to be drowned in a flood of boisterous high spirits. Yet the mere bulk of such pieces forces upon our attention a distinct if unattractive phase of our subject, so that this book may, like the phoenix, in aromatic odors end.

Travesty is a free, humorous reworking of a serious narrative which retains the characters and at least a recognizable amount of the subject matter of the original, but reduces everything to the level of bourgeois comedy or farce. The impulse toward travesty is almost as old as literature, but it was not an accident that in Italy, France, Spain, England, a wave of burlesque followed in the wake of the classical revival. Extreme and often wrong-headed veneration for the classics, the hardening of neoclassic dogmas of imitation, the extravagances of mythological poems, produced the logical reaction. The bolder spirits very early began to ask if nature had expended all its energy in the creation of the ancients, if moderns might not hope for an equal gift of genius, and there was born the quarrel of ancients and moderns which was to last for generations. A few at least of the men who wrote travesties may be regarded as the light cavalry in the army of the moderns. The influence of Scarron established the travesty as a popular form, and dozens of lesser men, without Scarron's talent and taste, set about debasing traditional idols and ideals with all the zest of modern biographers.

So far as England is concerned the critical significance of the movement should not be exaggerated. The most important representative, Charles Cotton, was as a writer of travesty far inferior to Scarron. The Elizabethan age, with its ethical reading of the ancients, its general moral seriousness and glowing idealism, gave way to the easy immorality, sophistication, and sometimes blunt common sense, of the Restoration. Travesties of the classics could hardly have flourished in the time of Spenser, and to remember that they did flourish in the time of Milton is to remember that Milton's soul dwelt apart. The majority of English burlesques, lacking the wit and critical seasoning which make a number of French pieces documents, if nothing more, in the history of taste, seem merely to have gratified a desire in writers and readers to abandon tragic passions and high imaginings and indulge, as Boileau said, in "le langage des halles." Travesties at their best were not exactly refined, and in England the reaction against puritanism contributed to a rather self-conscious coarseness.

In 1644 Scarron published his *Typhon,* which was not strictly a travesty, since it did not caricature any particular poem, but as a humorous treatment of a serious mythological subject it led the way for the *Virgile travesti.* The first books of that famous work appeared in 1648, and many imitations quickly followed. Scarron had seized upon the poet whose qualities lent most piquancy to burlesque, and Virgil was at first the chief victim. But there was plenty of other material available, and Ovid was soon undergoing a variety of metamorphoses, as in Richer's *Ovide bouffon* and the *Ovide en belle humeur* of D'Assoucy.[1]

While Scarron exerted some influence upon a few of the later English travesties, there were in English traces of at least a jocose or satirical handling of classical stories long before Scarron wrote. Pettie's prose adaptations of Ovidian and other tales were not very serious, and added abundant courtly and bourgeois elements. Whetstone's *Rocke of Regard,* also of 1576, tells the story of Venus, Mars, and Vulcan in a half-realistic manner—Vulcan being "a Croydon chuffe"—in order to illustrate "the discommodities of forst marriages." [2] We have noticed that Warner used mythological figures as a stalking-horse for homely satire. Marston's assertion regarding his tale of Pygmalion at least shows that he could entertain the notion of a mythological burlesque, though not of the bourgeois kind.

We should not pass by the highly unromantic prose version of the story of Hero and Leander in Nashe's *Prayse of the Red Herring* (1599).[3] Though Nashe has only respect for Marlowe he turns his back on passion

---

[1] See Victor Fournel's introduction to his edition of *Le Virgile travesti* (1858); S. E. Leavitt, "Paul Scarron and English Travesty," *S. P.*, XVI, 108.

[2] Ed. Collier, page 131. Peend's poem of 1565 (see the Appendix) contained a brief version of the story in much the same vein. Indeed there is a similar "explication" in the *Ovide moralisé* (ed. De Boer, iv. 1538).

[3] *Works,* ed. McKerrow, III, 195 ff. In addition to Marlowe and Chapman Nashe evidently made use of Ovid. One may recall Ben Jonson's burlesque puppet play on Hero and Leander in *Bartholomew Fair* (Act V), which belongs to the same tradition as Shakespeare's Pyramus and Thisbe.

and splendor.[4] His alert common sense observes a difficulty in the traditional tale: why did Leander have to swim instead of taking a boat? The parents, he says, were unfriendly, and the towns were "at wrig wrag." Short work is made of courtship and of Hero's scruples. Nashe's slangy mockery is sometimes vivid and amusing, sometimes merely crude. When Hero found her lover on the beach, "sodden to haddocks meate" ("drowndead," as a later inhabitant of Yarmouth expressed it), and was about to kiss his "blew iellied sturgeon lips," the waves carried the body out again. "At that she became a franticke Bacchanal outright, & made no more bones but sprang after him, and so resignd up her Priesthood, and left worke for Musæus and Kit Marlowe." The gods' interest in the lovers is burlesqued, like everything else. Instead of Chapman's metamorphoses, Leander becomes the fish called "ling," Hero a "Cadwallader Herring," while the old nurse, "a shrewish snappish bawd," is turned into mustard seed. Thus it is that "the red Herring and Ling, neuer come to the boord without mustard, their waiting maid."[5]

The first real travesty appears to have been *The Innovation of Penelope and Ulysses,* by James Smith. It was included in the doggish *Wit Restor'd* of 1658, but evidently written in or before 1640. Thus, although it is in the farcical bourgeois vein of the imitations of Scarron, it seems to have preceded both the *Typhon* and the *Virgile travesti.*[6] The poem's chief merit is the light-heartedness characteristic of its reverend author's unclerical muse. Penelope and Ulysses and the Trojan war are brought down to the level suggested by this greeting to the absent husband:

---

[4] There is at least one touch not unworthy of Marlowe: "Yet towards cocke-crowing she caught a little slumber, and then shee dreamed that Leander and shee were playing at checkestone with pearles in the bottome of the sea."

[5] In earlier chapters we have noticed that the injection of humor or satire into mythological poems was one of the marks of the transition from the Elizabethan to the Jacobean manner. In addition to examples just cited in the text there were such later pieces as the *Salmacis and Hermaphroditus* of 1602, Drayton's *Man in the Moone,* and Basse's *Urania.* See also, in the Appendix, *The Metamorphosis of Tobacco,* 1602; Brathwait's *Birth of Tobacco,* 1617; Henry Hutton's *Follie's Anatomie,* 1619. One might notice the fanciful or burlesque use of mythology in Dekker's *A Knights Coniuring* (1607), in particular the burlesque story of Orpheus and Eurydice (ed. Rimbault, Percy Society, 1842, pp. 24–25).
I can only mention the use of mythology as a framework in satire of a more literary kind, the critical survey of poets. The form was made popular by Boccalini, and the best-known English example is Suckling's *Sessions of the Poets;* see Spingarn, *Cambridge History of English Literature,* VII, 273–74, and *Critical Essays of the Seventeenth Century,* I, xxiii. Such writing is of course remote from the travesties we are considering, but the satirical adaptation of the old roll call of poets springs from the same irreverent impulse.
[6] For the text of the *Innovation* see *Musarum Deliciæ* (Hotten, London, 1874), I, 255 ff. A commendatory piece has the signature of Philip Massinger, who died in March, 1640.
For the influence on Mennes and Smith of satirical and facetious French verse, see, for example, Spingarn, *Critical Essays of the Seventeenth Century,* III, 310–11.

My pretty Duck, my Pigsnie, my Ulysses,
Thy poor Penelope sends a thousand Kisses . . .

Stricken with love-longing, Ulysses washes his hands and hastens home-
ward, while Penelope

had her shoes rub'd over with Lamp blacking,
Her new rebato, and a falling band,
And Rings with severall poesies on her hand.

At the feast a song in praise of blacksmiths is sung, "collected out of
Homer, Virgill and Ovid"; it has the lusty classical refrain "Which
Nobody can deny." The narrative is furnished with burlesque footnotes.[7]
The only respect in which the *Innovation* fails to conform to the later
convention is that it does not burlesque one particular poem, although it
has obvious and avowed connections with Ovid's epistle. Some of the
commendatory lines, including the author's own, show that the novelty
was appreciated. Massinger, more friendly than critical, declares that the
Culex showed more art than the *Aeneid,* and as for the *Innovation,*

Methinks I do behold in this rare birth
A temple built up to facetious mirth.

Smith's verse-letters and other pieces are written in a vein of colloquial
jocoseness, with occasional burlesque references to mythology, and here,
whether or not the idea was original, he applied his normal style to a
traditionally lofty theme.

There is hardly any better proof of the strong stomachs possessed by
some of our ancestors than *The Loves of Hero and Leander,* which
perhaps first appeared in 1651.[8] In addition to the almost inevitable
allusion to *Venus and Adonis* (the amorous horse this time), there is
some burlesque of *Hero and Leander,* of the crudest kind.[9] Some lines

---

[7] A *Carmen Heroicum* in *Wit Restor'd* (page 153) has still more remarkable footnotes.
One may be quoted to indicate how far we have moved from *Endimion and Phœbe:*
"Endimion was a handsome young Welshman, whom one Luce Moone lov'd for his
sweet breath; and would never hang off his lips: but he not caring for her, eat a bundance
of toasted cheese, purposely to make his breath unsavory; upon which, she left him
presently, and ever since 'tis proverbially spoken (as inconstant as Luce Moone.) The Vatican
coppy of Hesiod, reades her name, Mohun, but contractedly it is Moone. *Hesiod. lib. 4.
tom. 3."*
This last sentence marks the arrival of sophisticated scholarship.
[8] It was reprinted in 1653, and, bound up with Heywood's translation of the *Ars
Amatoria,* in 1662 and later years. See above, p. 187, n. 25, for references to articles by
Mr. A. M. Clark, which straighten out bibliographical puzzles. The title of the 1662 edition
is: *Ovid De Arte Amandi and the Remedy of Love Englished As also the Lovs of Hero &
Leander, A mock-Poem. Together with Choice Poems, and rare pieces of Drollery.*
[9] The motives burlesqued are Leander's swim (including the fish playing round him and
the dalliance of Neptune), and the metamorphosis of the lovers into a crab and a flounder,
inspired doubtless by Chapman or Nashe. Leander's telling of the story of Cophetua to
Hero might have been suggested by Chapman's tale of Teras, though there is no actual
similarity.

may refer to the popular literary firm of Mennes and Smith, and seem to recognize the pair as models of the new style.[10]

Richard Flecknoe at any rate paid open tribute to Dr. Smith, "whose muse so bonny is and blithe," and to Mennes, in his *Diarium* (1656). In the same work Flecknoe mentions Scarron and imitates a passage in the *Virgile travesti*.[11] He appears to be one of the earliest links between the native tradition and the foreign. From this time onward travesties sometimes reveal the direct or indirect influence of Scarron, but, unless they name their model or clearly imitate him, influence is hard to prove. The formula was easy to apply, after a fashion, and the English writer of travesty had no more need to know Scarron than the composer of a limerick to have read Lear.

In 1664 appeared Charles Cotton's *Scarronides,* a travesty of the first book of the *Aeneid;* a version of the fourth book was added later. The work was extremely popular and stirred up a host of imitators. The title acknowledges a debt to Scarron, and Cotton follows him in choice of subject, in meter, in the constant use of comic anachronisms; there is also some direct borrowing. But there is little in the piece that might not have been as it is if Scarron had never written. Cotton in general is closer to the earthy buffoonery of Smith than to the barbed satirical wit which strikes through the genial irreverence of Scarron. This is Scarron's invocation of the muse, in part:

> Petite muse au nez camard,
> Qui m'as fait auteur goguenard,
> Et qui, quoique mon mal empire,
> Me fais pourtant quelquefois rire,
> Dis-moi bien comment, et pourquoi,
> Junon, sans honneur et sans foi,
> Persécuta ce galant homme,
> Sans lequel nous n'aurions pas Rome,
> Ni tous ces illustres Romains
> A qui nous baisons tous les mains.
> Elle fit bien la furieuse
> Contre personne si pieuse:
> Ils se fâchent donc comme nous!

[10] The dubious lines are these:
> Know all, I value this rich Gem,
> With any piece by C. J. M.
> Nay more then so, I'le go no less,
> Then any script of Friends, J. S.

The *Innovation* had contained allusions to the story of Hero and Leander (pp. 269, 277). In *Wits Recreations* of 1640 (reprint of Hotten, II, 106) an epigram *On a Coy Woman* recasts a distich of Marlowe's:
> She seems not won, yet won she is at length;
> In loves war, women use but halfe their strength.

[11] Leavitt, p. 110. For the mention of Smith, see *Musarum Deliciæ,* I, 7.

> Je ne les croyois pas si fous,
> Et les croyois être sans bile,
> Ces beaux dieux d'Homère et Virgile!

Scarron is not invariably delicate, but here we have a scholar and a gentleman permitting himself a holiday from orthodox respect for antiquity, employing both sophisticated and affectedly naïve irony to reduce mythological beings to the humdrum level of prose. Cotton was a scholar and gentleman also, but he produces a daub of coarse liveliness:

> But oh, my Muse! put me in mind,
> To which o' th' Gods was he unkind:
> Or, what the Plague did Juno mean,
> (That cross-grain'd, peevish, scolding Quean,
> That scratching, cater-wawling Puss)
> To use an honest Fellow thus?
> (To curry him like Pelts at Tanners)
> Have Goddesses no better Manners?[12]

If one reads more than a few pages one may wonder how even a fond editor of Cotton can describe the work as "exceedingly witty."[13] Cotton's travesty of Lucian, *The Scoffer Scofft* (1675) is equally dull and coarse.

In 1664 the first book of the *Iliad* was travestied by J. Scudamore, as *Homer à la Mode.* In the following year Scarron's *Typhon* was translated as *The Gyants War with the Gods,*[14] and the second book of the *Aeneid* was burlesqued by R. Mounsey under the now conventional title of *Scarronides.* Passing over some other minor pieces we may notice a burlesque *Hero and Leander* of 1669 which has been attributed to Wycherley. The work does not seem to reveal any debt to Scarron's *Léandre et Héro* (1656), but it does apparently hark back to Marlowe's elaborate descriptions of Leander and the temple, and perhaps Marlowe's dialogue as well.[15]

In 1672–73 John Phillips translated the fifth and sixth books of *Le Virgile travesti* as *The Maronides, or Virgil Travesty.* As a rule he followed Scarron closely, though he substituted English for French allusions. But from this time onward Ovid was the most popular victim. In 1673 appeared *Ovidius Exulans,* a travesty of five epistles from the

[12] *Poetical Works of Charles Cotton* (London, 1765), p. 6. It is pleasant to read that Denham, having burlesqued as well as translated Virgil, burned the travesty, "sayeing that 'twas not fitt that the best poet should be so abused" (Aubrey's *Brief Lives,* ed. Clark, I, 218; *Works of Sir John Denham,* ed. T. H. Banks, p. 42, note 181).
[13] John Beresford, *Poems of Charles Cotton* (1923), p. 8.
[14] This translation is attributed to John Phillips by the *D.N.B.* and the *Cambridge History of English Literature* (IX, 268), but Mr. Leavitt thinks it unworthy of Phillips' linguistic knowledge and experience as a translator (page 113).
[15] *Works of Wycherley,* ed. M. Summers, IV, 76, 84 ff. M. Charles Perromat does not accept the notion of Wycherley's authorship (*William Wycherley,* Paris, 1921).

Heroides. The author calls himself "Naso Scarronnominus," and mentions Scarron in his preface, but his work, which applies the common formula, gives no evidence of any special debt. He declares that he has not written in order to get credit, or pay a bookseller, or flatter a patron, but out of spite, because he sees daily such elaborate pieces of nonsense creeping out under patronage, and wonders "whether this would pass among them that dote on such Rubbish Learning." The work has no more subtlety than its fellows. Leander would go to Hero on the Bankside if the Thames were not so plaguy rough. Laodamia grieves in this fashion:

> Before that I could fetch my Scarf,
> Your nimble feet had reach'd the Wharf.
> Nay you were got quite out of hear-
> Ing, e're the Cat could lick her ear . . .

If *Ovidius Exulans* is dull, *The Wits Paraphras'd* (1680) falls into the category of the dull and obscene.[16] It burlesques the translation of the *Heroides* (1680) done by Dryden, Flatman, and others. Not many shreds of Ovid are left. In the same year Alexander Radcliffe published an *Ovid Travestie.* His preface ridicules *The Wits Paraphras'd* and its author, "an unlucky Pretender to Poetry." Radcliffe burlesqued some epistles from the *Heroides;* the number was increased in later editions. The popularity of the work was doubtless owing to the fact that Radcliffe was one of the most obscene of his tribe.

There is no need of prolonging a catalogue of such drolleries, since their general character is much the same. It is clear that while a few paid lip service to Scarron, and while Scarron must have encouraged the growth of travesty in England, no English writer had the talent, or perhaps the desire, to emulate his real cleverness. Besides, the simple tricks which the English writers relied upon—anachronism, coarseness, general vulgarizing of theme and characters—were, as we have seen, being practiced before Scarron wrote. Even the continental travesties need not be taken too seriously as a reaction against idolatry of the ancients, since it is only in an age of faith that a feast of fools can be enjoyed, and the English pieces were mostly the hasty scribbling of pot-poets. In the whole mass of tawdry stuff one can find hardly anything that approaches the satirical neatness of Butler's famous lines:

> The Sun had long since in the Lap
> Of Thetis, taken out his Nap,
> And like a Lobster boyl'd, the Morn
> From black to red began to turn.

---

[16] There is a dedication signed "M. T." The Bodleian Catalogue gives the piece to Matthew Stevenson.

CONCLUSION

WHATEVER conclusions have emerged from this study may, I fear, have been repeated so often, since they were first announced in the introduction (and admitted as obvious), that perhaps nothing should be added here to delay the reader's arrival at the Appendix. Yet a few main threads may be picked up. To begin with, one might ask why, with the age of full-blown classicism looming directly ahead, Milton should be counted as the last poet of the classical Renaissance in England. Or, and more probably, one might wonder why so many excellent stopping places before Milton had been overlooked.

In a large sense, of course, no major tradition ever ends, and mythology is a part of the great stream of Latin culture in European poetry. But tradition, like the river of Heracleitus, is not the same from one moment to the next. Only at certain points, when the normal process of change is hastened by some far-reaching alteration in philosophic outlook, or by some poetic genius of masterful originality, the old tradition becomes unrecognizable as the old tradition, and a new era begins. So the Renaissance tradition, although in Milton's last poems it has changed so greatly from what it was two generations before, is still itself and not something else.

But the age of Dryden—I am not speaking strictly in terms of chronology—despite obvious outward and some inward marks of continuity with Renaissance culture (as in critical theory), is essentially different. The character of the body of poetry which we have surveyed permits, indeed insists, that the line be drawn between Milton and Dryden. For the substance of Milton's mind is largely a combination of Renaissance humanism and medievalism; there is no such mixture in the writings of Dryden and his fellows. They are classical, after a fashion, but their modes of thought, feeling, and expression have no tincture of the medieval. Thus our outline begins with the most modern of medieval poets, and ends with the most medieval of late Renaissance poets, and in all that lies between Chaucer and Milton we have observed the fusion, complete or incomplete, of the medieval and the classical.

Mythology bulks largest in Spenser and Milton. The medievalism of Spenser is axiomatic, that of Milton less so. Both poets are of course acutely conscious of new and disturbing ideas, and in some aspects of his thought Milton is a vigorous radical, of the humanistic, not the modern humanitarian variety. Milton does not, like Spenser, allow himself to dally with the romance of chivalry, he is not in the allegorical tradition of the *Roman de la Rose*. Yet he is partly medieval in the nature of his reaction to the new mathematical and mechanical philosophies which were pushing God and man out of the real world, in his conception of reason and will, both divine and human, in his bringing of learning and science to the aid of theology, in his mixing of Ovid and the Bible, gods and angels.

But it was not the most Catholic or catholic elements of the medieval tradition that dominated Milton. Chaucer rested in the bosom of a religion and a religious philosophy which had settled most ultimate questions and left him free to look with clear eyes at human nature and life; though the same fact keeps him from ranking with the greatest. Spenser, by temperament and the accident of chronology, wandered between two worlds, and, unlike the Victorian wanderer, did not suffer greatly. The Protestant strain in him was too slight to make him a propagandist, or to spoil his enjoyment of the world of sense, and he derived poetical strength from the large and liberal Catholic tradition. But a cleavage already shows itself in him. Even if he is not often troubled by inner conflicts he is at any rate several different poets, not the fully integrated, foursquare personality of Chaucer. For Milton, in his time and with his nature, there could be no such amiable neutrality. Between the Catholic reformation and the puritan reformation it was left only to God and the angels (and some quiet latitude men) to be lookers-on. In Milton—to ignore modifying factors for the moment —we have, not the simple faith and mellow humanity of Chaucer, nor Spenser's mixture of orthodox conformity and poetic idealism, but the militant and all-embracing Manicheism of some of the fathers and their successors, the puritans. Thus the medieval synthesis and its gradual break-up are reflected even in the classical mythology of the three greatest non-dramatic poets of the three eras of the English Renaissance. Chaucer's attitude toward myth is usually one of serene and untroubled acceptance. In Spenser there is an unconscious equilibrium between the sometimes contradictory instincts of moralist and artist. Though Milton both as moralist and artist belongs to the Renaissance tradition, in him the tradition has become morally stricter and artistically more disciplined; his praise is given to Spenser the moralist, and he is himself driven, by the accumulated force of puritanism, to conscious and uneasy compromises. Milton's compunctions were not felt by Dante.

Spenser and Milton contained within themselves, in varying proportions, all the diverse impulses of the Renaissance. Mythological poems proper, of infinitely smaller compass than *The Faerie Queene* and *Paradise Lost,* were mainly the expression of a single impulse, Italianate paganism. Yet an especially English and Protestant inability to be completely and naturally pagan was revealed in various ways, in the self-conscious revolt of Marlowe, the moralizing of Shakespeare, the Platonic idealism of Drayton, the half-mystic sublimations of Chapman. Marlowe and Shakespeare were imitated by a host of young men intoxicated with sensuous delights and verbal sweetness. But the seeds of most such poems were planted in shallow soil, and the Muses' garden was soon filled with weeds which, along with effete Petrarchism, were banished at least from the foreground of poetry by Donne's complex fusion of wit, intellect, passion. The mythological poem in its very nature rarely touched the level of major poetry on which the best metaphysicals moved..

Both in these minor epics of the Renaissance convention and in Chaucer and Spenser, mythology is inextricably mixed with, and deeply colored by, the most heterogeneous unclassical matter. Such mixtures, whether conscious or unconscious, restrained or unrestrained, are essentially medieval, since Gothic art is distinguished from the classical by its acceptance of incongruity. The result is as different from Hellenic purity as Notre Dame, or even St. Paul's, is different from the Parthenon. The Gothic qualities so pronounced in Spenser are visible even in Jonson and Milton, the chief classicists (along with Landor) in English literature, and the fact is a testimony to the strength of the medieval and native tradition.

When we turn from the Renaissance to the Augustan age we find no medieval mixtures, no pseudo-classic columns with gargoyles, or even angels, on top. And what do we have in the way of mythology? Travesties; mock-heroic poems; translations and paraphrases, sometimes fine if one likes Augustan rhetoric; mythological allusions equally numerous and frigid. Of mythological poetry there is little of any kind, and nothing that lives. While much of the more or less unclassical mythology of earlier writing is alive, some of it among the supreme beauties of English poetry, our one classical age yields barren husks. What virtue has gone out of the classicists? Instead of cathedrals, as it were, we have Canova. (I am speaking, of course, of the handling of myth.) Milton was no doubt the destruction as well as the consummation of Renaissance art; no one could go further along the path he trod. But the splendor of Milton, the opulence of Spenser, were inseparable from their conception of the nature and function of poetry.

Milton was the last English poet who had the mastery of knowledge which justified him, like Dante, in the claim to be a teacher of mankind. While the humanistic and aesthetic values of the classical tradition were united with the religious and ethical force of the Middle Ages, Milton was still possible. But the new philosophies, beginning with Descartes, had been undermining the ground on which Milton stood, had been killing the essence of the classical tradition, of religion, of poetry.[1] Besides, while for Milton poetry and knowledge were still one, as they had been for Dante, science had set out on its own independent path, which was to lead beyond the horizon of any one man, any one poet. Through the division of labor the unacknowledged legislators of the world had lost their leadership.[2] Milton is a poet; Dryden is a man of letters.

To return from these spacious but necessary platitudes to the matter in hand, the moral for us is that, other things being equal, classic myth is alive in English poetry only when, in spite of Malherbe,[3] it is not treated in a neoclassic manner.[4] In short, we come back to the truism that, for good or ill, the English genius has been incurably romantic. In mythological narrative the one kind which was to be of major importance was that which derived its imaginative and spiritual strength from the Middle Ages, namely, the allegorical or symbolic. When the imagination awoke again in poetry, when Keats and Shelley turned to ancient myth, it was to revive that kind, and mythology, alive once more, was as remote as ever from the classical in conception and style.

One distinction must be reiterated, that mythology and the classical tradition are not the same thing. That is one phase of the problem which Milton presents, for, as Mr. Gilbert Murray among others has remarked, the external classicisms in Milton are "so conspicuous as really to divert a reader's attention from the main stream of classical tradition flowing through him. And it is the main stream that matters."[5] After glancing at the opening scene of *Hamlet*, Mr. Murray continues:

---

[1] See G. Lanson, "L'influence de la philosophie cartésienne sur la littérature française," *Revue de métaphysique et de morale*, IV (1896), 517–50.

[2] See Max Eastman, *The Literary Mind* (New York, 1931), pp. 123 ff.

[3] See above, page 123.

[4] As regards style and diction, while the texture of Milton's epic verse is more Latin and rhetorical than Greek, his occasional excesses only emphasize his frequent achievement of a wholly classical "rightness." In any case it seems hardly fair to blame him for eighteenth-century Miltonese.

[5] *The Classical Tradition in Poetry* (1927), p. 22.

I have merely tried to show, first, that in an author of markedly classical leanings, like Milton, there is, besides the obvious classicisms, a great mass of classical influence—that is, extremely ancient traditional influence—which passes unnoticed; and next, that the same is true of a very different author, such as Shakespeare, who is commonly supposed to represent the opposite tendency. But we remain confronted by the difficulty that, when we try to reckon up the amount of unnoticeable and perhaps unconscious classical influence that exists in these authors, we have no proper instrument for detecting it. We do not really know what we are looking for. We can see the classicism that stands out as alien against the ordinary style of English poetry; but how are we to recognize the elements in that ordinary style which are the direct though unconscious fruit of ancient influence and have been in poetry from the beginning?

This book has not attempted to answer that unanswerable question, it has been occupied with one of the various things which successive generations of poets and readers considered to be an element of classicism. That there is such a difference as Mr. Murray describes seems to us obvious, yet it was not so obvious in the sixteenth, seventeenth, and early eighteenth centuries. Mythology in English poetry has often been a blessing, often too a curse, but always it has been, so to speak, an accident. It belongs, to vary a phrase of Denham's, to the clothes, not the garb, of the ancients. Perhaps, however much native or romantic coloring it acquires, mythology in English poetry always remains an exotic. Yet, for those who, surveying poetry of the past or present, regard it only as a curse, it is well to pause and consider how infinitely poorer that great body of poetry would be without it.

> The intelligible forms of ancient poets,
> The fair humanities of old religion,
> The Power, the Beauty, and the Majesty,
> That had her haunts in dale, or piny mountain,
> Or forest by slow stream, or pebbly spring,
> Or chasms and wat'ry depths; all these have vanished.
> They live no longer in the faith of reason!
> But still the heart doth need a language, still
> Doth the old instinct bring back the old names.[6]

"That," as Mr. Rylands says, in quoting the passage, "is the conclusion of the whole matter. Poetic diction is no more than a consecrated code of symbols and passwords, the language of the heart. Whether it be the rose or Rhodope—

> still
> Doth the old instinct bring back the old names." [7]

[6] *Wallenstein*, Part I, II. iv. 123 ff. (*Works of Coleridge*, ed. J. D. Campbell, 1909, p. 257). See *Guy Mannering*, c. 3.
[7] *Words and Poetry*, p. 89.

APPENDIX

APPENDIX

This appendix has two main objects, first, to provide a chronological conspectus of mythological poems (and a few related works in verse and prose) up to 1680; and, secondly, to include brief accounts of a number of minor works not discussed in the text. The list aims, of course in vain, at something like completeness, within necessarily arbitrary limits, since hardly any book of the period is free from mythology. In its original manuscript state this appendix had swollen into another volume, and it has been reduced to more tolerable size by the exclusion of nearly all ballads, lyrics, and brief pieces generally, and of almost all formal translations from classical poems except some few mentioned in the text. Up to 1600 all translations of Ovid's *Metamorphoses* and *Heroides* are included. A few other items not covered by these general exceptions appear on account of some special significance.

For the sake of uniformity titles are almost always given as they appear in the *Short-Title Catalogue* of Messrs. Pollard and Redgrave. Exceptions to this rule comprise titles of books printed after 1640; titles of books not published or not extant; a few cases in which a title is abridged or given in full.

No attempt has been made to supply full references and bibliographical information. "Text" means a reference to the earlier pages of this book. For the titles of Bartlett, Hazlitt, Palmer, Scott, see Bibliography, "General." "Collier," unless a title is given, means *A Bibliographical and Critical Account,* etc., 4 vols., New York, 1866.

1475? William Caxton, The recuyell of the historyes of Troye.
      Text, p. 32.

ca. William Caxton, Thhistories of Jason.
1477.

1480. William Caxton, Ovyde hys booke of Methamorphose.
      Text, p. 33.

1490. William Caxton, Eneydos.
      Text, p. 33.

1508? Robert Henryson, The traitie of Orpheus.

1518? This boke treath of the lyfe of Virgilius.
      The legendary life of Virgil the wizard. See under 1562, and Palmer, p. 117.

1520– A lire of love etc.
1540?   A poem of 273 lines, printed by Mr. Padelford along with many others from MS. Rawlinson C. 813 (*Anglia,* XXXI, 1908, 385 ff.). The date of the MS is placed between 1520 and 1540; some of the poems are much older. The first

35 lines of our piece describe the judgment of Paris. The author proceeds, in exuberantly aureate language, to praise love and women and especially his own "redolent flowre." The medieval flavor is strong. The poet borrows from an odd pair, Tibullus and Hawes. See W. Bolle, *Anglia*, XXXIV, 275, 290, 299–300, 306; and Padelford, *Anglia*, XXXV, 185.

1521. Brian Anslay, The boke of the Cyte of Ladyes.

The book contains many stories of goddesses, etc. A translation of Christine de Pisan's *Livre de la Cité des Dames*, which itself is modeled on, and borrows largely from, Boccaccio's *De Claris Mulieribus*. See text, p. 32.

1526. The letter of Dydo to Eneas.

Printed in Pynson's edition of Chaucer, 1526. Apparently a free and abridged paraphrase of the epistle in the *Heroides*, whether direct or not. See E. Hammond, *Chaucer*, p. 436.

Before La conusaunce damours.
1531.   A poem containing thirty pages of rhyme royal, printed by Pynson. To gain inspiration for a poem in honor of "dames and pusels" the writer calls on a young woman and her friends. The hostess tells in thirty stanzas of not unpleasing verse the story of Pyramus and Thisbe. It is a close paraphrase, direct or indirect, of Ovid; the chief departure, a medieval one, is the expansion of *audacem faciebat amor* into a couple of stanzas on the power of love. At the end of the story comes a discussion of love, with contributions from "Reason" and "Thought-and-hevynesse." There is an allusion to the *Troilus* of "our ornate Chaucer." The poem was said by Collier (IV, 161) to be from the French— as the title might suggest—but I do not know any original.

1536– The C. hystoryes of Troye.
1545.   A translation of Christine de Pisan's *L'Epistre d'Othea*, probably done by the printer, Robert Wyer.

1553. The faythfull and true storye of the destruction of Troye, compyled by Dares Phrigius, which was a souldier while the siege lasted, Translated into Englyshe by Thomas Paynell. (Palmer, p. 40).

Before   Henry Parker, Lord Morley (d. 1556), translated, but did not publish, Boccaccio's
1556. *De Claris Mulieribus*. Brief extracts are in Waldron's *Literary Museum*, 1792.

1557. Giovanni Battista Gelli, Circes. *Tr.* out of Italyon H. Iden.
Text, p. 35.

1557. Songes and sonettes, written by Henry Haward late Earle of Surrey, and other.

Tottel's *Miscellany* contains many amatory poems employing myths; for some of these see text, p. 56. Other pieces of classical interest are a translation of the opening lines of Penelope's epistle to Ulysses (*Heroides*); Wyatt's *Song of Iopas*; and Grimald's *Ciceroes Death* (from Beza's Latin), one of Grimald's two experiments in blank verse. See also text, p. 27.

1560. The fable of Ovid treting of Narcissus.
Text, p. 48.

1561. The nine ladies worthy.

A piece on famous heroines, printed in Stow's edition of Chaucer, 1561. See Skeat, *Chaucerian and Other Pieces*, p. xii; Hammond, p. 441.

How Mercurie with Pallas, Venus and Minarua, appered to Paris.

Also in Stow. See Skeat, p. xiii; and *Romaunt of the Rose: Minor Poems*, p. 33; Hammond, p. 427.

1562– A boke intituled Perymus and Thesbye.
1563. Entered to W. Griffith, *Stat. Reg.*, I, 215. Warton mentions a quarto on the same theme, licensed in 1562 to T. Hacket (*History of English Poetry*, 1871, IV, 297). See *Gorgeous Gallery*, ed. Rollins, pp. 198, 203; Chambers, *William Shakespeare*, I, 363.

1562? Virgilius. This boke treateth of the lyfe of Virgil.
   An account of the wizard. See under 1518.

1563. A myrroure for magistrates.
   This edition contained Sackville's *Induction*. Text, p. 60.

Before Sir Thomas Chaloner (d. 1565) wrote, but apparently did not publish, a render-
1565. ing of the epistle of Helen to Paris (*Heroides*). Printed in *Nugae Antiquae* (1804), II, 372–89.

1565. The fyrst fower bookes of P. Ouidius Nasos worke, intitled Metamorphosis. *Tr.* into Englishe meter by A. Golding.

1565. The pleasant fable of Hermaphroditus and Salmacis [*tr.*] by T. Peend.
   Ovid is treated rather freely in 166 lines of jog-trot verse. The rest of the 340 lines expound the allegory. Hermaphroditus represents youthful purity, Caria the world, Salmacis all the allurements of vice. A similar interpretation is given in the *Ovide moralisé* (ed. De Boer), iv. 2284 ff. There are also euhemeristic explanations of Actaeon and other figures which go back at least as far as Fulgentius and Servius. Apparently with the help of the *Ars Amatoria* (i. 269 ff.) Peend rebukes the "folysh fyts" of passionate women, citing such examples as Venus, Hero, Juliet.
   Peend says that he gave up a projected version of the *Metamorphoses* on being "prevented" by another—evidently Golding. One is not left inconsolable. Brydges prints extracts in *Brit. Bibl.*, II, 344; I used the Bodleian copy of Peend. See L. Rick, *Ovids Metamorphosen in der englischen Renaissance*, pp. 32–35.

1565– Very pleasaunte sonettes and storyes in myter.
1566. First edition of *Handful of Pleasant Delights* (1584). See *Handful*, ed. Rollins, introduction. On particular ballads, text, above, p. 58.

1566. William Painter, The palace of pleasure [vol. I].
   Text, p. 35.

1566. John Partridge, The notable hystorie of two famous princes Astianax and Polixena.
   A piece of about 220 long lines, written ostensibly to show the horrors of war. Though said by the author to be a translation, it seems to be based on those parts of Seneca's *Troades* (in Heywood's translation) which deal with Astyanax and Polyxena. Use is made of the speech of Achilles added by Heywood to the original. Some details, especially about Polyxena, are possibly from *Metam.* xiii. 449 ff., or Lydgate, *Troy Book*, iv. 6635 ff., 6684 ff. Brief extracts are given in Collier, III, 147.

1566. Thomas Underdowne, The excellent historye of Theseus and Ariadne.
   I have not seen the whole poem. It is described, with excerpts, in Brydges, *Brit. Bibl.*, II, 534, and Collier, IV, 183. The myth receives a strongly didactic and misogynistic coloring.

1567. The XV. bookes of P. Ouidius Naso, entytuled Metamorphosis. *Tr.* into English meeter by A. Golding.
   Text, p. 70, and see index.

304 MYTHOLOGY AND THE RENAISSANCE TRADITION

1567. William Painter, The palace of pleasure [vol. II].
Text, p. 35.

1567. James Sanford, The amorous and tragicall tales of Plutarch.
A prose version of Plutarch's five tales of love. See *Moralia*, ed. Bernardakis, IV, 463 ff.; *Morals*, ed. Goodwin (Boston, 1878), IV, 312–22. The translator's epistle censures "the fruites which spring of hote Loue and fleshly lust." The volume contains also a version of parts of Heliodorus, beginning with bk. iv.

1567. George Turberville, The heroycall epistles of Pub. Ouidius Naso, in Englishe verse . . . With A. Sabinus aunsweres.
The *Stat. Reg.* for 1566–67 (I, 328, 329, 335) has three entries to Denham for epistles of Ovid. These were doubtless a precautionary announcement of Turberville's work, though one or two may have appeared separately. See H. E. Rollins, *M. P.*, XV (1918), 519. The book has been reprinted by Mr. Boas (Cresset Press, 1928).

1567. George Turberville, Epitaphes, epigrams, songs and sonets.
Text, pp. 53–54.

1568. William Fulwood, The enimie of idlenesse. Teaching how to indite epistles.
This manual gives a model poem, of ten stanzas, the "story of Pigmalions ill," in which the myth is applied to the case of an unhappy lover; the hard-hearted statue does not come to life. For a piece on Troilus and Cressida see Rollins, *P. M. L. A.*, XXXII, 391.

1568. Thomas Howell, The arbor of amitie or pleasant poems.
————— Pleasant sonnets and prettie pamphlets.
Text, pp. 54, 59.

1569. W. Hubbard, The tragicall and lamentable historie of Ceyx, kynge of Thrachine, and Alcione his wife.
Reprinted in Collier, *Illustrations of Old English Literature*, III (and see *Bibl. Acct.*, II, 143). Hubbard treats Ovid (*Metam.* xi. 346 ff.) freely, abridging the description of the storm, and omitting mythological machinery in the account of Alcyone's dream. Lines and phrases are frequently borrowed from Golding.

1570. B. G., Helen's epistle to Paris.
Hazlitt, p. 429. Warton (IV, 301) records the piece, calling it a "ballet." The title of course suggests translation or adaptation of Ovid.

1573. James Sanford, The garden of pleasure.
Re-issued in 1576 as *Houres of recreation* (Scott, p. 27). The book includes short tales and anecdotes, ancient and modern, such as those concerning the wife of Candaules; Mercury and Battus; Atalanta; the three Graces.

1574. Richard Robinson, The rewarde of wickednesse.
Described in Collier, III, 330; Brydges, *Censura Lit.*, IV, 36; *Mirror for Magistrates*, ed. Haslewood, pp. xxiii ff. I used the British Museum copy. The piece is strongly didactic and anti-Romanist. The author visits Hades and hears the confessions of sundry notable sinners, Helen, Pope Alexander VI, Tarquin, Medea, Tantalus, Midas, etc. One is reminded of the *Mirror*, and also of the dialogue of Ravisius Textor, *Earth and Age*, which Thomas Heywood translated in his *Pleasant Dialogues and Dramma's*.

1574– George Turberville, Tragical tales.
1575. Text, p. 54.

1575. W. Painter, The palace of pleasure beautified; Corrected and augmented.

1576. The paradyse of dainty deuises.
This popular miscellany included four poems, by Edwards, illustrating the cardinal virtues. They deal with the story of Damocles; a young man of Egypt and Valerian; Zaleuch and his son; and Spurina. See Rollins' ed., pp. 55 ff., and notes. Text, p. 34.

1576. George Gascoigne, The steele glas. A satyre, togither with the Complainte of Phylomene.
Text, p. 56.

1576. George Pettie, A petite pallace of Pettie his pleasure.
Text, p. 36.

1576. George Whetstone, The rocke of regard.
The book includes three moralistic poems, on Cressida, Medea, Venus and Vulcan (Collier's reprint, pp. 36, 108, 131). On the last, see text, p. 288.

1577. Stephen Batman, The golden booke of the leaden goddes.
Text, p. 32. Available in M. L. A. rotograph series, No. 76.

1577? " 'The historie of Leander and Hero, written by Musæus, and Englished by me a dozen yeares ago, and in print'. So mentioned by Abraham Fleming in his Virgil's Georgics, 1589. Not otherwise known." (Palmer, p. 74.) See Hazlitt, p. 410; Collier, II, 27.

1577. J. Grange, The golden Aphroditis.
A piece of prose fiction, with touches of euphuism, though more flowery than strictly euphuistic. The heroine, A. O., is a daughter of Diana and Endymion, and there is much decorative mythology. Like Pettie's shorter tales, the story is full of love-making and letter-writing.

1578. A gorgious gallery of gallant inuentions.
Text, pp. 50, 53.

1579. H. C., The forrest of fancy.
A miscellany of prose and verse, described in Brydges, Restituta, III, 456; Collier, II, 30; Koeppel, Quellen und Forschungen, LXX (1892), 44–46; Scott, pp. 36–38. A few short tales about such characters as Eteocles and Polynices (this inspired perhaps by the Senecan translations); King Antigonus; Meleager.

1579. A poor Knight, his pallace of priuate pleasures. Written by a student in Cābridge. And published by J. C. Gent.
Reprinted by Sir H. Ellis, Three Collections of English Poetry of the Latter Part of the Sixteenth Century (Roxburghe Club, 1845). A piece of thirty pages uses the dream-allegory to describe, somewhat in the manner of Lydgate or Googe's Cupido Conquered, a battle between the forces of Diana and Cupid and a trial before the gods. There is also a poem of nearly two hundred lines, which combines broadside style with historical detail, The lyfe and death of Maister, T. Cicero. Cf. Lydgate, Fall of Princes, ed. Bergen, vi. 2948–3276.

1579. Thomas Salter, A mirrhor mete for all mothers, matrones, and maidens, intituled the mirrhor of modestie.
Reprinted in Collier, Illustrations of Old English Literature, I. The author is indignant that women able to read Prudentius and other Christian poets should prefer "Lascivious bookes of Ovide, Catullus, Propercius, Tibullus, and in Virgill

of Eneas, and Dido; and amonge the Greeke poettes of the filthie love (if I maie terme it love) of the Goddes themselves, and of their wicked adulteries and abhominable fornications, as in Homer and suche like" (p. 17). There are classical anecdotes of a moral turn, and a quite unclassical dialogue between Mercury and Virtue.

1579. Edmund Spenser, The shepheardes calender.
See index.

1580. Humfrey Gifford, A posie of gilloflowers.
Contains *A straunge historie,* which tells of Camma, Sinatus, and Sinorix (pp. 60–62 in original ed. of *Posie;* pp. 122 ff. in Grosart's reprint). Gifford's names in his book are Camna, Sinatus, Sinoris. The piece had been issued as a broadside ten years earlier. Mr. Rollins took this ballad to be the same as another issued in the same year (1569–70), *The Revenge yat a Woman of Grece toke of hym that slewe hyr husbounde* (see his *Analytical Index,* 2284 and 2452). But Mr. Baskervill suggested that "the publication of 2452 by Jones may have called forth another ballad on the same theme from the press of Arnold" (*M. P.,* XXIII, 1925–26, 123). This seems probable, for Gifford's ballad (if, as one may assume, it was *Sinorex, Caniu et Sinatus*) is based on *The Courtier* (Tudor Translations, pp. 236–37), while the title of the other, as Mr. Rollins points out, is summarized from the title in North's translation of Guevara, bk. ii, c. 5.

1581. William Goodyear, The voyage of the wandering knight.
Translated from the French of Jean de Cartigny. One of the illustrations of Folly's dominion over man is the Trojan war, which is outlined, in two and a half pages, from the judgment of Paris to the lonely old age and death of Helen. Apparently the ultimate source is Dictys. Extracts from other parts of the book are given in the *Retrospective Review,* I (1820), 250–58.

1581. Thomas Howell, Howell his deuises for his owne exercise, and his friends pleasure.
Text, p. 54.

1582. *Cal. St. Pap. Dom. Add.,* XII, 77, Oct. 14, 1582.
"John de Critz to Sec. Walsingham: 'Pardon my slackness in not sending oftener . . . Meantime I send two pieces, the one of St. John, the other a poetical story taken out of Ovid, where Neptune took Coenis by the seaside, and having ravished her, for some amends changed her into the form of a man. Take this little present in good part. I trust to send something better next time.'"
This irrelevant reference to pictorial art is included here for the sake of its atmosphere. See *D. N. B.* on De Critz.

1584. A handefull of pleasant delites by C. Robinson and diuers others.
See under 1565–1566, and text, p. 58.

1585. Robert Greene, Planetomachia.

1585? Thomas Procter, The triumph of trueth.
Reprinted in Collier, *Illustrations of Old English Literature,* II. There are classical tales of the didactic sort. Caesar's glory was "blemisht with desire of Lucre." "The Gretians Conquest" tells the story of the Trojan war in five pages. The account of the capture of Troy seems to follow Virgil; other parts suggest the *Heroides* or Dictys, though the matter was common property.

1586. John Shepery, Hyppolitus Ouidianæ Phædræ respondens.

1586. William Warner, Albions England.
The first edition, comprising four books and the prose tale of Aeneas. Text, p. 65.

1586. Helenæ raptus, Latinus, paraphraste T. Watsono.
Watson's Latin translation of the poem of Colluthus.

1586. Geffrey Whitney, A choice of emblemes and other deuises.
Emblems mostly taken from Alciati, and others. Dozens of myths are briefly
recounted and often allegorized. Reprinted by Henry Green, London, 1866.
See M. A. Scott, p. 470, and my index.

1587. Robert Greene, Euphues his censure to Philautus.
———— Penelopes web.
Text, p. 39.

1587. Mathew Grove, The most famous and tragicall historie of Pelops and
Hippodamia.
Ed. Grosart, 1878. See also Collier, II, 95, and *Catalogue . . . of Early English
Literature at Bridgewater House* (1837), p. 134. The poem occupies 44 pages
in Grosart. The story, taken perhaps from Diodorus Siculus (iv. 73), is amplified
with speeches, moralizing, descriptions, in the feeble, jog-trot style of Ovidian
poems of twenty years earlier. The author plagiarized somewhat from Tottel's
Miscellany (ed. Rollins, II, 112).

1587. The mirror for magistrates.
The edition containing lives of Roman emperors. Text, p. 64.

1587? Christopher Marlowe, The rape of Helen.
"Marlowe is credited with a translation of Coluthus which no longer exists"
(Palmer, p. 39). See *Marlowe's Poems,* ed. L. C. Martin, p. 22.

1587. Antonius Thylesius, Cassius of Parma his Orpheus. *Tr.* Roger Raw-
lyns.
Thirty-five lines tell the story of Orpheus (without Eurydice) to show that the
musician must work in order to reach the top of the tree.
The same translator produced a similar inspirational piece called *Nestor his
Antilochus.*

1587. George Turberville, Tragical tales.
See under 1574–1575.

1588.   In William Byrd's *Psalms, sonets and songs* appeared a piece of eight lines, a
translation of the opening portion of Ovid's epistle from Penelope to Ulysses.
The author is unknown. Reprinted in Bullen, *Some Shorter Elizabethan Poems*
(1903), p. 14; Arber, *English Garner,* II, 84.

1588. Sixe idillia.
Text, pp. 54–55.

1589. Thomas Lodge, Scillaes metamorphosis.
Re-issued in 1610 as *A most pleasant historie of Glaucus and Scilla.* Text, p. 81.

1589. George Peele, A farewell. Entituled to the famous generalls of our
English forces: Sir J. Norris & Syr F. Drake. Whereunto is annexed:
a Tale of Troy [in verse].
Text, p. 51.

1589. W. Warner, The first and second parts of Albions England, reuised
and corrected.
Second edition, containing bks. i–vi. Text, p. 65.

1590. Thomas Fenne, Fennes frutes.

An extraordinary hodge-podge, mainly in prose, heavily didactic, with scores of classical anecdotes from the usual sources, Plutarch, Justin, etc., some taken verbatim from Fleming's translation of Aelian. Somewhat in the manner of Valerius Maximus, tales are marshaled to illustrate temperance, modesty, etc. There is a detailed account of the Trojan war, citing Dares and Dictys. Fenne protests against the derivation of Britons from "such an unfaithfull stock" as the Trojans.

Forty pages of verse on "Hecubaes mishaps" also recount the Trojan story; the matter seems to be taken from Dares, Dictys, Lydgate, Ovid, Homer, Virgil.

1590. Edmund Spenser, The Faerie Queene [Bks. i–iii].
Text, chapter 5.

1590. Edmund Spenser, Muiopotmos.

The title-page of this poem in *Complaints* (1591) is dated 1590. Text, p. 108.

1590. William Vallans, A tale of two swannes.

Reprinted in Hearne's edition of Leland's *Itinerary* (vol. V). A topographical poem about Hertfordshire, with a slight mythological framework involving Venus and Mercury. Venus sits by a river side "Tuning her Lute unto the waters fall." See Carpenter, *Reference Guide to Spenser*.

1591. Thomas Bradshaw, The shepherds starre.

A much amplified "paraphrase upon the third of the Canticles of Theocritus, Dialogue wise." Inset is a piece of verse, *A Dialogue betwixt Hercules and the two Ladies, Voluptuous, and Vertuous,* with a reference to "Xenophon. li. 2. Memorabilium"; see Xenophon, ii. 1. 21 ff. Cf. Whitney, *Choice of Emblemes,* p. 40.

1591. John Clapham, Narcissus, siue amoris iuuenilis descriptio.

An elaborate didactic, allegorical version of the story, in Latin verse.

1591. Jo. M., Philippes Venus. Wherein is pleasantly discoursed sundrye fine and wittie arguments in a senode of the gods and goddesses assembled for the expelling of wanton Venus from among their sacred societie.

Esdaile, *English Tales and Prose Romances,* p. 96; Hazlitt, p. 365; Collier, III, 195.

1592. Abraham Fraunce, The third part of the Countesse of Pembrokes Yuychurch: entituled, *Amintas Dale.* Wherein are the most conceited tales of the pagan gods in English hexameters: together with their auncient descriptions and philosophicall explications.

The book has been made available in the M. L. A. rotograph series, No. 75. Inset in a pastoral framework are sixteen narratives in verse, the subjects roughly covering the fifteen books of the *Metamorphoses.* An extract from one tale is given above, p. 145. Most of the stories are fairly close paraphrases of Ovid, with more or less Italianate ornament and an occasional interpolation.

The prose sections constitute a dictionary of allegorized mythology. Innumerable and varied authorities are cited, many demonstrably at second hand; such references as those to Spenser, Boscán, Belleau, Tasso, seem to be Fraunce's own. His allegorical matter seems to be compiled chiefly from Vincenzo Cartari, Natalis Comes, an annotated edition of Ovid (Cambridge, 1584), and Leo Hebraeus.

1592. William Warner, Albions England. The third time corrected.
Books i–ix.

1593.   Gervase Markham "revised for the press 'Thyrsis and Daphne,' a poem not
         known to be extant (cf. *Stationers' Reg.* 23 April 1593)" (*D. N. B.*). The piece
         may have been pastoral or mythological or both.

1593. **Christopher Marlowe, Hero and Leander.**
         Entered to J. Wolf, September 28, 1593, but no edition is known previous to that
         of 1598. Text, chapter 6.

1593. **William Shakespeare, Venus and Adonis.**
         Text, p. 139.

1594. **Richard Barnfield, The affectionate shepheard.**
         The volume includes *Hellens Rape. Or a light Lanthorne for light Ladies*
         (*Poems*, ed. Arber, p. 38). The poem's 75 creaking hexameters suggest that the
         imitative Barnfield's idol of the moment was Abraham Fraunce. The Trojan saga
         receives some apparently original additions, such as Paris' "Aunt Amaryllis"
         and a variegated Elizabethan banquet.

1594. **George Chapman, Σκιὰ νυκτός. The shadow of night: containing
         two poeticall hymnes.**
         Text, p. 200.

1594. **T. H., Oenone and Paris.**
         The earliest known full-length imitation, or rather plagiarism, of *Venus and
         Adonis*. The "T. H." who apologizes for "the first fruits of my indeuours" may
         possibly be Thomas Heywood, although nothing definite is known of him as an
         author before 1598. But it is difficult to associate what seems to be wholesale theft
         with even the early career of a man who later spoke out indignantly against
         scribblers who pilfered from him. I have not seen the poem. For comments and
         excerpts see Sotheby's catalogue of the Britwell Court Library, March 24, 1925,
         pp. 36–38; *T. L. S.*, February 19, 1925, p. 124, April 9, 1925, p. 256; *Year's
         Work in English Studies*, 1925, pp. 183–84; J. D. Parsons, *Notes and Queries*,
         CLVII (1929), 39, 325; A. M. Clark, *Thomas Heywood*, 1931, p. 8, note.

1594. **I. O., The lamentation of Troy, for the death of Hector.**
         About 200 sixain stanzas, presenting a series of Trojan characters, Priam,
         Andromache, and others, lamenting in speeches of varying length. The initial
         idea perhaps came from Seneca's *Troades* or *Iliad* xxii, xxiv; the author praises
         Homer. Details and some verbal parallels suggest that the main source was
         Lydgate's *Troy Book*. The framework—the ghost of Troy appearing in a dream—
         and the gloomy subject recall the *Mirror for Magistrates*. There is a reference to
         Astrophel and Stella. Spenser is hailed as "the only Homer liuing." The influence
         of the new mellifluous style, especially Spenser's, is quite marked in elaborate
         similes; rhythm and style in general often suggest the sixains of Lodge and
         Shakespeare. There was a ballad in 1586 called *The lamentations of Hecuba and
         ye ladies of Troye* (Rollins, *Analytical Index*, 1464).

1594. **William Shakespeare, The rape of Lucrece.**
         Text, p. 149.

1595. **R. B., Orpheus his iourney to hell and his music to the ghosts.**
         A poem of 24 pages in sixains. In general it follows the orthodox story, with
         rather more action and less decoration than the new mode prescribed. Orpheus
         sings some lyrics about love. See the note on Colse, under 1596.

1595. **Richard Barnfield, Cynthia, with certaine Sonnets and the legend of
         Cassandra.**
         The author claims *Cynthia* as the first imitation of the verse of *The Faerie
         Queene*. Using the device of the dream-vision and a variation on the judgment of
         Paris, Barnfield achieves the inevitable compliment to Elizabeth.

Cassandra is a more ambitious piece, in 78 sixain stanzas. The poet tells of Cassandra's relations with Apollo, then with Agamemnon. After the murder of the king she laments, in prison, on such topics as fortune, ambition, chastity. Finally, with a knife "her purest soule was eased." There is an obvious debt to Shakespeare, especially *Lucrece.* (For Barnfield's imitation of Shakespeare and Marlowe, see Pooler's edition of *Venus and Adonis,* pp. ix–xii; Charles Crawford, *Collectanea,* First Series, and *Notes and Queries,* Ninth Series, VIII, 217, 277.)

Much of the Trojan matter seems to be taken from the *Recuyell* (ed. Sommer, pp. 509, 526 ff., 658 ff., 667, 673). For the death of Agamemnon external probability, and some parallels in detail, favor the *Agamemnon* of Seneca.

1595. George Chapman, Ouids banquet of sence.
Text, p. 203.

1595. Michael Drayton, Endimion and Phœbe. Ideas Latmus.
Text, p. 156.

1595. Thomas Edwards, Cephalus and Procris: Narcissus.
Edited, with a very full apparatus criticus, by W. E. Buckley (Roxburghe Club, 1882). On the identity of Edwards see Mrs. Stopes, *M. L. R.,* XVI, 209. *Cephalus and Procris* was entered October 22, 1593 (*Stat. Reg.,* II, 639).

The Ovidian fables are almost lost sight of on account of Edwards' endless elaboration and fanciful additions. Aurora's wooing of Cephalus follows *Venus and Adonis.* A few details suggest a knowledge of Pettie's romantic prose version. There are also such un-Ovidian episodes as a meeting between Procris and Lamia, and an uncivil swain's somewhat violent expression of admiration when he finds Procris asleep. The story of Narcissus is padded with a long account of women's efforts to captivate him, and with discussions of love and beauty. At times both poems achieve some mild charm and grace.

Edwards' debt to his models is obvious. He salutes Spenser, Daniel, Watson, Marlowe, Shakespeare. Marlowe is his chief creditor, for luxuriant description, arguments against chastity, myth-making, and many incidental phrases. There are over forty clear echoes or imitations of Marlowe's poem, not to mention other possible ones.

1595. John Trussel, Raptus I Helenæ. The first rape of faire Hellen.
The *Stat. Reg.* (II, 296) gives *Raptus Helenæ* [,] *Helens Rape by the Athenian Duke Theseus.* Though in the meter of *Venus and Adonis* and containing phrases borrowed from it, the poem is described as a plagiarism of Shakespeare's *Lucrece* (*T. L. S.,* July 9, 1931, p. 552). For a report of a copy in Marsh's Library, Dublin, see the letters from Mr. N. B. White in *T. L. S.,* July 7, 1927, p. 472, and July 16, 1931, p. 564. The volume which contained it included a copy of *Endimion and Phœbe,* a third in addition to the two already known.

1596. Sir John Davies, Orchestra, or a poeme of dauncing.
Text, p. 185.

1596. Peter Colse, Penelopes complaint.
For the Shakespearean puzzles connected with this poem see G. B. Harrison's edition of *Willobie his Avisa* (1926) and reviews of the book; F. S. Boas, *Marlowe and His Circle,* pp. 88–89; Chambers, *William Shakespeare,* I, 570. Mr. C. Crawford (*S. P.,* Extra Series, May, 1929) gives Nicholas Breton credit for various things—Breton is "Hadrian Dorrell" of *Willobie;* Peter Colse; and the "R. B." of *Orpheus his iourney to hell* (1595).

As verse *Penelopes complaint* is sad stuff. The plan of the numerous sections, and the moralizing, are indebted to *Willobie;* the significant subtitle is "A Mirrour for wanton Minions." The Homeric story is followed, at a distance, so far as it concerns Penelope, Telemachus, the wooers, and the return of Ulysses; Penelope and the wooers are much more articulate than they are in Homer (cf. the very different *Orchestra* of Davies). The letter of Penelope in the *Heroides* is used, and one section seems to be based on the epistle from Ulysses to Penelope which Sabinus added to Ovid (Colse, ed. Grosart, pp. 177–78).

1596. The auncient historie of the destruction of Troy, newly corrected by W. Fiston.
> An edition of Caxton's *Recuyell*.

1596. Dunstan Gale, Pyramus and Thisbe.
> The dedication is dated 1596; no edition is known earlier than that of 1617. The poem is in couplets, divided into forty twelve-line stanzas. A fanciful elaboration of Ovid, describing the childhood of the lovers, the agency of Venus and Cupid, etc. I do not find any certain evidence of a relation to earlier pieces on the same theme. *Venus and Adonis* is alluded to, and Gale's lion, like the boar, only wanted a kiss. There are many echoes and imitations of Marlowe, in the description of Thisbe, in conceits, gnomic lines, etc. The poem is a feeble effort in the conventional Italianate style.

1596. Edmund Spenser, The Faerie Queene [Bks. i–vi].
Text, chapter 5. See under 1590.

1597. G. B., Ludus Scacchiæ: Chesse-play. [Anon.] Containing also a poem [a translation of the Ludus Scacchiæ of H. Vida] Written by G. B.
> Vida's poem has a mythological framework. See R. W. Bond, *Poetical Works of William Basse*, pp. xxxix–xl; Brydges, *Brit. Bibl.*, I, 382.

1597. [   ] of Loues complaint; with the legend of Orpheus and Euridice.
> Lownes, the printer, has an epistle to Anthony Gibson (see under 1599). Collier's excerpts from the piece (II, 281–84) suggest the conventional manner. Some satire on women is put in the mouth of Orpheus.

1597. Robert Parry, Sinetes passions uppon his fortunes.
> Related to the story of Sinatus, Sinorix, and Camma? See Hazlitt, p. 697. On pp. xiii ff., in his edition of Robert Chester (see under 1601), Grosart gives extracts from Parry's work.

1598. Samuel Brandon, The tragicomœdi of the vertuous Octauia [and epistles].
> Both drama and epistles (exchanged between Antony and Octavia) are among the manifestations of interest in Garnier's *Marc Antoine* displayed by the Countess of Pembroke's circle. Daniel's *Cleopatra* had appeared in 1594.
> The epistles derive of course from Ovid, and more directly from Drayton. Brandon lacks dignity of feeling and style; his Octavia seldom rises above tedious moralizing and shrill nagging.

1598. Christopher Marlowe, Hero and Leander.
> The earliest known edition of Marlowe's fragment. See under 1593.

1598. George Chapman, Hero and Leander.
> An edition of Marlowe's fragment, with Chapman's continuation. Text, p. 205.

1598. John Marston, The metamorphosis of Pigmalions image; and certaine satyres.
Text, p. 177.

1598. Henry Petowe, The second part of Hero and Leander.
> A curious continuation of Marlowe. Petowe states, whether on good authority or not, that Marlowe's work was interrupted by his sudden death. A good part of the poem as well as the preface is taken up with mingled self-depreciation and praise of Marlowe. Petowe professes, doubtless with the license allowed romancers,

to have been "inriched by a Gentleman a friend of mine, with the true Italian discourse, of those Louers further Fortunes." The story is a mosaic of well-worn motives of chivalric romance; after a lifetime of felicity the pair undergo an Ovidian metamorphosis. There is an abundance of romantic rhetoric, drawn largely from Tottel's *Miscellany* (see Rollins' edition of Tottel, II, 112 ff.). There are echoes of Marlowe, a few of *Venus and Adonis;* the idea of Venus' anger at Hero may have come from the tale of Cupid and Psyche, to which Petowe elsewhere alludes. The poem is reprinted in L. Chabalier, *Héro et Léandre* (1911). Extracts are given in Rollins, in Dyce's edition of Marlowe (1858, pp. 398–401); I used the Bodleian copy of Petowe. For a sketch of chapbooks in a similar vein see A. T. Crathern, *M. L. N.,* XLVI (1931), 382.

1598. **Thomas Powell, Loues leprosie.**

Reprinted by Rimbault, *Ancient Poetical Tracts* (Percy Society, 1842). About 320 ll. in couplets, on the love of Achilles for Polyxena and his death at the hands of Paris. Based probably on Caxton or Lydgate; the style is suggestive of Lydgate on stilts. Along with aureate diction we have (p. 73) at least one distinct echo of *Hero and Leander* (ii. 9, etc.).

1599. **Samuel Daniel, A letter from Octauia to Marcus Antonius.**

Much superior to Brandon's epistles, which may have given Daniel some hints. There is not lacking the note of sober moral earnestness so characteristic of Daniel. A phrase in the argument may be echoed in *Antony and Cleopatra,* I. ii. 125–26; see *T. L. S.,* November 20, 1924, p. 776.

1599. **Anthony Gibson, A womans woorth, defended against all the men in the world.**

The large claims of the title-page are perhaps slightly weakened by addresses to various Maids of Honor, including Mistress Fitton. The book is translated from the French of the Chevalier de l'Escale (A. M. Clark, *Thomas Heywood,* p. 97). Some seventy authorities are named, from Orpheus to Bandello. The thesis is proved with many brief anecdotes or sayings about Penthesilea, Dido, etc. The section on beauty has a speech by Leander to Hero. Gibson praises Spenser and Daniel.

1599. **R. Linche, The fountaine of ancient fiction.**
Text, p. 32, and Scott, p. 76.

1599. **Thomas Moffett (Moufat, etc.), The silkewormes, and their flies.**

A long didactic poem on silkworms, clothes, etc., dedicated to the Countess of Pembroke by a well-known physician attached to her circle. An inset story, in twenty-three stanzas, tells of Pyramus and Thisbe; it seems to be a paraphrase, sometimes close, sometimes free, of Ovid. A marginal note on the metamorphosis refers to Natalis Comes. Extracts are given by M. L. Farrand, "An Additional Source for 'A Midsummer-Night's Dream,'" *S. P.,* XXVII (1930), 233 ff. I have not found evidence of such a Shakespearean relationship as Miss Farrand urges; see *M. L. N.,* XLVI, 144–47.

1599. **Thomas Nashe, Nashes Lenten stuffe.**
Text, p. 288.

1600. **Englands Helicon.**

The golden treasury of Elizabethan pastoral poetry contains Constable's piece (see next item) and many mythological-pastoral poems.

1600. **Henry Constable, The sheepheards song of Venus and Adonis.**

This lyrical poem has a special interest in view of the verbal parallels between it and Shakespeare's narrative. The date of composition is unknown. Most Shakespearean commentators have thought Constable the debtor (see the editions of Shakespeare's poems by Wyndham, Lee, Pooler, Feuillerat). Mr. Carleton

Brown (Tudor ed., pp. xi–xii) gives reasons for the contrary view. It would seem more natural for a short piece to summarize and echo a long one than for such an elaborate narrative as *Venus and Adonis* to be developed out of a lyrical pastoral. At any rate Constable's title and manner remind us that the theme belongs to the pastoral tradition. His "orped Swine," by the way, is doubtless from Golding (ed. Rouse, p. 170, l. 526).

1600. **F. L., Ovidius Naso his remedie of love.**

Described by Collier, III, 95. In addition to a freely expanded version of Ovid's poem, there is a translation of the Ovidian epistle of Dido to Aeneas and an answer to it. The answer is said to be the work of "the thrice renowned Sapho of our times," a phrase which suggests the Countess of Pembroke. But it is subscribed "Tout Seule," and the Countess did not become a widow until 1601.

1600. **Thomas Middleton, The ghost of Lucrece.**

A continuation of Shakespeare's poem, in the same stanza. It was discovered in 1920. See H. C. Bartlett, p. 158; *T. L. S.,* February 27, 1920, p. 144.

1600. **Samuel Nicholson, Acolastus his after-witte.**

Described by Collier (III, 58) as a pastoral poem with flagrant plagiarisms from *Venus and Adonis, Lucrece,* some of Shakespeare's plays, and from other authors. See Carpenter, *Reference Guide to Spenser,* p. 247; H. C. Bartlett, p. 158.

1600. **Cyril Tourneur, The transformed metamorphosis.**

Reprinted in *Plays and Poems of Tourneur* (ed. J. C. Collins, 1878, II, 169 ff.); I have not been able to consult Mr. Nicoll's edition, Fanfrolico Press, 1930. It may be mentioned here on account of its use of mythology, but it is perhaps the most harsh and obscure of Elizabethan satires, and need not be discussed. It seems to deal with the fear caused by papal machinations, with the later career of Essex, and other political and general topics, all in a hideous jargon.

1600. **John Weever, Faunus and Melliflora; or, the original of our English satyres.**

A recently discovered work, thus described in *T. L. S.,* June 12, 1924, p. 376: "It is the story, in rhyming couplets, of the loves of Faunus, son of Picus, the second King of Laurentes, and Melliflora, one of Diana's nymphs. Diana, in revenge for the desertion of her nymph, turns their son into a satyr. Brutus, when landing at Dover, is credited with having brought with him some satyrs, who, after running wild in Kent," " 'proved full stout hardy knights . . . As Spencer shewes.' " The subject matter, as thus outlined, suggests imitation of Warner as well as Spenser.

1600. **E. W[ilkinson] his Thameseidos.**

A pastoral-mythological-topographical poem which "may have imitated Spenser and influenced Drayton" (H. Taylor, *Topographical Poetry in England during the Renaissance, University of Chicago Abstracts of Theses, Humanistic Series,* V, 1926–27, 493–97). It tells of Neptune's unsuccessful pursuit of the chaste "Thamesis," and the ravishing of her nymph Medway by a satyr, etc.

1601. **Robert Chester, Loues Martyr; or, Rosalins complaint.**

Ed. Grosart, 1878. The piece opens with a half-medieval assembly of the gods. A very Italianate anatomical catalogue is put in the mouth of Dame Nature, who prays to Jove. See Irma R. White, *T. L. S.,* July 21, 1932, p. 532.

1602. **Francis Beaumont (?), Salmacis and Hermaphroditus.** Text, p. 180.

1602. **The metamorphosis of tabacco.**

Reprinted in Collier, *Illustrations of Early English Popular Literature,* and *Poems of Sir John Beaumont,* ed. Grosart (1869), pp. 275–321. The attribution to

Beaumont is doubtful. The poem is apparently accepted as Beaumont's by R. J. Kane, *Tobacco in English Literature to 1700 (Harvard University Summaries of Theses, 1929,* p. 163). A framework of pseudo-Ovidian myth is used for a light-hearted eulogy of tobacco. Cf. Brathwait, under 1617.

1603. **Hugh Holland, Pancharis.**

A piece in *terza rima*, reprinted in Collier, *Illustrations of Old English Literature,* II. Katharine, widow of Henry V, was so good that Diana came down to Windsor to see her. Venus also paid a visit, but was refused admittance. The rest of the poem tells how Venus and Cupid contrived to make the queen fall in love with Owen Tudor, and it ends with an Ovidian account of the elements reduced to order by Love. Chaucer and Lydgate are referred to (p. 34). A tree-list (pp. 20–21) perhaps alludes to Spenser's February eclogue. (For some lines by Holland in praise of Spenser, see H. E. Sandison, *M. L. N.,* XLIV, 161.) A debate on the relative happiness of maid, wife, and widow (pp. 38 ff.) was doubtless imitated from the playlet by Sir John Davies which was produced in 1602 and included in the 1608 edition of the *Poetical Rhapsody* (ed. Rollins, 1931, I, 247).

1606? **Michael Drayton, Poemes lyrick and pastorall: odes, eglogs, the man in the moone.**
Text, p. 163.

1607. **William Barksted, Mirrha the mother of Adonis, with certain eclogs by L. M[achin].**
Text, p. 183.

1607. **W. N., Barley-breake, or a warning for wantons.**

Ed. Grosart, 1877. A pastoral of native and old-fashioned flavor. The girl Euphema plays at barley-break with her friends. Old Elpin, disliking the freedoms of young Streton, calls her away, and later, as a warning, tells her the story of Jupiter and Callisto, in about 230 lines. The author follows Ovid in the main, though he had read Warner's version (see text, p. 65), to which he alludes. Euphema is deaf to the cautionary tale and is betrayed by Streton. When she returns in the same condition as Callisto, Elpin dies, and she stabs herself. Streton, pursued by wild beasts, finds his victim, while birds and beasts crowd around. One bird cries "A rope!" another "Goe hang thee in thy garters!" This last suggestion is followed, and Streton is finished by the birds and flies.

1607. **Richard Niccols, The cuckow.**

Fifty-one pages, in couplets, describe the birth of Flora; a gathering of birds to welcome Lady Ver; a contest between the "cuckow," which has sung unchaste songs, and Philomel or Casta, whose themes have been innocent. The contest takes place in a "bower of blisse" thronged by nymphs, ladies, knights, the chief member of the last group being "Vanitie," who is the favorite of the mistress of the bower. In this belated treatment of medieval motives, Philomel tells, in over forty lines, the story of her ravishment. The book has an allusion to Spenser's squire who had such a long search for a chaste woman; and there are other Spenserian echoes. See Carpenter, *Reference Guide,* p. 246; Brydges, *Restituta,* II, 1 ff.; Collier, *Catalogue of Bridgewater House,* p. 220.

1608. **W. Bettie, The historie of Titana and Theseus.**

I have not seen the piece. Chambers (*William Shakespeare,* I, 363) says that Titania is not a fairy but a mortal princess.

1609. **F. Baconi De sapientia veterum liber.**
Text, p. 240.

1609. **Thomas Heywood, Troia Britanica, or Great Britaines Troy.**
Text, p. 187.

1609. Edmund Spenser, Two cantos of mutabilitie.
Text, p. 117, and see index.

1610. Giles Fletcher, Christs victorie, and triumph.
Text, p. 165.

1611. Richard Brathwait, The golden fleece.
A sermon in verse, of about thirty-six pages, "shadowing under this title of Golden Fleece, the reward of a sincere and prouident pilgrim, who with Iason endureth patiently the surging Sea of persecution . . . " Appended elegies on Narcissus and Aeson are cautionary tales based on Ovid.

1611. George Chapman, The Iliads of Homer.
First complete edition.

1611. Sir David Murray, The tragicall death of Sophonisba.
Reprinted by the Bannatyne Club, Edinburgh, 1823. Murray evidently took his subject matter from Painter's *Palace of Pleasure,* since the version of Bandello in Painter contains moralizing and rhetorical elements which are absent from Livy's brief account (Livy, bk. xxx, cc. 13–15; Painter, ii. 7, vol. II, pp. 236 ff., in Jacobs' ed.). (Bandello, by the way, had followed Livy and the fifth book of Petrarch's *Africa;* see *M. L. N.,* XXXII, 374–75, *M. L. R.,* XX, 191, and XXI, 195.) Murray's twelve hundred lines have a minimum of action and maximum of rhetoric. As befitted both a "Scoto-Brittaine" and a tutor of royalty, Murray was one of the wiser sort who preferred Shakespeare's *Lucrece* to *Venus and Adonis,* and he faithfully follows his model.

1611. Sands Penven, Ambitions scourge, described in the morall fiction of Ixyon.
Hazlitt, p. 453. I have not seen this work, but the title is equally suggestive and satisfying.

1606– William Basse, Urania.
1612. Text, p. 190.

1612– Michael Drayton, Polyolbion.
1622. Text, p. 164, note.

1612. "A booke to be prynted when it is translated and further Alowed. Called. *Les Metamorphoses, D' Ovide De nouueau traduytes en Ffrancois* avec. *xv. Discours. Contenans L'explication Morales Des fables."*
Stat. Reg., III, 489. I do not know any record of the book's being published.

1612. The passionate pilgrime.
See index.

1613. H. A. (editor?), The scourge of Venus.
Ed. Grosart, 1876. Another version of the story of Myrrha. For a clearing-up of the uncritical legend which made "H. A." the Austin whom Heywood denounced for stealing his translations of the *Ars Amatoria* and *De Remedio Amoris,* see A. M. Clark, "Thomas Heywood's 'Art of Love,'" *Library,* Fourth Series, III (1923), 210 ff.
The 161 six-line stanzas are abundantly padded with dialogue, soliloquy, and psychological analysis of prolix simplicity. The author is not averse to lingering over erotic details, but amply atones by referring to "God's holy Bible" and by expressing horror. The opening lines reveal a debt to *Venus and Adonis,* and the whole poem, wherever it sticks to Ovid, is full of phrases from the useful Golding. It is said to have first appeared in 1613, though the edition of 1614 is the earliest extant; it was, unaccountably, reprinted in 1620.

1613. William Browne, Britannia's pastorals [bk. i].
Text, p. 172.

1613– Thomas Milles, The treasurie of auncient and moderne times.
1619. An immense prose miscellany compiled from Mexia and similar sources. There
are classical stories without end. Chapter 33, in the fourth book, rejects the view
that the Trojan matter is fabulous, and appeals to the eyewitnesses Dares and
Dictys, as well as to Homer, Herodotus, Euclid. Skeptics are advised to visit the
ruins of Troy.

1613. S[amuel] P[age], The love of Amos and Laura.
This non-classical poem (of which the second edition, 1619, was dedicated to
Izaak Walton) is included here because of its wholesale plagiarism from *Hero
and Leander*. The chief matter of the piece is based on Leander's pleading; there
are the usual decorative imitations, and dozens of lines echo Marlowe. *Venus and
Adonis* also receives some attention.

1614. George Chapman, Andromeda liberata. Or the nuptials of Perseus
and Andromeda.
Text, p. 212.

1614. The life and death of Hector.
A modernization, in thirty thousand lines, of Lydgate's *Troy Book*. The attribution to Thomas Heywood has been thoroughly disposed of (J. S. P. Tatlock,
P. M. L. A., XXX, 691 ff.; A. M. Clark, *T. L. S.*, October 2, 1924, p. 612; *Thomas
Heywood*, pp. 340–41; C. A. Rouse, *P. M. L. A.*, XLIII, 1928, 779 ff.). To
mention only one detail which will illustrate the degree of the writer's literacy,
he refers to Petrarch as "Patricke Franke." Now Heywood was the first Englishman to quote the Italian text of Dante (*S. P.*, XX, 176), and he mentions
Petrarch several times (*S. P., loc. cit.*, and *Exemplary Lives*, p. 99, "the famous
Italian Poet, Francis Petrarch." The *Life and Death* is cheap hack work, but its
appearance tells something about popular taste.

1614– J. M., The newe metamorphosis.
1615? A huge unpublished MS, described, with extracts, by Mr. J. H. H. Lyon,
A Study of The Newe Metamorphosis (Columbia University Press, 1919). It was
begun in 1600 and apparently completed about 1614–15. Mr. Lyon is inclined
to assign the work to Gervase Markham.
It is an extraordinary jumble which "mingles classical figures and motifs with
medieval legends, with metrical romances, with the ribald jests of the *fabliau*,
with the witchcraft theme, and with the erotic and intricate intrigue of the
novelle" (Lyon, p. 34). The author's first intention, a pseudo-Ovidian framework,
gave way to other devices as he proceeded. A number of poets, such as Sidney and
Spenser, are laid under contribution, and *Venus and Adonis* is paralleled "with
some closeness."

1615. Richard Brathwait, Loves labyrinth, or the true lovers knot.
In *A Strappado for the Diuell*, ed. Ebsworth (1878), pp. 252 ff. This very long
poem deals with "the disastrous fals of two star-crost Louers Pyramus & Thysbe."
"Varietie of inuention," if not "proprietie of passion," fills about twenty-three
hundred lines. Among un-Ovidian episodes is a meeting between Thisbe and
Silvanus, who is a sort of Comus; on her refusing his offers, he asks how a
vestal comes to be roaming in the gloaming, and later sends a lion after her.
The chief embellishment is rhetoric. "Thysbe address'd to die, yet long in dying,"
addresses everything in sight, and when her breath has happily departed ten
more pages are devoted to lamentations from wood-nymphs and parents.
Erotic pieces in the same volume (*The Ciuill Deuill, Frankes Anatomie, The
Wooer*) contain clear echoes of *Hero and Leander*, but Brathwait's talent was too
pedestrian and slipshod to learn much from Marlowe. In *Loves labyrinth* he could
catch the note of Leander's argument, could strew mythological conceits and

gnomic lines everywhere, but these things had become commonplaces. (Hero is mentioned on p. 303; and see pp. 88–89.) Some faint echoes of *Venus and Adonis* appear in the first two of the erotic pieces mentioned, and perhaps in the long poem. In *The English Gentlewoman* (ed. 1641, p. 349), among his precepts for female conduct, Brathwait includes an injunction against reading about Venus and Adonis.

The *Strappado* contains also *The Epistle of Hyppolitus unto Phedra*, in the semi-Ovidian fashion revived by Drayton. Ovid had neglected to write a *suasoria* in favor of chastity, and Brathwait's hero seems to owe something to Seneca's play. His notes in the volume refer twice to Senecan drama, though not to the *Hippolytus*. Cf., in this Appendix, John Shepery's Latin piece of 1586.

1615? **George Chapman, Homers Odysses.**
First complete edition.

1615. **T[homas] E[vans], Œdipus: Three cantoes. Wherein is contained: 1. His unfortunate infancy. 2. His execrable actions. 3. His lamentable end.**
Palmer, p. 100; Collier, I, 321, and *Catalogue of Bridgewater House*, p. 115.

1616. **George Chapman, The divine poem of Musaeus.**
Text, p. 210.

1617. **That which seems best is worst. Juvenals tenth satyre: with Virginias death. By W. B[arksted?].**
Text, p. 185, note.

1617. **R. Brathwait, The smoaking age.**
The section called "The Birth of Tobacco" uses mythology in the manner of the work which doubtless inspired his own, the *Metamorphosis of Tobacco* of 1602. "Tobacco" is an illegitimate son of Bacchus and Proserpine, who is changed by Jove into a plant and by Pluto banished from Hades to earth, where he receives his bad name, derived from that of his father. Brathwait's sentiments are in harmony with his royal master's, and contrary to those of the *Metamorphosis*. See Matthew W. Black, *Richard Brathwait* (Philadelphia, 1928), p. 70.

1617. **Leonard Digges, The rape of Proserpine. Translated out of Claudian in Latine, into English verse.**
In dedicating the poem to his sister, Digges remarks that it was intended for her "as a Patterne for a piece of Needle-work," for which no poet would be more suggestive than Claudian. The translation sometimes becomes free elaboration, especially in picture-making. Thus two lines (i. 257–58) are expanded into nearly twenty, and into the embroidery are woven the story of Narcissus and "the thorne-prick't goddesse loue to Adon." The Elizabethan luxuriance is not unattractive.

The three prose prefaces set forth a threefold allegory, historical, natural, allegorical, in the manner of the *Ovide moralisé*, etc. They are taken, with hardly any alteration, and without acknowledgment, from the Italian (*Il Ratto di Proserpina di Claudiano da Giovan Domenico Bevilacqua in ottaua rima tradotto . . . Con gli argomenti, & Allegorie di Antonino Cingale. Palermo, MDLXXXVI*).

1617. **Dunstan Gale, Pyramus and Thisbe.**
See under 1596.

1618. **J. Brinsley, Ouids Metamorphosis *tr.* grammatically, etc.**
A school version, mentioned here because of its didactic and allegorical notes. See G. W. McClelland, *Schelling Anniversary Papers* (1923), pp. 189 ff., 207.

1618. **James Shirley, Ecc[h]o and Narcissus.**
Stat. Reg., III, 618. Text, p. 195.

1619. The wisedome of the ancients. *Tr.* Sir A. Gorges.
Translation of Bacon's work of 1609.

1619. Henry Hutton, Follie's anatomie: or satyres and satyricall epigrams.
Reprinted by Percy Society, 1842. The volume contains "a compendious History of Ixion's Wheele" which is of some slight interest as regards the beginnings of mythological travesties. The piece is in much the same style as the satires, so that, though not strictly a burlesque, it often reads like one:
> Hermes did trudge, a iolly foote-mans pase,
> T'inuite the Rectors of the Spheres sublime.

The whole poem is gritty with legal jargon. The end is didactic. There is a conventional Shakespearean allusion—"chast Adonis blush"—and a possible echo of Marlowe in the lines "The modest queen . . . " (p. 51).

1620. The destruction of Troy. *Tr.* out of the second booke of the Aeneads by Sir T. Wrothe.
Quite free and un-Virgilian, according to Collier, IV, 290.

1621. R. Brathwait, Natures embassie.
Ed. Ebsworth (1877). The book contains a series of didactic satires, or partly satirical sermons, attached to mythological figures, and modeled perhaps on Bacon's *De Sapientia Veterum*. Through the "deuine Morals" embodied in fable "the very heathen Poets" taught virtue and reproved vice (p. 31).
There follow three "funerall Elegies, concerning sundry exquisite Mirrours of true loue," namely, Hero and Leander, Pyramus and Thisbe, and Dido. The first reveals a trace of Marlowe, and echoes a couplet from Chapman's continuation (Sest. iii, ll. 231–32). The account of Dido uses Virgil and Ovid. Moral lessons are summarized at the end.
Another series of mythological satires follows the same plan as the first. The array of authorities is as heterogeneous as ever, including Gregory's commentary on *Job*, Boethius, Alanus de Insulis. All the pieces are old-fashioned.

1621. George Sandys, Ovid's Metamorphosis.
The first five books. No copy extant. See Hazlitt, p. 430; Brydges, *Censura Lit.*, VI, 132.

1622. Patrick Hannay, The nightingale. Sheretine and Mariana, etc.
Reprinted in *Minor Caroline Poets*, I. Preceding the 1,680 lines of *Philomela* is the calm statement that it "is to be sung (by those that please) to the tune set down before in the frontispiece." There is abundant padding, though actual departures from Ovid's story are slight. The opening recalls Gascoigne's tale. Nearly a hundred lines describe the mythological pictures in Philomela's gown. The general style suggests Turberville, and the structure of the stanza is an invitation to bathos which the poet commonly accepts. But, in this poem and *Sheretine*, there are echoes of Marlowe: e.g., p. 626, ll. 361–62; p. 627, l. 432; p. 663, l. 169; p. 665, ll. 269–70. Cf. Marlowe, i. 184, ii. 8–9, i. 428, i. 167–68. For a probable allusion to *Venus and Adonis*, see p. 633, ll. 929 ff.

ca.   On a manuscript, which Mr. Candy has ascribed to Milton, containing stanzas
1623? about Ovidian engravings, see text, p. 252, note.

1624. Thomas Heywood, Γυναιϰεῖον.
Text, pp. 190, 242.

1626? (pub. 1651). William Bosworth, The chast and lost lovers . . . Arcadius and Sepha.
Text, p. 193.

1626. James Gresham, The picture of incest.
Ed. Grosart, 1876. Over seven hundred lines, in couplets, on the story of Myrrha. A number of phrases establish one more debt to Golding. The poem

follows Ovid more closely than its predecessors of 1607 and 1613, though speeches are expanded and decorative details added. Gnomic lines are frequent enough to satisfy the moral sense. The most obvious characteristic of Gresham's style is the use of compound epithets, which are of varying success—"her azure-veyned necke"; "sence-delighting-rare-delitiousnesse"; "tree-chang'd-mothers-barke."

1626. George Sandys, Ovid's Metamorphosis.

1628. The true history of the tragicke loves of Hipolito and Isabella, Neapolitans. Englished.

> Taken from *Histoire des tragiques Amours d'Hipolite et d'Isabelle,* 1597 (A. H. Upham, *French Influence,* p. 369). The work, which I have not seen, included "the tale of Narcissus out of Ovid's third booke of his Metamorphosis."

1628. Phineas Fletcher, Venus and Anchises (Brittain's Ida).

> Text, p. 167. A slip in *S. T. C.* assigns the poem to Giles Fletcher the younger.

1628. Henry Reynolds, T. Tassos Aminta. Englisht. To this is added Ariadne's complaint in imitation of Anguillara.

> Reynolds, the friend of Drayton, supplies a close link with the Italianate Ovid. *Ariadne's Complaint* is a paraphrase of one of the interpolated passages in Anguillara's "translation" of the *Metamorphoses* (bk. viii, pp. 136 ff., in edition published at Venice, 1575). Anguillara apparently developed his story from the epistle in the *Heroides,* and the episode of Bacchus in the *Fasti* (iii. 459–516), perhaps drawing also upon the *Ars Amatoria* (i. 527 ff.) and the tale of Olimpia in Ariosto. For details see *M. L. N.,* XLI (1926), 510. Cf. *Narcissus,* below, under 1632.

1632. Martin Parker, The nightingale warbling forth her owne disaster, or, the rape of Philomela.

> The man destined to be a popular laureate here essays a literary flight, and commendatory verses, more candid than tactful, express surprise at the erudition displayed. But, though a detail or two may have come from Ovid, the piece is almost wholly a versification of Pettie's prose tale. For details see *M. L. N.,* XL, 486–88. The bird's singing to the poet in a grove recalls the poems of Gascoigne and Hannay on the same theme. Daniel Price, author of one of the commendatory pieces, died in 1631; see *D. N. B.*

1632. Henry Reynolds, Mythomystes . . . The tale of Narcissus.

> *Mythomystes* was entered and presumably printed in 1632. Reynolds says the poem on Narcissus was "diuerse yeares since, put into English," and that he has paraphrased Ovid "after my owne way," but this piece also is a more or less free paraphrase of Anguillara. Reynolds is at least quite successful in reproducing in English the liquid movement of the Italian. Ovid's 170 lines (*Metam.* iii. 341–510) become 504 in Italian, 448 in English. *Narcissus* was reprinted in *Englische Studien,* XXXV (1905), 260 ff., and in the Orinda Booklets (J. R. Tutin, Hull, 1906).
>
> The poem is appended to *Mythomystes* as an illustration of Reynolds' mystical and allegorical theory of poetry. He expounds the geographical, physical, moral, and divine senses of the allegory in the medieval manner of a seventeenth-century Platonist and Cabbalist. See text, p. 243.

1632. George Sandys, Ovid's Metamorphosis Englished, mythologiz'd, and represented in figures. An essay to the translation of Virgil's Æneis. Text, p. 243, and see index.

1633. Abraham Cowley, Poetical blossomes. Text, p. 196.

1637. Thomas Heywood, Pleasant dialogues and dramma's.
Text, pp. 190, 243.

1637. Shakerley Marmion, A morall poem, intituled the legend of Cupid and Psyche.
Text, p. 231.

1637. John Milton, A maske [Comus] presented at Ludlow Castle, 1634.
Text, pp. 258, 264.

1638. John Milton, Lycidas.
Text, p. 263.

1639. Jean Ogier de Gombauld, Endimion. An excellent fancy, interpreted by R. Hurst.

> The plot of this once popular *roman à clef* makes Keats's poem seem meager. Incidentally, we have here an aërial voyage, and Endymion, though devoted to Diana, stirred by the appearance of a mortal maiden whom he had seen before. Rossetti had a copy, and supposed that "Keats had probably never seen it. If he had, he might really have taken a hint or two for his scheme, which is hardly so clear even as Gombauld's, though its endless digressions teem with beauty" (A letter quoted in Hall Caine, *Recollections of D. G. Rossetti*, London, 1882, p. 181). See the poem of Henry Vaughan, *Works*, ed. L. C. Martin, I, 48.

1639. George Rivers, The heroinæ: or the lives of Arria, Paulina, Lucrecia, Dido, etc.

> A prose work dedicated to Lady Dorothy Sidney. The story of Lucrece employs Augustine's famous argument. That of Dido is quite un-Virgilian, and Rivers vindicates her honor by showing that Virgil's matter was fabulous. Each tale is followed by arguments pro and con regarding the problem involved (cf. G. Pettie, in 1576). Verbal quotations show a debt to Heywood's *Gunaikeion* (pp. 128–30) for the story of Aretaphila; Heywood also (p. 152) had given references for the un-Virgilian account of Dido, etc.

1640 or earlier? James Smith, The innovation of Penelope and Ulysses.
Burlesque. Pub. 1658. Text, p. 289.

1640. Thomas Heywood, The exemplary lives and memorable acts of nine the most worthy women of the world.
Text, p. 190, note.

Before 1642. Sidney Godolphin, [A translation of part or all of *Aen.* iv].
Text, p. 233.

1642. Sir Francis Kynaston, Leoline and Sydanis.

> *Minor Caroline Poets*, II, 70 ff. This non-classical poem is mentioned on account of its abundant mythology and its echoes of Marlowe. E.g., cf. p. 72, ll. 92 ff. (the enamorment), with Marlowe, i. 91–96, 157 ff.; p. 113, l. 1720, with Marlowe, i. 338; etc. Finsler (*Homer in der Neuzeit*, p. 282) remarks: "Für die Trojasage verweist Kynaston ausdrücklich auf Dares." There is an occasional echo of Spenser.

1645. John Milton, Poems, both English and Latin.

1646. J. Shirley, Narcissus.
See under 1618.

1647. Thomas Stanley, Poems and translations.

    The volume contained translations from Theocritus, Ausonius, etc., reprinted in 1651.

1647. Sir Robert Stapylton, Musaeus on the loves of Hero and Leander.

    This formal translation may be mentioned because, while the author does not seem to have known Marlowe—at any rate does not mention or echo him—he frequently echoes Chapman's translation of 1616. Natalis Comes is quoted in the notes. The volume also contained versions of the two epistles of Ovid on Hero and Leander.

1648. Sir Richard Fanshawe, Il Pastor Fido . . . with an addition of divers other poems.

    The volume contained a translation of *Aen.* iv. Text, p. 233.

1649. Robert Baron, An apologie for Paris.

    Ninety-six pages of prose tell of the judgment of Paris in the vein of pastoral romance. There is a long prose version of the story in a French Ovid of 1539 (above, p. 50, note 7), pp. 9–24; though Baron does not seem to owe anything specific to it he may have used it or some similar elaboration. His particular figures for the forces of Greeks and Trojans testify to the spirit of Dictys and Dares (the figures differ in many books; cf. Burton, *Anatomy,* Bohn's Popular Library, I, 59). Apart from quotations the tale has obvious echoes of Warner, *Venus and Adonis, Henry IV,* Pt. I, etc.

    Baron's notorious piece of plagiarism, *The Cyprian Academy* (1647), had contained abundant mythology, including pictures of Daphne and Apollo, Venus and Adonis, Hero and Leander.

1651. William Bosworth, Arcadius and Sepha.
    See under 1626.

1651. Thomas Hall, Wisdoms conquest, or, an explanation of the thirteenth book of Ovids Metamorphoses, containing that curious and rhetoricall contest between Ajax and Ulysses, for Achilles armour: where is set forth to the life the power of valour, and the prevalence of eloquence.

    An edifying work by a schoolmaster, citing such authorities as Sabinus, Golding, Sandys. "The scope and drift of this Fable and fiction is, to shew the folly of those, who preferre Strength before Policy, Warriours before Scholars, and Weapons before Wisdome," etc. See under 1655.

1651. The lovs of Hero and Leander.
    Travesty. Text, p. 290.

1651. Sir Edward Sherburne, Salmacis . . . the rape of Helen, etc.
    Text, p. 237.

1651. Thomas Stanley, Anacreon. Bion. Moschus, etc.
    Text, p. 236, and see under 1647.

1652. The gallery of heroick women. Written in French by Peter Le Moyne, of the Society of Jesus. *Tr.* into English by the Marquesse of Winchester.

    A collection of tales, with moral reflections, from *La Gallerie des Femmes Fortes,* Paris, 1647. Among the classical heroines are Panthea, Camma, Artemisia, Zenobia, Lucrece, etc.

1655. Thomas Hall, Phaetons folly, or, the downfal of pride: being a translation of the second book of Ovids Metamorphosis . . . where is lively

set forth the danger of pride and rashness, with the safety of moderation . . .
> A schoolbook, with moral lessons. Natalis Comes is referred to.

1655. The rape of Lucrece, committed by Tarquin the sixt; and the remarkable judgments that befel him for it. By . . . Will. Shakespeare gent. Whereunto is annexed, the banishment of Tarquin: or, the reward of lust. By J. Quarles.
> Hazlitt, pp. 493, 546; Collier, III, 252; H. C. Bartlett, pp. 8–9.

1658. N. Billingsley, ΚΟΣΜΟΒΡΕΦΙΑ, or the infancy of the world . . . with a taste of poetical fictions.
> The latter section is an ample taste in the form of a series of poems on Jupiter, Apollo, and other mythological figures, apparently based on Cartari or some such book. One religious poem, *Genethliacon*, seems to be an imitation of Milton's *Nativity*.

1658. The passion of Dido for Æneas, translated by Edmund Waller and Sidney Godolphin.
> Text, p. 233, note.

1658. John Jones, Ovid's invective or curse against Ibis . . . translated . . . and the histories therein contained . . . briefly explained . . . with natural, moral, poetical, political, mathematical, and some few theological applications.
> A number of interpretations are taken from Natalis Comes. Sandys is sometimes cited, and his explanation of the tale of Tereus and Progne is used (see text, p. 57, note). It was presumably the same Jones who translated *Hero and Leander* (*Notes and Queries*, Third Series, VII, 435).

1658. James Smith, The innovation of Penelope and Ulysses.
> Burlesque. See under 1640.

1660. Philander, The history of Tarquin and Lucretia.
> Hazlitt, p. 456.

1664. Charles Cotton, Scarronides; or Virgile travestie.
> Text, p. 291.

1664. James Scudamore, Homer à la mode.
> Travesty. Text, p. 292.

1665. Charles Cotton, Scarronides.
> Including travesty of *Aen.* iv.

1665. Lanii triumphantes, or the butchers prize. Being a description of the famous battel, between Achilles, a butcher of Greece, and Hector, a weaver of Troy, occasion'd by the rape of a daughty damosell y-clep'd Hellen the bright.
> Obviously a travesty. The title is quoted from Catalogue No. 265, Pt. x, of Pickering & Chatto (item 8497).

1665. R. Mounsey, Scarronides: or, Virgil travestie.
> Text, p. 292. Hazlitt, p. 403.

1665. Typhon, or the gyants war with the gods.
> Travesty. Text, p. 292.

1667. John Milton, Paradise lost.
Text, chapter 15.

1669. W. Wycherley (?), Hero and Leander.
Travesty. Text, p. 292.

1671. John Milton, Paradise regained: Samson Agonistes.
Text, chapter 15.

1672. Cataplus, or Aeneas his descent into hell.
Travesty.

1672. Chaucer's ghoast: or, a piece of antiquity. Containing twelve pleasant fables of Ovid penn'd after the ancient manner of writing in England. Which makes them prove mock-poems to the present poetry . . . By a lover of antiquity.
The tales are those of Pygmalion; Actaeon; Jupiter, Juno, and Tiresias; Apollo and Coronis, etc. This precious lover of antiquity should have been haunted by the ghosts of both Chaucer and Gower, for the tales are lifted from the *Confessio Amantis* "with few and slight modernizations, but enough to render them easily intelligible" (Lounsbury, *Studies in Chaucer*, III, 118–19). See Caroline Spurgeon, *Five Hundred Years of Chaucer Criticism and Allusion*, I, 248.

1672. John Phillips, The Maronides, or Virgil travesty.
A translation of the fifth book of Scarron; followed in 1673 by a translation of the sixth. Text, p. 292.

1673. Ovidius exulans.
Travesty. Text, p. 292.

1675. Charles Cotton, The scoffer scofft.
Travesty. Text, p. 292.

1680. The wits paraphras'd.
Travesty. Text, p. 293.

1680. Alexander Radcliffe, Ovid travestie.
Text, p. 293.

BIBLIOGRAPHY

BIBLIOGRAPHY

Authorities and references cited in the text and footnotes constitute of course only a small part of the relevant material consulted, and the following bibliography is almost wholly limited to a selection from those citations. References pertaining to more than one chapter are mostly assembled in the first general section.

I may here go through the formality of giving a list of the abbreviations used in notes, appendix, and bibliography:

E. E. T. S., Early English Text Society; *J. E. G. P., Journal of English and Germanic Philology; M. L. N., Modern Language Notes; M. L. R., Modern Language Review; M. P., Modern Philology; P. M. L. A., Publications of the Modern Language Association of America; P. Q., Philological Quarterly; R. E. S., Review of English Studies; S. P., Studies in Philology; S. T. C., Short-Title Catalogue* (see below, Alfred W. Pollard); *T. L. S., London Times Literary Supplement.*

GENERAL

Flora R. Amos, *Early Theories of Translation.* Columbia University Press, 1920.

The Golden Asse of Apuleius, trans. William Adlington, ed. Thomas Seccombe. New York, 1913.

Lodovico Ariosto, *Orlando Furioso,* ed. S. Debenedetti. Bari, 1928.

English Works of Roger Ascham, ed. W. A. Wright. Cambridge University Press, 1904.

Henrietta C. Bartlett, *Mr. William Shakespeare.* Yale University Press, 1922.

Sir Egerton Brydges, *British Bibliographer.* London, 1810–14.

——— *Censura Literaria.* London, 1805–09.

——— *Restituta.* London, 1814–16.

Arthur H. Bullen, *Some Longer Elizabethan Poems.* London, 1903.

Robert Burton, *The Anatomy of Melancholy* (Bohn's Popular Library). London, 1923.

Cambridge History of English Literature. Cambridge University Press, 1908–16.

(V. Cartari), *Vincentii Chartarii Rhegiensis Imagines Deorum . . .* Moguntiæ [Mainz], 1687.

William Caxton, *Eneydos. E. E. T. S.,* 1890.

——— *Recuyell of the Historyes of Troye,* ed. O. Sommer. London, 1894.

Alexander Chalmers, *Works of the English Poets*. London, 1810.

Sir Edmund K. Chambers, *William Shakespeare*. Oxford: Clarendon Press, 1930.

Alfred F. B. Clark, *Boileau and the French Classical Critics in England*. Paris, 1925.

John Payne Collier, *A Bibliographical and Critical Account of the Rarest Books in the English Language*, 4 vols. New York, 1866.

———— *Catalogue . . . of Early English Literature at Bridgewater House*. London, 1837.

———— *Illustrations of Old English Literature*, 3 vols. London, 1866.

Natalis Comes, *Mythologiae*. Patavii [Padua], 1616.

William J. Courthope, *History of English Poetry*. London and New York, 1895–1910.

Samuel Daniel: Poems and A Defence of Rhyme, ed. A. C. Sprague. Harvard University Press, 1930.

Dante Alighieri, *La Divina Commedia*, ed. C. H. Grandgent. New York and Boston, 1913.

Englands Helicon, ed. Hugh Macdonald. London, 1925.

Omnia Divini Platonis Opera Tralatione Marsilii Ficini . . . Lugduni [Lyons], 1548.

Georg Finsler, *Homer in der Neuzeit*. Leipsic and Berlin, 1912.

Finley M. K. Foster, *English Translations from the Greek*. Columbia University Press, 1918.

Abraham Fraunce, *Third part of the Countesse of Pembrokes Yuychurch*. London, 1592.

Fabius Planciades Fulgentius, *Mythologiae* and *Liber de Expositione Virgilianæ Continentiæ* (in *Mythographi Latini*, ed. T. Muncker, Amsterdam, 1681).

George S. Gordon (ed.), *English Literature and the Classics*. Oxford: Clarendon Press, 1912.

———— *Virgil in English Poetry*. Oxford University Press, 1931. (Not seen.)

John Gower, *English Works*, ed. G. C. Macaulay. Oxford: Clarendon Press, 1901.

Works of Robert Greene, ed. A. B. Grosart, 1881–86.

Walter W. Greg, *Pastoral Poetry and Pastoral Drama*. London, 1906.

Herbert J. C. Grierson, *Cross Currents in English Literature of the XVIIth Century*. London, 1929.

Otto Gruppe, *Geschichte der klassischen Mythologie und Religionsgeschichte während des Mittelalters im Abendland und während der Neuzeit*. Leipsic, 1921.

Giambattista Guarini, *Il Pastor Fido*, ed. G. Brognoligo. Bari, 1914.

———— *Il Pastor Fido*, trans. Sir Richard Fanshawe. London, 1676.

William C. Hazlitt, *Hand-Book to the Popular, Poetical, and Dramatic Literature of Great Britain*. London, 1867.

Elizabeth Holmes, *Aspects of Elizabethan Imagery*. Blackwell, Oxford, 1929.

Violet M. Jeffery, *John Lyly and the Italian Renaissance*. Paris, 1928.

Max H. Jellinek, *Die Sage von Hero und Leander in der Dichtung*. Berlin, 1890.

Otto L. Jiriczek, *Specimens of Tudor Translations from the Classics*. Heidelberg, 1923.

Sir Sidney Lee, *Elizabethan Sonnets*. London, 1904.

————— *The French Renaissance in England*. New York, 1910.

Leo Hebraeus, *Dialoghi d'Amore*, ed. S. Caramella. Bari, 1929.

Works of Lucian, trans. H. W. and F. G. Fowler. Oxford University Press, 1905.

Lydgate's Troy Book, ed. H. Bergen. E. E. T. S., 1906–10.

Works of John Lyly, ed. R. W. Bond. Oxford: Clarendon Press, 1902.

John W. Mackail, *The Springs of Helicon*. New York, 1909.

John M. Manly, "Chaucer and the Rhetoricians." *Proceedings of the British Academy*, XII (1926), 95 ff.

Gilbert Murray, *The Classical Tradition in Poetry*. Harvard University Press, 1927.

Works of Thomas Nashe, ed. R. B. McKerrow. London, 1910.

Elizabeth Nitchie, *Vergil and the English Poets*. Columbia University Press, 1919.

Ovid, *Metamorphoses*, ed. R. Ehwald. Leipsic, 1919.

————— *Opera*, ed. R. Merkel. Leipsic, 1853–66.

Le Metamorfosi di Ovidio, Ridotte da Giouanni Andrea dell'Anguillara, in ottaua rima, impressione quinta. Venice, 1575.

Shakespeare's Ovid Being Arthur Golding's Translation of the Metamorphoses, ed. W. H. D. Rouse. London, 1904.

Ovid's Metamorphosis Englished, Mythologiz'd, and Represented in Figures, by George Sandys. Oxford, 1632.

Henrietta R. Palmer, *List of English Editions and Translations of Greek and Latin Classics Printed before 1641*. London, 1911.

Works of George Peele, ed. A. H. Bullen. London, 1888.

The Phœnix Nest, ed. H. Macdonald, London, 1926; ed. Hyder E. Rollins, Harvard University Press, 1931.

Alfred W. Pollard and G. R. Redgrave, *A Short-Title Catalogue of Books Printed in England, Scotland, & Ireland, and of English Books Printed Abroad 1475–1640*. London, 1926.

Edward K. Rand, *Ovid and His Influence* (with bibliography). Boston, 1925.

Herbert Read, *Reason and Romanticism*. London, 1926.

Leo Rick, *Ovids Metamorphosen in der englischen Renaissance*. Münster i. W., 1915.

John M. Robertson, *The Problems of the Shakespeare Sonnets*. London, 1926.

Hyder E. Rollins, *Analytical Index to the Ballad-Entries in the Registers of the Company of Stationers of London*. S.P., XXI (1924), 1 ff.

Pierre de Ronsard, *Œuvres*, ed. Ch. Marty-Laveaux. Paris, 1887–93.

Herbert J. Rose, *A Handbook of Greek Mythology* (with bibliography). London, 1928.

George H. W. Rylands, *Words and Poetry*. London, 1928.

George Saintsbury (ed.), *Minor Caroline Poets*. Oxford: Clarendon Press, 1905–21.

Sir John E. Sandys, *A History of Classical Scholarship*. Cambridge University Press, 1903–08.

Walter F. Schirmer, *Antike, Renaissance und Puritanismus*. Munich, 1924.

Franck L. Schoell, see under "Chapter X."

Mary A. Scott, *Elizabethan Translations from the Italian*. Boston, 1916.

Seneca's Tragedies, trans. F. J. Miller (Loeb Classical Library). London and New York, 1917.

Seneca His Tenne Tragedies, ed. T. S. Eliot (Tudor Translations). London and New York, 1927.

Servii Grammatici . . . commentarii, ed. G. Thilo and H. Hagen. Leipsic, 1878 *et seq.*

Sir Philip Sidney, *The Countesse of Pembrokes Arcadia*, ed. A. Feuillerat. Cambridge University Press, 1912.

E. E. Sikes, *The Greek View of Poetry*. London, 1931.

K. C. M. Sills, "Virgil in the Age of Elizabeth." *Classical Journal*, VI (1910–11), 123 ff.

Gregory Smith, *Elizabethan Critical Essays*. Oxford: Clarendon Press, 1904.

Joel E. Spingarn, *Critical Essays of the Seventeenth Century*. Oxford: Clarendon Press, 1908–09.

———— *Literary Criticism in the Renaissance*. New York, 1908.

Elmer E. Stoll, *Poets and Playwrights*. University of Minnesota Press, 1930.

Complete Works of Joshua Sylvester, ed. A. B. Grosart. 1880.

Torquato Tasso, *La Gerusalemme Liberata*, ed. P. Papini. Florence, 1922.

———— *Jerusalem Delivered*, trans. E. Fairfax, ed. H. Morley. New York and London, 1901.

John S. P. Tatlock, "The Siege of Troy in Elizabethan Literature." *P.M.L.A.*, XXX (1915), 673 ff.

Tottel's Miscellany, ed. Hyder E. Rollins. Harvard University Press, 1928–29.

Alfred H. Upham, *The French Influence in English Literature, from the Accession of Elizabeth to the Restoration*. Columbia University Press, 1908.

P. Vergili Maronis Opera, ed. F. A. Hirtzel. Oxford, 1900.
Thomas Warton, *History of English Poetry*, ed. W. C. Hazlitt. London, 1871.
Thomas Watson, *Poems*, ed. E. Arber. London, 1895.
Enid Welsford, *The Court Masque*. Cambridge University Press, 1927.
Geffrey Whitney, *A Choice of Emblemes*. Leyden, 1586.

CHAPTER I

John E. Wells, *A Manual of the Writings in Middle English* (with supplements). Yale University Press, 1916 *et seq*.
Benoit de Sainte-Maure, *Le Roman de Troie*, ed. L. Constans. Paris, 1894–1912.
Ella Bourne, "Classical Elements in the *Gesta Romanorum.*" *Vassar Mediæval Studies*. Yale University Press, 1923.
————— "The Mediæval Wanderings of a Greek Myth." *J. E. G. P.*, XXIV (1925), 184–94.
Works of Chaucer, ed. W. W. Skeat. Oxford: Clarendon Press, 1926.
Geoffrey Chaucer, *Troilus and Criseyde*, ed. Robert K. Root. Princeton University Press, 1926.
Domenico Comparetti, *Vergil in the Middle Ages*, trans. E. F. M. Benecke. London and New York, 1895.
L. Constans, "L'épopée antique." Petit de Julleville, *Histoire de la langue et de la littérature française*, I, 171 ff. Paris, 1896.
John D. Cooke, "Euhemerism: A Mediaeval Interpretation of Classical Paganism." *Speculum*, II (1927), 396 ff.
Cornelia C. Coulter, "Boccaccio's Acquaintance with Homer." *P. Q.*, V (1926), 44–53.
Walter C. Curry, "Astrologising the Gods." *Anglia*, XLVII (1923), 213 ff.
————— "The Judgment of Paris." *M. L. N.*, XXXI (1916), 114–16.
Dares Phrygius, *De Excidio Troiae Historia*, ed. F. Meister. Leipsic, 1873.
Dictys Cretensis, *Ephemeris de Historia Belli Troiani*, ed. F. Meister. Leipsic, 1872.
Eneas: roman du XIIe siècle, ed. J.-J. Salverda de Grave. Paris, 1925–29.
Edmond Faral, *Les arts poétiques du XIIe et du XIIIe siècle*. Paris, 1924.
————— *Recherches sur les sources latines des contes et romans courtois du moyen age*. Paris, 1913.
Robert D. French, *A Chaucer Handbook*. New York, 1927.
Gesta Romanorum, ed. H. Oesterley. Berlin, 1872.
Nathaniel E. Griffin, *Dares and Dictys*. Baltimore, 1907.
————— "Un-Homeric Elements in the Medieval Story of Troy." *J. E. G. P.*, VII (1907–08), 32 ff.
N. E. Griffin and A. E. Beckwith, *The Filostrato of Giovanni Boccaccio*. University of Pennsylvania Press, 1929.

Dudley D. Griffith, *A Bibliography of Chaucer, 1908–24.* University of Washington Publications, 1926.

Foster E. Guyer, "The Chronology of the Earliest French Romances." *M. P.,* XXVI (1929), 257 ff.

Charles H. Haskins, *The Renaissance of the Twelfth Century.* Harvard University Press, 1928.

French Haynes, *Shakespeare and the Troy Story. Howard College Bulletin,* LXXX, No. 3 (1922), pp. 67–131.

Laura A. Hibbard, *Mediæval Romance in England.* New York, 1924.

Archibald A. Hill, "The Traditional Development of a Character" [Diomede]. *Essays and Studies in English and Comparative Literature by Members of the English Department of the University of Michigan,* pp. 1–25. University of Michigan Press, 1932.

John of Salisbury, *Opera Omnia* (Migne, *Patrologiæ Latinæ,* CXCIX. Paris, 1900).

Edgar C. Knowlton, "Notes on Early Allegory." *J. E. G. P.,* XXIX (1930), 159 ff.

August C. Krey, "John of Salisbury's Knowledge of the Classics." *Transactions of the Wisconsin Academy of Sciences,* XVI, Part 2 (1910), 948 ff.

M. Manitius, "Beiträge zur Geschichte des Ovidius und andrer römischer Schriftsteller im Mittelalter." *Philologus,* Supplementband VII (1899), 723 ff.

John C. McGalliard, *Classical Mythology in Certain Mediaeval Treatments of the Legends of Troy, Thebes, and Aeneas. Harvard University Summaries of Theses, 1930,* pp. 200–03.

Sanford B. Meech, "Chaucer and an Italian Translation of the *Heroides." P. M. L. A.,* XLV (1930), 110 ff.

———— "Chaucer and the *Ovide Moralisé." P. M. L. A.,* XLVI (1931), 182 ff.

F. J. Miller, "Ovid's *Aeneid* and Vergil's." *Classical Journal,* XXIII (1927–28), 33 ff.

John R. Moore, *Literary Paganism in the Poetry of France and England from Hildebert of Tours to Chaucer. Harvard University Summaries of Theses, 1931,* pp. 235–39.

Charles G. Osgood, *Boccaccio on Poetry.* Princeton University Press, 1930.

Ovide moralisé, ed. C. de Boer. *Verhandelingen der Koninklijke Akademie van Wetenschappen te Amsterdam.* Afdeeling Letterkunde, Nieuwe Reeks, Deel XV. 1915 *et seq.*

Gaston Paris, "Chrétien Legouais et autres traducteurs ou imitateurs d'Ovide." *Histoire littéraire de la France,* XXIX (1885), 455 ff.

———— *La poésie du moyen age.* Paris, 1903.

Philomena, ed. C. de Boer. Paris, 1909.

Piramus et Tisbé, ed. C. de Boer. Paris, 1921.

Edward K. Rand, "The Classics in the Thirteenth Century." *Speculum*, IV (1929), 249 ff.

John R. Reinhard, "Chrétien de Troyes: A Bibliographical Essay." *Essays and Studies in English and Comparative Literature by Members of the English Department of the University of Michigan*, pp. 195–231. University of Michigan Press, 1932.

Robert K. Root, "Chaucer's Dares." *M. P.*, XV (1917–18), 1 ff.

W. B. Sedgwick, "The *Bellum Troianum* of Joseph of Exeter." *Speculum*, V (1930), 49 ff.

The Seege or Batayle of Troye, ed. M. E. Barnicle. *E. E. T. S.*, 1927.

Edgar F. Shannon, *Chaucer and the Roman Poets*. Harvard University Press, 1929.

John W. Spargo, *Studies in the Transmission of the Mediaeval Popular Tale* [on popular legends concerning Virgil the wizard]. *Harvard University Summaries of Theses, 1926*, pp. 182 ff.

Karl Voretzsch, *Einführung in das Studium der altfranzösischen Literatur*. Halle, 1925.

"Thomas Waleys," *Metamorphosis Ovidiana moraliter explanata*. Paris, 1509.

Julius Wirl, *Orpheus in der englischen Literatur*. *Wiener Beiträge*, XL, 1913.

CHAPTER II

Percy S. Allen, *The Age of Erasmus*. Oxford: Clarendon Press, 1914.

Matteo Bandello, *Novelle*, ed. G. Brognoligo. Bari, 1910–12.

François de Belleforest, *Histoires tragiques*. Lyons, 1583 *et seq*.

John M. Berdan, *Early Tudor Poetry*. New York, 1920.

Giovanni Boccaccio, *De Claris Mulieribus*. Berne, 1539.

———— *De Genealogia Deorum*. Venice, 1511.

Roberta F. Brinkley, *Arthurian Legend in the Seventeenth Century*. Baltimore and London, 1932.

Walter L. Bullock, "The Precept of Plagiarism in the Cinquecento." *M. P.*, XXV (1927–28), 293 ff.

J. Douglas Bush, "The Classical Tales in Painter's *Palace of Pleasure*." *J. E. G. P.*, XXIII (1924), 331 ff.

———— "Pettie's Petty Pilferings from Poets." *P. Q.*, V (1926), 325 ff.

———— "*The Petite Pallace of Pettie his Pleasure*." *J. E. G. P.*, XXVII (1928), 162 ff.

Ingram Bywater, "Four Centuries of Greek Learning in England" (1894). *Oxford Lectures on Classical Subjects*. Oxford: Clarendon Press, 1919.

P. G. C. Campbell, "Christine de Pisan en Angleterre." *Revue de littérature comparée*, V (1925), 659 ff.

Baldassare Castiglione, *The Courtier*, trans. Sir Thomas Hoby (Tudor Translations). London, 1900.

William Caxton, *Ovyde Hys Booke of Methamorphose*, ed. S. Gaselee and H. F. B. Brett-Smith. Blackwell, Oxford, 1924.

Christine de Pisan, *The Epistle of Othea to Hector,* trans. S. Scrope, ed. G. F. Warner. Roxburghe Club, 1904.

A. C. Clark, "The Reappearance of the Texts of the Classics." *Library,* Fourth Series, II (1922), 13 ff.

Carey H. Conley, *The First English Translators of the Classics.* Yale University Press, 1927.

Cornelia C. Coulter, "The Genealogy of the Gods." *Vassar Mediæval Studies.* Yale University Press, 1923.

Sir Thomas Elyot, *The Governour,* ed. H. H. S. Croft. London, 1883.

Arundell Esdaile, *A List of English Tales and Prose Romances Printed before 1740.* London, 1912.

C. R. L. Fletcher, *Collectanea,* First Series. Oxford Historical Society, 1885.

Geoffrey of Monmouth, *Historia Regum Britanniae,* ed. Acton Griscom. London and New York, 1929.

George S. Gordon, "The Trojans in Britain." *Essays and Studies by Members of the English Association,* IX (1924), 9 ff.

Richard Grafton, *Chronicle or History of England,* ed. Sir Henry Ellis. London, 1809.

H. L. Gray, "Greek Visitors to England in 1455–56." *Haskins Anniversary Essays.* Boston, 1929.

Edwin Greenlaw, "The Battle of the Books." *Studies in Spenser's Historical Allegory.* Baltimore and London, 1932.

Montague R. James, "Greek Manuscripts in England before the Renaissance." *Library,* Fourth Series, VII (1927), 337 ff.

A. Jeanroy, "Boccace et Christine de Pisan: Le *De Claris Mulieribus* principale source du *Livre de la cité des dames.*" *Romania,* XLVIII (1922), 93 ff.

Emil Koeppel, *Studien zur Geschichte der italienischen Novelle in der englischen Litteratur des sechzehnten Jahrhunderts. Quellen und Forschungen,* LXX, 1892.

Mathilde Laigle, *Le livre des trois vertus de Christine de Pisan.* Paris, 1912.

Louise R. Loomis, *Mediaeval Hellenism.* Lancaster, Pennsylvania, 1906.

———— "The Greek Renaissance in Italy." *American Historical Review,* XIII (1907–08), 246 ff.

Francis O. Matthiessen, *Translation: An Elizabethan Art.* Harvard University Press, 1931.

J. Bass Mullinger, *The University of Cambridge.* Cambridge University Press, 1873–1911.

William Painter, *The Palace of Pleasure,* ed. Joseph Jacobs. London, 1890.

The Paradise of Dainty Devices, ed. Hyder E. Rollins. Harvard University Press, 1927.

George Pettie, *A Petite Pallace of Pettie his Pleasure,* ed. Sir I. Gollancz. London, 1908.

Marie Josèphe Pinet, *Christine de Pisan.* Paris, 1927.

Polydore Vergil's English History, from an Early Translation, ed. Sir H. Ellis. Camden Society, 1846.

Martha H. Shackford, *Plutarch in Renaissance England.* Wellesley College, 1929.

Walter F. Schirmer, *Der englische Frühhumanismus.* Leipsic, 1931.

John Speed, *The History of Great Britaine.* London, 1627.

John Stow, *Annales, or, A Generall Chronicle of England.* London, 1631.

M. P. Tilley, "A Variant of Homer's Story of Ulysses and the Sirens." *Classical Philology,* XXI (1926), 162–64.

Malcolm W. Wallace, *The Birthe of Hercules.* Chicago, 1903.

Wilson's Arte of Rhetorique, ed. G. H. Mair. Oxford: Clarendon Press, 1909.

Harold O. White, *Plagiarism and Imitation in English Literature, 1558–1625. Harvard University Summaries of Theses, 1930,* pp. 218–21.

CHAPTER III

F. Brie, "Zu Warners 'Albions England.'" *Archiv für das Studium der neueren Sprachen,* CXXVII (1911), 328 ff.

J. Douglas Bush, "Classical Lives in the *Mirror for Magistrates." S. P.,* XXII (1925), 256 ff.

———— "Classic Myths in English Verse, 1557–89." *M. P.,* XXV (1927), 37 ff.

———— "A Note on William Warner's Mediaevalism." *M. L. N.,* XLIV (1929), 40–41.

———— "The Tedious Brief Scene of Pyramus and Thisbe." *M. L. N.,* XLVI (1931), 144 ff.

Thomas Corser, *Collectanea Anglo-Poetica.* Chetham Society, 1860 *et seq.*

Complete Works of George Gascoigne, ed. J. W. Cunliffe. Cambridge University Press, 1907–10.

A. H. Gilbert, "The Source of Peele's *Arraignment of Paris." M. L. N.,* XLI (1926), 36 ff.

A Gorgeous Gallery of Gallant Inventions, ed. Hyder E. Rollins. Harvard University Press, 1926.

Georg Hart, *Ursprung und Verbreitung der Pyramus-und-Thisbe-Sage.* Passau, 1889.

———— *Die Pyramus-&-Thisbe-Sage in Holland, England, Italien & Spanien.* Passau, 1891.

A Handful of Pleasant Delights, ed. Hyder E. Rollins. Harvard University Press, 1924.

Marguerite Hearsey, "The MS. of Sackville's Contribution to the *Mirror for Magistrates," R. E. S.,* VIII (1932), 282–90.

John W. Hebel and H. H. Hudson, *Poetry of the English Renaissance.* New York, 1929.

Poems of Thomas Howell, ed. A. B. Grosart. London, 1879.

Howell's Devises, ed. Walter Raleigh. Oxford: Clarendon Press, 1906.

Hans Huf, *William Warner, Albion's England. Quellenuntersuchungen zu den ersten Büchern.* Munich, 1912.

Violet M. Jeffery, "The Source of Peele's 'Arraignment of Paris.'" *M. L. R.,* XIX (1924), 175 ff.

Otto L. Jiriczek, "Die erste englische Theokritübersetzung." *Jahrbuch der Deutschen Shakespeare-Gesellschaft,* LV (1919), 30 ff.

Emil Koeppel, "Chaucers 'Romaunt of the Rose' und Sackvilles 'Induction.'" *Archiv für das Studium der neueren Sprachen,* CI (1898), 145–46.

A Mirror for Magistrates, ed. J. Haslewood. London, 1815.

Hyder E. Rollins, *Analytical Index.* See under "General."

——— "New Facts about George Turberville," *M. P.,* XV (1918), 513 ff.

——— "The Troilus-Cressida Story from Chaucer to Shakespeare." *P. M. L. A.,* XXXII (1917), 383 ff.

Roxburghe Ballads, ed. W. Chappell and J. W. Ebsworth. London, 1871 *et seq.*

George Turberville, *Epitaphes, Epigrams, Songs and Sonets,* ed. J. P. Collier. London, 1867.

E. Witz, *Die englischen Ovidübersetzungen des 16. Jahrhunderts.* Leipsic, 1915.

CHAPTER IV

Charles R. Baskervill, "Some Evidence for Early Romantic Plays in England." *M. P.,* XIV (1916–17), 229 ff., 467 ff.

Antonio Belloni, *Il Poema Epico e Mitologico.* Milan, 1912.

Giovanni Boccaccio, *Il Ninfale fiesolano,* ed. A. F. Massèra. Torino, 1926.

——— *Opere Volgari.* Florence, 1827 *et seq.*

Juan Boscán, *Las Obras,* ed. W. I. Knapp. Madrid, 1875.

Donald L. Clark, *Rhetoric and Poetry in the Renaissance.* Columbia University Press, 1922.

Francesco Colonna, *The Strife of Love in a Dream (Hypnerotomachia,* Book I), ed. Andrew Lang. London, 1890.

R. H. Coon, "The Vogue of Ovid since the Renaissance." *Classical Journal,* XXV (1929–30), 277–90.

Clyde B. Cooper, *Some Elizabethan Opinions of the Poetry and Character of Ovid.* Menasha, Wisconsin, 1914.

Francesco Flamini, *Studi di Storia Letteraria Italiana e Straniera.* Livorno, 1895.

Hector Genouy, *L'élément pastoral dans la poésie narrative et le drame en Angleterre, de 1579 à 1640.* Paris, 1928.

Edwin Greenlaw, see under "Chapter V."

Frederick Hard, see under "Chapter V."

The Complete Works of Thomas Lodge, ed. Sir Edmund Gosse. Hunterian Club, 1883.

Percy W. Long, "A Detail of Renaissance Criticism." *M. L. N.*, XV (1900), 84 ff.

Susannah J. McMurphy, see under "Chapter V."

Gilbert Murray, *Tradition and Progress*. Boston, 1922.

N. Burton Paradise, *Thomas Lodge*. Yale University Press, 1931.

Rudolph Schevill, *Ovid and the Renascence in Spain*. University of California Publications, 1913.

John Addington Symonds, *Italian Literature (The Renaissance in Italy)*. London, 1909.

Guy A. Thompson, *Elizabethan Criticism of Poetry*. Menasha, Wisconsin, 1914.

Robert Withington, *English Pageantry*. Harvard University Press, 1918–20.

CHAPTER V

Frederic I. Carpenter, *Reference Guide to Spenser*. University of Chicago Press, 1923.

Alice Parrott, "A Critical Bibliography of Spenser from 1923–1928." *S. P.*, XXV (1928), 468 ff.

Charles R. Baskervill, "Dramatic Aspects of Medieval Folk Festivals in England." *S. P.*, XVII (1920), 19 ff.

———— "The Genesis of Spenser's Queen of Faerie." *M. P.*, XVIII (1920–21), 49 ff.

H. M. Belden, "Two Spenser Notes." *M. L. N.*, XLIV (1929), 526 ff.

Josephine W. Bennett, "Spenser's Garden of Adonis." *P. M. L. A.*, XLVII (1932), 46–80.

———— "Spenser's Hesiod." *American Journal of Philology*, LII (1931), 176–81.

H. H. Blanchard, "Spenser and Boiardo." *P. M. L. A.*, XL (1925), 828 ff.

J. D. Bruce, "Spenser's *Faerie Queene*, Book III, canto vi, st. 11 ff., and Moschus' Idyl, *Love the Runaway*." *M. L. N.*, XXVII (1912), 183–85.

Albert S. Cook, "The House of Sleep." *M. L. N.*, V (1890), 9 ff., 22.

C. C. Coulter, "Two of E. K.'s Classical Allusions." *M. L. N.*, XXXV (1920), 55–56.

W. P. Cumming, "The Influence of Ovid's *Metamorphoses* on Spenser's 'Mutabilitie' Cantos." *S. P.*, XXVIII (1931), 241 ff.

R. E. N. Dodge, "Spenser's Imitations from Ariosto." *P. M. L. A.*, XII (1897), 151 ff.; XXXV (1920), 91–92.

Joachim du Bellay, *La défense et illustration de la langue francaise*, ed. L. Séché. Paris, 1905.

Edwin Greenlaw, "Some Old Religious Cults in Spenser." *S. P.*, XX (1923), 216 ff.

———— "Spenser's Fairy Mythology." *S. P.*, XV (1918), 105 ff.

———— "Spenser's 'Mutabilitie.'" *P. M. L. A.*, XLV (1930), 684 ff.

———— "Two Notes on Spenser's Classical Sources." *M. L. N.*, XLI (1926), 323 ff.

Frederick Hard, "Spenser's 'Clothes of Arras and of Toure.'" *S. P.*, XXVII (1930), 162 ff.

Merritt Y. Hughes, "Spenser and the Greek Pastoral Triad." *S. P.*, XX (1923), 184 ff.

———— *Virgil and Spenser.* University of California Publications, 1929.

———— "Virgilian Allegory and 'The Faerie Queene.'" *P. M. L. A.*, XLIV (1929), 696 ff.

Viola B. Hulbert, *Spenser's Twelve Moral Virtues "According to Aristotle and the Rest."* *University of Chicago Abstracts of Theses, Humanistic Series*, V (1926–27), 479 ff.

———— "A Possible Christian Source for Spenser's Temperance." *S. P.*, XXVIII (1931), 184 ff.

Harry S. V. Jones, "The *Faerie Queene* and the Mediæval Aristotelian Tradition." *J. E. G. P.*, XXV (1926), 283 ff.

———— *A Spenser Handbook.* New York, 1930.

R. W. Lee, "Castiglione's Influence on Spenser's Early Hymns." *P. Q.*, VII (1928), 65 ff.

Charles W. Lemmi, "The Symbolism of the Classical Episodes in *The Faerie Queene.*" *P. Q.*, VIII (1929), 270 ff.

————"The Influence of Trissino on the *Faerie Queene.*" *P. Q.*, VII (1928), 220 ff.

Susannah J. McMurphy, *Spenser's Use of Ariosto for Allegory.* University of Washington Publications, 1924.

W. P. Mustard, "E. K.'s Classical Allusions." *M. L. N.*, XXXIV (1919), 193 ff.

———— "E. K.'s Note on the Graces." *M. L. N.*, XLV (1930), 168–69.

———— "Note on Spenser, *F. Q.*, V. 5. 24." *M. L. N.*, XX (1905), 127.

Frederick M. Padelford, "The Virtue of Temperance in the Faerie Queene." *S. P.*, XVIII (1921), 334 ff.

William L. Renwick, *Edmund Spenser.* London, 1925.

Alice E. Sawtelle, *The Sources of Spenser's Classical Mythology.* Boston, 1896.

Edmund Spenser, *Poetical Works*, ed. J. C. Smith and E. de Selincourt. Oxford, 1912. (Quotations are made from this text.)

———— *Works*, ed. W. L. Renwick. London, 1928 *et seq.*

———— *Works*, ed. H. Todd. London, 1805.

———— *The Faerie Queene*, Book I, ed. L. Winstanley. Cambridge University Press, 1924. Book II, ed. L. Winstanley. Cambridge University Press, 1914.

P. Vergili Maronis Opera, ed. O. Ribbeck. Leipsic, 1895.

CHAPTER VI

C. F. Tucker Brooke, *The Life of Marlowe and The Tragedy of Dido.* London and New York, 1930.

C. F. Tucker Brooke, "The Reputation of Christopher Marlowe." *Trans-actions of the Connecticut Academy of Arts and Sciences*, XXV (1922), 347 ff.

J. Douglas Bush, *"Hero and Leander* and *Romeo and Juliet." P. Q.*, IX (1930), 396–99.

———— "Notes on *Hero and Leander." P. M. L. A.*, XLIV (1929), 760 ff.

L. Chabalier, *Héro et Léandre*. Paris, 1911.

Una M. Ellis-Fermor, *Christopher Marlowe*. London, 1927.

M. H. Jellinek, see under "General."

Gertrud Lazarus, *Technik und Stil von Hero und Leander*. Bonn, 1915.

Works of Christopher Marlowe, ed. C. F. Tucker Brooke. Oxford: Claren-don Press, 1910. (Quotations are made from this text.)

Marlowe's Poems, ed. L. C. Martin. London and New York, 1931.

Musaeus, *Hero and Leander,* ed. C. Dilthey. Bonn, 1874.

John Addington Symonds, *Studies of the Greek Poets*. London, 1893.

Frederick Tupper, "Legacies of Lucian." *M. L. N.*, XXI (1906), 76–77.

CHAPTER VII

J. Douglas Bush, "Notes on Shakespeare's Classical Mythology." *P. Q.*, VI (1927), 295 ff.

Sir Sidney Colvin, "The Sack of Troy in Shakespeare's 'Lucrece' and in Some Fifteenth-Century Drawings and Tapestries." *A Book of Homage to Shakespeare*. Oxford University Press, 1916.

Wilhelm Ewig, "Shakespeare's „Lucrece."" *Anglia,* XXII (1899), 1 ff., 343 ff., 393 ff.

Edgar I. Fripp, *Minutes and Accounts of the Corporation of Stratford-upon-Avon,* Vol. III. Oxford University Press, 1926.

———— "Shakespeare's Use of Ovid's *Metamorphoses." Shakespeare Studies*. Oxford University Press, 1930.

Sir Sidney Lee, "Ovid and Shakespeare's Sonnets." *Elizabethan and Other Essays*. Oxford: Clarendon Press, 1929.

Leo Rick, "Shakespeare und Ovid." *Jahrbuch der Deutschen Shakespeare-Gesellschaft,* LV (1919), 35–53.

Robert K. Root, *Classical Mythology in Shakespeare*. New York, 1903.

Shakespeare, *Poems,* ed. Carleton Brown, Tudor ed., New York, 1913; ed. A. Feuillerat, Yale University Press, 1928; ed. C. H. Herford, Eversley ed., New York, 1906; ed. Sir Sidney Lee, Oxford, 1905; ed. C. K. Pooler, Arden ed., Indianapolis, n. d.; ed. A. von Mauntz *(Gedichte von William Shakespeare),* Berlin, 1894; ed. George Wyndham, London, 1898.

Complete Works of Shakespeare, ed. W. J. Craig. Oxford University Press, 1916. (Quotations are made from this text.)

Hazelton Spencer, "Shakespeare's Use of Golding in 'Venus and Adonis.'" *M. L. N.*, XLIV (1929), 435 ff.

Bruno E. Werner, "Venus and Adonis. Beitrag zur stilgeschichtlichen Betrachtung Shakespeares." *Das Inselschiff,* VI (1925), 99 ff. (Not accessible.)

340 MYTHOLOGY AND THE RENAISSANCE TRADITION

H. M. Belden, "Alanus de Insulis, Giles Fletcher, and the 'Mutabilitie' Cantos." *S. P.*, XXVI (1929), 131 ff.

Poems of William Browne, ed. Gordon Goodwin (Muses' Library). London and New York, n. d.

Michael Drayton, *Endimion and Phœbe*, ed. J. W. Hebel. Blackwell, Oxford, and Boston, 1925.

Minor Poems of Michael Drayton, ed. Cyril Brett. Oxford: Clarendon Press, 1907.

Oliver Elton, *Michael Drayton*. London, 1905.

Poetical Works of Giles and Phineas Fletcher, ed. F. S. Boas. Cambridge University Press, 1908.

J. W. Hebel, "Drayton and Shakespeare." *M. L. N.*, XLI (1926), 248–50.

Emil Koeppel, "Die englischen Tasso-übersetzungen des XVI. jahrhunderts." *Anglia*, XI (1889), 11 ff., 333 ff.

Frederic W. Moorman, *William Browne*. *Quellen und Forschungen*, LXXXI, 1897.

Venus & Anchises (Brittain's Ida) and Other Poems by Phineas Fletcher, ed. Ethel Seaton. Oxford University Press, 1926.

CHAPTER IX

Morse S. Allen, *The Satire of John Marston*. Columbus, Ohio, 1920.

William Barksted, *Mirrha*, etc., ed. A. B. Grosart. 1876.

Poetical Works of William Basse, ed. R. W. Bond. London, 1893.

Francis Beaumont (?), *Salmacis and Hermaphroditus*. *Shakespeare Society's Papers*, III (1847), 98 ff.

J. Douglas Bush, "The Influence of Marlowe's *Hero and Leander* on Early Mythological Poems." *M. L. N.*, XLII (1927), 211 ff.

————— "Musaeus in English Verse." *M. L. N.*, XLIII (1928), 101 ff.

Arthur M. Clark, "A Bibliography of Thomas Heywood." *Oxford Bibliographical Society Proceedings and Papers*, I, Part 2 (1925), 97 ff.

————— "Thomas Heywood's 'Art of Love' Lost and Found." *Library*, Fourth Series, III (1923), 210 ff.

————— *Thomas Heywood*. Blackwell, Oxford, 1931.

Abraham Cowley, *Essays, Plays and Sundry Verses*, ed. A. R. Waller. Cambridge University Press, 1906.

Complete Poems of Sir John Davies, ed. A. B. Grosart. London, 1876.

Thomas Heywood, *Troia Britanica*. London, 1609.

Works of John Marston, ed. A. H. Bullen. London, 1887.

R. G. Martin, "A Critical Study of Thomas Heywood's *Gunaikeion*." *S. P.*, XX (1923), 160 ff.

Works of James Shirley, ed. Alexander Dyce. London, 1833.

CHAPTER X

George Chapman, *The Iliads of Homer* (Temple Classics). London, 1901.

————— *The Odysseys of Homer* (Temple Classics). London, 1906.

The Works of George Chapman: Poems and Minor Translations. London, 1875.

T. S. Eliot, *Homage to John Dryden.* London, 1924.

J. B. Emperor, see under "Chapter XI."

Gertrud Lazarus, see under "Chapter VI."

Alfred Lohff, *George Chapman's Ilias-übersetzung.* Berlin, 1903.

H. M. Regel, "Über George Chapman's Homerübersetzung." *Englische Studien,* V (1882), 1 ff., 295 ff.

Franck L. Schoell, *Études sur l'humanisme continental en Angleterre.* Paris, 1926.

Percy Simpson, "Ben Jonson on Chapman." *T. L. S.,* March 3, 1932, p. 155.

Janet Spens, "Chapman's Ethical Thought." *Essays and Studies by Members of the English Association,* XI (1925), 145 ff.

George Williamson, *The Donne Tradition.* Harvard University Press, 1930.

CHAPTER XI

Norman Ault (ed.), *Elizabethan Lyrics.* London, 1925.

———— *Seventeenth Century Lyrics.* London, 1928.

Poems of Thomas Carew, ed. A. Vincent (Muses' Library). London, 1899.

Poems of Charles Cotton, ed. John Beresford. London, 1923.

Poems of Abraham Cowley, ed. A. R. Waller. Cambridge University Press, 1905.

Poems English, Latin, and Greek of Richard Crashaw, ed. L. C. Martin. Oxford: Clarendon Press, 1927.

Poems of John Donne, ed. H. J. C. Grierson. Oxford: Clarendon Press, 1912.

Poetical Works of William Drummond of Hawthornden, ed. L. E. Kastner. Edinburgh, 1913.

John B. Emperor, *The Catullian Influence in English Lyric Poetry circa 1600–1650.* University of Missouri Studies, 1928.

Robert S. Forsythe, *"The Passionate Shepherd;* and English Poetry." *P. M. L. A.,* XL (1925), 692 ff.

Herbert J. C. Grierson, *Metaphysical Lyrics and Poems of the Seventeenth Century.* Oxford: Clarendon Press, 1921.

Poetical Works of Robert Herrick, ed. F. W. Moorman. Oxford: Clarendon Press, 1915.

Violet M. Jeffery, "Source of the 'Complaint of the Satyres against the Nymphes.'" *M. L. R.,* XIX (1924), 56 ff.

Beatrice Johnson, "Classical Allusions in the Poetry of Donne." *P. M. L. A.,* XLIII (1928), 1098 ff.

Ben Jonson, ed. C. H. Herford and P. Simpson. Oxford: Clarendon Press, 1925 et seq.

Poems & Letters of Andrew Marvell, ed. H. M. Margoliouth. Oxford: Clarendon Press, 1927.

Mario Praz, see under "Chapter XII."

Poems of Sir Walter Ralegh, ed. A. M. C. Latham. London, 1929.

Poems of Thomas Randolph, ed. G. Thorn-Drury. London, 1929.
Poems of Edmund Waller, ed. G. Thorn-Drury (Muses' Library). London, 1901.
George Williamson, see under "Chapter X."

CHAPTER XII

Flora R. Amos, see under "General."
John Conington, "The English Translators of Virgil." *Miscellaneous Writings,* ed. J. A. Symonds, London, 1872, I, 137 ff.; and *Quarterly Review,* CX (1861), 38–60.
Sir Richard Fanshawe, *The Fourth Book of Virgil's Aeneid,* ed. A. L. Irvine. Blackwell, Oxford, 1924.
Poems of Sidney Godolphin, ed. William Dighton. Oxford: Clarendon Press, 1931.
John W. Mackail, "Sir Richard Fanshawe." *Studies of English Poets.* London, 1926.
Mario Praz, "Stanley, Sherburne and Ayres as Translators and Imitators of Italian, Spanish and French Poets." *M. L. R.,* XX (1925), 280 ff., 419 ff.
Henry Thomas, "Three Translators of Góngora." *Revue hispanique,* XLVIII (1920), 180 ff.

CHAPTER XIII

Francis Bacon, *De Sapientia Veterum. Works,* ed. Spedding *et al.* (Boston, 1860), XIII, 75 ff.
H. M. Briggs, "Tasso's Theory of Epic Poetry." *M. L. R.,* XXV (1930), 457 ff.
Charles H. Herford, see under "Chapter XIV."
Ovid's Metamorphoses Translated by the most Eminent Hands [Dryden, Addison, Garth, *et al.*]. London, 1717.
Alexander Pope, *The Iliad of Homer,* ed. G. Wakefield. London, 1796.
William Prynne, *Histriomastix.* London, 1633.
Sir Walter Ralegh, *History of the World.* Oxford University Press, 1829.
Austin Warren, *Alexander Pope as Critic and Humanist.* Princeton University Press, 1929.

CHAPTER XIV

David H. Stevens, *Reference Guide to Milton from 1800 to the Present Day.* University of Chicago Press, 1930.
Herbert Agar, *Milton and Plato.* Princeton University Press, 1928.
E. G. Ainsworth, "Reminiscences of the *Orlando Furioso* in *Comus.*" *M. L. N.,* XLVI (1931), 91–92.
E. C. Baldwin, "An Instance of Milton's Debt to Virgil." *J. E. G. P.,* VII (1908), 85–86.

BIBLIOGRAPHY 343

Robert Bridges, *Collected Essays, Papers, etc.* Oxford University Press, 1928.

J. D. Bruce, "A Note on *Paradise Lost* (book vii, ll. 463–474)." *Englische Studien*, XLI (1909), 166 ff.

Friedrich Buff, *Miltons Paradise Lost in seinem Verhältnisse zur Aeneide, Ilias, und Odyssee.* Hof a. S., 1904.

J. Douglas Bush, "Notes on Milton's Classical Mythology." *S. P.*, XXVIII (1931), 259 ff.

W. Connely, "Imprints of the *Aeneid* on *Paradise Lost*." *Classical Journal*, XVIII (1922-23), 466 ff.

Albert S. Cook, "Notes on Milton's Ode on the Morning of Christ's Nativity." *Transactions of the Connecticut Academy of Arts and Sciences*, XV (1909), 307 ff.

Mabel Day, "Milton's 'Il Penseroso' ll. 17–18." *M. L. R.*, XII (1917), 496–97.

A. S. Ferguson, "'Paradise Lost,' iv, 977-1015." *M. L. R.*, XV (1920), 168–70.

Edwin Greenlaw, "'A Better Teacher than Aquinas.'" *S. P.*, XIV (1917), 196 ff.

———— "Spenser's Influence on *Paradise Lost*." *S. P.*, XVII (1920), 320–59.

J. W. Hales, "Milton and Ovid." *M. P.*, I (1903–04), 143–44.

James H. Hanford, *A Milton Handbook* (with bibliography). New York, 1926.

————"The Youth of Milton." *Studies in Shakespeare, Milton, and Donne, by Members of the English Department of the University of Michigan.* New York, 1925.

Kathleen E. Hartwell, *Lactantius and Milton.* Harvard University Press, 1929.

Charles H. Herford, "Dante and Milton." *The Post-War Mind of Germany and Other European Studies.* Oxford: Clarendon Press, 1927.

Ben Jonson, *Masques and Entertainments*, ed. Henry Morley. London, 1890.

Walter MacKellar, *The Latin Poems of John Milton.* Yale University Press, 1930.

Prose Works of John Milton, ed. J. A. St. John (Bohn Library). London, 1910

Poetical Works of John Milton, ed. David Masson. London, 1874.

Poetical Works of John Milton, ed. W. A. Wright. Cambridge University Press, 1903. (Quotations are made from this text.)

Milton, *Paradise Lost*, ed. A. W. Verity, Vol. II. Cambridge University Press, 1929.

———— *Poems upon Several Occasions*, ed. Thomas Warton. London, 1785.

O. H. Moore, "The Infernal Council." *M.P.*, XVI (1918–19), 169 ff.; XIX (1921–22), 47 ff.

Charles G. Osgood, *The Classical Mythology of Milton's English Poems.* New York, 1900.

———— "Milton's Classical Mythology." *M. L. N.*, XVI (1901), 282–84.

———— "Paradise Lost 9. 506; Nativity Hymn 133–53." *American Journal of Philology*, XLI (1920), 76–80.

George R. Potter, "Milton's Early Poems, the School of Donne, and the Elizabethan Sonneteers." *P. Q.*, VI (1927), 396 ff.

Sir Walter Ralegh, see under "Chapter XIII."

Sir Walter Raleigh, *Six Essays on Johnson.* Oxford: Clarendon Press, 1910.

Robert L. Ramsay, "Morality Themes in Milton's Poetry." *S.P.*, XV (1918), 123 ff.

Edward K. Rand, "Milton in Rustication." *S.P.*, XX (1922), 109 ff.

E. H. Riley, "Milton's Tribute to Virgil." *S.P.*, XVI (1929), 155 ff.

George Sandys, *Ovid's Metamorphosis;* see under "General."

———— *A Relation of a Iourney begun An: Dom: 1610.* London, 1627.

M. E. Seaton, "Milton and the Myth of Isis." *M.L.R.*, XVII (1922), 168 ff.

John S. P. Tatlock, "Milton's *Sin* and *Death.*" *M.L.N.*, XXI (1906), 239–40.

George C. Taylor, "Shakspere and Milton Again." *S.P.*, XXIII (1926), 189 ff.

Alwin Thaler, "The Shaksperian Element in Milton." *Shakspere's Silences.* Harvard University Press, 1929.

E. M. W. Tillyard, *Milton.* London, 1930.

CHAPTER XV

Poetical Works of Charles Cotton. London, 1765.

George Kitchin, *A Survey of Burlesque and Parody in English.* Edinburgh and London, 1931.

S. E. Leavitt, "Paul Scarron and English Travesty." *S.P.*, XVI (1919), 108 ff.

Musarum Deliciæ. J. C. Hotten, London, 1874.

Paul Scarron, *Le Virgile travesti,* ed. V. Fournel. Paris, 1858.

Œuvres de Scarron. Paris, 1786.

Albert H. West, *L'influence française dans la poésie burlesque en Angleterre entre 1660 et 1700.* Paris, 1930. (Not seen.)

INDEX

INDEX

Gombauld, Jean Ogier de, 320
Góngora, Luis de, 78, 236
Goodyear, William, 306
Googe, Barnabe, 55, 58, 305
Gorboduc, 41, 63
Gordon, George, 39
Gorgeous Gallery of Gallant Inventions,
    50–53, 303, 305
Gorges, Sir Arthur, 318
Gosse, Sir Edmund, 184
Gosson, Stephen, 246, 272
Gower, John, 22, 32, 50, 150, 323
Grafton, Richard, 40, 64
Grange, John, 305
Graves, Thornton S., 52
Gray, H. L., 43
Gray, Thomas, 92, 259
Greene, Robert, fiction, 34, 37, 39, 71, 143,
    189, 306–07; poems, 144, 173, 217, 222
Greenlaw, Edwin, 39, 79, 98, 102–03, 114–
    15, 117–18, 269
Greg, W. W., 73, 84, 173, 185
Gregory the Great, Pope, 17, 318
Gresham, James, 318–19
Grey, Lady Jane, 44
Grey, William, 43
Grierson, H. J. C., 123, 225, 254, 258
Griffin, Bartholomew, 71, 126, 221
Griffin, Nathaniel E., 9
Grimald, Nicholas, 302
Griscom, Acton, 39
Grocyn, William, 44
Grosart, A. B., 178, 311
Grosseteste, Robert, 43
Grove, Mathew, 307
Gruppe, Otto, 17, 31, 68
Guarini, Giambattista, 84, 103, 134–35,
    217, 321
Guarino, Battista, 26, 46
Guazzo, Stefano, 30, 38
Guevara, Antonio de, 34–36, 306
Guido delle Colonne, 9, 17–18, 21, 31–33
Gunthorp, John, 43
Guyon, Sir, 96–97, 102–03, 105, 114–15,
    122, 266

H., T., 177, 309
Hacket, Thomas, 49, 303
Haemon, 56, 193
Hales, J. W., 283
Hall, Arthur, 28, 45
Hall, John, 60–61
Hall, Thomas, 244, 321–22
Hamlet, 61, 151, 155, 181, 280, 297
Hammond, Eleanor, 302
Handful of Pleasant Delights, 50, 58–59,
    84, 137, 303, 306
Hanford, James H., 251–52, 264, 266, 268–
    69
Hannay, Patrick, 162, 318–19

Hard, Frederick, 78, 110
Harington, Sir John, 70, 127, 187, 213
Harrison, G. B., 95, 147, 310
Hart, Georg, 50, 58
Hartwell, Kathleen E., 266, 272, 280, 284
Harvey, Gabriel, 113, 117, 135, 155, 162
Harvey, Richard, 41
Haskins, Charles H., 11–12, 18–19
Haslewood, J., 304
Hawes, Stephen, 302
Haworth, Peter, 35
Haynes, French, 56
Hazlitt, W. C., 301, 304–05, 308, 311, 315,
    318, 322
Hazlitt, William, 96, 148
Hearsey, Marguerite, 61
Hebe, 164, 183–84, 255, 257
Hebel, John W., 62, 156–57, 159, 163
Hector, 8, 31, 33, 188, 309, 322
Hector, Life and Death of, 316
Hecuba, 51, 308–09
Heffner, Ray, 111
Helen of Troy, 4, 7–9, 49, 53, 55, 97, 107,
    129, 136, 187–88, 220, 259, 278, 303–04,
    306–07, 309–10, 321–22
Heliodorus, 27, 304
Henry IV, 321
Henryson, Robert, 14, 54, 56, 301
Hephaestus (*see also* Vulcan), 188
Hera (*see also* Juno), 278
Heraclides Ponticus, 264
Herbert, George, 226, 256
Hercules, 34, 60, 63, 65, 91, 94, 97, 145,
    189, 200, 217, 255–56, 270, 278, 308
Herford, Charles H., 223–24, 247, 263,
    266–69
Hermaphroditus, 140, 144, 166, 181–83,
    237, 303, 313
Hermes, *see* Mercury
Hermes Trismegistus, 188, 265
Hermione, 282
Hero, 56, 78, 124–38, 145–46, 160, 163–64,
    166, 180, 182, 184, 205–11, 251, 288–93,
    303, 305, 311–12, 317–18, 321, 323
Hero and Leander (Marlowe), 80, 110,
    119, 124–38, 139, 144, 146–47, 149, 153,
    155, 158, 163, 177, 179, 181, 189, 192,
    205–09, 214, 232, 244, 251, 258, 309,
    311
    influence, general, 124–26, 155, 163, 166,
    177, 190, 195, 197, 216, 267, 290–92,
    296, 310–12, 316–18, 320–21; Bark-
    sted, 184; Beaumont, 182; Bosworth,
    193–94; Browne, 174–75; Chapman,
    205–10; Drayton, 125, 159–64; Ed-
    wards, 126, 310; Phineas Fletcher,
    167–70; Marston, 179–80; Milton, 267,
    273; Nashe, 126, 288–89; Peele, 53;
    Shakespeare, 125, 137, 143–46, 152
Hero and Leander, The Loves of, 290, 321